BEST OF RIVALS

BEST OF RIVALS

Joe Montana, Steve Young, and the INSIDE STORY behind the NFL's Greatest Quarterback Controversy

Adam Lazarus

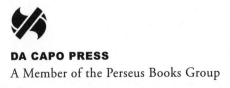

DA CAPO PRESS
A Member of the Perseus Books Group

Editorial production by Lori Hobkirk at the Book Factory.
Book design by Cynthia Young at Sagecraft.

Cataloging-in-Publication data for this book is available from the Library of Congress.
ISBN: 978-0-306-82135-6

Published by Da Capo Press
A Member of the Perseus Books Group
www.dacapopress.com

Da Capo Press books are available at special discounts for bulk purchases in the U.S. by corporations, institutions, and other organizations. For more information, please contact the Special Markets Department at the Perseus Books Group, 2300 Chestnut Street, Suite 200, Philadelphia, PA 19103, or call (800) 810-4145, ext. 5000, or e-mail special.markets@perseusbooks.com.

10 9 8 7 6 5 4 3 2 1

For Mom,
who also always wanted to be nearby,
and also wanted to race onto the field,
but thankfully never did.

Contents

Prologue

MAY 12, 1987

Steve Young walked into the San Francisco 49ers locker room unprepared: he forgot to bring a pair of cleats. So with his new team's three-day mini-camp in Redwood City about to begin, he tracked down the 49ers equipment manager, Bronco Hinek.

"Tampa Bay didn't send his shoes in time, and he apparently thought a pair would be provided by the team," Hinek said. "When I told him they wouldn't, I suggested he borrow a pair of Joe's. Steve was a little embarrassed, but they both wear the same size."

Young reluctantly laced up Joe Montana's cleats, took the practice field, and spent an hour displaying his talents for Bill Walsh and the rest of the 49ers coaching staff. When the workout was over, Walsh and Young walked back into the locker room, where they ran into the cleats' rightful owner.

"Hi, Joe," Walsh shouted. "I'd like you to meet Steve Young. Steve, Joe Montana."

"This was definitely not the way I envisioned meeting Joe Montana," Young later recalled. "Frankly, I didn't know how he'd react. Maybe he would think I was walking right in and trying to take over. I mean, the guy is a legend."

The two men shook hands then chatted for a few minutes—all the while Young subtly retreating toward a nearby wall: the back of the shoes he was wearing bore Montana's number 16 written in red ink.

Soon the conversation came to an end, prompting another handshake and a parting of the ways. But not before Montana had one final comment for his presumed understudy.

"Steve, when you're finished, just throw the shoes back in my locker."

Those size-eleven cleats wouldn't be the last thing Steve Young took that Joe Montana wanted back.

Crystal Joe

It was like this guy is touched by God, he's designed to
play for the 49ers. He's gonna be indestructible.

*—Carmen Policy on Joe Montana's return
from major back surgery in 1986*

It's funny," **Joe Montana wrote** in August 1986, "I've spent a lot of time
thinking about life after football; maybe it's because I turned thirty in June."
But even before that milestone—and well after it—the San Francisco 49ers
star quarterback was repeatedly reminded that he would not play football
forever.

On June 1, 1986, ten days before his thirtieth birthday, Montana underwent what the press called a "secret" surgery on his throwing shoulder: nobody
outside of the San Francisco 49ers organization knew about the arthroscopic
procedure until two weeks after it was performed.

That spring, the two-time Super Bowl Most Valuable Player (MVP) had admitted to reporters that the injury—which had also been accompanied by
bruised ribs, courtesy of the New York Giants during a playoff loss in
December—was so painful that weeks passed before he was able to pull a shirt
over his head.

Still, for the 49ers and their fans, there was little to be concerned about regarding the injury.

"He had persistent pain in the shoulder when he was throwing," the team's orthopedic surgeon Dr. Michael Dillingham said. "We scoped his shoulder and cleaned out a small piece of cartilage. His rotator cuff and tendons were OK. . . . He has good range of motion and reasonable strength. If he keeps going like this, he'll do well. I'm optimistic."

Apart from the promising diagnosis and Dillingham's assurance that Montana could resume throwing in three or four weeks, Montana's reputation as one of the game's most durable passers left little doubt who would be under center for the 49ers. After all, since taking over as the club's starter in 1980, Montana had missed only two games.

For his part, the minor surgery hardly left Montana bedridden or in a dispirited state: twelve days after the procedure Montana and teammates Dwight Clark, Ronnie Lott, and Riki Ellison went to a studio in Sausalito to sing backup vocals for Huey Lewis and the News' recording of "I Know What I Like."

And by late July, Montana was effortlessly humming forty-yard passes downfield to receivers during the team's training camp at Sierra Community College in Rocklin, California.

"It felt good; it felt real good," Montana said. "I threw a little harder than I expected to."

But it didn't take long for a backache to crop up, forcing him to walk delicately and miss several practices. Once the preseason schedule neared, he returned to his familiar position behind center Fred Quillan, and even took over the holding duties on extra points and field goals. Bill Walsh, the 49ers head coach, justified the move by saying, "People like John Brodie did it their entire careers and never were hurt."

But soon enough Walsh rethought the decision.

Three days after San Francisco thumped the Los Angeles Raiders 32–0 in their preseason opener, 49ers guard Guy McIntyre accidently stepped on Montana's ankle during a drill and he was carted off the field so X-rays could be taken. Walsh said he was expected to miss only a few days of practice.

"It's nothing serious," Montana explained.

In fact, that week Montana was far more angered with the "detailing" vandals had done to his $70,000 Mercedes-Benz 500 SEC in the parking lot at Sierra College. As if to add insult to injury, someone poured gray paint all over the hood, bashed in the windshield, and dented the body in several places.

"I don't want to talk about it," he told reporters. "I don't even want to think about it. I don't want to see it."

Eventually Montana's ankle became a much greater concern than his abused sports car. In addition to that week's game against the Rams, he missed the team's final two preseason contests and was fitted for a cast.

"I'm not worried about Joe's ankle," said team physician Michael Dilling-ham. "But we'd like it to heal faster, so we are going to immobilize it until Wednesday or Thursday."

The ankle improved, San Francisco waived third-string quarterback Mike Moroski, and Montana was deemed ready to go for the season opener, despite missing nearly four full weeks of practice and having some pain in his foot when he pivoted off the ankle.

"[It] is getting better slowly," Montana said the first week of September. "It's one of those things you've got to practice with. It will take a long time to heal this way, but it's the only way I can do it."

The 49ers opened the 1986 regular season on the road against the Bucca-neers and a familiar face: Steve DeBerg—Bill Walsh's starting quarterback in San Francisco during 1979 and 1980 and therefore Joe Montana's competi-tion during his first two seasons in the National Football League (NFL).

"We were roommates, we just really got along extremely well, and we be-came good friends immediately," DeBerg recalled years later. "The thing that we enjoyed the most was competing with each other and just competing in general. It became really a great relationship. It's not always true when people compete against each other that they have a real good friendship: me person-ally, I'd rather compete against my best friend than anybody and have fun do-ing it. And that was the kind of relationship Joe and I had."

Late in the 1980 season, Montana permanently wrested away the starter's job from DeBerg, and the 49ers traded away the California native. By 1984 DeBerg wound up in Tampa Bay as the starting quarterback. But the follow-ing year, the Buccaneers signed Steve Young, a superstar in the crumbling United States Football League (USFL). Instantly, the franchise's players, coaches, owner, and fans saw Young as the savior and DeBerg as expendable.

"I could almost feel what [DeBerg] was going through," Joe Montana wrote in the summer of 1986. "When the Bucs decided to sign Steve Young, the high-priced quarterback from the Los Angeles Express of the USFL, I knew what he must have been thinking. He had to be dying inside."

Despite Young's superior athletic gifts (and his million-dollar-per-season contract), DeBerg beat out the talented, yet unpolished passer during the pre-season and earned the starter's job for Tampa Bay's Week 1 showdown against San Francisco. But DeBerg threw a franchise-record seven interceptions that day and late in the first half, the fans at Tampa Stadium began to cheer, "We Want Steve Young! We Want Steve Young!"

While Young watched the entire game from the sidelines—and reportedly gestured to the crowd to halt the chant—Montana dispelled any concern re-lating to his injured shoulder, back, and ankle. He led the 49ers offense to a pair of first-quarter touchdown drives, taking a 14–0 lead into halftime. With the San Francisco defense hounding DeBerg—they also recorded three sacks to go along with the seven interceptions—and Montana completing thirty-two of forty-six attempts for 356 yards, the 49ers looked every bit the Super Bowl contender.

"I was very pleased with the outcome, although I think the game was tougher than the score indicates," Walsh said about his club's 31–7 win. "It was good to prove our ability to get into the end zone. It was an excellent effort, up to our highest expectations."

Nevertheless the 49ers didn't leave Tampa completely unscathed. Despite stellar passing statistics and his fiftieth career victory as a starting quarterback, Joe Montana had a tough return to the playing field. In addition to suffering a slightly sprained knee, Montana was reportedly bothered by headaches, which were likely caused by the Florida heat and humidity. Neither seemed to slow him down, though: only once before had Montana ever completed thirty-two or more passes in a single game.

At some point during the win over the Bucs, Montana rolled to his left and released a pass to the right, awkwardly twisting his lower back in the process. He showed no signs of pain and the twenty-four-point lead—not the yet-to-be-realized injury—was the only reason why backup Jeff Kemp entered the game in the fourth quarter.

"There was a little disbelief initially, because Joe reported on Monday (after the Tampa Bay game) without complaining of his back to me," Walsh told reporters later that week.

But Montana sat out the Tuesday practice, as the 49ers prepared for the Los Angeles Rams, and the next day Walsh announced that Kemp would start against their National Football Conference (NFC) West rival.

"Montana's injury doesn't merely raise serious questions about the outcome of the Rams game," *San Francisco Chronicle* columnist Lowell Cohn wrote. "It throws Joe's entire future into doubt. As football players go, he is a slight man, not built for bone-crushing contact. The beating he has taken over the years may have caught up with him.

"That would be a shame," he continued, "because Montana may be the best quarterback who ever lived, certainly one of the most pleasurable to watch. The 49ers have to face the fact that his body is growing fragile, that he is, in fact, becoming Crystal Joe."

At Anaheim Stadium, San Francisco's defense held the Rams great running back Eric Dickerson in check (nineteen carries, seventy-eight yards) and replacement Jeff Kemp completed nineteen of twenty-four attempts, including a sixty-six-yard third-quarter touchdown pass to wide receiver Jerry Rice. Midway through the fourth quarter the game was tied at 13. But the Rams drove ninety-two yards over eleven plays in the final six minutes to set up a game-winning eighteen-yard field goal by Mike Lansford, and with that the 49ers were 1–1.

From his Redwood City home, Montana watched the game while lying on his back to ease the pain of spasms that had not dissipated following time spent in a portable traction unit and injections of anti-inflammatory medicines.

"I should be there, huh?" he told a 49ers official on the phone during half-time.

Not long after hanging up the phone, Montana checked into St. Mary's Hospital: a CT scan late in the week proved surgery was necessary.

Early Monday on September 17, a team of orthopedic surgeons led by Dr. Arthur A. White cut into Montana with two specific purposes: to remove a large, central portion of the disk that cushioned the lower vertebrae (L5) of the spine; and to split the L5 and S1 vertebrae "in order to create a larger opening in the canal that carries the nerve fibers of the spinal cord." According to the team's physicians, Montana was born with abnormally small openings for the nerves, a condition called stenosis.

So many local fans flooded the hospital with calls of sympathy and questions about where to send flowers, cards, and letters that a special hotline was established with instructions and daily updates on Montana's condition.

He may have only just turned thirty, had been a resident of the city for less than eight years, and was born more than twenty-five hundred miles away, but Montana had become the city's greatest sports idol. That legacy surfaced after guiding the championship-starved, oft-hapless 49ers—San Francisco's only truly "original" team[1]—to victories in Super Bowl XVI and Super Bowl XIX. By the mid-1980s, San Francisco sports fans professed an unprecedented, undying, and unconditional love for Joe Montana.

"Because of the 49ers' history and origination the man who would lead them to a championship was destined to be a new hero and [Montana] was," recalled Art Spander, who covered San Francisco sports for more than five decades.

"I can safely say that after that 1984 season when Joe won his second Super Bowl (and beat Dan Marino in the game), he was the most popular sports figure in San Francisco sports history," *San Jose Mercury News* sports columnist Mark Purdy added in 2012. "After winning just one Super Bowl, he was a real fan favorite and kind of a cult figure, almost, but the second Super Bowl put

---

[1] Major League Baseball's San Francisco Giants and the NBA's San Francisco/Golden State Warriors were the city's other professional sports franchises. Both had been transplanted from East Coast cities—the Giants from New York in 1958 and the Warriors from Philadelphia in 1963.

him over the top. I think people have a view of the Bay Area as a quirky place that doesn't treat sports the same way as the rest of the country. That's correct, and I think it's in a good way—fewer people make athletes into idols or plan their lives around sports.

"However, when Walsh and Montana combined to put those Super Bowl teams on the field and did it in such a unique way, I think the Bay Area elevated them both as Northern California pop culture icons almost along the lines of the Grateful Dead or Francis Ford Coppola or Clint Eastwood because Bill and Joe seemed to exemplify what Bay Area residents think about themselves—that they are smarter and cooler and more creative than people in other parts of the country. Joe was all of that. And you could definitely argue that if in 1986 you had put Joe at a table signing autographs alongside tables with Jerry Garcia and Coppola and Eastwood and only had Bay Area citizens in the room, the longest line would be at Joe's table."

If there had ever been such a line, Bill Walsh wouldn't have to wait in it. He also didn't have to call the special hotline established at St. Mary's Hospital for news on his quarterback's condition. Upon the team's return from Anaheim, Walsh visited Montana.

"He's still sleepy and somewhat sedated," Walsh said. "He's in excellent spirits and asking for pizza already. . . . Hospital pizza, I don't think, would be that attractive." (Local fans actually began sending or ordering pizzas to the hospital after Walsh mentioned Montana's appetite.)

Collectively, the team of surgeons said that the two-hour procedure went well, announcing via a statement, "Everything looks great for a successful recovery."

But not everyone was quite that optimistic. One Bay Area doctor, provided with the details of the operation, told the *San Jose Mercury News*, "That sounds good for Joe. That sounds like a classic herniated disk, and there is an 89 or 90 percent chance that he will make a good recovery. But if I were Joe Montana, I wouldn't play football again. For you or I to get along with that is no big deal. It would be successful surgery, and we would be very content for the rest of our lives. But if we were going to carry sacks of concrete or get tackled by 250-pound monsters, I'm not sure the back would hold up."

Even one of the team's physicians, Dr. Robert Gamburd, told reporters, "We'll have to wait and see about whether he'll ever play again."

"I thought he was finished," Montana's mother, Theresa, later said. "I was in his hospital room the day after the operation. They wheeled him in, sat him up, or at least tried to. I could see the pain in his eyes. I wanted to cry, but not in front of him. Ronnie Lott was in the room, Dwight Clark, Wendell Tyler. They couldn't hold the tears back. A day later I asked him, 'What do you want to do?' He said, 'I want to play football again.' The next day he was up doing exercises, the day after that he was working with weights, small stuff mostly, but at least he was doing something."

Their franchise quarterback declared out for the entire season, and perhaps forever, the 49ers considered acquiring another quarterback.

Walsh—who, looking ahead to the next season, insisted that Montana would "start and play . . . I think he'll return to greatness"—inquired with the Oilers about Jim Everett, their unsigned, third-overall draft pick whose salary demands were far more than Houston wanted to spend. Coincidently, the Oilers' asking price for Everett was also far more than the 49ers wanted to spend.

Bob Gagliano, a former backup for the Chiefs and starter for the Denver Gold of the USFL, was brought in for a tryout, as was Ed Luther, a journeyman recently cut by Atlanta.

But one name soon garnered more attention than all the others.

"As the 49ers go quarterback shopping, they should think of Steve Young," *San Francisco Chronicle* columnist Glenn Dickey wrote the day after Montana's surgery.

"Young has the mobility that 49er coach Bill Walsh prizes in a quarterback—he even was used as a running back at times by the Los Angeles Express—and he's an accurate passer who led the nation in passing as a collegian. Young would fit even better than Jim Everett into Walsh's ball-control passing scheme. He is, in fact, much like Joe Montana when Montana first came to the 49ers."

Dickey—who also pointed out that 49ers offensive coordinator Mike Holmgren was Young's coach in college—wasn't the only one intrigued by Young. Walsh even called Buccaneers head coach Leeman Bennett about the raw quarterback.

"I do not believe he is available," Walsh said, "although we have great regard for him."

Walsh was right: Young wasn't available. The following Sunday in Detroit, with Steve DeBerg nursing a sore elbow, Young started for Tampa Bay and helped the Bucs snap a horrific nineteen-game road losing streak.

St. Mary's released Montana on Monday, September 22, the day after the Jeff Kemp-led 49ers toppled the New Orleans Saints 26–17 in their home opener. One of his surgeons, Dr. Arthur White, acknowledged that Montana was experiencing some numbness in his foot—a condition that was possibly permanent—but might return to the field far sooner than expected.

"The absolute soonest would be two months, and that would be a phenomenal effort," said White. "I believe there's less danger now that he has more room in his spine to take those hits."

The rehab process began right away: less than a week after the surgery, Montana worked out on a Nautilus machine and began walking long distances.

Not surprisingly, without Montana, the 49ers endured a roller-coaster stretch.

They steamrolled the Miami Dolphins, intercepting Dan Marino four times in a 31–16 win, then defeated the winless Indianapolis Colts 35–14, as Jerry Rice grabbed three second-half touchdown passes from Kemp, who threw for 274 yards. He had won his third straight start.

"I definitely had fear for my job," Montana later admitted.

But they also squandered a ten-point fourth-quarter lead at home, losing to the Vikings in overtime, then began a brutal stretch of four road games in the span of five weeks. Against the 5–1 Atlanta Falcons, the offense struggled. Following a Roger Craig touchdown on the opening possession, the 49ers produced just three field goal attempts (only one of which kicker Ray Wersching made), and the game ended in a 10–10 tie.

The news got only worse when they returned to California. During the game against Atlanta, Kemp injured his hip and would miss the next two weeks. Halfway through the 1986 season, the 49ers had already lost two starting quarterbacks due to injury. Mike Moroski, who had been cut by the team in the preseason and re-signed after Montana's back injury, took over for Kemp.

A pair of fourth-quarter interceptions returned for touchdowns, first by Ronnie Lott, then another by Tory Nixon, allowed the 49ers to escape Milwaukee County Stadium with a 31–17 win over the 1–6 Packers, but another subpar effort from the offense one week later in New Orleans dropped them to 5–3–1. With a little more than one month remaining in the regular season, San Francisco trailed the Rams by two games in the race for the NFC West crown.

Still, all was not bleak by the Bay.

Joe Montana's recovery from back surgery was well ahead of schedule. Although he suffered a near-disastrous fall in the family's Foster City condominium—hearing one-year-old Alexandra fall out of her crib, the first-time father rushed from another room to his daughter, unsuccessfully trying to hurdle a childproof gate blocking a staircase—Montana rehabbed with a vengeance.

"This is like anything else that people love to do," he said. "It's the same as a person who breaks his foot skiing. As soon as he can, he is back on the slopes because he loves to ski. It's the same for me. I love the game. Everybody's a little nervous. I'm a little nervous. But I don't want to baby myself to the point where I sit out. That's just not me."

Within weeks of the surgery he was jogging, swimming, weight-training, and running agility drills. After one month, he resumed throwing and returned to team practices. Midway through the first full week of November, Walsh named Montana the starter for the 49ers home game against the St. Louis Cardinals.

"We had to make sure we were properly and appropriately covered in every facet of his return, from the standpoint of the evaluations of all the doctors working with the 49ers, and obviously, with his surgeons," Walsh said. "The assessment of everyone was in 100 percent agreement on this matter."

The physical state of the back wasn't the only issue Montana, Walsh, and the team's front office dealt with. Throughout the recovery, Montana struggled to cope with his absence from the game, the possibility that he might never heal, and—should he return to the field—concern over both his productivity and safety.

"I thought something could happen in the surgery," Montana admitted during a press conference. "I mean, they were talking about my spinal column. It was scary to me. Afterward, the morphine messed up my mind. At times, the walls were blurry, I saw double, I slurred my words. I said to Jennifer (his wife), 'Will I come back? I don't know if I can come back. Will I ever be healthy?' She said, 'There's nothing to worry about.' She was stronger than I was.

"You start thinking crazy. I just wanted to walk normal, be able to play with my kids, live a normal life. I had talks with Jennifer and my parents about never playing again, but after I stopped the medication those talks subsided."

Still, at one point during the process, Montana even met with his accountant to discuss his finances should he never play again: "It was crushing. It was killing me," he admitted. "I went through states of depression."

But the moment he entered the game, Montana's depression, fears, and doubts were all distant memories. As had been the case for years, Joe Montana the Person contrasted with Joe Montana the Quarterback.

"He was different on the field," 49ers owner Eddie DeBartolo Jr., said. "Off the field he was very outgoing, court jester, always playing tricks in the locker room. At team dinners he'd [inhale] helium balloons and joke around. That was just his way. . . . But once he strapped on his helmet, he was a different person. There was no fooling around: he was the boss, he was the general. And what he said went."

"When he stepped on the field," teammate Steve Bono later remembered, "at that point in his career because he was so popular, he was more comfortable on the field than he was walking down the street. Because he knew his element when he was on the field. He was protected."

In his return to the team, fifty-five days removed from major back surgery, the 49ers already held a 13–3 advantage when Montana lofted a deep post pass over the middle of the field to Rice who hauled in the forty-five-yard touchdown. The Candlestick crowd and 49ers sideline did not, however, immediately burst into celebration: Cardinals defensive lineman Al "Bubba" Baker blasted Montana just as he threw the pass, but the quarterback promptly stood up and was seen smiling.

"A lot of times, when I'd get hit, I'd be asked by one of our guys or their guys, 'You, OK?' And I'd say, 'Yeah.' One other time somebody told me, 'I took it easy on you that time,'" Montana said. "You can't worry about it. If you play, you're going to get hit. You can't worry about a guy from this direction or that direction because, if you do, you're going to forget about what you're supposed to be doing back there."

"The phrase I used," Mark Purdy recalled years later, "was it was like being at the circus where the guy's on the high-wire, and everybody doesn't want him to fall, but the fact that they know he *can* fall makes it like you're holding your breath the whole time. Every time a guy got near Joe—because nobody really knew what was going to happen—it was a big deal."

Two Candlestick Park spectators in particular—Montana's wife and his surgeon—were most worried, especially after the quarterback endured a sack and two roughing-the-passer penalties. Jennifer Montana admitted that she had cringed when her husband took hits from St. Louis defenders on three consecutive plays, as did Dr. White, who during a conference call that week said Montana was "crazy" for returning to football.

"I told Joe from the first day I met him that I don't recommend that people I do surgery on go back to anything that is way out of control—that they should stay in control of their spines the rest of their lives."

Montana and Rice hooked up on a third forty-plus-yard touchdown, late in the third quarter, giving the 49ers a commanding twenty-point lead, but more so than his passing Montana's presence bolstered the spirits of his 49er teammates, who had only one victory in the previous month.

"It was just the fact that we had him," guard Randy Cross said after the 43–17 blowout. "Armies work hard for Lancelot, but they work even harder for King Arthur."

The 49ers would need a heroic effort over the next few weeks.

In a matchup with Joe Gibb's NFC East–leading Washington Redskins, the 49ers offense racked up huge chunks of yards—Montana set career highs with sixty attempts and 441 yards passing—but interceptions killed three drives, and they managed just two field goals in an ugly 14–6 loss on Monday Night Football.

A 20–0 victory over the Falcons pulled San Francisco within one game of passing the Rams for first place in the West, but then the New York Giants came to Candlestick. The Giants had suffocated the 49ers offense in the playoffs the previous December and had won ten of their last eleven games.

None of that seemed to matter by halftime as the 49ers took a 17–0 advantage. But the Giants defense shut out Montana and the 49ers in the second half, and scored three touchdowns in the third quarter, winning 21–17.

Much of the blame for the second half collapse fell at Montana's feet. One reporter noted that—post surgery—he was less inclined to scramble and make plays with his legs, opting instead to attempt throws prematurely: "The new Joe Montana is not quite the same as the previous version. He scrambles if necessary, but more carefully." Another accused him of rushing "his throws as if he was afraid of what would happen if Leonard Marshall or George Martin got a good hit on him."

Even Walsh admitted, "He hasn't had the scintillating days he's had in the past. He's OK physically, but not playingwise."

With three games left on the schedule, the 49ers had to win each one just for a shot at reaching the postseason. First up: the offensively challenged New York Jets, a club that had scored just three points in each of their previous two games. Again, neither Montana nor the offense was "scintillating," but they outgained the Jets by more than two hundred yards for a 24–10 win, then flew across the country and narrowly defeated the defending American Football Conference (AFC) champion, New England Patriots, 29–24.

A second straight win, coupled with the Rams heartbreaking overtime loss to the Miami Dolphins set up a winner-take-all showdown in the Week 17 season finale.[2]

"Most successful athletes do like to play this type of game," Montana said that week. "This is what you're here for. If it wasn't for the thrill of the game, and not knowing what's going to happen, then it would just be too easy. The people would lose interest, as the players would. This is what it's all about, this type of pressure."

A string of passes from Montana to Rice—including a forty-four-yard touchdown pass that Rice hauled in by leaping over Rams defenders Nolan Cromwell and Johnnie Johnson—yielded a 10–0 first-quarter lead.

"I think the return of Joe Montana and his ability to make the big plays is the key for them," Cromwell said.

----

[2] Heading into the final game of the regular season, the Rams were 10–5, the 49ers 10–4–1. Essentially, whichever team won eleven games would be declared the NFC West champion.

Los Angeles and quarterback Jim Everett—in September, the Rams gave up mulitiple players and high draft picks to acquire the rookie from Houston—cut into the deficit early in the third quarter with a touchdown run by Eric Dickerson. But San Francisco answered with a fourteen-play, ninety-two-yard touchdown drive that drained more than eight minutes off the clock.

In the second half the two clubs traded touchdown passes, but the 49ers defense picked off Everett three times, and the Rams late fourth-quarter touchdown didn't matter. The 49ers won the game 24–14 and claimed the NFC West for the fourth time in six years. When the fourth-quarter clock hit triple zeroes, Montana exuberantly spiked the ball.

"I've never done that before," said Montana, who completed twenty-three of thirty-six attempts for 238 yards and even scrambled for a critical seventeen-yard gain. "It was just the winning."

Montana's atypical display of emotion could be understood. Ever since returning from the surgery, some skeptics questioned how effective he was considering an apparently reduced mobility.

"I'm probably a little more cautious now," Montana said when asked about the differences between his play before the back surgery and after. "I don't feel that way, but everyone (the media) tells me. I hope this [performance] quiets the critics."

It did . . . for about two weeks.

Winning the NFC West earned San Francisco a much needed bye during the wild-card round, then set up a second consecutive postseason trip to the Meadowlands for a showdown with the Giants.

"The game will be a test of technique and tactics (the 49ers) against a powerful, awesome football team (the Giants)," Walsh told reporters a few days before kickoff. "That makes it interesting for the serious fan. Our defense is smaller, quicker, maybe not faster. It's the same with our offense. The game will be all tactics, but Joe (Montana) is a master of that."

The master started the week under the weather. On the Monday before the divisional playoff with New York, Walsh sent his flu-stricken starting quarterback home from practice, but Montana was back in action by midweek. Still, Montana continued to feel sick as he watched film of the Giants defense. The unit, coordinated by thirty-year-old Bill Belichick, had the NFL's Most Valuable Player Lawrence Taylor, three additional Pro Bowlers, allowed less than fifteen points-per-game, and recorded fifty-nine sacks that season.

But more than any of those figures, one statistic defined the 1986 Giants defense. In consecutive November games, not only did they knock the opposing team's starting quarterback—Philadelphia's Ron Jaworski (torn hand tendon) and Dallas's Danny White (broken wrist)—out of the game, they sidelined each one for the remainder of the season. The following week, they bashed the Vikings Tommy Kramer's hand and the Pro Bowler missed the next two games with a sprained thumb.

"We don't try to hurt or maim anyone," the Giants future Hall of Fame linebacker Harry Carson told reporters prior to the playoff game with San Francisco. "We've just got a solid defense."

With several early self-inflicted wounds by the 49ers, Carson, Taylor, and the Giants played more than just solid defense during a thirty-degree day in East Rutherford, New Jersey.

On the game's opening possession, Montana drove San Francisco to midfield, then hit Rice over the middle on a slant pattern. Having broken past cornerback Elvis Patterson and safety Herb Welch, Rice inexplicably dropped the football at the Giants 27-yard line, then compounded the mistake by trying to scoop it up, rather than simply falling on the football. New York's Kenny Hill recovered the fumble, ending the 49ers chance of taking an early lead.

"If I had put that one in," Rice said, "the crowd would have been quieted down, and we would have been able to get into our offense."

The Giants drove eighty yards for the game's first touchdown. San Francisco netted a field goal that narrowed the score to 7–3, but the offense never found its rhythm.

Hit by linebacker Carl Banks, Montana was unable to make a clean pass attempt to Rice in the second quarter, and Herb Welch grabbed the interception. Joe Morris rumbled forty-five yards on the next play for a Giants touchdown.

"When you hit people like we did, good things happen," Lawrence Taylor said afterward.

The 49ers next drive resulted in a three-and-out (along with two false start penalties), and soon New York capitalized again: quarterback Phil Simms's touchdown pass to Bobby Johnson gave the Giants a 21–3 advantage.

Two plays later, Taylor and the Giants defense delivered the knockout blow, literally and figuratively. With less than one minute remaining in the half, Montana dropped back to pass inside his own 10-yard line. Giants defensive tackle Jim Burt breached the middle of the 49ers offensive line and clobbered Montana just as the quarterback released a pass intended for Jerry Rice.

"He saw me coming. I came up square and hit him at full speed. My helmet came up under his chin, but I didn't fall on him," Burt said afterward. "After I hit him, I turned to see where the pass went because the crowd roared."

Lawrence Taylor hauled in the wobbly throw at the 34-yard line and raced down the sideline for essentially a game-clinching touchdown. Meanwhile, Montana lay on his side, unable to pick himself off the ground. Teammates,

49ers officials, and even Burt walked over to the fallen star. Immediately, the fear centered around Montana's back.

If Montana had a "career threatening" injury in September without even being touched, Burt's hit stirred up visions of the worst-case scenarios. But the medical staff realized Montana was suffering from a head injury, and his back was not the issue: Burt's hit launched Montana several feet and he fell on the hard, cold AstroTurf of Giants Stadium. Eventually Montana—who reportedly blacked out for a moment—stood up and was helped to the locker room, where he twice asked a security guard to call his wife to relay that he was all right.

"He was pretty groggy," said Dwight Clark, who talked to his friend at halftime. "He didn't know what happened to the ball. He didn't know they had scored. I think he was fine, but he was disoriented."

With Jeff Kemp taking Montana's place, the 49ers re-took the field in the third quarter but continued to be manhandled by the Giants defense and they were unable to cut into the fast-growing deficit.

"We were just devastated," Walsh admitted after the 49–3 drubbing. "We just self-destructed, and they destroyed us at the same time in the second period."

Montana didn't see the final thirty minutes of one of the most lopsided games in NFL playoff history. He spent the second half in the 49ers locker room with team doctor James Klint, before Dr. Peter Tsairis, chief neurosurgeon at Manhattan's Hospital for Special Surgery, was paged over the public address system. Late in the fourth quarter an ambulance pulled up to the entrance of the visitor's locker room and Montana—on a stretcher with a white towel over his head and sunglasses on his face—was gently placed inside and taken to Cornell Medical Center where he received a CT scan.

"He has a concussion, and his condition is normal," said Dr. Tsairis, who admitted that Montana had trouble staying awake. "He's still got a headache. He's coherent but a little groggy, which is normal for this kind of head injury. So we decided to keep him overnight. The plan now is that he'll leave tomorrow afternoon and fly home."

The next morning, Montana was released and with Dwight Clark—who did not leave with the team—flew home aboard owner Eddie DeBartolo Jr.'s private jet.

"He feels fine except for a slight headache," Clark told reporters. "He remembers a lot of the game, but we didn't talk too much football on the way home."

Walsh *was* talking football once he returned to California.

"This game reminds us we have to look at all positions," Walsh told reporters a day after the loss. "I think we need to add to the team to improve. . . . It was a very sobering experience. It might affect our evaluations of certain players."

In Walsh's mind, that even included Montana.

"Joe's situation does concern us, naturally. No question about that," Walsh told reporters a day after the loss to the Giants. "He is going to do a lot of work in the off-season. . . . He is going to have to come to camp bigger and heavier."

That simple statement allowed the imaginations of sportswriters and fans to run wild.

The clear-cut best player in college football that fall had been quarterback Vinny Testaverde. At 6-foot-4 and 230 pounds, the Heisman Trophy winner from the University of Miami (FL) fit Walsh's description perfectly.

"With Montana, who battled back from back surgery earlier this season, looking increasingly vulnerable," the *Chicago Tribune* reported in early January, "49ers' coach Bill Walsh is thinking ahead to grooming a replacement, perhaps even Heisman Trophy winner Vinny Testaverde. Through trades, the 49ers have stockpiled two picks in each of the first two rounds of the upcoming college draft, and Walsh is considering trading all of them for the first or second pick."

Walsh and the 49ers front office had already displayed a willingness and ability to pull off draft-day wonders before: in April 1985, they dealt a first-, second-, and third-round choice to New England to acquire the fifteenth overall selection, which they used on Jerry Rice.

Tampa Bay held the first overall pick, and their recently hired new head coach, Ray Perkins, was cryptic when asked about zeroing in on Testaverde.

"I saw no minuses with Vinny," said Perkins, who personally scouted Testaverde at the Senior Bowl. "He is everything they said he would be. But I have not seen our quarterback yet. A lot of people have said a lot of good things about him."

Perkins was talking about a twenty-five-year-old named Steve Young.

Over the next few months, Perkins and the Tampa Bay front office grew increasingly desperate for a bona fide star. In 1986, they held the top pick in the draft and squandered it by selecting Bo Jackson, who refused to sign and chose to play pro baseball instead. This year, Tampa Bay signed Testaverde to an enormous contract four weeks before the draft.

Losing out on Testaverde didn't end Walsh's interest in evaluating the quarterback position, nor did it entirely slow down the rumor mill. But as the sting of the crushing loss to the Giants faded, the "concern" over Montana seemed to diminish.

Less than three weeks after suffering the concussion, Montana returned to New York City to co-host *Saturday Night Live* with Chicago Bears superstar Walter Payton. Montana participated in a double-entendre-laden conversation with Dana Carvey's "Church Lady," and even managed not to break character as "Stu" during the bizarre, but hilarious "Honest Man" sketch beside Phil Hartman and Jan Hooks. Montana's comedy tour continued a month later at San Francisco's Moscone Center, where he appeared as the guest of honor at a "Super Roast," benefitting the City of Hope Hospital.

But it wasn't the quarterback's newly public taste for humor that encouraged Walsh and the 49ers front office. That spring, Montana improved his leg strength significantly and returned to his playing weight of 195 pounds, up from the 180 pounds he weighed following the back surgery. According to the *Boston Globe*'s Will McDonough, "Word out of the Niners office is that he is bigger and stronger than ever."

By mid-March, at the NFL owners' meeting in Maui, the 49ers brass delighted in telling reporters about the "new Joe [Montana]," as owner Eddie DeBartolo Jr. called him.

"We're assuming he'll be playing great football," Walsh announced. "I think Joe can be on top of his game for another five to eight years."

2

The Comeback Kid

D uring the mid-1980s, a reporter noticed a small scar above the right
side of Joe Montana's mouth. The inquisitive journalist asked San
Francisco's star quarterback about the origin of the blemish and was
surprised to discover that it did not result from a defensive end's sack or a linebacker's vicious tackle.

"I was bitten by a dog, I really was," Montana said. "It was when I was
about eight years old. He was my aunt's dog. He wanted to quit playing, and I
didn't."

Even as a small child Joe Montana was fearless, persistent, and indestructible.

Born on June 11, 1956, in New Eagle, Pennsylvania, Joseph Clifford
Montana Jr. cherished his parents, Joseph Sr. and Theresa. Years later, when
his fame and popularity rivaled any athlete's in the world, Montana shared
his favorite childhood memory with *Sports Illustrated*'s Paul Zimmerman:
"Playing ball in the backyard with his dad," Zimmerman wrote, "then coming into the kitchen, where his mother would have a steaming pot of ravioli
on the stove."

Traditional Catholic Italians, the Montanas raised their only child in the
blue collar Western Pennsylvania town of Monongahela. Both parents, however, worked in an office, the same office, rather than a steel mill or factory; a
few years after the birth of his son, Joe Sr. left his job as a telephone equipment installer to manage the local Civic Finance Company. Theresa was his
secretary.

The family was by no means wealthy, but Joe Sr. and Theresa did their best to make their boy think otherwise: "Working is for adults; a kid should be a kid," Joe Sr. told him. And in the Montana household, being a kid meant playing sports.

While in junior high school, Joe Jr. (called Joey by his parents) took a summer job as a caddy at the nearby country club. One day, his loop ran long, and he didn't show for warmups before his 6 p.m. Little League game.

"When Joey wasn't there at 5:45, Joe went after him," Theresa recalled years later. "He picked up Joey's baseball uniform at home, drove out to the country club, took him off the golf course, had him change clothes in the car, and got him to the ballpark in time for the first pitch. That night, Joey's father had a few words for him. He told him, 'We'll have no more of this, son. If you need money, I'll give it to you. If I can't afford it, you'll go without. You came close to letting your team down tonight—your team, their parents, your parents, your coach, and most of all, yourself.'"

Although Joseph Sr. hadn't participated in organized sports during his career at Monongahela High, he did play while in the navy. And from the very start, he introduced his boy to athletics.

"I weighed 130 pounds soaking wet in high school, but I did play sandlot baseball," Joseph Sr. once said. "[Joe Jr.] was brainwashed as a child. He constantly had a ball in his hand, be it a football, basketball, or baseball. Like all parents, I wanted to see him make good."

In Monongahela, Joseph Sr. even organized a neighborhood youth basketball team. He rented the gymnasium, arranged for local adults to teach fundamentals and run the drills, and drove the kids all over Western Pennsylvania and as far as Niagara Falls for tournaments.

Montana was exceptionally skilled at all sports, but the game he truly loved was basketball.

"It was just one of those sports to me—when you're playing, practice is more fun than football practice. It was just a game, every minute you were in it," he said in 2011.

His competitiveness—which became one of Montana's most enduring legacies—developed instantaneously. As much as he enjoyed playing sports, he enjoyed winning far more . . . and hated losing with a passion.

"He was a real competitor, [an] act-shy type of guy," remembered Michael Brantley, Montana's teammate at Waverly Elementary School, Finleyville Junior High, and Ringgold High, and his favorite target on both the football field and basketball court. "He didn't like losing at nothing, even when we'd be playing pickup games in the morning before school. He always wanted to win. Even when we played dodgeball. He hated to lose at that."

Although hoops were Montana's passion, and he excelled as a baseball pitcher—he threw three perfect games in Little League—football was his most natural gift. When he was eight years old (one year too young for the team) his father listed Joe Jr. as nine so he could play quarterback for the Monongahela Little Wildcats.

"I told Joe's dad when he was a very young kid, [Joe] was going to be an All-American," Wildcats coach Carl Crawley said decades later. "I lied. He was not an All-American, he was an All-Pro. I saw that when he was a young kid."

Aware of the special talent in front of him, Crawley, a former college defensive lineman and later an NCAA official, pushed the boy, encouraging him to play and practice hard, not run out of bounds, and fight for extra yardage.

"I've only missed one game in Joe's career," Theresa said. "That was when he was playing on a midget team, which had a game in Clairton. If I went, I would have had to drive alone since my husband was one of the coaches and he was going with the team bus. So I stayed home. When my husband returned from the game that night, Joe's helmet had a hole as big as an orange. I said then I'd never miss another game because if something happened to Joe I'd want to be nearby. And I never have."

In 1971 Montana earned a spot on Ringgold High's varsity football team as a sophomore. At the time, Ringgold's was a mediocre and disorganized program: the year before, the Rams didn't win a single game. But that season, under new head coach Chuck Abramski, Ringgold showed considerable improvement, posting a 4–6 record.

The next summer Montana was expected to compete for the varsity's starting quarterback position, but he did not participate in the team's rigorous summer weightlifting program, and his absence caused Abramski—who pejoratively called the teenager "Joe Banana"—to question his commitment.

"For me, competing in sports was a 365-day-a-year thing," Montana later said. "I was playing American Legion baseball, summer basketball. It was hard for Coach Abramski to accept that."

Although one of the primary goals of the summer training program was to build team camaraderie and prove the players' dedication, Abramski also wanted the quarterback there to strengthen a scrawny, 6-foot, 165-pound frame.

"He was a frail young man, but as frail as he was . . . I've never seen a guy with a vertical leap ever that that kid had," said Chuck Smith, a teammate and Ringgold lineman. "The thing that I remember most about Joe was how he threw the football. He just had an accuracy."

In training camp the junior battled with senior Paul Timko for the starting job. Despite Montana's superior throwing ability, Timko—6-feet-2 and

220 pounds, and a member of the summer weightlifting group—had the upper hand in the quarterback competition.

"Abramski wasn't stupid," said Timko. "He said he tried to pit us against each other. I didn't realize it at the time, but everything we did had Joe and I against each other. Every drill, every spring running, and it actually made me try harder. That's why we couldn't really like each other because we were pitted against each other."

Eventually Timko won the starter's role and was under center for Ringgold's 1972 season opener against Elizabeth Forward High School. The Rams lost by four touchdowns. The rough start to the season, coupled with an injury to tight end Dave Osleger convinced Abramski to switch Timko to tight end and insert Montana into the starting lineup for the next game at Monessen, a Western Pennsylvania powerhouse and a favorite to win the Big Ten conference title.

"When we went into Monessen, it was an awesome environment, it was a night game," fullback Keith Bassi remembered. "Their stadium was at the top of the hill. At that time we would dress at our home locker room in Monongahela, get onto a bus, and drive the ten miles to Monessen in order to play the game. And whenever you approached the stadium, you had to have your helmet on, because your bus was likely to be pelted by rocks or apples or tomatoes or whatever it might be in the hands of the kids and the fans at Monessen. It was a tough, tough crowd.

"One of the characteristics of Monessen was the football team would enter from the top of the stadium and come down the long stairs all the way to the field, then enter onto the field. Well, their squad—in contrast to our squad—looked like the legions of Rome coming into the amphitheater of the Coliseum. There we were, maybe thirty to forty kids . . . the stadium probably had about fifteen- to twenty-thousand people in it, which was typical of Western Pennsylvania high school football stands at that time, and we were just encircled by Monessen, and now here they came onto the field.

"We're standing on the field doing our warmups, and it's all that we could do to keep our jaws from staying wide open as we're watching this event unfurl. And I can remember Montana, just having his back to everything, just going on about business as though it was another day on our practice field. He was completely nonplussed about everything. It was almost as if he didn't notice what was going on around him because he was so focused on what it was he was doing."

In his first high school start, Montana completed thirteen passes for 255 yards and four touchdowns—one to his longtime teammate Michael Brantley and three to his former quarterback rival Paul Timko. The Rams and Greyhounds fought to a 34–34 tie that left local high school football fans completely stunned.

"Montana has the tools to be one of the best quarterbacks in the WPIAL next year, if not this season," Abramski told reporters that evening.

The trio of Montana, Timko, and Brantley gave Ringgold a prodigious passing attack in an era and a region dominated by the run. Montana accounted for twelve touchdowns in their next five games, as the Rams finished with a winning record of 4–3–2, reshaping the program's image. Over the next several months, Montana's body matured, reaching 6-feet-2 and nearly 180 pounds. The following season, Ringgold posted an 8–1 record and reached the WPIAL playoffs.

"In his senior year, the games at Legion Field were a happening," Ringgold's golf coach Bob Osleger said. "There was this flat bit of ground above the stadium, and Joe's father would stand there and watch the game, and all these college coaches and scouts would vie for position to stand near him. The whispers would start, about which college coaches were there that night, and I can see it so clearly now. Joe's dad would be standing there with his hands in his pockets and all these guys jockeying for position around him."

Named an All-American by *Parade* magazine, Montana was heavily courted by several major college football programs, but once Notre Dame offered the Catholic boy a scholarship, his mind was made up. In the summer of 1974, he left Monongahela for South Bend, Indiana, home of the reigning college football national champions.

Once there, however, Montana spent his freshman season as a tackling dummy for the varsity defense, absorbing brutal shots from his teammates, including two All-Americans, defensive tackle Mike Fanning and linebacker Greg Collins.

"If you ever wondered why I'm able to get up after [Mike] Singletary or [Steve] McMichael or [Mark] Gastineau pounds the crap out of me, I've got the Welcome Wagon boys from my freshman year at Notre Dame to thank for that," Montana wrote in his 1986 autobiography *Audibles: My Life in Football*.

The Fighting Irish won ten games that year, but two weeks before a narrow Orange Bowl victory over Alabama capped off the season, head coach Ara Parseghian surprisingly resigned. Green Bay Packers head coach Dan Devine was named his successor. Although Parseghian and his staff had recruited Montana to Notre Dame, the sophomore-to-be actually viewed the coaching change as a boost in his pursuit of the starting quarterback's job.

"I liked Ara, but I figured I had a better chance of starting under Devine," Montana wrote. "The new coach only added to my feeling that I should be playing. If an athlete says, 'Hey, that guy's great, he's better than me,' well, the guy is in big trouble. Once you start thinking that people are better than you, you start giving up. That's when you are destined to stay on the bottom.

Sometimes I look back and wonder where all my mental toughness came from. I've seen guys who seemed to be ten times stronger than me, but I always thought I was better."

Spring practices for the next season began in April 1975, and Montana started proving to everyone else that he was better than any other quarterback on the Notre Dame roster. In the annual Blue–Gold intra squad scrimmage, Montana ignored the rain to throw for 195 yards and three touchdowns during a 38–6 victory over the Blue team and fellow sophomore quarterback Gary Forystek.

"Forystek throws a little better than Montana," Devine told the *Chicago Tribune* that summer. "But Joe, well, Joe comes from a place where he was about the only show in town. And he acts like it. The kid has a certain flair. He does a few of the things that you expect to see in a kid with the name of Joe Montana."

Montana's fine spring was not enough to win the job, however, and Devine named Rick Slager—a junior who had missed spring ball due to an injury—the starter for Notre Dame's opener at Boston College. But Montana's chance to play would come just two weeks later. At Notre Dame Stadium, the Irish fell behind Northwestern 7–0 after a Slager interception provided the Wildcats with great field position.

Later in that first period, a defender bashed Slager on an option-keeper, knocking him from the game. Montana—self-described as "plenty nervous at first"—took command of the offense, and Notre Dame scored thirty-one unanswered points. The nineteen-year-old threw a touchdown to Mark McLane and rushed for another on a fourth-and-goal from the six to close out the victory.

Modest offensive outputs (three combined touchdowns against unranked teams) in Notre Dame's first two games and the spark Montana provided against Northwestern ignited a minor quarterback controversy in South Bend. Montana and Slager split quarterback duties the next Saturday in a 10–3 turnover-laden loss to Michigan State. Devine then named Slager the full-time starter the following week against North Carolina.

But Slager and the offense continued to struggle in Chapel Hill. With his team losing 14–6 midway through the final period and in danger of a second-straight loss, Devine turned back to Montana, who drove the Irish seventy-three yards for a touchdown and converted the game-tying two-point conversion. Minutes later, he completed the comeback with a short sideline pass to Ted Burgmeier, who broke through Bobby Trott's tackle and sprinted eighty yards for the game-winning score.

"I was excited," Montana later wrote, "but I didn't go overboard. I knew my fate was calculated on a week-to-week basis."

Montana was right to be cautious, especially after hearing his head coach speak to the media following the game.

"I thought both Rick Slager and Joe Montana did well," he said. "I love them both. We need them both. Montana's greatest supporter on the sidelines was Rick Slager, and vice versa."

Slager was named the starter for the following game in Colorado Springs, but the budding quarterback controversy was overshadowed that week by rumors that Devine would be fired to make room for a return by Parseghian. Amid those distractions, Notre Dame fell behind the Air Force Academy 30–10. Montana relieved Slager during the second half, however, and early in the fourth quarter he led the offense to three touchdowns, pulling off a fantastic 31–30 victory.

"Once we got going," Montana told the press that day, "everybody knew we could pull this out. You start thinking more in the fourth quarter, and your whole mental attitude is better."

After a second straight comeback, Montana was given his first college start a week later against the archrival Southern California Trojans. He completed just three passes, however, and threw two costly interceptions in a 24–17 loss. His tenure as starter didn't last long. During an easy triumph over Navy, Montana chipped a bone in his finger and missed the rest of the season.

The next year Slager won the Blue–Gold game MVP and ultimately the starter's job in spring practice, while Montana separated his shoulder during a drill just before the start of the 1976 season. Redshirted, Montana didn't play in a single game, but he did heal much earlier than doctors expected: his cast was removed after just three-and-a-half weeks, instead of the predicted six. The coaching staff even promised Montana that he could travel with the team if he returned to run scout team practices late in the season, which he did. But Montana dressed only for one home game.

"That season was frustrating, but I learned not to take anything for granted," Montana wrote. "Traveling with the team might seem trivial, but what was important was the knowledge at that point in my career that I really couldn't trust Dan Devine."

* * *

Starter or not, injured and in a sling or on the field directing improbable victories, Joe Montana's Notre Dame teammates loved him.

"[He was] just a regular guy who wanted to play hoops, go drink a beer," center Dave Huffman said. "We called him Joe Montanalow because he was the spitting image of Barry Manilow. In his senior year he moved into an apartment above a bar. When the bar closed down, we'd go upstairs to Joe's place. It was our after-hours joint."

Montana's personality and the string of fourth-quarter comebacks he engineered as a sophomore made the junior a popular choice for the next season's starting job. But after the Blue–Gold game, Devine instead named junior Rusty Lisch the starter as they entered the summer and reaffirmed his selection at the end of the preseason.

"He's a dedicated athlete," Devine explained in April. "[Lisch] doesn't do anything here except study and play football. He's tough . . . he's never been hurt."

Apart from his dedication and durability, Lisch—a 6-foot-4 dual threat from Belleville, Illinois—had quarterbacked the Irish's 20–9 Gator Bowl victory over Penn State the previous December.

But that promising résumé was not the only reason Montana—who later wrote that Devine "was wishy-washy. . . . He would never stick to one quarterback"—fell to third string on the depth chart, behind both Lisch and Gary Forystek.

"I think there were a lot of people who had seen him play, and certainly some of our coaches felt like he probably should be the starter," Notre Dame's offensive coordinator Merv Johnson said years later. "But he had that quality that made him great . . . a bad play, he could immediately put it behind him and not let it affect his play from there on.

"Coach Devine was old school and [if] a guy makes a bad play in practice, he'd like for it to really eat him up and bother him a lot more than it did Joe. But Joe was just the same guy. He just blew it off and went on to the next play. So it was a little hard for him to endear himself . . . to Coach Devine to get the starting role."

In early September Notre Dame faced the University of Pittsburgh. Despite the return to his native Western Pennsylvania, Montana did not play, as the Irish toppled the defending national champion Panthers 19–9. The next Saturday he again watched from the sidelines, this time while his teammates squandered a fourth-quarter lead and lost to Ole Miss, 20–13.

"When we lost to Mississippi with Joe on the bench, I thought, 'What a weird deal,'" said All-American tight end Ken MacAfee. "I mean, we all knew he could do it, he knew he could do it, but he wasn't playing. He was really down. I remember going to his apartment one night and he said, 'I'm just sick of this crap, sick of the whole thing.'"

The following week versus in-state rival Purdue, the preseason number-one Irish were headed for a second straight loss to an unranked opponent. Late the third quarter, Notre Dame trailed 24–14 when Purdue sophomore linebacker Keena Turner nabbed the second interception thrown by Rusty Lisch.

"We had them by the throat," remembered Turner, who would become Montana's San Francisco 49ers teammate through eleven seasons and four Super Bowl triumphs. "Joe comes in and [scores] two touchdowns and beats us. . . . So when I went to the Niners, I knew who he was."

Early in the fourth quarter, Montana took over for an injured Forystek, who had taken over for the ineffective Lisch. After an ugly, wobbly pass that was nearly intercepted—"Forget it, fellows," he told the huddle, "I had to get that one out of my system. We'll settle down now"—Montana completed nine of thirteen attempts for 154 yards. A touchdown pass to MacAfee tied the game at 24, and minutes later he hit wide receiver Kris Haines for twenty-six yards, setting up the game-winning touchdown run by Dave Mitchell.

"I won the quarterback job that day," Montana later wrote. "When I look back at it, I still have mixed feelings about the way the whole thing was handled. Sometimes I think it came down to luck . . . not my ability."

Luck or not, with Montana under center Notre Dame won the next eight games and finished the season ranked fifth in the nation, earning a Cotton Bowl showdown with the University of Texas. The Irish pounded the top-ranked Longhorns 38–10 to claim the school's tenth national championship. The next autumn, however, Montana—a team captain and short-lived preseason Heisman Trophy favorite—and the Irish dropped their first two games. Despite the slow start, by the end of the 1978 season the senior quarterback secured a place in college football mythology.

Eight consecutive wins, followed by a painful 27–25 loss to Southern Cal—an official's dubious call ruined Montana's nineteen-point second-half comeback—earned the Irish a repeat trip to the Cotton Bowl, albeit under starkly different circumstances.

When Notre Dame defeated Texas to win the national championship in January 1978, the weather in Dallas had been unseasonably cold, but nothing like what they encountered the following year for their showdown with ninth-ranked Houston. On New Year's Eve, a freak ice storm hit Dallas. Power lines and tree branches snapped under the chunks of ice, fifty thousand homes lost electricity, and at least two fatalities were reported.

Despite closed roads, minus-six-degree wind chill temperatures, thirty mile per hour winds, a blanket of ice on the AstroTurf, and nearly forty thousand no-shows to the sold-out game, the annual Cotton Bowl Classic kicked off on time at 1 p.m. New Year's Day.

Benefitting from harsh winds at the offense's back, the Irish took a 12–0 first-quarter lead. Houston answered with two touchdowns and two field goals, taking a 20–12 advantage just before halftime. A pair of Montana interceptions aided the Cougars resurgence. The windy and frigid conditions—as well as the rock salt scattered across the field to break up sheets of ice—contributed to the second-quarter woes, but there was another handicap for the Irish: earlier in the week, Montana had caught the flu, making him more susceptible to the nasty elements.

"It was almost impossible to feel the ball through our frostbitten fingers," Montana wrote. "At the half, I arrived in the locker room shaking uncontrollably. My temperature had dropped to ninety-six degrees. This was really strange; I couldn't control my body. The doctors and trainers covered me with blankets and coats. I began drinking as much chicken soup as I could. As my body warmed, that feeling I had had earlier—not wanting to play because of the cold—disappeared. I wanted to go back and take another shot."

But when the players left the locker room for the second-half kickoff, Montana did not join them. And, trailing 20–12 during the second period, the Irish free fall continued. Houston scored a pair of third-quarter touchdowns, increasing their lead to 22.

"We saw Joe sitting on the athletic table as we were walking out [of the locker room], and he wasn't coming with us," wide receiver Kris Haines recalled. "Everybody's kind of like, 'Oh God, now we're finished,' which is a bad attitude to have, but that's the kind of response guys had."

While Montana remained in the locker room throughout the third quarter, buried in blankets, gulping down chicken soup, Dan Devine received frequent updates on the health of his quarterback.

"Rick Slager was in law school then, and he was a graduate assistant coach on the sidelines with me," Devine said years later. "His job was to run into the locker room every five minutes to see what Joe's temperature was. He'd come back and say, 'It's up to 97,' and five minutes later I'd tell him to run in and find out again."

Late in the third quarter, with the Irish still behind 34–12, Montana's temperature approached normal, and he emerged from the locker room.

"When Joe came back to the field, I started thinking this was a fairy tale," Kris Haines said. "Here he comes again. He's done it so many times before."

After a partially blocked Houston punt was returned for a touchdown, Montana inched Notre Dame closer with a two-point conversion. The Irish defense then forced another punt, and Montana soon rushed for a short touchdown and added another two points via a pass to Haines. With less than five minutes remaining, the deficit was just six.

Notre Dame stopped Houston's next possession on a fourth-and-short, giving Montana the ball back with only twenty-eight seconds left. He scrambled for eleven, then once again hit Haines near the sideline for ten more yards. An incompletion stopped the clock with two seconds remaining.

"The coaches just waved their hands at us . . . 'Call whatever you want to call,'" running back Vagas Ferguson remembered years later. "Kris Haines had told him, 'I can beat this guy, I can beat this guy.' And Joe got on the ground and drew a little thing on the ground and said 'Kris, you do this, Vagas, you clear and do this, and Kris you go right to that spot there, and I'll hit you.' And it worked out that way. Last play of the game, and he drew it up on the ground. People don't believe that, but I sat there and watched him do it."

Montana broke the huddle, took the snap, rolled right to escape a defender's grasp, and slung a pass to the corner of the end zone, where a diving Haines made the game-winning grab.

"It couldn't have been a more perfect pass," Haines said. "It looked low and outside, but that's where it was supposed to be. It was so clutch."

Kicker Joe Unis nailed the extra point, completing the icy miracle. The winning sideline—those not frozen or racing for the warmth of the locker room—went crazy. But for Montana, the 35–34 victory was bittersweet, and not just because the game was his last in a Notre Dame uniform.

"Reporters were asking me if I realized that we had just played in a classic football game," Montana wrote in 1986. "Yeah, maybe we did, but other things were running through my mind. It was a time for reflection. During the last three years at Notre Dame, Devine had really done nothing to boost my confidence. In fact, he had never given me much credit until now. Why couldn't he have been easier? Why do coaches play games with people's minds? I guess I'll never know because I never went back and talked to him about it.

"Maybe I learned a lesson. It is part of my nature to give someone the benefit of the doubt, to think they mean well. My stay at Notre Dame changed my attitude. Devine never let me know what he was up to. Believe me, after that Houston game, my conversion from a believer to a skeptic was complete.

"But sitting in that locker room, in the middle of a great celebration, it occurred to me that no coach wants to give you credit while you are playing for him. Maybe Devine was playing mind games with me, but maybe it was strategy. He had the ability to keep me on edge, keep me on my toes."

*   *   *

In September 1978, NFL draft guru Gil Brandt, provided *Sport* magazine with a college football All-American preview and a roster of future NFL stars. Brandt, the Dallas Cowboys ultra-successful vice president of Player Personnel, gave high marks to Southern California offensive tackle Anthony Munoz, Missouri tight end Kellen Winslow, and a two-sport star from Michigan State, wide receiver Kirk Gibson. The lone quarterback on his list of top NFL prospects was Notre Dame's Joe Montana.

"I can remember making the college rounds in the spring of '74, when all the talk was about 'where Montana will go,'" Brandt wrote. "Almost from the beginning at Notre Dame, he demonstrated that he was a leader and a great competitor. . . . Statistically, Montana doesn't look that impressive. I suppose you'd have to be inside the Notre Dame huddle when he calls a play. His teammates just know he's going to make it work. He has a quality that reminds me of Roger Staubach: he finds a way to win."

The following spring, in the 1979 NFL draft, Brandt's Cowboys passed on Montana three times in the first three rounds. So did every other team with a first-, second-, or third-round draft choice until the San Francisco 49ers pulled Montana off the board with the eighty-second overall selection. And even that choice was a reluctant one.

In January, the 49ers had hired Stanford University's Bill Walsh as their new head coach. With the team's third-round pick, Walsh wanted to select Cardinal quarterback Steve Dils, winner of the annual Sammy Baugh Trophy. At the urging of the franchise's scouting director Tony Razzano and vice president John Ralston, Walsh grudgingly selected Montana.

"We kept going back and forth, and Tony kept insisting on Montana," Ralston said years later. "Bill yelled at me and said, 'Get me one more recommendation on Joe Montana.' I called Dan Devine, the coach at Notre Dame, and he said, 'John, if I had Joe Montana, I'd still be head coach in Green Bay.' That was enough for Bill. He took Montana. But when the Vikings drafted Dils a few picks later, bang! Bill slammed his fist down on the table and said, 'Dammit, I knew we should have taken Steve.'"

And when Montana arrived at the 49ers first training camp, his physique (or lack thereof) didn't relieve Walsh, who years later admitted that local fans had asked him, "Where'd you get this guy who looks like a Swedish placekicker?"

Even Walsh's boss Eddie DeBartolo Jr. had his doubts. Walsh informed DeBartolo—a Notre Dame alum—of the selection on draft day, in the team's grossly undersized Redwood City headquarters at 711 Nevada Street. Initially, the 49ers owner approved.

"Bill came out a little bit before the third round, and we started talking. He said, 'What do you think about this kid from Notre Dame?' Jokingly, I said, 'How can you ever go wrong with somebody from Notre Dame?'" De-Bartolo recalled years later. "The next morning I was meeting Joe Montana. [He was] quiet, subdued, little, frail-looking, nothing that I expected. He was very gentlemanly—we talked about Notre Dame, we talked about some of the old haunts we used to go to that were still around—he was just a normal guy. But he certainly didn't look like a franchise quarterback, let me put it that way."

Following a difficult negotiation period—the front office and his agent couldn't agree on a contract so Montana was shopped to other teams—

Montana signed with the 49ers in July. That 1979 season, he started one game and played briefly in four others, occasionally spelling starter Steve De-Berg, Montana's friend, roommate, and heated rival in everything from basketball and tennis to late night games of ping pong and Mattel's baseball video game.

"[DeBerg taught me] to be resilient and persevere because it gets tough," Montana said in 2011. "I never heard him complain. He was another one of those guys who'd compete with you walking down the street, who was in front of who, by a step. It was fun to be around Steve . . . but he would fight back. I don't care what happened to him, how good or bad it was going, he's battling until they take him out."

As Montana began grasping the offense and the pro game, the 49ers coaching staff did start to take DeBerg out. Walsh carefully chose moments to replace the veteran, inserting Montana in low-pressure situations, past midfield and near the opponent's goal line.

"Coach Walsh was grooming Montana to be his quarterback, so he brought Joe along kind of slow, and he would put him in situations where he would have a real good chance of success," DeBerg recalled years later. "Sometimes it was a little frustrating for me. There was one or two times I know that they had a signal for me to fake an injury so that Joe could go in [for] some kind of trick play. It was Bill Walsh's way of bringing Joe along and building his confidence and preparing him to be a great player."

Eventually, Walsh began benching DeBerg in favor of Montana, even in the middle of drives. During Week 7 of the 1980 season, DeBerg threw two interceptions against the Los Angeles Rams, both of which were returned for touchdowns. After the second turnover put the Rams ahead 34–7, Montana took the field. Walsh never told DeBerg he was being replaced, then justified the move to the press by saying, "Steve was pretty banged up." DeBerg denied any injury.

"I was lucky. Bill was grooming me to become the 49ers' quarterback of the future—I hoped!" Montana later wrote. "I felt bad for Steve; he was my friend. Bill might have been handpicking situations for me to build my confidence, but what was that doing to DeBerg? Inside he must have been going nuts, but he never said anything. He never complained. He had to believe he was better than me, but even if he didn't, he was too much of a competitor to ever admit it. The way they were treating Steve would have driven me crazy."

The undesirable quarterback-swapping continued throughout Montana's second season, as both players started a handful of games and played in several others. By late November, San Francisco's two-year record under Walsh was just 6–22.

"DeBerg has the knowledge and background to do the job, and Montana is the better athlete," Walsh said prior to the 49ers Week 13 matchup with New England. "I prefer Montana the nearer we are to the opponents' goal line and DeBerg when we're looking for ball control. DeBerg has more of a grasp of what we're trying to do. He's not an active player; he throws the ball well, but he's not at all an active, quick quarterback."

The next day Walsh announced that Montana would start against New England. The twenty-four-year-old rewarded his head coach with three touchdown passes in a 21–17 upset victory over the 8–4 Patriots. A thigh bruise knocked Montana out of the game in the second half, but he begged Walsh to let him return to close out the victory.

"He said he wanted to play some more," Walsh said. "So I let him go."

The following week, Walsh also kept Montana in the lineup during a miserable first half—twenty-one yards and zero points from the offense—at home against the 0–14 Saints. Trailing 35–7, Montana marched the offense eighty-eight yards, capping off the series with a short touchdown run. San Francisco then scored touchdowns on their next three possessions to tie the game at 35. In overtime, the Saints could not make a first down and punted. Montana then drove the 49ers from their own 34 to the Saints 19. Four plays later, Ray Wersching's thirty-six-yard field goal completed the largest second-half comeback in NFL history.

"Joe was simply outstanding," Walsh told biographer David Harris. "This was the game where his teammates learned to believe in him."

As much as his teammates were beginning to believe in him, Montana was becoming a believer of the 49ers scheme, as well. Walsh, a protégé of the great Paul Brown, trained the 49ers in what became known as the "West Coast Offense," a system centered around short, strategically designed passes that methodically advanced the ball downfield.

"There was a purpose to the things that were being done," Montana explained years later. "It wasn't that I couldn't throw the ball down the field; [Walsh] didn't like throwing the ball down the field because it was a low percentage pass unless it was done in the right circumstance, like a blitz or you've got man-to-man coverage, no safety deep. His was a high percentage completion [offense]. 'Look, I'm going to give you someone down the field, basically, and I'm going to give you two guys down here who are going to try to influence the people covering you. And if they don't respect these guys underneath, just give them the ball.

"It's funny how defenses think, because you hand the ball off to a running back and he gains four yards on first down and everybody's saying that's not good: you can't give up four yards on a run on first down. Well, if you drop back and throw on first down and you're looking down the field, dump it off, and you gain four yards, the defense has in their minds, 'Well, we pretty much stopped them, that was a good hold.' Well, you got the same four yards, it doesn't really matter how you accomplish it; it's just find a way to get it done. And that's what it takes a quarterback in that position to understand."

Although he was raised in blue collar Western Pennsylvania, was shy and introverted around the press, and preferred spending his days on the basketball court or football field and his nights throwing back a few beers with his pals, Montana meshed perfectly with Walsh's deep, philosophical approach to the barbaric sport.

"I wanted to play the game as more of a chess game," he once told NFL Films. "One move's going to lead to another, and you're not always going to get the king immediately: four yards here, five yards there, ten yards . . . is as wearing, if not more, on a defense as one seventy-yard touchdown. And that was more my style than anything."

The marriage of Montana and Walsh's styles produced a Cinderella season in 1981. The 49ers posted a 13–3 record, toppled the New York Giants, then faced "America's Team," the Dallas Cowboys, in an epic NFC Championship Game. Largely due to three Montana interceptions, Dallas owned a 27–21 advantage when the 49ers took possession at their own eleven-yard line with less than five minutes remaining in the game.

"Our confidence was super with [eighty-nine] yards to go," said Montana. "We knew we could move the ball. "There was never any doubt. There was plenty of time. There was no need to worry."

A handful of Lenvil Elliot runs, Freddie Solomon's fourteen-yard pickup on a wide receiver reverse, followed by a critical sideline completion to Dwight Clark put San Francisco at the Dallas twenty-five. Another clutch pass to Solomon and a short run by Elliott pushed San Francisco to the Dallas six. From there, Montana rolled right, twice hesitated with the ball—"I was thinking of throwing the ball away, but I saw him come open," he said—then floated a high pass into the end zone. A leaping Dwight Clark pulled in the ball, resulting in the most memorable reception in NFL history, "The Catch."

The 49ers won the NFC title, and two weeks later at the Silverdome in Pontiac, Michigan, defeated the Cincinnati Bengals 26–21, clinching their first NFL championship in franchise history. Montana completed fourteen of twenty-two attempts, rushed for the game's first score, tossed a touchdown pass, and was named the MVP of Super Bowl XVI.

The career-defining achievement, the accolades, and the instant worldwide attention—he became the first person to appear on the covers of *Sports*

Illustrated, *Time*, and *Newsweek* in the same week[1]—hardly satified Montana's roaring, competitive fire.

"I talked to some of my friends from Pittsburgh, particularly [four-time Super Bowl champion] Rocky Bleier," Montana said. "They told me, 'The more you win, the sweeter it gets.' 'Well, I've got ten fingers . . . and ten toes,' Rocky said. And I think any athlete feels this way—that the more you win, the more you want to win. He said once you're there (in the Super Bowl), and you come back the next year, the way you can feel successful inside is if you get there again. If you do it again, it becomes something that you feel you have to do each year if you want to feel successful as a team."

By these lofty new standards, Montana and the 49ers next two seasons were failures. But in 1984, San Francisco returned to the Super Bowl to play the Miami Dolphins, led by another Western Pennsylvania quarterback product, record-setting, second-year passer Dan Marino. Much to the disdain of the viewing audience and the ABC television network, however, the game never approached its pregame hype as a shootout between the NFL's two brightest young stars. Instead, Montana threw for three touchdowns, ran in a fourth, and the 49ers trounced Miami, 38–16.

"Dan Marino's a great young quarterback," Walsh told reporters that evening, "but my feeling, our feeling, is that Joe Montana is the greatest quarterback today, maybe the greatest of all time."

Despite the success, the accolades, and sudden talk of a surprising dynasty, behind closed doors not all was well within the organization. Out of the public eye, Montana's relationship with his head coach was as strained and untrusting—often more so—as his relationships with Ringgold's Chuck Abramski and Notre Dame's Dan Devine. Regardless of Walsh's public praise and a mutual respect the two men felt for each other, they remained privately distant. According to David Harris's biography, *The Genius*, Montana felt that Walsh didn't appreciate him or respect his talents and efforts. Montana also believed that his fate wasn't quite his own: it belonged to Walsh. So, with each victory, each division title, each Super Bowl championship, one question bubbled under the 49ers' surface: Who was the true catalyst of the blossoming dynasty? The quarterback or the coach?

"I think when it started off, it was easy: Joe was a third-round pick, Bill was the new coach," 49ers advisor Carmen Policy remembered. "I think moving forward, Joe Montana could have really loved Bill Walsh, if Bill Walsh

---

[1] Eight years earlier, the Triple Crown–winning horse Secretariat was the first "athlete" to appear on the cover of *Sports Illustrated*, *Time*, and *Newsweek* all in the same week, but Montana was the first *human* athlete to do so.

would have not become so obsessed with the idea that the success was the product of his efforts and his genius. I think he saw—like so many other people did—Joe, as a third-round pick.

"I think maybe Walsh, instead of seeing the diamond in the rough, he may have saw a carbon that he shined up to the level of a diamond. And I always felt that that wasn't quite fair to Joe, and I think Joe always respected Bill: Joe's that kind of guy, he's old fashioned in many respects."

Complex, cynical football relationships were commonplace for Walsh. Just a few years earlier, as a member of Paul Brown's Cincinnati Bengals staff, Walsh was passed over for promotion to head coach, then fired by Brown's successor, Tiger Johnson. Many—including Walsh—believed Brown secretly campaigned against his promotion and even blacklisted him in the years that followed.

"Bill never would get close to his players because he'd have to cut them, and you want to be able to make an objective decision and make a decision that's in the best interest of the team. He would say that too often too many coaches keep veteran players one year longer than they should, and it hurts the team," said Guy Benjamin, a quarterback who played for Walsh at Stanford and with the 49ers.

"Bill would talk to us about retiring, being out on the top. You don't want to be the old pro that just kind of hangs around and a memory of your former self, resting on your laurels, he'd always say that. . . . Having said all that, after it's over with, after you're retired, he really would step forward and seek out to continue that relationship, and change the relationship into a personal relationship. And if a player did not respond in that way, Bill would very much be distraught over that. He very much wanted to have close, personal relationships with his players; he's very loyal to his former players, was open in a number of ways. He was always open. He was a very different man and had very different relationships, once you stopped playing for him."

After a disappointing 4–4 start to the 1985 season, the defending Super Bowl champion 49ers rebounded with five wins in the final six weeks to earn a wild card berth and a trip to East Rutherford, New Jersey, to play the New York Giants. That year, Montana missed just his second professional game due to injury. A sprained shoulder sidelined him in Week 9 against Philadelphia.

That wasn't the only injury Montana suffered that season, however. In training camp, his lower back began to ache and a CT scan revealed scoliosis—a twist in the vertebrae. He sat out the team's final two exhibition games before the start of the regular season, and received physical therapy throughout the year.

"I think Joe is going to be fine," the team's physician Dr. Michael Dillingham said that August. "This injury is certainly nothing to get alarmed about, and we have some things we will do during the season to assure that his back remains healthy."

To earn a spot in the postseason, the 49ers had to win their regular season finale against the Cowboys at Candlestick Park. Trailing Dallas 13–0 midway through the second period, Montana fired two touchdown passes to Dwight Clark, and the 49ers came back to win 31–16. During the victory, however, Montana pulled a muscle in his ribs, and throughout the following week the pain worsened, especially when he tried to run. The agony intensified when a cold he caught forced him to cough and sneeze. Reluctantly, Montana agreed to take a series of eight pain-killing injections.

"The pain was very bad, but I didn't want to take any shots because I don't like needles," Montana wrote in 1986. "I can't stand the feeling of a needle going into my body, so I usually avoid any kind of shot as long as possible."

On game day, Montana's availability remained in doubt. He barely practiced late in the week, and tight end Russ Francis didn't expect him to play.

"Joe wouldn't say much about it," Dwight Clark said, "but he was in excruciating pain all week. If he just coughed or sneezed, it killed him. And now he had to try to throw a football."

In a stout defensive battle, the host Giants clung to a 17–3 lead late but still feared the opponent's battered quarterback and his penchant for legendary fourth-quarter comebacks.

"I looked into Montana's eyes," Giants nose tackle Jim Burt said, "and it seemed like even at the end he was going to get it done."

Montana—who was sacked four times—completed twenty-six passes for 296 yards, but the Giants defense kept San Francisco out of the end zone and ended the 49ers bid for a Super Bowl repeat.

"The only time my ribs hurt was when I dropped back to pass and when I followed through," Montana said. "They didn't hurt when I released the ball."

Although Walsh noticed Montana was in pain, he told reporters that he never once considered replacing his quarterback.

"It unquestionably affected Joe, but not enough to keep him out," Walsh said. "When you come this far with Joe Montana, you're not going to take him out when he can still function reasonably."

Great Expectations

Eight-year-old Steve Young yearned to play quarterback for his elementary school football team, the North Mianus Cowboys.

"But the coach's son played quarterback, too," Young recalled years later. "So I played running back."

In his first game against the Belhaven Buzzards, Young lined up in the backfield, took a handoff from the coach's son, and sprinted around the end of the line where a much larger defender grabbed his neck, harshly yanking him to the ground. Watching from the stands, his mother, Sherry Young—"twenties-aged lady, in a dress, on a football field, purse on her shoulder, big sunglasses, high-heeled shoes aerating the field," Young remembered—raced onto the field. But not toward *her* child.

"She started shaking this big kid by the shoulders and telling him, 'Don't ever hit my son that way again,'" he remembered. "I'm lying there on the ground, trying to catch my breath and thinking, 'Aw, Mom, not here, in my first game.' But that was the last game I played running back."

Steve Young got his wish, becoming his team's starting quarterback.

The great-great-great-grandson of Mormon patriarch Brigham Young, Jon Steven Young was born in Salt Lake City, Utah, on October 11, 1961. Eight years later, the Young family moved east when Steve's father, a lawyer for the Anaconda Wire and Cable Company, was transferred to New York City.

Although LeGrande Young made a fine living as a corporate attorney and raised his family in the wealthy Greenwich, Connecticut, suburbs—"the low rent district," according to Steve Young—his children felt no sense of entitlement. For years, LeGrande, whose nickname was "Grit," successfully convinced his children that he made only six dollars a day.

"I grew up mowing lawns for the country-club set," Steve Young said. "They made me feel out of place then, and I still feel awkward with that crowd."

The eldest child, Steve wanted a new purple Schwinn Sting-Ray bicycle as a boy. To raise money, he delivered the *Greenwich Times* to neighbors after school. Eventually, he passed the paper route to his younger brothers, Tom, Mike, and Jimmy, and his sister Melissa.

"We thought we were the poorest people in the world," Melissa remembered years later.

In between school, his paper route, jobs at the nearby country club and the ice cream parlor, and Mormon bible study classes in Scarsdale, New York, Young played sports. Slightly bigger and faster than his classmates, he played with older kids, which, despite his athleticism, always put him at a disadvantage. "I never felt like I was the good one," he remembered. "I was pushing so hard to be good. . . . At that point, you just don't know how truly gifted you are."

Once he reached Greenwich High School, Young was a three-sport star: an excellent left-handed pitcher and centerfielder, a point guard on the varsity basketball team, and an elusive quarterback for the Cardinal football team.

As a senior, during the 1978–1979 school year, he captained all three teams, dated the prettiest girl in school (Christy Fichtner, who would be crowned Miss USA seven years later), won the Harvard Book Award for English, and was a National Merit Scholar, despite a course load of advanced placement (AP) classes. He entered college two credits shy of sophomore standing.

"He had the whole package," said Terry Lowe, Young's AP calculus teacher. "He kept to the rules of his life and was always a model student. He carried himself with honor, dignity, and modesty."

Modest also best described Young's throwing ability as a high school quarterback. In head coach Mike Ornato's offense, Young excelled as an option quarterback, but rarely threw the ball. A two-year total of 1,928 rushing yards, consecutive seven-win seasons, and a berth in the 1979 Fairfield County Interscholastic Athletic Conference (FCIAC) championship game meant there was little need for another offensive approach.

"Steve was never outstanding as a passer and did not have a particularly strong arm, but he was a great, great runner," Ornato later said. "He had excellent speed, and he was a deceptive, slashing type of runner."

Young's physical gifts and wealth of academic achievements drew attention from major Division I college football programs, including Syracuse,

West Virginia, and North Carolina. But Young's limited skills as a passer and his speed and athleticism meant schools recruited him to play either running back, wide receiver, or defensive back. Young only wanted to play quarterback, however, and one school was willing to at least let him try—the university his great-great-great grandfather founded, the same university where his father had been a star fullback in the 1950s.

"I remember looking at him on film, and he never threw the football; he ran the option and was a great runner, a great athlete, so we had some interest in him from that standpoint," Brigham Young University's head coach LaVell Edwards said in 2011. "I spoke at a [Mormon] church function, a youth meeting, to the people of that New York area. Steve Young conducted it. He was in high school at that time. And I remember how impressed I was with him and how poised he was.

"At the end of the season, during recruiting, I went back up there in January to visit with him and his family. We weren't sure about his passing, dropback. The passing he had done had been mainly option, on the run, on the move. But we wanted him in the program because if he couldn't be a quarterback he could certainly play any number of other positions. He said, 'The only commitment I want from you is that I have a legitimate chance to be a quarterback before you move me to another position.' Of course we told him that would be the case."

The season before Edwards and his staff recruited Young, the BYU Cougars set a school record for victories and lost the Holiday Bowl to Indiana by just a single point. Their 11–1 record marked the fourth consecutive season in which BYU won at least nine games. During that same stretch, the Cougars began churning out excellent, NFL-caliber quarterbacks. In 1976, Gifford Nielsen threw for 3,192 yards and twenty-nine touchdowns and was named an All-American. Three years later, Nielsen's replacement, All-American Marc Wilson, led the nation in passing, finished third in the Heisman Trophy race, and was a first-round draft choice of the Oakland Raiders.

"If you want to be a quarterback," Young later said, "this is the place."

But when Young arrived in Provo in the summer of 1980, Edwards already had a stable packed with quarterbacks. He fell to eighth on the team's depth chart and came to regret his choice of schools.

"After five days of summer camp," Young said. "I was so frustrated I called my dad and told him that was it. I'm coming home. I quit. He said, 'You can quit, but you can't come home.' No quitters. It was a low that my dad helped me through. I don't know that I ever called him again and said I was going to quit, no matter how hard it was."

Determined not to give up, Young remained in Provo for his freshman year and returned in the fall of 1981, but the coaching staff considered moving him to defensive back.

"I really liked Steve Young's potential, even though he was an option quarterback in high school and was still learning how to be a drop back guy in our system," quarterback coach Ted Tollner remembered. "There were some fundamentals, mechanics, that I really liked along with his athleticism. [LaVell Edwards] said he had a chance to start on defense, and we needed some help. So I talked to Steve . . . and he basically said to me, 'If you think I can be a quarterback, I really want to be a quarterback. So I can be patient for a year.'"

Tollner persuaded Edwards to keep Young on offense, and he eventually rose to second-string, where he backed up Jim McMahon, fresh off perhaps the finest single season in the history of college football history.

As a junior in 1980, McMahon threw for 4,517 yards and forty-seven touchdowns, shattering the NCAA records. In that year's Holiday Bowl against Southern Methodist and their "Pony Express" backfield, he rallied the Cougars from a twenty-point deficit with less than four minutes remaining to win 46–45. McMahon's Hail Mary to Clay Brown on the game's final play capped the miraculous comeback.

McMahon returned for his senior season and was again one of the nation's premier passers. He threw thirty touchdowns, finished third in the Heisman Trophy balloting, and guided the Cougars to a second consecutive Holiday Bowl victory.

"I thought [Steve Young] was anxious to get out there, but I also understood that the guy in front of him was a very good player," Tollner remembered. "Jim was an outstanding player that had different kind of traits . . . a lot of them very similar to Steve, but he was obviously further along at that point. He knew that by observing, watching Jim, he could grow that way. But he also wanted to play. The bottom line is you gotta get on the field to really grow."

Despite tremendous differences in values, personality, and backgrounds—one journalist described McMahon as "a Catholic with a fondness for four-letter words, a cold beer, Coke, and chewing tobacco, who was immediately at odds with the institution"—Young found in McMahon a model to emulate. Or at least a quarterback model to emulate.

"I really didn't know how to throw back then," Young later said. "I learned to throw at Brigham Young, mostly from Jim McMahon. We were about the same size and had the same athletic abilities. It was really good for me, because he had no bad habits. . . . I mean, naked golf, that's different."

"Their private lives were different," Tollner said. "But on the football field, I thought he was very eager to learn from what Jim did to make him successful. It was not a close relationship. . . . I didn't observe it as being close, but I observed it as being respectful of each other."

A first round draft choice by the Chicago Bears, McMahon left Provo after his 1981 senior season. The media and Cougar fans expected Young to fill the gapping void and carry on the school's tradition of All-American quarterbacks.

"I am not Jim McMahon," Young said prior to the 1982 college season. "Nor do I want to be Jim McMahon. I'm always asked what it's like to follow all the great BYU quarterbacks—Gifford Nielsen, Marc Wilson and of course, old McMahon. I'm always asked if I'll be better than McMahon. The answer is yes. I'm always asked if I can fill his shoes. No—Jim's a [size] ten; I'm a twelve."

Just two weeks into his career as the Cougars starter, Young didn't seem to measure up.

After an easy 27–0 victory over University of Nevada–Las Vegas (UNLV) in their season opener, BYU traveled east to play the sixth-ranked Georgia Bulldogs and superstar running back Herschel Walker. That game—against the highest ranked opponent in the fifty-eight-year history of the BYU program—offered the Cougars an opportunity for the Western Athletic Conference (WAC) program to earn national respect by defeating a Southeastern Conference (SEC) powerhouse. But Georgia's defense and a heavy rainstorm stifled Young, who threw six interceptions, the last of which came in the final minute as the Cougars trailed 17–14 but were in range of a game-tying field goal.

"He had a real bad second game. It was also my second game as quarterback coach there," said Mike Holmgren, who was brought in that season to succeed Tollner. "He threw six interceptions against Georgia, and I told him on Monday, 'Steve, this had better get better or I'm back at San Francisco State, and I don't know where you are.'"

The following week—in front of the largest sports crowd in the history of the state of Utah—Young's scrambling produced ninety-seven yards and three rushing touchdowns, but the Cougars still fell to Air Force 39–38, their first home defeat in nearly six years.

"I played my heart out and tried to play up to my expectations," Young later said. "I felt if I lived up to them, people would have to be pleased. [Jim McMahon's] success set a standard for me, so the pressure was there. But that was good because I wanted to be good."

Despite the Cougars worst start since 1975, Young remained confident in his abilities and growing familiarity with the offense. BYU recovered to win seven of their next eight games and earned another trip to the Holiday Bowl. But there the Ohio State Buckeyes pounded the Cougars, 47–17.

"We were getting beat quite soundly," Edwards remembered. "And in the game [Young] went to throw the ball and got hit from his blind side, they really flattened him. He got the wind knocked out of him, and so I went out, and they got him back on his feet, and he walked off. . . . There's less than a minute left in the game, maybe time for one or two plays. I'm standing there on the sideline, and he comes up and taps me on the shoulder. He says, 'Coach, I gotta go back in there.' I said, 'No, Steve, you've had enough, a nice year, you've come a long way. . . . ' He looked at me and said, 'Coach, they're going to win the game, but I don't want to let them think they defeated me.'"

Young earned the respect of his teammates and head coach that day, but for many quarterback-spoiled Brigham Young football fans he still had a lot to prove.

"Expectations were high, and immediately people compared me to McMahon," Young wrote years later. "I remember walking in downtown Provo after our 8–4 season and hearing fans say, 'Steve Young sucks.'"

The following season, Young silenced his detractors.

After a narrow season-opening loss to Baylor—in which he threw for 351 yards and ran for 113 more—Young directed BYU to victories in their next ten games and a sixth consecutive outright WAC title.

The 1983 Cougars team was loaded with talent on both sides of the ball, including All-American tight end Gordon Hudson and linebacker Todd Shell, whom the San Francisco 49ers selected in the first round the next spring. But their quarterback was the centerpiece.

Young led the nation that year in passer rating, touchdowns, yardage, and completion percentage, and finished second to Nebraska's Mike Rozier in the Heisman Trophy voting. But even more than his passing brilliance, Young's persistence and courageous style of play became his trademark.

"He just worked so hard and had such talent and there's no question that his running ability and athleticism enabled him to do some great things, some remarkable things at that position," backup quarterback Robbie Bosco remembered. "And he's such a tough guy. I can remember one game, we're playing Utah State at home, and he gets a concussion, gets hit hard in the first quarter, and he can't even stand out there.

"So I get to go in the game and we go down and we score and I'm thinking, 'This is great, I'm going to get to play the whole game.' All of a sudden, I'm getting ready to go back in, and Steve says, 'I'm in bro, I'm going back in.' I don't even know if the coaches knew that he was going back in! But he wasn't going to sit out any games."

That day, at home against the instate rival Aggies, Young set an NCAA record by throwing a touchdown in his nineteenth consecutive game. With less than two minutes remaining and the Cougars still trailing 34–31, Young guided the offense from their own 33-yard line to the Utah State 21. From there he scrambled for twenty more yards, then rushed for the game-winning score with just eleven seconds remaining.

"A year ago," LaVell Edwards said, "Steve would put so much pressure on himself to be another McMahon. I told him he didn't have to be. All we wanted him to do was be as good as he could be, and that would be good enough to be Brigham Young's quarterback."

* * *

The last play of Steve Young's collegiate career was an improbable game-winning touchdown pass that came in the closing seconds of his team's thrilling bowl victory. Only Young wasn't the one throwing the football.

With thirty-one seconds remaining and BYU trailing Missouri by three, Young—whose passing had driven the Cougars eighty yards to the Tigers' red zone—handed off to Eddie Stinnett. The running back meandered a few steps to his right, turned left, then threw the ball back across the field where Young had sneaked behind the defense and was wide open. Young caught the ball at the 14-yard line, followed a pair of blockers towards the goal line, then crossed into the end zone just as a Missouri defender knocked him to the ground. The touchdown gave BYU a 21–17 victory and lifted them to seventh place in the *Associated Press* poll, the highest finish in school history.

In the days leading up to the game, Young's willingness to duck his head, take on tacklers, and run with the football had been celebrated nearly as much as his prowess as a passer. Not only did the daring trick play punctuated with a crushing hit from a defender seal the game for the Cougars, it was a fitting end to Young's tenure as the team's quarterback.

"I don't wear a pink skirt out there," Young told the *Associated Press*'s Will Grimsley prior to the Holiday Bowl. "I'm not anxious to get hurt, but I don't mind getting my nose bloodied and banged up a bit. It makes you feel like part of the game—like Roger."

The Roger he was referring to was Dallas Cowboys icon Roger Staubach. As a child in Connecticut, Young had rooted for Staubach's Cowboys, his Mianus elementary school's namesake.

"Ever since I've played football, Roger has been my idol," he said. "He's such a composed player, never gets rattled, always in control of the situation, leadership. Besides, I like what I read about his normal life, just a real nice, down-to-earth guy, a family man, good example for kids."

Even after he left Greenwich to begin his career at BYU, while visiting his uncle in Centerville, Utah, Young held up a Cowboys jersey, proclaiming, "This is the future!"

Young's athleticism and gaudy passing numbers as a senior (71.3 percent completion, 33 touchdown passes, 316 yards passing per game) convinced scouts that he was destined for NFL stardom. And as he was finishing his double major in business finance and international relations (3.4 grade-point average) Young was considered a lock as a top pick in May 1984's NFL draft.

The Cincinnati Bengals owned the first selection, and the team's general manager Mike Brown scouted Young at the Senior Bowl in Hawaii. Three weeks later the Bengals new head coach, Sam Wyche, personally worked Young out. Wyche, the former 49ers offensive coordinator—and Joe Montana's tutor in San Francisco from 1979 to 1982—returned from Provo convinced that Young was the quarterback he needed to build a winner.

"We obviously thought he would fit into the West Coast offense, 'cause I was running the exact same thing that Bill [Walsh] was; the only thing I changed was I made it no-huddle," Wyche said years later. "We had negotiated with Leigh Steinberg, who was his agent. Mike Brown was literally at the airport or going to the airport, and he called Leigh to make sure that they were going to meet in Salt Lake City to sign the deal.

"He couldn't get a hold of Steinberg, and then he tried to call Steve Young, couldn't get a hold of Young and said, 'This doesn't seem right.'"

There was indeed a reason why Brown couldn't reach either Young or his agent: the newly formed United States Football League.

Founded in May 1982, the USFL began playing games the following March and outbid the NFL for several college superstars. Heisman Trophy winner Herschel Walker went to the New Jersey Generals, All-American wide receiver Anthony Carter signed with the Michigan Panthers, and University of Miami star quarterback Jim Kelly joined the Houston Gamblers, a year before the team played a single game.

After a lackluster first season marred by dwindling attendance figures, the Los Angeles Express and their self-proclaimed "self-made billionaire" owner J. William Oldenburg wanted to make a similar big-name acquisition. Like the Bengals, they targeted Young.

To try and lure Young away from the NFL, Express general manager Don Klosterman appealed to Young's competitive fire. He hired Sid Gillman, the former San Diego Chargers head coach considered to be the father of the modern passing game, as offensive coordinator, then drafted and signed three star college offensive linemen, Oregon's Gary Zimmerman, Texas's Mike Ruether, and Baylor's Mark Adickes. And in mid-January, Klosterman also drafted and signed All-American tight end Gordon Hudson, Young's close friend and favorite receiver.

"First of all, they made the football argument that behind Ken Anderson in Cincinnati he would sit," Leigh Steinberg remembered. "And [with the

Express] he'd be able to play immediately, he would have coaching with the best quarterback coaches available, he would have a great line, he would be able to flourish and learn at the quarterback position. And Steve was all about participation. He didn't want to sit behind anybody, because his life was about participation."

But football talent and Young's college roommate weren't Klosterman's only key bargaining chips.

"They knew he really wanted to be a lawyer, and they proposed to us that they would help him get into law school in Los Angeles. They knew that we were charitably oriented, and they offered to pay for a scholarship, fund one, for someone at BYU. And we started negotiating a contract. One morning I was at the Express at nine in the morning, and we finished at seven the next morning. It was sort of a simple process, because we were up at Don Kloster-man's house. At one point he was so tired he jumped into the pool.

"I would keep Steve and LeGrande updated, and the dollars were just un-believable, they kept expanding and expanding. And it was simple: Steve didn't want to play in the USFL; he wanted to play in the NFL, so I just had to say no. And every time I said no, they enhanced the offer."

By the end of Klosterman and Steinberg's negotiation session in the Hollywood Hills, the Express agreed to pay Young an intricate four-year $40 million contract that included a $2.5 million signing bonus, a $1.5 million tax-free loan, and an annuity starting at more than $30 million. Rumors of the enormous offer quickly spread, and both the NFL and USFL made last-ditch efforts to land the quarterback. Joe Namath and Howard Cosell—each a part of ABC's USFL broadcast team—called Steinberg, urging Young to sign with Los Angeles. NFL commissioner Pete Rozelle called Steinberg, lobbying Young to sign with Cincinnati. Young also received a call from his idol, Roger Staubach, who advised him to "always be humble [and] pray about it a lot."

Three days later, Young signed the deal with Los Angeles.

"I don't want to look like I'm money-hungry," he told *Sports Illustrated*. "That's not what I based my decision on. Look at my alternative, the NFL—living in Cincinnati and sitting behind Ken Anderson. Who knows if I'd get a chance for three or four years?"

Almost immediately, Young began to regret his decision.

Raised to be frugal—the photograph accompanying his *Sports Illustrated* feature revealed a hole in his sock—Young became the poster boy for 1980s excess. The media paid little attention to the charitable elements of his con-tract with Los Angeles (besides the BYU scholarship and money set aside for Mormon missionaries, he also tithed ten percent of the earnings to the church) and focused on the overall $40 million dollar figure.

"The big money really depressed Steve," Grit Young said. "He couldn't cope with it. He had always seen himself as a little old guy. Down to earth. The money was a nemesis to him, and I don't think he's ever gotten over it."

The burden of the largest individual contract in sports history made up only a part of Young's angst. Advice from LeGrande—"You signed a contract. You have to honor it"—compelled him to continue, but passing up the NFL weighed on him.

"He woke up the next day," his mother Sherry said, "and he had given away his dream."

Young—who signed his contract one day after the Express lost to the Birmingham Stallions—debuted in the sixth game of the season. He threw an interception and a touchdown, and Los Angeles lost to Herschel Walker's New Jersey Generals, 26–10. The Express fell to 2–4.

"I felt good about it, but we have to get some wins on the board. LA is not a patient town," Young said. "If I can live up to what I expect—probably a forty-for-forty day with no interceptions and six touchdowns for five hundred yards—I'm happy. But I've got to feel like I did what I could. Pressure is something that you can either shrug off or put on yourself and make it worse. I have tried to alleviate a lot of it and just go out there and have fun. I think if I keep that realistic attitude I'll be OK."

The Express lost two of their next three games, but behind Young they rebounded to win seven of their final nine contests, earning a spot in the USFL playoffs. In the postseason-clinching victory over Oakland, Young completed fourteen of sixteen passes for 195 yards and a touchdown, and dazzled the miniscule Los Angeles Coliseum crowd by hurdling over linebacker David Shaw, then outrunning a pair of defensive backs for a go-ahead forty-seven-yard touchdown run. The performance earned the Mormon quarterback the league's ironically sponsored Miller Lite Beer Player of the Week award.

In the first round of the playoffs Los Angeles beat the defending league champion Michigan Panthers, then lost in the semi-finals to Arizona. The next winter, they opened the 1985 season with high hopes. Express head coach John Hadl—an All-Pro for the Los Angeles Rams and Sid Gillman's AFL championship-winning quarterback with the San Diego Chargers—had equally high hopes for Young.

"He was inconsistent throwing the ball last season," Hadl said. "He didn't get a chance to read coverages. He's doing that now. He runs a 4.5 forty-yard dash, and could play running back, receiver, or free safety on our team. We've been working on throwing the ball deep. He was criticized for not doing that last year, but we really didn't have the time to work on that. We're working on that every day. He's throwing the ball very well."

The opening game of the 1985 season pitted Young against another high-priced college superstar quarterback—Jim Kelly, who had spurned the Buffalo Bills in 1983 and won the USFL MVP in his first year with the Houston Gamblers. Despite the marquee matchup of the league's two top quarterbacks on that late February day, less than twenty thousand people attended the game. The massive Los Angeles Coliseum was so empty that, according to Young, "We had to whisper in the huddle so the other guys wouldn't hear our plays."

The scant few who did see the game—ABC chose to broadcast the Tampa Bay Bandits 35–7 win over Orlando rather than the Gamblers-Express game—saw an exhilarating shootout. After trailing early, the Express rallied to take a 33–13 lead with just ten minutes remaining in the game. But Kelly—who set a professional record with 574 yards passing—tossed three long touchdown passes to complete a 34–33 comeback victory.

"What can I say about Kelly?" Young said. "He drops back and throws it, guys are running around everywhere—holy smoke, I thought I was back at BYU. I'd love to play with an offense like that. But ours is better balanced. In the end, I think ours will be better."

Unfortunately for Young, as the 1985 USFL season unfolded, the Express offense didn't get much better. Los Angeles won just three of their final seventeen games, scoring ten points or less in nine of those losses. But far worse than the team's miserable last-place record, or the knee injury that cost Young three starts that season, was the financial state of both the Express and the USFL.

Television ratings and attendance plummeted. Forced to compete with the outrageous salaries of Young, Kelly, Herschel Walker, Doug Flutie, and the league's top-paid stars, several teams claimed huge financial losses. And the league's largest market, Los Angeles, became the league's largest sinkhole. Lawsuits against J. William Oldenburg and two of his companies cost the Express owner millions and—after courts ruled he could not sell the franchise—the USFL took control of the team.

Young and his $40 million contract were blamed for the team and the league's financial woes.

"Get rid of him," New Jersey Generals owner Donald Trump told one reporter, "He's the most overrated player in football. I'd sue him for damages for not playing half this season."

The Express's resources were so drained that while heading to a game the team bus driver pulled over on the side of the road, demanding he be paid for the first time in weeks. A trainer paid the driver $500 cash and the team continued to Los Angeles's Pierce Community College where they played the Arizona Wranglers in front of eighty-two hundred people.

Following the 21–10 loss, Young addressed reporters on a dirt hill, and the team debriefing took place in a dusty shed. Players jokingly asked each other whose mother was driving the carpool that week. *Los Angeles Times* reporter Chris Dufresne noted, "You half expected Los Angeles Express players to throw their helmets in the air and shout: 'two, four, six, eight, who do we appreciate?'"

"I wasn't mad," Young later said. "But it got to the point where nobody cared about the games anymore. Nobody ever asked me a football question. I decided I didn't care about the money anymore. I just want to get in the NFL."

In the weeks after the merciful end to the Express's season, agent Leigh Steinberg leveraged Young's release from the contract.

"In a period of less than fifteen months, $4.7 million was paid to Steve Young," USFL commissioner Harry Usher said. "That's a lot of money, maybe an all-time record. But if he's unhappy in L.A., well, that pains me a lot."

The league granted Steinberg and Young permission to negotiate with the Tampa Bay Buccaneers—who acquired the quarterback's rights in the 1984 supplemental draft—and within a month a deal was reached. The USFL agreed to release Young from his contract (provided he pay a sum believed to be over $1 million) and the Buccaneers agreed to pay him six consecutive one-year deals, worth roughly $1 million per season.

"This is a new experience," Young said. "I'm excited, yet apprehensive. I feel better now because I know what I'll be doing. I could sit in Provo, Utah, all my life and be comfortable but never grow that way. It's important to know what you are going to do. I just want to be a positive part of the team, and I'll have a lot of catching up to do to be ready to help the other guys."

The Bucs certainly needed help. They were 8–24 during the previous two seasons, had hired a new head coach, Leeman Bennett, and would lose the first nine games of the 1985 season.

"I didn't have any idea that the franchise was as bad as it was from the standpoint of weight rooms and spending money," Bennett remembered. "The attitude down there at that time was that this is a cheap organization and so on and so forth, and that rubs off on the players, and they looked at it that way and understood it that way.

"We were happy to get Steve Young, and we all knew he was a tremendous athlete and thought he could play quarterback. I think there were a lot of expectations placed on him to carry a bad football team. And rookie quarterbacks can't do that, and that's what he was."

While Young learned the system, well-traveled veteran Steve DeBerg quarterbacked the Tampa Bay system. A 1977 draft pick of the Dallas Cowboys, DeBerg also tutored Young, who eagerly listened to veterans, particularly one who had learned under Young's boyhood idol.

"I made it to the NFL in the first place because Roger Staubach took me under his wing and explained things to me," DeBerg later said. "He showed me what was going on. I wouldn't have ever made it in the NFL if he hadn't done that. So I always felt like since that's how I made it in the NFL to begin with, I should do the same thing. . . . I just felt secure in my ability to help the other quarterback."

DeBerg's willingness to teach young quarterbacks had come at a great price. After leaving San Francisco, where Joe Montana permanently replaced him late in the 1980 season, DeBerg went to Denver. Three years later, John Elway, the top pick in that year's draft, took DeBerg's job, and the Broncos traded him to Tampa Bay. Young was now the third college superstar groomed to supplant DeBerg. Nevertheless, he still mentored the rookie.

"We never had a rivalry," DeBerg said years later. "We had a very healthy competition, and we both enjoyed competing. We were excellent friends, and I still consider Steve a good friend."

Young made his NFL debut in Week 12 of the 1985 season, completing sixteen passes and rushing for sixty yards in an overtime win over Detroit. But in December, he completed less than half his attempts, threw eight interceptions, and the Bucs lost all four of their games, scoring an average of less than twelve points each week.

Entering his first NFL training camp in the summer of 1986, Young battled with DeBerg for the starter's role, each trading off snaps during practice and exhibition games. By late August, the coaching staff selected DeBerg, who displayed a much better handle of the offense.

Throughout his entire football career, Young's remarkable athleticism was an asset. Even at the highest professional level, he was one of the fastest players on the field, routinely running the forty-yard dash in 4.5 seconds. And he ran as fearless and confident as any running back in the game.

"I don't think there's any question about [Steve Young's] arm being plenty strong enough to play, and win, in the NFL," Lee Bennett said. "(But) Steve was unsettled. He wasn't poised, and he showed no confidence. He was helter-skelter."

"I'd rather get beat up and play than not play at all," Young told the *St. Petersburg Times* during Buccaneers training camp. "I put in my lumps last year, and my feeling was, 'We'll catch you on the rebound.' I just love fighting. I don't know what I'll do when I get out of football. I gotta hit something."

Although he was raised in a white collar, affluent, Connecticut suburb, was charismatic and insightful around the press, and preferred spending his free time speaking to Mormon Church groups, Young played the game with an impulsive, undisciplined, and reckless style.

"He was like a wild man," Steve DeBerg said in 2012. "He just was so will-ing to give up his body, taking off and running. Just doing things that weren't typical of the quarterback position . . . he would run like a running back; he was a very exciting player, that's for sure."

His bravery and self-sacrifice—though noble and greatly admired by his teammates—became problematic, first in Los Angeles, and later on in Tampa Bay. Seeking out linebackers and safeties and courting contact increased the chance of injury to a defenseless position already fraught with danger. Young may have welcomed, even craved, contact, but the Buccaneers front office and ownership wanted their $1-million-per-season investment to last.

"As time goes on, I think he'll learn how to get down and not take some of the licks he took," Leeman Bennett said after Young's NFL debut against De-troit. "They got some good ones on him, and some were to the extent that they were pretty vicious-type tackles. I don't know if the Lions went after him to indoctrinate him to the NFL or what, but they went after him pretty good."

Young's fearless attitude as a ball carrier was only part of the reason some experts, including three-time NFL Coach of the Year Chuck Knox, suggested that Bennett convert Young to running back. Young lacked maturity inside the pocket and abandoned passing plays much earlier than the offense re-quired.

"Steve would actually look at the rush," DeBerg said later, "and he was a good runner. But he was passing up a lot of successful plays if he'd have just kept his vision beyond the rush in making his reads. Sometimes his number-one receiver would be open, and he was back there scrambling around."

Besting Young in their summer-long quarterback competition earned De-Berg both a start in the Buccaneers season opener and what the press automat-ically assumed was a measure of revenge: Tampa Bay's opponent in Week 1 was DeBerg's former team, the San Francisco 49ers, still coached by Bill Walsh and quarterbacked by Joe Montana.

"I have no resentment," DeBerg said that week. "I enjoyed playing in San Francisco and learned more from Walsh than any coach. And Joe was my roommate and best friend. That trade was the best thing that ever happened to me, because I knew how good Joe Montana was going to be. I'm glad be-cause, otherwise, I could have been backing him up all these years."

Still, several reporters showed more interest in DeBerg's unrefined yet gifted backup than his reunion with his former head coach and close friend.

"Young quarterbacks will do that because they are not tight with their teammates yet," Walsh said. "They don't have confidence in their line. But a running quarterback is a great weapon to have."

Walsh's greatest protégé, however, wasn't quite as enamored with the scrambler's talents.

"I think Young put too much pressure on himself by trying to show everything to everybody all at once," Montana told reporters that week. "I still tend to leave the pocket too early, and my linemen always let me know about it."

Montana's linemen did not have to scold him very often in the 49ers-Buccaneers Week 1 showdown: the four-time Pro Bowl quarterback stayed tethered to the pocket throughout most of the game. As a result, Montana completed thirty-two of forty-six passes for 356 yards in a 31–7 victory.

Montana's counterpart and former roommate fared far worse in the ninety-degree weather.

In "probably the worst game I've ever had," DeBerg threw seven interceptions. But the local fans who chanted for Young to replace DeBerg never got their wish. The only quarterback substitution seen that day at Tampa Stadium came in the fourth quarter, when Montana, who suffered a (seemingly) harmless tweak of his lower back, was replaced by his backup Jeff Kemp.

Two more interceptions from DeBerg and another decisive home loss the following week prompted Leeman Bennett to turn back to Young. Although he completed just six passes, Young managed to lead the Buccaneers over Detroit 24–20, earning their first road victory in nearly three years.

"We feel awfully good," Young said. "But we realize we have to play the same way the next week and the week after that and keep building confidence in ourselves."

From that point on, Young remained the starter throughout the Buccaneers regular season, but aside from a 38–24 victory over the equally dreadful Buffalo Bills, Tampa Bay did not win another game. Following a second consecutive 2–14 season, Leeman Bennett was fired and replaced with Ray Perkins, the former New York Giants and University of Alabama head coach. Perkins's first task was to take inventory of the players on Tampa Bay's roster.

"My findings, which I reported to my owner, were we were not real big, not strong enough to compete in the National Football League, and we were too slow," Perkins told reporters. "Nor did we have a quarterback who could get us to the Super Bowl."

That assessment, coupled with the team's rights to the first overall pick in the 1987 NFL draft, convinced the Buccaneers to pursue Heisman Trophy winner Vinny Testaverde. A prototypical pocket-passer with perfect size, Testaverde starred for the University of Miami, a quarterback-factory that produced NFL starters Jim Kelly and Bernie Kosar. Perkins publicly praised Young during the team's spring minicamp, but by late March the organization was already negotiating with Testaverde's agent.

"Coach Perkins and I spoke briefly about the upcoming draft, and he told me not to worry about it," Young said that spring. "I feel it will resolve itself soon. I don't feel, though, that I will be on the team next season if they decide to draft Vinny; this team has too many needs to stockpile talent at quarterback.

"A quarterback's image is tied to team success, and that can be frustrating. It makes you want to play tennis or golf," he added. "And I know the excitement about me being here has worn off."

As he had two years earlier in Los Angeles, an unsatisfied and exasperated Steve Young wanted out.

"I went to [owner Hugh] Culverhouse and said, 'Look, Steve came here because you promised security and stability,'" Leigh Steinberg recalled years later. "Now you're going to draft Vinny Testaverde, so obviously you're going to trade Steve, but let me make this point abundantly clear . . . you made him a series of promises you can't fulfill. You owe it to us to allow us to designate where he'd like to go next."

Culverhouse and the Buccaneers agreed, and word quickly spread that the twenty-five-year-old quarterback was available. Several teams showed an interest, most notably the San Francisco 49ers, whose offensive coordinator Mike Holmgren had been Young's quarterback coach at BYU. But the reputation of the 49ers head coach most intrigued Young and Steinberg.

"I explained to Steve that if you have an opportunity to go to San Francisco and be coached by Bill Walsh, it will definitely change your career and help you be an even better quarterback," recalled DeBerg, a former student of Walsh's. "Bill Walsh was a really great quarterback coach."

Even though both the St. Louis Cardinals and San Diego Chargers reportedly offered first-round draft choices in exchange for Young, the Buccaneers and 49ers began negotiating. Four days before the 1987 NFL draft—with Testaverde already inked to a six-year, $8.2 million deal—Tampa Bay dealt Young to San Francisco in exchange for a second-round pick (fiftieth overall), a fourth-round pick (106th overall), and $1 million.

"So the thought was, we looked around, and Bill Walsh is coaching the 49ers. And we started discussions with Bill Walsh. Bill Walsh works him out at a secret workout in Provo," Steinberg said. "Bill told him that Joe Montana had a bad back and probably would never play again. And that [Young] would go into this sophisticated system and Bill would work on his passing skills and all the rest of it and [he'd] go to a storied franchise.

"The *only* choice I knew he would never make is a choice that wouldn't let him play. And we never would have gone there except for the fact that Joe Montana was going to retire."

Stirring Something Up

I must be a masochist or something. My dad always said
I loved third-and-10 . . . maybe third-and-20, actually
trying to replace those two guys.

*—Steve Young on following Jim McMahon
in college and Joe Montana in the NFL*

Despite Joe Montana's size and strength improvements—his bench
press increased by fifty pounds during the spring of 1987—once the
Tampa Bay Buccaneers started shopping Steve Young, Bill Walsh
didn't hesitate. He called owner Eddie DeBartolo Jr. and team vice president
Carmen Policy, who were in Jamaica.

"Bill's trying to do this trade with Culverhouse for Steve Young," Policy recalled. "So Eddie said, 'I watched him, he's a good kid, [but] is he too damaged—USFL, Tampa Bay? Can you salvage him, Bill?'

"Bill says this guy's great. He can be the next Joe Montana, but he's even
better because he has more athletic skills. He's naturally better.'"

According to Carmen Policy, Walsh's heavy interest in a phenom such as
Young was deep-rooted.

"I think that was part of it with Bill as a personnel guy," Policy said years
later. "In his mind, Joe was always the third-round pick. Steve was always a
high first-round pick. I always thought in my mind, that he always factored

53

that in as he was looking at it. . . . He never told us; we found out later that he promised Steve he'd be starting no later than the beginning of the 1988 season."

But contrary to the assurances Walsh had provided, Montana—who was vacationing in Italy when the trade for Young was made—had no intentions of stepping away from the game.

"If I had wanted to retire, I would not have come back after surgery," Montana told the press upon return from Europe. "Why would I have gone through all the agony of fighting back and going through the headache I ended up with? . . . No matter who is on the team, it's always going to be competitive. No matter if it's Steve Young or Vinny Testaverde. I still have the same feeling of working against the other person and myself. [Young] came here and said, 'I'm not here to sit on the bench.' Well, neither am I.

"Sure, you wonder what they (the organization) are thinking. Did they bring in the guy intentionally to take my place? After a serious injury, the organization looks at you, no matter what they say, and thinks, 'It can't be too much longer.' When I sit back and think about it, it makes me mad, but I have to look at it from their point of view. They have a winning tradition since Bill's been here. It's hard to look at it like that, though. Retirement is hard to think about. I'm getting older. That's reality. I want to make it as difficult as I can to replace me."

In early May, Montana joined his teammates for a three-day minicamp, and from the moment he set foot on the field at the team's practice facility he quashed any notion that retirement was imminent.

"I remember the first time we got out to practice," Steve Young said years later. "Joe came running out, and I thought, 'Man, he doesn't look real hurt.' And he practiced and I thought, 'Crap, he's not hurt at all.' And I knew I was in for a little bit of a haul here. It was definitely difficult."

Montana's presence was not the only difficulty that Young endured during his first few practices as a member of the San Francisco 49ers. His passing failed to impress anyone that week, including John Paye, the Stanford quarterback San Francisco drafted that spring.

"Steve was the least accurate of the five quarterbacks," recalled Paye, whose family hosted Young in their Menlo Park home during the summer of 1987. "Sometimes I remember commenting to my dad or a friend of mine, 'Golly, Steve doesn't throw the ball that well.' We'd get into quarterback meetings, and we'd be watching tape, and Steve would bounce pass a ball to a receiver who was running a comeback. And we would kind of laugh just because Steve was not a natural thrower, and it magnified itself in some of those settings in minicamp and training camp."

Despite all he had achieved as a passer—especially at BYU, where he had led the nation in passing yardage, touchdown passes, and completion percentage as a senior—Young struggled with his mechanics and his confidence, even after four seasons as a professional. Slowly, however, by simply watching Montana's nonchalant, yet precise style of quarterbacking, Young found his rhythm.

"When I was in college, everyone was supposed to throw like Dan Marino, and all I knew was when I threw like Dan Marino I wasn't very strong, and that my arm hurt. But that's how I threw it, and I played a few years in the pros trying to throw like that, and it was not till I got to see Joe Montana and his big, long motion around [that] I said, 'He's won Super Bowls. I'm just gonna do it that way.' I suddenly got a much stronger arm, much more accurate. It changed a lot for me in the things that I could do. And it's just something dumb like that. As far back as I remember I was trying to do something that wasn't natural to me, and it was like Joe allowed me the freedom to do it: to say, 'It's ok, I'm doing it, and you're fine.'"

Following the productive three-day minicamp, Montana remained in town for the summer. In previous offseasons he had returned to his home in Southern California, but this year Montana stayed in his Bay Area home, to which he added a new weight and workout room.

By the first week of training camp, Walsh and 49ers offensive coordinator Mike Holmgren fawned over his practices and one reporter wrote that Montana "was bouncing around the practice field like a pogo stick, zinging passes downfield, talking it up to teammates, and acting generally as though he had hummingbird blood in him."

In August, the 49ers and Kansas City Chiefs kicked off the NFL's exhibition season in Canton, Ohio, home of the Pro Football Hall of Fame. Montana, scheduled to play eighteen to twenty minutes, completed nine of his fourteen attempts for 120 yards, but Walsh quickly pulled him from the field following a hard hit from a Chiefs defender. He briefly returned but soon met his quota of pass attempts and was replaced by Young.

Still learning the offense, Young's scarlet and gold debut was not terribly impressive—he connected on only five of his fourteen attempts for forty-five yards, was sacked three times, and nearly threw an interception. But late in the third quarter he avoided a Chiefs defender, sprinted to the sideline, and hit tight end John Frank with a perfect sixteen-yard completion that gave the 49ers a first down.

"I feel confident I'll be here a long time," Young told reporters after the 49ers 20–7 exhibition win. "There's not going to be any dropoff, whether Joe's in the game or not."

A week later, back in the Los Angeles Coliseum where he had wowed small crowds as a member of the Express, Young's confidence grew. With Montana dressed but not in the lineup (in practice that week he had reaggravated the chest injury suffered against Kansas City), San Francisco overpowered the Raiders 42–16. Young completed twenty of his twenty-seven passes for 247 yards, but as usual, his legs garnered much more attention.

"There were times in that first year that it was like, 'Well, God, if Joe can't last, I can throw the ball better than Steve: I'm gonna be the guy in front of Steve," John Paye remembered. "But everything became clearer after our exhibition game that year against the Raiders. It was down in the Coliseum and up until that time, everything was not live on the quarterback, and I remember Steve in that game having his first big, explosive, Michael Vick-like play. I think it was a bootleg, and all of a sudden he just took off and ran away from first the defensive lineman, and then ran away from the linebackers, and then he made a defensive back miss, and all of a sudden it was like, 'Wow that was a [thirty-four-]yard gain by our quarterback going straight. Steve is running north and south as a quarterback whereas up until that time most of the quarterbacks playing [didn't] . . .

"Montana was very nimble but we were always taught that Montana would always go more east and west . . . then run out of bounds and avoid the hit, whereas Steve would plant then go north and south and, boom, [thirty-four] yards."

The run (one of six that gained sixty-one yards, leading all 49ers rushers) impressed his teammates and the crowd at the Los Angeles Colissuem but not necessarily his offensive coordinator.

"He still thinks too much about the run," Holmgren told reporters the next day. "I want him to get to a point where he's like Joe. He just naturally goes through the progression of receivers, dinks the ball off to a back, or if the run is there, he takes it intuitively. . . . [But] I thought Steve did some awfully good things on Saturday night. . . . He had a third-down pass to Tony Hill that was one of his best throws. It had a nice touch, good velocity, and he threw it over the middle, which takes a certain amount of technique. And his thirty-four-yard run was excellent. He had two options to pass on that play. Run was the third option, and he showed that he isn't looking to step out of bounds and that he can make people miss."

Montana recovered from the chest strain and returned to the field in time for San Francisco's next preseason game against Dallas. With Montana missing on his first seven pass attempts (he finished the day five-of-sixteen for forty-six yards) the Cowboys won 13–3. The offense played noticeably better in their next game, a 17–3 win over San Diego, but in their final preseason tune-up the 49ers were thrashed, 34–10. Even with Jerry Rice returning from the broken finger that cost him most of the preseason, the first-team offense could score only one touchdown despite playing the majority of the game.

"We've got a long week ahead of us," said Dwight Clark, who battled back from three knee surgeries that offseason. "As Bill said after the game, there were a lot of things we were awful at. And we've got to get it together in the next eight days."

The 49ers opened the 1987 regular season in Pittsburgh where they faced the Steelers, the team Montana followed as a child. But from the outset, his visit to Three Rivers Stadium, located less than twenty miles north of his childhood home in Monongahela, was a sour homecoming.

His second pass of the game was intercepted, and on the next series, a Roger Craig fumble was returned fifty yards for a Steelers touchdown. The 49ers managed a field goal, but the offense did not convert on a single third down until midway through the third quarter, and San Francisco fell behind 20–3. Two more interceptions by Montana offset a pair of second-half touchdown passes, and the 49ers fell 30–17.

"We were that bad," said tackle Keith Fahnhorst. "When you turn the ball over like that, you start pressing."

Just like the rest of the team, Montana was not immune to Bill Walsh's criticism, which once again centered around the quarterback's perceived lack of mobility or willingness to scramble.

"He wasn't quick or explosive. He didn't have sharpness in his movement," Walsh said. "I thought he was physically fatigued."

Montana—who braved his fear of needles and took two anti-inflammatory injections that season to relieve pain from the 1986 back injury— naturally disagreed, "I wasn't tired at all. . . . I didn't even break a sweat."

Some experts accounted for the Steelers dominance by pointing out that Pittsburgh's defensive coordinator was Tony Dungy, a former safety who played for Walsh in San Francisco during the 1979 season, which was Walsh's first season with the 49ers. By that reasoning, the 49ers would be at an even greater disadvantage a week later in Cincinnatti: Sam Wyche was still the Benglas head coach.

"Sam is clearly the brightest coach in the game today and certainly the most innovative," Walsh said prior to the 49ers–Bengals Week 2 matchup at Riverfront Stadium. "I think we're a little bit dated in our style of football. I think we've been at a high water mark, at a zenith of effectiveness a few years ago, and people have caught up with us. That's why I appreciate Sam so much. He's ahead of the game, to be honest with you."

Having missed out on Steve Young with the top selection, Wyche found a more than capable Plan B in the second round of the 1984 draft, another All-American left-handed passer named Norman "Boomer" Esiason. In Wyche's system, Esiason became a Pro Bowler by his third season, and just days before the Bengals game against San Francisco the organization rewarded him with a new contract that made him one of the game's highest-paid players. And through two quarters against the 49ers, Esiason looked to be worth every penny.

Three field goals and a forty-six-yard touchdown pass from Esiason to Rodney Holman gave the Bengals a 20–7 halftime lead. Walsh—perhaps trying to upgrade his "dated" offense—chose to feature the running game in the first half. Cincinnati's defense contained Roger Craig, however, and Montana misfired on all four of his first-quarter passes. The 49ers didn't score until late in the second period when Mike Wilson beat rookie Eric Thomas on a thirty-eight-yard touchdown.

"Hey, I want to know who has the guts on this team," Walsh told his team at halftime.

That challenge from the head coach—combined with an offensive strategy aimed at picking on Eric Thomas—gave San Francisco new life. Less than three minutes into the third quarter, Montana hit Jerry Rice on a thirty-four-yard touchdown pass, again over Thomas, narrowing the gap to 20–14.

A pair of field goals from both kickers preserved Cincinnati's six-point lead through most of the second half, but with less than two minutes remaining, the 49ers took possession deep in their own territory. Two incompletions, a sack by nose tackle Tim Krumrie, and a punt seemingly guaranteed the 49ers an 0–2 start.

But fifty-four seconds still remained, and the 49ers possessed two time-outs. Three kneeldowns by Esiason reduced the clock to six seconds, leaving Wyche with a difficult decision.

Because the Bengals were on their own 30-yard line, taking an intentional safety really wasn't an option. And in Wyche's mind, neither was the more conventional play.

"A punt definitely is a six-second play," Wyche said afterward, "but you have a long snap, your punter has to make the catch, you have to get it off, they've got a chance to run it back or make the block."

Instead, Wyche—hoping to either gain the first down or at least use up the remaining six seconds—called a sweep with running back James Brooks, who was lassoed by 49ers defensive end Kevin Fagan.

"The guard and offensive tackle pulled, and I saw the daylight," Fagan said. "Their whole team seemed to be loafing, like they had the game won. I don't think anyone touched me."

San Francisco took over on downs at the Bengals 25, and because Fagan had brought Brooks to the turf so quickly, only two seconds had rolled off the clock.

Equipped with a four-receiver set—Dwight Clark, Mike Wilson, and John Taylor to the left, and Rice to the right—Montana was amazed by the pre-snap read. The Bengals had again matched up rookie Eric Thomas one-on-one with Rice.

"I was supposed to go to the corner, but at the last minute Joe pointed straight downfield," Rice said. "It was something we just came up with before the snap of the ball. . . . I just felt like I knew what Joe wanted."

Montana dropped back to pass, surveyed the left (trips) side of the field, pivoted to his right, and fired the ball downfield for a wide-open Rice, who leapt in the air, pulling down the game-tying score with no time remaining on the clock.

"Guys were throwing their helmets all over the place," Montana said. "They seemed to forget about the extra point."

Wyche also forget—he ran across the field to congratulate his mentor Bill Walsh on the victory—but with Montana holding, Ray Wersching nailed the kick, and San Francisco won.

"Vintage Joe Montana," left tackle Steve Wallace remembered years later. "It changed our whole season, because we were five seconds away from being 0-2."

The joy from the "Hail Jerry" as it was dubbed by the press ("The Catch II" was also used) should have traveled with the 49ers on their cross-country flight. But momentum from the victory came to a halt; two days after returning from Cincinnati, at the Veterans Memorial Senior Center in Redwood City, by an eighteen to eleven count (with many voters abstaining) the players supported a league-wide NFL Players Association (NFLPA) strike. Although the two sides disagreed on several issues, the NFLPA's chief dispute with the owners was over unrestricted free agency, still not yet a part of the collective bargaining agreement.

"I think we all agreed that (owner) Eddie DeBartolo has treated us well here," the team's co-player representative and starting offensive tackle Keith Fahnhorst said. "It's certainly not the 49ers going on strike against him. But we're not an isolated entity here."

While talks between negotiators for the owners and players continued during the week, some 49ers reported to the team's headquarters while others held makeshift practices at nearby Cañada College. Meanwhile, each NFL front office scrambled to fill its roster with "scab" players.

On his weekly Friday KFOG radio show, *Ultimate Armchair Quarterback*, Montana, who stood to lose $62,500 per week, didn't deny he was considering not siding with the union, of which he was not a member: "There is always that possibility," he said.

That week's full slate of games was cancelled, but the following week the league announced the games would continue with or without the striking players. And on Friday, October 2, 1987, three days before the 49ers scheduled Monday Night Football game against the defending Super Bowl champion New York Giants, twenty-seven picketers, including Jerry Rice, Randy Cross, and Steve Young, stood outside the 49ers offices, wearing or holding protest signs.

"The main reason I'm here is not because of [NFLPA executive director] Gene Upshaw or the other 1,550 members of the union," Cross said. "I'm here for the fifty guys I play with."

At the same time a handful of players, including Montana, met at Stanley's Deli near the team's practice facility to discuss their plan to continue playing. But there they were talked out of their decision by, of all people, head coach Bill Walsh.

"We want to avoid division within the team," Walsh told the press. "At this point, we're still a team operating as a unit, and hopefully will remain so."

But once the rest of the team and the media learned that eight players had even considered abandoning the strike, the damage was done. And Montana was at the center of the story.

"This isn't going to affect how I think of Joe as a player," guard Guy McIntyre said. "But it might with regard to respect. When you have people play as a team, you don't expect them to just play one half. And it's the same way in a strike. You have to ask yourself, 'Can you trust a man in the trenches?' We'll have to see."

"I was a friend of his before the strike, and I'll be a friend of his after the strike," Riki Ellison said. "I'm just disappointed. It wasn't that hard to miss one week, one paycheck. It's not like we're all on skid row."

With quarterback Bob Gagliano under center—in the third quarter, the 49ers sent in Mark Stevens, a Canadian Football Leaguer who had recently applied to be a mailman, to run the wishbone offense, prompting laughter from both Walsh and Giants head coach Bill Parcells—the "Phony-Niners" toppled the Giants in the Meadowlands, 41–21. Although it was a nationally televised playoff rematch between clubs that had won three of the previous seven Super Bowls, nearly fifty thousand seats at Giants Stadium were empty.

Two days later, Montana, Roger Craig, Dwight Clark, and eight more 49ers reported to work, a move that was met with resentment by union leaders and many players across the league.

"I would like to say that, even though I'm not a member of the union, I've always been sympathetic to the cause," said Montana. "Up until this time, I have honored the strike out of deference to my teammates. Now that I've learned that several of my teammates have decided to return to practice, and because of the fairness that I have received in the past from Mr. DeBartolo (owner Ed DeBartolo Jr.) and the 49ers' organization, I have decided to return also. This is an individual decision and in no way am I trying to influence any other players in their decision."

That Sunday, before a crowd of less than nine thousand, the Falcons hosted the 49ers in Fulton County Stadium. And in one of the most bizarre games in team history—every time Montana and the "real" 49ers built a sizable lead, they were replaced by "scabs," only to return when the win was in danger—the 49ers won 25–17.

The strike, however, eventually ended. More and more players (including stars such as Lawrence Taylor, Eric Dickerson, and Steve Largent) crossed the picket line, and after twenty-four days, the NFLPA ordered all players to return, despite not reaching a new agreement. By the middle of the 1987 season's fifth week, most of the original 49ers resumed practicing. To their surprise, they found themselves alone atop the NFC West.

"It just so happens that the scab guys were pretty good . . . they won every single game," said Steve Wallace. "And so when you come back from all of that, now you're saying, 'Hey, this is not too bad, we're 4–1.'"

The full complement of 49ers returned to the field on October 25, just in time to take on the toughest part of the schedule: back-to-back road games against division rivals, the Saints and the Rams. With Montana tossing three touchdown passes and the defense limiting the Saints to field goals instead of touchdowns, the 49ers escaped New Orleans with a 24–22 victory.

That day, Steve Young made his regular season debut with the San Francisco 49ers, an inauspicious start to say the least.

Late in the second period, with the 49ers ahead 14–3, Montana returned to the huddle, following a discussion with Walsh during the two-minute warning. Then he jogged back to the sidelines, pointing to his helmet.

"Yeah, there was dirt in my helmet," said a wry Montana, well aware that the game was being played on AstroTurf in the Superdome. "Yeah, that's right. There was grass in it. Oh. We're indoors? OK."

It was all a ruse.

While Montana feigned an equipment problem, Young sprinted onto the field, called a play, and broke the huddle, in an attempt to catch the Saints defense off guard. But Young never had a chance to carry out the play-action and subsequent bootleg to the opposite side. Saints linebacker Pat Swilling swallowed up the quarterback before he even attempted the fake handoff to Roger Craig. Following the nine-yard sack, Montana retook the field.

"[Young] miscalled the formation," Walsh said later that day. "Do you believe that? He was supposed to send somebody in motion, and he didn't do it. He had nobody to throw to."

But the botched trick play didn't keep Young on the sidelines forever. A week later in Anaheim, Young closed out the 49ers 31–10 win over the Rams with a kneeldown. And during a 27–20 win the following Sunday against Houston, Young produced his first positive yardage in a regular season game for the 49ers. Late in the second quarter, Young again replaced Montana for one play, a quarterback draw that netted fifteen yards.

"Everything went right," Young said. "They just put the play in (the game plan) for me yesterday."

The 49ers coaching staff would soon be creating a game plan entirely around Young.

Still fulfilling the duties of holder on field goals and extra points, Montana sprained a joint on the index finger of his throwing hand while holding the ball in practice for kicker Ray Wersching. The ball—not Wersching's foot—hit Montana's finger when he didn't pull his hand out of the way of the kick.

Montana played through the pain that day, but the next morning his knuckle was so swollen he couldn't practice.

"He is very doubtful for this game," Walsh told the press on Thursday, "so Steve got all the work today."

That fact was not lost on *St. Petersburg Times* reporter Tom Zucco, who half-joked in his column that Young "slipped Ray Wersching a couple of bucks."

"Yep, Ray's a rich man today," Young remarked facetiously.

Toward the end of the week, Walsh declared Montana available as a reserve, stating that because Young took the bulk of the snaps, he would start Sunday's home game against the Saints.

"Joe is a legend, and he's hard to replace," left guard Jesse Sapolu said, "but Steve has the potential to be a legend."

In less than ten minutes of play, Young lived up to his teammates' expectations.

Trailing the Saints 3–0 midway through the opening period, the 49er offense approached midfield, where Young couldn't find any open receivers and took off running around the left end. Four yards past the line of scrimmage, however, Saints linebacker and fellow USFL alum Vaughan Johnson clobbered him.

"I know better than to run head-on into a linebacker," said Young, whose eyes, according to Johnson, instantly became glazy. "I wanted to make sure we moved the ball, but I'm sure the coach will tell me to use better judgment next time."

Young initially walked to the wrong huddle after the play, and had to be redirected by teammate Mike Wilson. But he remained in the game, and three handoffs and another scramble (which picked up nine yards) pushed the 49ers across midfield. Then, at the Saints 46-yard line, Young dropped back to pass, stumbled to one knee, regained his balance, and heaved a pass downfield for Jerry Rice, who hauled in the bomb for the game's first touchdown.

An elated Young celebrated by punching the air above him and sprinting for the end zone to celebrate with Rice. Then he headed to the sideline.

"You don't look so good," noted Dr. James Klint, the team physician who had diagnosed Montana's concussion during the 49ers playoff loss ten months earlier. "Do you know what state you're in?"

"I not only know what state I'm in, I can name the capitals," Young replied.

"I don't believe you. Take a seat."

While the 49ers defense set about protecting their 7–3 lead, neither Young nor Montana made Walsh's next decision easy.

"When Walsh had to make the move to replace Young with Montana, Steve tried to push in front of Joe," the *San Francisco Chronicle*'s Lowell Cohn reported. "Montana stood right in front of Walsh as if to say, 'Don't forget about me.' Finally, Walsh tapped Montana on the side and gently pushed Young away."

With Young hazy, dizzy, and reportedly wondering why the team went to the locker room at the end of the first quarter (it was halftime), Walsh had no choice but to insert Montana and his sprained finger. But as the game wore on, Young—when he wasn't pleading with Walsh to return to the field—was coherent enough to relay signals to Montana from the sideline.

"It's always upsetting when you can't play," Montana admitted. "You hate to miss a game. But Bill had to make a judgment."

Montana's return didn't infuse new life into the offense right away: his second pass of the game was bobbled by tight end Ron Heller and intercepted by the Saints. The next two 49er drives also ended with a Montana interception and another San Francisco miscue—a blocked field goal returned sixty-one yards for a Saints touchdown. At the start of the fourth quarter, San Francisco was behind 23–14.

But the 49ers offense regained their form in the final period. Ray Wersching's field goal narrowed the deficit to six points, and with just over three minutes to play, Montana hit Heller with a twenty-nine-yard touchdown pass, giving San Francisco the lead.

New Orleans responded, and Morten Andersen nailed a forty-yard field goal (his ninth in two games against the 49ers that year) and reclaimed the lead, 24–23. Left with a minute to play, Montana drove San Francisco to the Saints 40, a few yards shy of Wersching's field goal range. With eighteen seconds and no timeouts remaining, Montana scrambled for nine yards, but the clock continued to tick—a Saints player allegedly kicking the ball after

Montana was tackled didn't help—and there wasn't enough time to attempt the game-winner.

New Orleans's victory not only snapped their seven-game losing streak at Candlestick Park, but it pushed them within one game of the division lead.

"I can't say the Saints are a better team than we are," Roger Craig offered. "We made a lot of mistakes, but this is no time to point fingers. We've got to forget about this game."

For the 49ers' two slightly bruised quarterbacks, the site of their next game held memories that they had preferred to forget, as well. San Francisco was scheduled to face rookie phenom Vinny Testaverde and the Buccaneers at Tampa Stadium. In that very same venue, during the 49ers 31–7 road win over Tampa Bay less than fifteen months earlier, Montana had wrenched his lower back, an injury that nearly ended his career and still caused numbness in his left leg and foot.

Steve Young didn't have quite such an isolated dour memory of "The Big Sombrero," as Tampa Stadium was dubbed, but he didn't have many positive ones, either.

"There was a lot of emotion the last year and a half there," said Young, who lost all but one of his final eight starts at Tampa Stadium. "Those were tough times. You were battling week after week just to keep your head above water."

Despite his own individual struggles (completing just 53 percent of his passes, throwing thirteen interceptions and just eight touchdowns) and an abysmal 2–14 record, Young had been the team's best player the previous season. And even though he returned to town wearing the opponent's jersey, the *St. Petersburg Times*, which voted him the team's 1986 MVP, honored him with a portrait of the quarterback in Bucs' orange and white.

"This means a lot to me," Young said. "It could have been easy for me to quit, but I feel like I fought hard all season long."

Young received the portrait during a ceremony at halftime, by which point San Francisco held a 17–10 advantage over the surprisingly competitive 4–5 Buccaneers. Early in the third quarter, however, the 49ers started to pull away. Montana hit Rice on a three-yard score, his third of the game and eleventh of the season.

"They played more man-to-man, and it was a surprise to me," said Rice, who added seven catches and 103 yards to his gaudy season totals. "One-on-one, it's hard for a defensive back to cover a good receiver, it doesn't matter who it is. Joe really put the ball right on me today; he did a fantastic job. I've got a real good chemistry with Joe. I know if the opportunity is there, he will get me the ball."

The following week in Cleveland, Rice hauled in another seven catches for 126 yards and three more scores in the 49ers 38–24 win. But the day belonged to Montana, who completed nearly 75 percent of his passes, threw for a season high 342 yards, and connected with Dwight Clark on a forty-yard score that made his close friend the 49ers all-time leader in receiving yards. The quarterback even ran the ball four times for forty-three yards, the second highest total of his career and easily the most gained in a game since his spinal surgery. That statistic did not slide by the media, which still constantly questioned Montana's ability and/or willingness to scramble.

"I thought I answered that question a long time ago by coming back and playing the rest of the year . . . the only time I ever hear about my back is when someone from the press brings it up," Montana said afterward. "If you were a quarterback, would you be running if you had guys like Jerry Rice, Dwight Clark, and Mike Wilson getting open all the time? We're not made to run the ball here. We try to find someone to throw it to. If I have to run, I run. Like any quarterback, when you're running you're looking for someone to throw to. If anyone doesn't like that, it's too bad."

It was unquestionably a great day for Montana, especially considering the opposition. Not only did the Browns have the NFL's top-ranked defense, but Walsh had also recently showered more praise on Cleveland's quarterback, Bernie Kosar, than on his own.

"[Kosar] is big, he's active, he's resourceful," Walsh said the previous Tuesday. "In evaluating the Tampa Bay game, we felt this was Montana's best game of the year. . . . I'm not sure that stands up to Kosar."

"Sometimes," 49ers general manager John McVay remembered years later, "Bill—being a master psychologist—would use certain terms and certain phrases or words and so on to keep guys on their toes."

At 9–2 and one win shy of clinching a playoff berth, Walsh could afford to play mind games, especially given how his star quarterback responded.

In early December during a twenty-seven-degree day at Lambeau Field in Green Bay, Wisconsin, Montana completed his first seventeen pass attempts against the Packers. Added to the five straight he hit at the end of the win over Cleveland, Montana set a new NFL record with twenty-two consecutive completions, a mark that would stand for seventeen years. Montana's third consecutive game with at least two touchdowns and three hundred yards passing maintained his NFL lead in both categories. He also set a career high with twenty-nine touchdown passes, all in just ten starts.

"Those aren't the important things," said Montana, who learned of his consecutive completions record only when Steve Young told him in the locker room. "Getting to the Super Bowl is."

A week later that goal seemed well within reach.

On ABC's Monday Night Football, the 10–3 Chicago Bears visited Candlestick for a showdown between two of the NFL's powerhouses. Chicago's defense—the fabled unit that led the Bears to their first and only Super Bowl title—wasn't quite as dominant as it had been in 1985. But head coach Mike Ditka still had future Hall of Famers Mike Singletary, Dan Hampton, and Richard Dent anchoring a defense that ranked second in the NFL.

"We'll just have to get rid of the ball quicker," Montana said that week. "They have been getting to the passer."

Montana did not have many opportunities to test his theory, however—he wouldn't survive the first quarter. Ironically, against a defense that led the NFL with fifty-six sacks through just twelve contests, it was a collision with a teammate that would send Montana to the sidelines.

On the 49ers second drive of the game, Montana retreated into the pocket to fake a handoff to Roger Craig. Noticing a blitzing safety, Montana tried to avoid the Chicago defender and dump the ball off to Rice, but he tangled his right foot up with Craig's left and fell hard to the ground where he remained for several minutes. Initially, Montana complained to team trainer Lindsy McLean about his knee, but as he hobbled toward the sideline, he felt pain in the back of his leg.

"I said, 'There goes the season,'" recalled 49ers owner Eddie DeBartolo Jr., who was watching the game from a luxury suite at Candlestick. "We got a report from the bench. When they said it hurts behind the kneecap, I guess that's the first sign of a cruciate ligament (injury). When you think of that, you say good-bye."

Aided by a crutch, Montana crawled onto a golf cart bound for the locker room.

"When Joe went down," Young said. "I just ran and got my helmet."

Very early on, Young—whose injured college teammate Jim McMahon watched from the sidelines wearing a black leather jacket—did not look like a rusty backup quarterback summoned in the middle of the game. On his first play, he scrambled past Richard Dent for eighteen yards, nearing the Bears goal line. Two plays later, he floated a touchdown pass to Rice.

"I think it helped me that I'd played against the Bears last year," Young said. "It got me over that whole image of playing against them. I went up there last year, faced them when they were going to the playoffs, had a chance to look Mike Singletary and the rest of them in the eyes. I felt during the week if I got a chance to play, I'd be okay. I knew I wouldn't be awed."

Two Ray Wersching field goals, six first-half turnovers by the Bears, and Young's clutch third down, thirteen-yard touchdown pass to Clark sent San Francisco into halftime ahead 20–0. As his team headed for the locker room, Bears head coach Mike Ditka gave the middle finger to the Candlestick Park crowd then chucked his chewing gum into the stands, where it landed in a woman named Terry Ornelas's hair. In addition to his team's awful first-half performance, Ditka had become enraged by 49ers fans who had thrown ice at him and his players on the sidelines. San Francisco police found the green wad the next day and registered it as "evidence" in a possible battery charge.

"Any time anybody throws something at me," an irritable Ditka told reporters, "I'm going to throw something back."

Ditka's mood didn't improve any once the second half began. Minutes into the third quarter, the 49ers defense forced a Chicago punt, which defensive back Dana McLemore returned eighty-three yards for a touchdown. Young then connected with Rice for two more touchdowns to cap off a 41–0 blowout.

"I'm not just resting between games, but I'm really pressing to play—I'm ready to play," Young told the large crowd of reporters that surrounded him after the game. "I try to figure Joe . . . in team meetings, I listen to the questions he asks, and I watch how he acts with the coach. During practice, I get 25 percent of the work. For the rest, I try to figure what Joe would do in a particular situation."

But Young admitted that he didn't always follow that mantra. Several times he prematurely abandoned a play and chose to improvise. And on plays when he ran the ball beyond the line of scrimmage, he didn't try to avoid hits and sometimes he actively sought them. He even attempted to block 267-pound Dan Hampton on a reverse carried out by Rice.

"You can't sit back on your heels against the Bears. You've got to make things happen," Young added.

Young's great performance in the 49ers victory softened the blow of Montana's injury, which doctors deemed a strained hamstring and hyper-extended knee. And with the NFL's best record, the 49ers didn't need to rush Montana back.

The veteran sat out the next Sunday, and Young again excelled, albeit against one of the NFL's worst teams, the 3–10 Atlanta Falcons. Two second-half touchdown passes to Rice—the first of which moved Rice past the NFL's previous single-season record of eighteen—and the defense's second consecutive game without allowing an offensive score gave San Francisco a 35–7 win.

Once again, however, Young's boldness—aided by his feet—most excited the fans and media. Early in the final period, already up by three touchdowns, the 49ers drove across the Falcons 30-yard line. In the huddle Young called a pass play intended for tight end John Frank, but Atlanta's defense bottled him up, prompting the quarterback to look elsewhere.

"It seemed like the whole [right] half of the field was open," said Young.

Young tucked the ball and bolted beyond the line of scrimmage, toward the goal line, where he leapt over Falcons safety Tim Gordon for a twenty-nine-yard score.

"I felt like I was playing with Thumper," guard Bruce Collie said in a post-game interview. "He's a damn rabbit. He was a lot better than he was last week. He gets downfield so fast. He definitely adds a different aspect to the game than we have with Joe. If nobody's open, he's not going to wait; he'll take off."

Entering the final game of the regular season at 12–2, the 49ers owned the best record in the NFL. But because New Orleans stood at 11–3 (and the clubs had split their two regular season contests), the 49ers still had not clinched the NFC West let alone a first-round bye or homefield advantage throughout the playoffs.

Meanwhile, Montana's hamstring had improved to the point that he returned to practice by the middle of the week, leaving Walsh with a difficult decision. After waffling on naming a starter—early in the week he had said it would be Young, next he had suggested it might be Montana, then he had declared he might wait until kickoff—Walsh finally settled on Young for the team's regular season finale versus the Los Angeles Rams.

The Rams had endured a very disappointing 1987 season. Under head coach John Robinson, they had qualified for the playoffs each of the previous four seasons, but a 1–7 start—in the midst of which they traded away disgruntled All-Pro running back Eric Dickerson—would end that streak. Five wins in a row had helped them climb back to respectability, but upon their arrival at Candlestick for Week 16, they had been relegated to the role of a spoiler, hoping to ruin their in-state rival's shot at a division title.

They would be disappointed in that regard, as well.

In the first half, Steve Young completed ten of thirteen passes for three touchdown passes (the first capping a ninety-nine-yard scoring drive) and the 49er defense continued to suffocate the opposition, allowing just 145 yards of total offense in a 48–0 defeat of the Rams. It was the third consecutive week in which the 49ers defense did not surrender an offensive score.

By the middle of the second quarter, with the score 27–0, the game was clearly a blowout, but fans still had the return of Montana to look forward to.

"We decided before the game that Joe would play one half, and it was likely that the best half would be the second," Walsh said. "Joe needed to sharpen his game, and he felt fine. It was our right to play him."

For Montana, two reasons justified risking another injury in a game that was already decided with his team so close the playoffs. The first was a concern over rust.

"It would [have] been about five weeks since I played, so it was good to be in there," he said. "Just the timing in a game situation, getting used to people moving around you."

The second concern was the possibility of another great performance from his backup, Young. "Yeah, that was part of it," Montana conceded.

With Young watching from the sidelines, Montana quarterbacked the 49ers offense in the second half. Although he threw only nine passes—completing six—he looked sharp, tossing two touchdown passes. The second, a forty-six-yarder to Mike Wilson at the start of the fourth period, was Montana's thirty-first of the season, breaking the franchise record set by John Brodie in 1965.

After the game, reporters could no longer contain themselves and flat-out asked Young if there was now a rivalry between the two quarterbacks.

"I hope so," Young said Sunday night. "I try to make it as competitive as I can with a nine-year veteran and three-time All-Pro. I've always kind of cringed at backing up."

Rivalry or not, there was no question about who would start the 49ers divisional playoff game at Candlestick. With Montana healthy, Young admitted that he knew he'd be watching the postseason from the sidelines . . . "as long as Joe doesn't do anything dumb the next couple weeks."

*　*　*

In the NFC's lone wild card playoff, the Minnesota Vikings went into the Louisiana Superdome and pounded the Saints, 44–10. During the first half, journeyman quarterback Wade Wilson threw two touchdown passes, and former University of Michigan star Anthony Carter added two more (one via an eighty-four-yard punt return and another on a halfback pass from Allen Rice), as the Vikings went on to spoil the Saints' first postseason game in franchise history.

The dominant victory confounded many across the NFL. New Orleans had entered the game having won their final nine games to earn the NFL's second-best record (one win less than the 49ers). The Vikings, an 8–7 club that finished the regular season with three losses in their final four games, surprised both Las Vegas oddsmakers (the Saints had been seven-point favorites against Minnesota) and the 49ers coaching staff.

"We spent a lot of time on the Redskins, as you might guess," Bill Walsh said, "but obviously, we did take a look at Minnesota."

Walsh had expected the Saints to beat Minnesota, which, given the playoff seeding, would have sent the Washington Redskins to Candlestick Park for the second round of the postseason. Instead of the Redskins, who now drew Chicago, the 49ers would host the Vikings on Saturday, January 9, 1988. A matchup of San Francisco's offense against Minnesota's defense garnered all the pregame attention from the media.

Vikings defensive coordinator Floyd Peters was the man charged with slowing down the 49ers prolific offense. To do that, Peters and the Vikings turned to an elite group of pass rushers: Henry Thomas, Stafford Mays, Keith Millard, Doug Martin, and All-Pro Chris Doleman.

"I'm getting tired of hearing how great the 49ers are," Doleman said. "They put their clothes on the same way we do. They don't have any halos over their head, no wings on their back. . . . Do you think Bubba Paris can block me? Do you think their guards can handle (Keith) Millard? Do you think their right tackle can handle Blood (defensive end Doug Martin)? I don't think so."

Doleman, who that season earned his first of eight trips to the Pro Bowl, even went so far as to say "[Joe Montana] ain't no great quarterback," a statement he backtracked from, explaining, "If you can stop Montana from doing the things he likes to do, then the 49ers aren't as effective."

The Vikings' confidence partially stemmed from a 27–24 overtime victory in Candlestick a year earlier, a game that Montana had missed while he recovered from his spinal surgery.

Minnesota's brash talk didn't faze either the 49ers offensive line— "games are played on the football field, not in the media," Bubba Paris said—or Montana, who was busy digesting a Walsh game plan that included ninety-seven different passing plays, at least twenty of which were new that week.

Another wrinkle that Walsh added centered on his backup quarterback's exceptional athleticism. Specific plays were also installed for Steve Young.

"Steve could come into the game in certain situations (to utilize his running ability)," Walsh said. "But Joe is our starter. We don't want to take continuity away from a quarterback who took us to two Super Bowl championships."

But the tweaks to the offense didn't only include play design or specific packages intended to take advantage of Young's speed.

"The emphasis with Joe this week is if there's no one open to throw to, run and wait for something to happen," Young explained that week. "You don't waste any time, because the Vikings' pass rush will get to you if you wait."

From the moment the trade with Tampa Bay was completed, Bill Walsh, Mike Holmgren, and even Young himself had hoped Montana's quarterback style and tendencies would rub off on the raw quarterback. Now, it was the other way around.

During the first period of their NFC divisional playoff, Minnesota and San Francisco traded field goals. Aided by a pass interference penalty, the Vikings took the lead on tight end Carl Hilton's seven-yard touchdown catch early in the second quarter, then added a field goal after Montana and the 49ers could not get a single first down against the Viking defense.

"I could sense he got frustrated early," Keith Millard said. "I saw him keep looking to see who was hitting him. I remember a couple times I hit him, and he got up pretty slow. I just think he couldn't take it anymore."

"I don't think he's as effective a scrambler as he's been in the past," Floyd Peters added.

Behind 13–3 with less than eight minutes remaining before halftime, Montana compounded the 49ers' problems on the very next series when he unloaded a pass for Dwight Clark at the San Francisco 45-yard line. Vikings nickelback Reggie Rutland cut in front of Clark, picked off the pass, and sprinted untouched into the end zone for a touchdown.

"I just threw it behind," Montana said. "It was a bad throw."

The Vikings defense produced three-and-outs on each of the 49ers next two possessions, and the ten-and-a-half-point favorite 49ers went to the locker room at halftime behind 20–3.

For the NFL's top scoring unit, a seventeen-point hole wasn't insurmountable. But the 49ers had no answer for the Vikings defensive strategy.

"It was frustrating because they took us out of our game plan," Montana said. "They got us out of our running and passing combinations. Our play-action pass was nonexistent. It was kind of ridiculous."

Fourth-year safety Jeff Fuller sparked San Francisco with an interception-turned-touchdown at the start of the third quarter, cutting the Vikings lead to ten. But the 49ers first offensive series of the second half once again did not produce any points. Trailing 27–10—Minnesota scored another touchdown on their ensuing offensive series—and with time running out on the 49ers' season, Walsh did the unthinkable: he sent Joe Montana to the bench.

"I told him I didn't like doing it," Walsh said. "I have great regard for him as a football player, but I had to change the chemistry, make a move. I couldn't afford sentiment at that time."

"You're always surprised when you get pulled," Montana said after completing twelve of twenty-six attempts for 109 yards. "Steve runs a little better than me in the open field. . . . After I was on the sideline for a while I could see what (Walsh) was trying to do. He was trying to stir something up. Steve's biggest thing is he gains more yardage when he runs. It wasn't happening for me."

Montana handled the benching with class and dignity, but inside he felt anger, embarrassment, and hurt.

"He was (angry)," Clark later said. "That's his thing. His whole life is bringing teams back from the depths. The greatest comeback kid of all time. But who knows if he could have done it that day? A lot more things went wrong that game than just the quarterback position."

Although the 62,547 fans at Candlestick were stunned, even appalled, by Walsh's move, it looked brilliant from the start. On the first snap, Young found Craig out of the backfield for a thirty-one-yard gain. After a few plays—one of which had been an eleven-yard touchdown run by Young that was called back because of a holding penalty—Young finally scored the 49ers first offensive touchdown, darting across the goal line from five yards out.

"The 49ers' thinking was immediately, we need a speed guy to elude the pass rush, *then* throw down the field, which is backwards," left tackle Steve Wallace remembered. "He could stare down Chris Doleman, and see what was going on and then make a play, where that was Joe's blind side."

In the fourth quarter, Young moved the offense from their own nine-yard line past midfield, then was picked off by cornerback Carl Lee. On the next series Young scrambled for forty-two yards, but again the 49ers were unable to put points on the board as kicker Ray Wersching missed a lengthy field goal attempt. Still, the substitution yielded noticable results, and San Francisco threatened to rally.

"Young changed everything," Minnesota defensive line coach Paul Wiggin said. "You need a .22 to bring him down."

With only a few minutes remaining, Young led the 49ers into Minnesota territory for the fourth time in the second half and fired a sixteen-yard touchdown pass to tight end John Frank, pulling the 49ers within nine points.

But with time expiring, the deficit proved too great. Minnesota left Northern California with a shocking 36–24 victory.

"Our offense just never got going," said Young, who completed twelve of seventeen passes for 158 yards and finished as the team's leading rusher with seventy-two yards. "We never got in our groove. I mean, when we're on . . . I don't know. Little things kept happening. We continually stubbed our toe."

Following his third consecutive postseason loss—and a third consecutive postseason start in which he could not lead the 49ers offense to a single touchdown—Joe Montana sat solemnly in the locker room at Candlestick Park.

Young walked over, pulled up a stool, and then sat across from Montana as the two carried out what Young called "quarterback talk."

"We go through certain plays. Sometimes you question yourself, what you did," Montana said. "Maybe we were trying to comfort each other. Maybe he was trying to comfort me."

Joe Cool and Mr. Hyperactivity

B oth of Bill Walsh's long-standing marriages—one to his wife, Geri, and the other to his quarterback, Joe Montana—were on the rocks during the winter and spring of 1988.

"Geri and I are separated, but it's more of a value relationship related to our needs personally," he announced in late March. "She's a professional (interior designer). She has an excellent career. My career has taken me through many long and difficult years. We're reflecting, both of us. That's the extent of it. This can happen to people our ages on occasion. . . . Divorce is the last thing on either of our minds."

Gossip around the Bay area indicated that Walsh was having an affair with Kristine Hanson, a September 1974 *Playboy* centerfold who covered sports for Sacramento's KCRA-TV.

He denied the claims—"There is no third person involved"—but years later, Walsh biographer David Harris wrote that the two had periodically lived together as far back as 1985.

During those same months, in the wake of the staggering playoff loss to Minnesota, another not entirely unrelated rumor centered on Walsh and the 49ers family.

On March 18, the 49ers gave Walsh a two-year, $2.7 million contract to remain as head coach. But it was what the organization took away from him that made news: he would no longer serve as the team's president.

"[Eddie DeBartolo Jr.] was pretty much convinced that Bill should go, maybe go period," said Carmen Policy, who along with DeBartolo conceived the new arrangement on the upper deck of a chartered yacht to the Caribbean. "Ultimately, my advice was, 'I don't think that's right; I think what you should do is basically try everything in your power to bring him back to the environment that surrounded him when he was *the* coach, the guy that really we all thought of as probably the best in the NFL, maybe one of the best ever in the NFL.

"We went back and forth and he says, 'Well I don't want him dealing with suites, and I don't want him dealing with marketing.' . . . Bill was so afraid of outside influences coming in and somehow, someway impacting the organization that he wanted control over anything. . . . He was just so concerned about so many things outside of coaching. So [DeBartolo] really thought I should take care of it; I should call Bill in, talk to him about a transition."

Upon his return from a ski trip to Aspen, Colorado, Walsh scoffed at the suggestion that the issues surrounding his personal life were the reason for the change. He also dismissed the notion that the change was punishment for the loss to Minnesota.

"[Bill] certainly had his fights with Eddie, and one of them was after that 1987 season when Eddie stripped him of his president's title," David Harris noted. "Eddie went apoplectic. Eddie was a great owner according to Bill, because he put enormous resources into the team, but in return Eddie wanted to go the Super Bowl every year and win it and would roast Bill's ass when that didn't happen. And 1987 was a paramount example of that."

In the realignment of the front office, the presidency title was given to De-Bartolo, who, as Policy explained would, "take more control of the organization on a day-to-day basis."

DeBartolo's first task as president was to deal with yet another rumor that complicated the 49ers' future. Within days of benching Joe Montana in favor of Steve Young during the playoff loss to Minnesota, speculation grew that Walsh was ready to divorce his Joe Montana.

The San Diego Chargers, preparing for the retirement of future Hall of Famer Dan Fouts, approached San Francisco about acquiring Montana. Walsh did not deny the reports, but made certain to tell both Montana and the press that San Diego had approached them about the deal—they weren't "shopping" the quarterback.

"I won't mislead you that we never talked to San Diego and that Montana's name came up, but a lot of names came up, including their players," Walsh said, a week before he officially lost his title as team president. "I put him in the same category as I would every other player. He's special, there's no doubt about it. And I suppose we could say that we'd never trade Montana. But I don't like saying that because, at some point in the future, I would suppose that mutually it would be done."

DeBartolo admitted that the club would "have a narrow mind, or be shortsighted not to listen," but he clearly didn't want to part with the franchise's centerpiece and asked for a king's ransom in return.

Chargers owner Alex Spanos called DeBartolo to inquire about Montana's availability. The *San Jose Mercury News* reported that, pressed for a price, DeBartolo demanded two first-round draft choices and linebacker Billy Ray Smith, the Chargers MVP the previous season. Spanos countered with two first-round selections and backup running back Gary Anderson, but DeBartolo then suggested he speak with Walsh, who he said "runs my organization."

"After we get through the '87 deal and Bill's back on board, he's hell-bent on trading Joe. And we understood later what happened: he had promised Steve that he was going to be the starter," Policy remembered years later. "Bill was trying to do everything he could to clear the decks to follow through with his promise and do what he wanted to do, and he felt he had to get Joe out of there. I also think [Bill] resented Joe's closeness to Eddie. I think that Bill felt that the locker room was his, and the players' affection and hatred belonged to him, and it shouldn't go outside of the locker room to anyone else in the organization, even the owner.

"I warned him," Policy added. "I said, 'Look, Bill, no one's getting in your way in terms of making personnel decisions. But when you're talking about Joe Montana, the starting quarterback, the icon, this is a whole different scenario. And you better be right, and you better get a blockbuster deal.'"

Although trade talks soon died, just before leaving for a spring vacation in Europe and the Grand Cayman Islands, Montana told DeBartolo, "Eddie, if it's going to help the football team, then trade me."

"[Joe's] a friend of mine," DeBartolo said. "He, Dwight Clark, and Ronnie Lott, that group that I call 'kids,' they're all my friends. I was really a baby in football when they came up."

DeBartolo had already set a precedent of siding with Montana over his head coach. In 1984, Walsh reportedly refused to give Montana the salary he wanted, but DeBartolo agreed to meet the quarterback's demands.

That decision came shortly after the twenty-seven-year-old Montana—who still had not missed a single game due to injury—nearly took the 49ers back to the Super Bowl: they lost a close NFC title game in Washington. Five years later, Montana's already uncertain tenure at quarterback became even more so, especially that February when he underwent another surgery, this time to relieve inflammation in the bursa sac of his throwing elbow.

For the second consecutive year, Montana's training was critical to his future, the 49ers Super Bowl dreams, and Walsh's decision about whom to start. And again, Montana dedicated himself to adding weight and durability to his frame. That offseason, routinely at 5:30 a.m.—"And I am not a morning person"—Montana was running hills in Redwood City, lifting weights, biking, even boxing, under the tutelage of local fitness expert Ben Parks.

"We'd do things like run up the stairs in my house," Montana said. "I don't know how many times a day, but we need a new rug."

When training camp opened, Montana claimed to have added nearly ten pounds of muscle to his upper body and was near his peak playing weight of two hundred pounds.

"I'm in a position to lose the job," he admitted in late July. "He (Young) is going to push, and he's going to push, but the competition is great. And I love it."

To Young, that competition was every bit as valuable.

"I've learned a lot from Joe, but I think I'm at a point now where I need to play to get any better," Young said. "Joe's the starter, so I've got to beat him out. Joe's been All-Pro and all-everything for a long time. I have a lot to do, but I'd like to think I could beat him out."

From the moment training camp opened, Walsh gave Young ample opportunities to earn the job.

Walsh was still fairly enamored with Young's athleticism and speed, both of which would pose a tremendous threat to opposing defenses and exasperate opposing coaches attempting to game plan. Publicly he stood by Montana, but he repeatedly hinted at a change.

"Joe last year was the premier quarterback, but when Steve had an opportunity to play, he was a very exciting and explosive performance. . . . Steve is so charismatic and exciting that he can actually push Joe for the job. And if Montana were to unfortunately stumble, Steve would be there to pick up the pieces."

Walsh couldn't help but talk out both sides of his mouth. Prior to the 49ers first preseason game—an extremely long, ten-thousand-mile trip east to London to play the Dolphins—Walsh told one reporter, "The last thing we want is a quarterback controversy because the quarterback does need total confidence in his team and his role."

But that same week, during an interview with NBC, Walsh created now-international sports headlines by explaining, "We have a quarterback controversy. We have two good quarterbacks. We're going to have to select between Steve Young and Joe Montana."

The exhibition game only further fanned the flames.

At London's Wembley Stadium, Montana—who missed parts of practice earlier in the week due to soreness in his elbow, a lingering effect from the off-season surgery—started the rematch of Super Bowl XIX. He attempted just five passes, two of which were dropped, two of which were completed, then spent the remainder of the game on the sideline.

"I guess it's sort of a long way to come for (two possessions)," Montana said.

Young replaced him early in the second quarter and picked up right where he left off following the playoff loss to Minnesota. On his first drive, Young scrambled twice for nineteen yards, found Rice for a forty-one-yard completion, and, with linebacker Hugh Green in his face, floated a short touchdown pass to fullback Tom Rathman. Later, with Young completing long passes, one to John Taylor and one to tight end Ron Heller, the 49ers added two more touchdowns to take a 21–20 lead. Perhaps Young's finest highlight of the day, however, came not as a ball carrier or as a passer. On a key third-and-2 inside the Dolphins redzone, Young handed off to running back Doug DuBose, who pitched the ball to John Taylor on a reverse. Young threw himself into a Miami defender, springing Taylor for the first down that set up the go-ahead touchdown.

"I ran a reverse in practice last week in Rocklin and tried to make a block, and everyone laughed at me," Young said. "I figured no more of that, I'll try to give it my best shot."

Both head coaches, Walsh and the Dolphins Don Shula, praised Young for the performance, as did Miami linebacker Rick Graf, who told reporters, "I'd rather face Montana than Young."

Upon returning to the States (Miami came back to win the preseason game, 27–21), Walsh continued to arouse speculation.

"I think it would have to be acknowledged there will be a controversy related to the quarterbacks this year," Walsh said. "There is now, I believe. There was toward the end of last season and certainly after the last game and going into this year. It will continue. I would have to be terribly naïve and all of us would be rather tongue-in-cheek if we didn't accept that. I would have to be awfully dogmatic and bullheaded if I were to say that only Joe would be considered this year as the starting quarterback. That would make life easier and simpler, but it wouldn't necessarily be the best eleven men."

Walsh believed that fear was the most powerful motivating tool at his disposal.

"You never thought that Joe would be in a quarterback controversy," tight end Brent Jones said in 2011. "Here's a guy who brought world championships to the San Francisco 49ers. But interestingly enough, in looking back now, and understanding what Bill Walsh's management style was, it was actually right in line with the way that he wanted his team to be run. The 49ers under Coach Walsh, down to a player, nobody was ever comfortable in their position. There was always a backup pressing you. . . .

"He understood what made each guy tick, but he also understood the competitive desire of the business and the competitive dynamics, where if you could have a strong backup to a guy that was working hard and pushing him and leaving you with an uncertainty, no matter how great you were performing. There's nothing worse than you're out there playing your butt off and Bill Walsh is complimenting your backup and saying what a great a job he is doing. So thinking back, I think Bill had a quality backup or somebody to push a guy at every single position other than quarterback. And then I don't think it was possible for him to find somebody, and then he found Steve."

Despite Walsh's reputation as a brilliant psychologist and motivator, he also seemed genuinely undecided about which player gave the 49ers the best opportunity to win.

Montana—whom Walsh called "the best technician in football"—may have been reasonably healthy and entering his tenth season in the West Coast system, but that summer, San Francisco's offensive line faced several uncertainties. Veteran Keith Fahnhorst reluctantly retired, Bubba Paris came into training camp overweight, and former Pro Bowler Fred Quillan was dealt to the Chargers. As he proved in the loss to Minnesota, Young's speed and elusiveness could disguise those flaws. And Young's blossoming confidence—which he explained grew exponentially during his relief effort in playoffs—again motivated the front office to consider making a trade.

"I know they were actively trying to trade Joe . . . and I don't think they were able to strike a deal," remembered quarterback Bob Gagliano, who started one game for the 49ers the previous season during the players' strike and by training camp was competing with former Stanford standout John Paye for a roster spot.

With Montana, Young, and Paye on the roster, Gagliano, the soon-to-be thirty-year-old former Chief, spoke to offensive coordinator Mike Holmgren about a trade or his release, so he might find work elsewhere.

"I had approached Mike about, 'Hey, I'm going to go to Bill and say please give me an opportunity to go hook up somewhere, because if we wait too long it's going to be tough.' And Mike said, 'Just hold off, just hang in there a little bit longer.' So I knew that there was something in the works."

No trade was to be made, however, and as the preseason carried on, so did the competition.

"Controversy has disrupted this quiet town twenty-five miles north of Sacramento, where the San Francisco 49ers prepare for the football season," Joan Ryan of the *San Francisco Examiner* explained prior to the 49ers next exhibition game. "In the 7-Elevens and Burger Kings, in the auto garages and hardware stores, people are choosing up sides. Steve or Joe? Joe or Steve?"

The next three games essentially resulted in a draw. Against the Raiders, Montana was superb, producing three scores and completing twelve of fourteen passes, for 166 yards in just one half.

"I think Joe was really fired up for this one," Rice remarked. "You don't want to challenge Joe."

But Montana sat out the next exhibition against Denver, giving Young a turn. He threw two touchdowns, ran for sixty yards on only four carries, and silenced the crowd at Mile High Stadium with a five-yard touchdown run in which he dodged a blitzing linebacker, headed toward the goal line, then dove into a pile of Denver defenders for the 49ers first score.

"It took a lot of guts to do what he did on that touchdown. This guy wants it," wide receiver Wes Chandler said.

A week later, the 49ers faced San Diego, and both quarterbacks were outstanding. Playing the entire first half, Montana threw a touchdown to Rice, completed eleven of his eighteen attempts, and even ran for thirty-six yards. But Young again stole the spotlight. Shredded for 265 yards and five scores by the unheralded quarterback duo of Babe Laufenberg and Mark Malone, the 49ers pass defense forged a seventeen-point early third-quarter deficit that Young was asked to erase. And he did so, thanks to a trio of fourth-quarter touchdown drives, the first of which ended with his twelve-yard touchdown pass to Dokie Williams. The 49ers escaped with a 34–27 victory.

One exhibition game now remained before the 49ers regular season opener against the New Orleans Saints in the Superdome. And by halftime of that preseason finale against the Seahawks, the incumbent's grip on the gig grew even more tenuous. Seven-of-fifteen for just seventy-nine passing yards (thirty-two of those yards came on a screen pass to Roger Craig), the Montana-led offense did not score throughout the entire first half.

"It seemed like we were running around for thirty minutes with our shoes on the wrong feet," Randy Cross admitted.

"It's not my job to criticize," Montana added before briskly leaving the locker room at game's end. "It wasn't a good day overall."

It *was* a good day, though, for Young. On three consecutive drives in the third period, the Young-led 49ers offense scored touchdowns. Granted, each time a Seattle miscue provided the 49ers with tremendous field position, deep inside Seahawks territory. But when San Francisco trailed by a single point in the middle of the final period, Young drove the offense fifty-six yards for the game-winning score, a nineteen-yard touchdown to Calvin Nicholas.

After the 49ers 27–21 win, Walsh's decision was now eminently more difficult than it had been just a month earlier. No one could claim that Montana had lost the starter's job. Facing the opposition's first string defense throughout the preseason, he was thirty-for-forty-seven, for 378 yards, one touchdown, zero interceptions in essentially a game-and-a-half's time. More importantly, the 49ers did not employ their entire arsenal: in the preseason, teams do not utilize the full extent of their playbook to prevent regular season opponents from scheming a successful game plan.

Still, with Young under center, the 49ers scored far more points, and in consecutive weeks he directed the game-winning fourth-quarter touchdown drive. And he did so with, at times, borderline NFL talent: instead of Rice, Young completed passes to Nicholas, Williams, and Wes Chandler, none of whom would survive the regular season. Of course that also meant that Young's late-game preseason heroics usually came against defensive lineups that featured many players that would eventually be cut.

"A lot of times quarterback troubles are negative," Young told press following his win over Seattle. "In this case it could be good. Because as long as Joe plays football there won't be any question about who's the leader, who's done what, or who's been where."

* * *

Montana and Young brought disparate skill sets and outlooks on playing the position of quarterback to the field. Methodically picking apart the opposing defense with deadly precision, while occasionally sidestepping—not necessarily running away from—the pass rush enabled Montana to bring a pair of Super Bowl trophies to San Francisco. Young, a left-handed passer who struggled mightily with accuracy in his first few seasons with the 49ers, was impatient in the pocket, eager to tuck the ball, employ his running back–like skills, and engage linebackers and defensive backs, rather than avoid them.

The difference in their athletic strengths and weakness, however, couldn't compare to the difference in their backgrounds and demeanors.

In every way imaginable, Montana epitomized his nickname, "Joe Cool." On the football field, he was never rattled, whether in the face of a blitzing linebacker or a twenty-eight-point halftime deficit. And out of uniform, the blue-collar Catholic Western Pennsylvania product, was equally relaxed, as he drove one of his sports cars—by the late 1980s Montana owned a Corvette, a BMW, a Mercedes-Benz 500 SEC, a Porsche 928, a Ferrari 308, and a Ferrari Testarossa—off to go and have a beer with or play practical jokes on his buddies.

Young—a Mormon from Connecticut who despite millions of dollars in the bank drove a beatup 1965 Oldsmobile Cutless until it died with more than 270,000 miles on the odometer—displayed an unwavering intensity. Teammate and Pro Bowl guard Guy McIntyre, later characterized Young as "nervous" in the huddle.

"I think a sense of urgency is a great way to describe him," said Brent Jones, Young's road-trip roommate. "There were even times when I would be like, 'Relax, we're up by a couple touchdowns, have some fun, enjoy the moment.' And I think that that was not necessarily built into his mindset. . . . One of the things we used to talk about was . . . look around, take in the moment, appreciate your teammates, look at the coaches, look at the fans, they're cheering for you, be aware of that, because sometimes he was so siloed and so focused that he'd miss out on some of the more exciting things that were going on."

Still, contrasting playing styles and even the contrasting personalities alone were not enough to create a quarterback controversy worthy of national interest. For that to happen, another element was necessary.

"People always think that we fought," Young said years later. "We never had a cross word, never had an argument, and I've always said to people that it went as well as it possibly could with two hypercompetitive people. But it wasn't easy; it was difficult, difficult for both of us."

"It's not that there was bad blood," Montana said in 2011. "I guess the only way you can explain it is if you go to work every day in an office . . . you're not always best friends with the guy sitting next to you. You're friends, but you're not best friends. And while we were friends, we wouldn't hang out together. . . . It had nothing to do with the game or the competition; it's just our personalities are different."

At the time, the way in which both Montana and Young spoke about the issue through the press only stirred up more friction.

"I remember in training camp that year, Steve refused to call himself the second-string guy," Brent Jones remembered. "He even made a quote, and I'm sure this didn't go over well with Joe, but he said, 'I'm 1-B.' So there's 1-A [Montana] and 1-B [Young]."

During that same training camp, Montana attempted to explain his relationship with Young as segregated: personally it was amicable; professionally, that was another matter.

"We're friends, Steve and I," Montana told *Sports Illustrated*'s Ralph Wiley. "But out on the practice field, if he doesn't hate me as much as I hate him, then there's something wrong."

There was already an innate discord between the two—an aging, battered legend trying to fend off the advances of a younger, stronger challenger—so Montana's use of word "hate," or Young staking his claim to the starter's job, was provocative.

"[Joe] was so competitive—and you know players will try to beat each other at Tiddlywinks—it was such an affront to him," Young's agent, Leigh Steinberg remembered. "It really put a tension, suspicion, distrust, into that relationship between Steve and Joe from the start. Steve was like the younger brother who venerated Montana and loved Joe. Joe was a proud competitive incumbent who didn't want Steve there."

Even within the confines of the team's facilities, passive-aggressive warfare was employed. Both lobbied for more repetitions in practice, then complained to third-string quarterback John Paye while their competition ran the offense. And when Paye wasn't either man's confidant, the media was.

That season, a member of the press was pulled aside by Montana, who said that Young had covertly erased portions of practice film in which Young threw a bad pass or made the wrong read. Within a week, Young pulled aside that same person to inform them that Montana was spreading false rumors about him erasing practice films to hide mistakes from the coaching staff.

"As a journalist, you're like, 'Well, this is really great for people like me,'" the member of the press later recalled. "But are we in junior high, or what's the deal? . . . I still can't really believe that those two guys, that accomplished, did that. But that was the atmosphere."

* * *

Instead of parsing his words and tiptoeing around the issue—as he had for the previous six months—Bill Walsh forcefully and unambiguously announced his starting quarterback for the 49ers regular season opener in New Orleans.

"Montana will start," Walsh told reporters during the postgame press conference following the preseason finale against Seattle.

Although disappointed, Steve Young gracefully accepted his head coach's decision.

"There's room for improvement," he said. "It's tough (to dislodge Montana). You've got to carry a brighter torch all the time."

But Young wouldn't have to wait very long for an opportunity to play.

With Montana making his ninety-ninth regular season start, the 49ers toppled the Saints in Week 1, 34–33. Three touchdown passes—in the span of eight minutes—built the 49ers a lead just large enough to survive a late rally from the Saints. The offensive performance was even more remarkable considering Montana's physical state.

Late in the second period, at the end of a scramble, Montana's throwing elbow—the same one that had been operated on that spring—was sandwiched between Saints linebacker Sam Mills and the hard AstroTurf of the Superdome. Montana was seen shaking his right arm, but the injury didn't prevent him from, seconds later, throwing an (incomplete) Hail Mary at the end of the first half. And after icing down the elbow in the locker room during halftime, Montana fired his trio of scores, each of which Montana called "helicopters . . . they were going end over end."

By the end of that same period, the elbow swelled to the "the size of a tennis ball," and Montana had to be removed from the game. This time, however, Young's relief effort didn't exactly overshadow Montana: he completed just one pass for four yards and, while trying to escape a sack in the end zone, was flagged for intentional grounding, resulting in a safety that cut the team's advantage to just five.

"Young was shaky in relief," *Sacramento Bee* reporter Jim Jenkins noted. "Walsh is probably praying for a speedy Montana recovery."

A few days before another lengthy plane ride east, this time to New Jersey to play the Giants in Week 2, Walsh was apprehensive about starting Montana, who had resumed throwing midweek.

"I felt that I could have thrown both those days," Montana told the press on Friday, "but it was obvious who they were going to go with. You can't get ready when you only throw the ball six times a day in practice. They were going to yank me last week against the Saints, but the game got tight, and they didn't want to make a change unless they had to. Sure it's tough. It's like someone's waiting for you to screw up. You're afraid of having a bad series."

By Saturday night, word leaked to the press that Young would start with Montana available if necessary. Indirectly, the head coach admitted that he made the move because Young practiced with the first team offense and Montana—who Walsh declared "90 percent" healthy—did not.

Young made enough plays with his arm (eleven-for-eighteen, 115 yards) and legs (five rushes, 48 yards) to send the 49ers into halftime tied at ten. But twice the Lawrence Taylor-less Giants—L. T. was serving a four-game drug suspension—sacked Young, who fumbled away the football. And late in the first half Walsh approached Montana on the sideline, saying, "Be ready to play in the second half."

"I wasn't sure he was serious," said Montana. "'I was shocked . . . but I wasn't going to argue."

Montana replaced Young at the start of the second half, and his passing set up a Mike Cofer field goal that snapped the 10–10 tie, but late in the fourth quarter, the Giants Phil McConkey returned a punt to the San Francisco 15-yard line, where Phil Simms threw the go-ahead touchdown pass to Lionel Manuel.

Although the situation wasn't nearly as grim as it had been a year earlier against the Bengals—in addition to having the ball, more than a minute-and-a-half remained—the 49ers looked buried. Their previous four possessions had yielded no points. The Giants defense allowed Rice (who dropped two passes, including a certain touchdown) only thirty-one yards on three receptions. And as for Montana, the last time he appeared at Giants Stadium he left via an ambulance.

None of that bothered Montana. Neither did what happened next. On first down, from their own 23-yard line, Rice, running a quick slant, dropped a perfect pass, his third of the day. The next play, Montana fumbled the snap, which center Randy Cross fell on for a one-yard loss. Now it was third-and-11, with less than a minute remaining. Walsh called a play, "76 All Go," which he described as "the ugliest play in football . . . you say a prayer and leave the huddle."

For Walsh and the 49ers, their prayer was immediately answered.

"76 All Go" was essentially a "Hail Mary." All four of Montana's receivers—two to his left, two to his right—would run fly patterns, straight up-field toward the end zone. Each receiver was covered man-to-man by a Giants defensive back while two safeties and a linebacker occupied the middle of the field for support.

Montana heaved a picture perfect fade pass down the right sideline, which Rice caught in stride and streaked seventy-eight yards for the game-winning score. (Giants defenders Mark Collins and Kenny Hill crashing into one another and falling to the ground guaranteed Rice's unimpeded path to the end zone.) Joe Cool had done it again, leading the 49ers to a 20–17 comeback win.

"Just as we planned," Montana said in the post-game press conference.

Interest in the 49ers electrifying comeback—the second last-minute Week 2 miracle in as many seasons—died out quickly, however. Instead, reporters pressed both Montana and Young for comments about Walsh's two-quarter-back system.

"I really wanted to play the second half because I thought I had a feel for the game. . . . I thought things were going well," Young said. "(Using two quarterbacks) wasn't real pretty, but it worked. Obviously, both of us would have liked to play the whole game. But we've won a couple of games, and both of us have seen a lot of action, so maybe that's a good sign."

"Joe's really been a man about this," Walsh said. "Steve, too, but it's harder for Joe because he's been the starter for so long. They both want to play, but they also want to do what's right for the team. That's the way it's been here. There are no overwhelming egos that have to be satisfied."

Winning managed to slightly mute the quarterback controversy: a triumphant win over the powerhouse Giants in front of a boisterous Meadowlands crowd meant less grist for the rumor mill.

But respite from the turmoil wouldn't last long. The following week, Montana threw three interceptions—one of which was returned for a touchdown—and the 49ers were defeated 34–17 by Atlanta in Candlestick Park. This time, none of the principals could divert attention away from the issue by pointing out a victory. Especially since Montana explicitly stated that the quarterback controversy had impacted his play, making him more cautious and hesitant.

"I'm not going to go out there and take advantage of things and make some tight throw that I would normally throw, because I don't want to come out of the game," Montana stated that week during a conference call with Atlanta reporters. "You don't want to think that way, but that's the way you end up reacting. You end up going, 'Oh, well, this is too tight. I'll just dump the ball to a back or the tight end,' which is a tough way to play the game."

The 49ers offense, however, was not timid during the next two games, a 38–7 blowout of Seattle, and a seven-point home victory over the Lions. In those consecutive wins Montana completed two-thirds of his passes for 494 yards and four touchdowns, and San Francisco's record improved to 4–1. Still, any perceived quarterback harmony was again short-lived.

In Week 6, the two-time defending AFC champion Denver Broncos arrived at Candlestick. Gusting winds, which at one point carried back judge Tom Sifferman's hat forty-two yards across the field, forced the 49ers to rely almost exclusively on running back Roger Craig. They were ahead 13–6 in the fourth quarter, but Montana, who had scored the game's only touchdown via a six-yard quarterback draw, fumbled a snap near midfield, setting up Denver's game-tying touchdown.

Curiously, although neither team could effectively throw the ball—"The wind had to be really bad for a guy like John Elway to quit throwing the ball," Montana noted—Walsh pulled Montana in favor of Young with 3:17 remaining in the game.

"It's no big deal," said Montana, who had played through flu-like symptoms. "I'm used to it now."

"It was the wind," Walsh explained. "We thought Steve's ability to run, if necessary, would help, and he throws the ball harder."

Saddled with a first-and-20 after a holding penalty, Young didn't have many opportunities to showcase a superior arm strength. Two runs and a sack—all the while chants of "We Want Joe" rippled throughout the home crowd—meant a quick three-and-out. Soon, the game went to overtime, which Montana began, then left due to a rib injury he suffered following a sack by Denver's Andre Townsend.

Young's first pass attempt upon taking over was an ill-advised, cross-field toss to fullback Tom Rathman, which was intercepted at the 32-yard line. It didn't help that two 49ers receivers had lined up incorrectly.

"The receivers (Rice and Wilson) were supposed to switch," Young explained. "We were running out of time so we couldn't get it fixed. It was just a mistake."

A stout effort from San Francisco's defense put the ball right back in Young's hands a few minutes later, but another, far more costly miscue dealt San Francisco a second home loss in four weeks.

From his own end zone, Young took a three-step-drop and slung a pass to the left side, intended for Rice. At the 12-yard line, the football skidded off

Rice's fingertips and right into the hands of Broncos' defensive back Steve Wilson.

"It was a good pass. . . . Only the ball was here, and my body was there," Rice said. "It was really my fault. We're taught not to tip the ball into the air like that."

"There's no excuses," said Young. "The wind was a factor, but not an excuse. You have to be very precise throwing in the wind."

Two plays later, barefooted kicker Rich Karlis ended the game with a twenty-two-yard field goal, leaving the entire football world asking just one question: How could a team coached by offensive guru Bill Walsh, equipped with the NFL's most versatile running back in Roger Craig, the game's premier pass catcher, Jerry Rice, and not one, but *two* star quarterbacks fail to put points on the scoreboard?

"Next week, if we score five touchdowns, it won't be discussed anymore. Our offense is very sound," Young told reporters.

Such a performance didn't take place the following week against the Los Angeles Rams. In fact, had it not been for a 190-yard effort by Craig—who not only became the NFL's leading rusher at the end of Week 7, but shared the league lead in receptions as well—the 49ers would have squandered a ten-point halftime lead and dropped another game.

Still, early in the final period, it was largely Montana who propelled San Francisco to a 5–2 start.

The bruised ribs Montana suffered late in the loss to Denver didn't prevent him from starting the next game in Anaheim—although he received multiple shots of a painkiller in his elbow during the week and Novocain injections in his chest prior to kickoff. That news, in addition to the one-hundred-degree Southern California heat, which made it even more difficult for Montana to breathe with his rib injury, forced Walsh to replace Montana with Young early in the third quarter.

"Nobody likes to be taken out," Montana said. "But under the circumstances, it was one of the few times I welcomed it."

Montana also didn't mind the substitution once he saw how Steve Young performed in his place. On consecutive series, he misfired on both of his pass attempts, was unable to produce a single first down, and nearly gave the football away, fumbling a snap. Not long after, Walsh re-inserted Montana, who threw an interception.

After the Rams scored a touchdown, San Francisco now trailed 21–17. But Montana didn't flinch. In the final period, staring down a third-and-19 from his own nine-yard line, he completed a thirty-one-yard pass to former Canadian Football League star Terry Greer, who hung on to the ball despite a vicious hit from a Los Angeles defender.

Mainly keeping the ball on the ground, the 49ers then drove the length of the field. Craig finished off the game-winning ninety-three-yard drive with his third rushing touchdown of the day.

"That was a great pass by Montana [to Greer]," said Walsh. "I thought [Joe] played an excellent game."

"Look, there's definitely a difference," Randy Cross said of the 49ers two-quarterback system. "But contrary to expert opinions, this is Joe Montana's offense. And I'm sure the guys on the other side of the field today will attest to that. It's not Steve Young's fault. He's the greatest Steve Young there is. Joe Montana is just a great quarterback."

But as great as Montana was, his body continued to betray him. The elbow that was operated on in the spring, then later sidelined him in New Orleans, remained a handicap and reduced his participation in the team's practices leading up to a Monday night battle in Chicago against the NFL's premier defense. Montana's health, coupled with the Bears defensive strategy—a preference for man-to-man coverage often left a scrambling quarterback unaccounted for—meant Young would be "on call" for Walsh.

But there was another reason why Walsh ached for chances to put Young out on the field.

"We really need Steve to come in and have a big game for us, so we can rest Joe," Walsh said two days before the Monday night game at Soldier Field. "We're just beating Joe to death, and if we don't give him a chance to recover, he won't be there when we need him later in the season. . . . That's been a problem. Steve hasn't responded when he's gone in. He just hasn't been in sync. He's been too hyper. But he knows that, and I think he'll get over that."

Walsh planned to use Young in spot duty, a series here, a series there, but in pregame warm-ups, he pulled a muscle in his back, and Walsh's confidence in his throwing ability waned.

By the end of the opening quarter, Walsh wasn't in need of a quarterback contingency plan. Montana picked apart a Bears defense that had allowed a combined twenty-three points in their previous four games. He threw for ninety-eight yards on six of eight attempts, including a textbook post pattern touchdown to Rice that put the 49ers ahead 7–0. More importantly, Montana wasn't sacked once.

The Bears adjusted their approach to feature more zone coverages, and Montana, unable to find openings in the secondary, completed just seven of his next twenty-one attempts. He also endured four sacks, was knocked down on several other plays, and threw a costly interception just before halftime. And with Roger Craig and the rushing attack equally stymied during the cold night by Lake Michigan, the 49ers offense fell silent.

"You've got to feel shocked," said Montana. "I mean you have to go into every game feeling you can move [the ball]. If you don't, you're beat."

A touchdown run by Young's collegiate mentor Jim McMahon followed by a Chicago field goal lifted the Bears to a 10–7 halftime lead. In the third quarter the 49ers defense sacked McMahon for a safety, narrowing the gap to just one. Later on, John Taylor's punt return set the offense up at Chicago's 35-yard line, but on the ensuing third down, Montana underthrew fullback Tom Rathman and the 49ers settled for a fifty-one-yard field goal attempt, which Mike Cofer missed. A fourth-down stop by San Francisco's defense with less than three minutes to play earned the 49ers one more opportunity for another fantastic comeback, but rather than entrusting the outcome of the game to his two-time Super Bowl MVP, Walsh pinned the 49ers hopes on Young. Walsh explained that the move was made because Montana was "totally fatigued."

"Fatigued? No, I don't think so," Montana responded. "I just wasn't having too good a night. Sometimes I wasn't setting up well. Sometimes I got hit; some passes I hurried. You want to be perfect with the ball when you know it's a big play, and you're trying to touch it over there and you don't throw it hard enough. I made a bad throw at the end (a swing pass to Tom Rathman) and I guess he (Walsh) felt it was time to do something."

Montana also insisted that the accumulation of injuries to his ribs and elbow were not a factor: "If I was hurting to the point where I couldn't play, I'd say something—especially in a game like this."

Young's scrambling could muster only a few yards, and on fourth-and-short a swing pass to Craig didn't capture the first down. The 49ers lost.

Just a few years earlier, the scene—Walsh substituting a reasonably healthy Joe Montana prior to the last-minute, potential game-winning drive—would have been inconceivable. And Walsh choosing an unproven, unseasoned quarterback with three career victories as the replacement made the move only more bizarre and more painful for Montana to accept.

"It's tearing my guts out," Montana admitted to his wife, Jennifer, according to a *Sports Illustrated* article a few years later.

But the latest unsuccessful installment of musical quarterbacks did nothing to discourage Walsh on Young or his belief that Montana needed a rest. In fact, upon the team's return to San Francisco, the head coach made a fairly stunning announcement. He was considering sitting Montana completely.

"(Montana's) readiness concerns me," Walsh said. "He has great heart and tremendous courage, so if you were to ask Joe, he will say he's 100 percent and ready. I have to look at it and see how he is. He needs a rest, to be honest with you. He needs a week off. . . . That can be viewed as bad judgment on my part for saying that. It's a good story that way. But honestly he needs to take a break. He's been taking a lot of hits, a lot of shots, and he's a 190-pound quarterback.

"So I'll look at it closely this week. I'm going to have to look closely at just how he moves and how he feels. A year ago Steve Young gave us some great performances, and he's going to have to do that this year when called upon. I'm hoping that [Montana's back injury] will be alleviated. It may or may not be."

Not only did Montana's back not heal, it got worse: as he pulled away from the line of scrimmage during practice, a lineman accidently stepped on his foot, which twisted his already painful spine, resulting in muscle spasms.

Although Walsh said Montana would "be fine" and waited until near the end of the week to officially announce it, Young was named the starter for Week 9. On game day, Montana would not even be in uniform.

"Steve looks good," Walsh declared. "Once he's in the saddle, so to speak, he becomes a little different, like most players. He gets to really assert himself. We have a lot of confidence in how he'll play and how he'll do. Once he's in sync, he'll be fine. He has been in the past."

Besides his own self-assurance and that of his head coach—neither of which wavered, even after his disastrous outing against Denver—Young had also slowly earned the trust of many teammates.

"It's tougher for Steve when he has to come off the bench and play," Rice said. "Now, he has a chance to get mentally ready. I'm looking forward to Steve having a good game."

* * *

Ten months removed from their 36–24 victory over the 49ers in the playoffs, the Minnesota Vikings returned to Candlestick Park the day before Halloween, 1988.

At 5–3 the Vikings had struggled in previous weeks, most notably a twenty-point home loss to the downtrodden Green Bay Packers. But Minnesota still had Anthony Carter, who had burned the 49ers that January, and a pass rush loaded with sack specialists.

"(The Vikings) have one of the top defenses," Steve Young said that week. "You have to be very aggressive and let loose."

Young and the 49ers' play calling quickly applied that philosophy, but the inaccuracy and inconsistency that had marked his previous few appearances continued. He completed only four of his first eleven attempts, overthrowing some open receivers, bouncing passes at the feet of others. Scant sounds of boos cascaded down from the stands at Candlestick Park.

"I guess I wasn't much of anything in the first half," he acknowledged later. "I was rusty. I expected some of that. We were trying to throw deep, and it wasn't quite there."

On the sideline, dressed in jeans and a long-sleeve black shirt, Montana provided Young with encouragement.

"Joe helped me through the game, especially in the first half when things weren't going well," said Young. "He would say, 'Don't worry, just let the plays be themselves. Don't try to do too much; don't try to do something spectacular.'

"It wasn't good that Joe was hurt, but it sure was great to know I would get the second half," Young added. "It helped my confidence. I think 80 percent of NFL games are won or lost in the last ten minutes, and that's when any quarterback wants to be in there. I'm just happy I got the whole game, knew I was getting the whole game."

With San Francisco trailing 7–3 to start the third period, Young found his rhythm, marching the 49ers on an efficient and impressive ninety-seven-yard scoring drive. His eighteen-yard completion to Terry Greer set up a Roger Craig touchdown run.

Minnesota reclaimed the lead as Wade Wilson connected with Carter for a sixty-seven-yard touchdown. But the 49ers needed just nineteen seconds to match the score. On a first-and-10 from his own 27, Young faked to his left, pointed downfield, then lobbed a pass to a wide-open John Taylor, who caught it at the Minnesota 35, spun away from a defender, and raced the rest of the way to the end zone.

"It was a good throw," Taylor said. "It just hung, and fortunately the free safety didn't get there in time."

Although Jerry Rice missed a huge portion of the game with nagging ankle and heel injuries, Young threw the ball with tremendous precision in the second half, completing ten of his final fifteen passes, and finishing the game with 232 passing yards, a personal best in San Francisco.

Again, the Vikings bounced back, eventually turning a Craig fumble into a touchdown to take a 21–17 advantage. As the fourth-quarter clock dwindled, the Vikings defense clamped down on Young, sacking him twice and allowing the 49ers just two total yards on a critical drive. But a poor punt by Minnesota with just over three minutes remaining, gave the 49ers the ball back at their own 43-yard line, trailing by four points.

Young's six-yard scramble followed by a short completion to Mike Wilson (which was ruled incomplete then declared a catch by Instant Replay), set the 49ers up with a third-and-short, as the clock approached the two-minute warning.

Young dropped into the pocket and on his third step cocked his arm as if to throw a pass to the left, but pressure from the Vikings elite pass rush started to consume him. Offensive linemen Jesse Sapolu, Randy Cross, Guy McIntyre, and Harris Barton shielded him just long enough for the lefty to duck his head and spin around 360 degrees, completely away from the mass of players.

"[Tim Newton] had him around the belly," Vikings defensive end Al "Bubba" Baker said. "The next thing I know, he squirted out of there. I've seen whistles on shorter plays. That run was mostly Steve Young's intestinal fortitude. The guy wasn't throwing like Joe (Montana). He had to rely on his strength—his athletic ability. He should have gotten maybe ten yards. Not up the middle of the field, up the sideline. That's something Roger Craig does. I don't think Joe (Montana) could've made that run. He probably would have slid ten to fifteen yards upfield."

Beyond the line of scrimmage and having been aided by a diving effort from Tom Rathman that impeded three Vikings—"Woody (to his team-mates, Rathman resembled Woody Harrelson's character on *Cheers*) gave me a block"—Young weaved laterally across the field. He escaped the grasp of All-Pro defensive end Keith Millard, but not without first juggling the ball, which Millard nearly knocked out of his grasp. Then he hurdled a second All-Pro, cornerback Carl Lee, and continued to move diagonally toward the sideline. At the thirty-five, Young, mouth agape, pulled up to avoid both safety Brad Edwards and his 49er teammate Guy McIntyre (who provided another great block) while simultaneously freezing approaching linebacker Chris Martin.

"Anytime I was on the field in those years, I had to get going. I couldn't wait around. It didn't matter what I did, I had to do it fast," Young remembered in 2011. "I just started to go and then almost fumbled it and started to go again, then I got to the sidelines and thought, 'Can't go out, let's cut back,' and then got a block. . . . It was as if it was unfolding for me, too. I was like, 'I don't know, we're just going here, and there, and the next place. . . . '"

Watching the play develop from above, Holmgren cheered his former BYU pupil on so enthusiastically that he broke his hand pounding the Plexi-glas that lined the 49ers press box.

"I haven't done anything like that since I was coaching high school—during a halftime pep talk when I punched a blackboard and found out there was a brick wall right behind it," he admitted. "It's kind of embarrassing. But Steve's run was just amazing."

While blood rushed to his offensive coordinator's hand, Young stiff-armed Jesse Soloman; Jerry Rice, in a brief cameo at the end of the game, helped finish off the Vikings linebacker. From there, both the drama and Young hit full stride.

"Steve's running style mirrors his personality," Randy Cross said that day. "He's intense, churning, aggressive. If Joe was in that situation, he'd be cool and calculated. I'd hesitate to apply those words to Steve Young. He's not a cool and calculated surgeon. He's the last guy I'd want to operate on me, especially if he's in a hurry. He's very intense, very hurried for a quarterback. He looked like he was about to die of a heart attack going into the end zone. It was extremely ugly, but the final spasm was all he needed to get in."

Young's feet, not a heart attack, *did* almost prevent him from crossing the goal line. At the 7, with no Vikings left to avoid, outrun, or escape, Young stumbled and nearly fell down, just shy of the end zone.

"I was so embarrassed," he remembered years later. "I was so tired and so overwrought—so much emotion went into playing whenever I played back then—and it was the end of the game; my legs gave out. It was like, 'After all that, I'm going to stumble on my will . . . and not score.' I just remember thinking, 'Just get to the end zone! Just get to the end zone!'"

Young, who beat writer Charles Bricker referred to as "Mr. Hyperactivity" in the next morning's edition of the *San Jose Mercury News*, did get to the end zone . . . barely. At the 2-yard line, rather than try to keep upright, he simply dove across the goal line to score the go-ahead touchdown.

"Steve is a frustrating guy in that we seem to be out of sync, but on the other hand, he makes these great athletic plays," Walsh said in his post-game press conference. "We can have success with him. It's just getting him into a coordinated mode. I'm hoping we'll get it together for him because he's a great athlete."

Ahead 24–21 by way of Young's incredible score, the 49ers defense preserved victory. The win seemed to salvage the 49ers' sinking ship. But it only further muddled the quarterback situation.

"I don't know," Young said that evening. "If I'm back on the bench, so be it. Joe supported me today. When I came off the field, he told me what was going on when we didn't do well. I'll be supporting him next week if he's in the game. My attitude is positive. Very positive.

"Joe is one of the all-time great quarterbacks, everybody knows that. I just want to do what I can. I think that in time, it will all work itself out."

Monday, at his regular meeting with the media, Walsh hinted that, because Montana was not fully healed, he expected Young to start Sunday's game.

The next morning, the *San Francisco Chronicle*'s cover story—beneath the above-the-fold headline "Montana Feels He May Be Traded"—reported that Montana believed Walsh was ready to push him out of town.

"I can't say, but I think maybe he's ready to get rid of me," Montana told the *Chronicle*'s C. W. Nevius. "The way it comes across to me is that Bill wants to play Steve. You just can't let him have any opening because he's going to take advantage of it. I just tried not to come out. Where you usually say, 'Just give me a breather for a play or two,' I would just stay in. Finally, when it was affecting my throwing, I didn't have a choice."

Montana also implied that a trade might be on the horizon.

"I would hate it, I've played here so long that if my career was ending, I want to end it here," Montana added. "They probably tried to do it last year. I don't know what happened with that story. It comes down to the fact that if I feel I can play somewhere else, I'd at least try to fulfill some things to my-self. Because when it's over, it's over. There is no second chance."

For the first time since the acquisition of Young in April 1987, Mike Holmgren publically commented on the growing controversy. Montana's sug-gestion, that Young was "too caught up in the competition with me," prompted the offensive coordinator to respond, "I think Joe is over-analyzing a bit."

Holmgren did, however, hint that he too was becoming frustrated with the instability at the position.

"I've never been a big fan of the two-quarterback system. You lose your most effective way of doing things. But we seem to have a two-quarterback system. All I can say is I've made my feelings known."

Holmgren's subtle acknowledgment simply verbalized an obvious concern. But after Montana's wife, Jennifer, spoke out, fans and the media could see just how complicated the issue had become.

One reporter told Jennifer that Holmgren said that he didn't consider Joe the backup, under any circumstance: "As long as he's healthy, he's the starter."

"Why don't they tell Joe that," Jennifer answered. "Bill certainly hasn't made this any easier."

Any preference Walsh had for Young over Montana—due to his athletic gifts or age or the fact that Young was left-handed, just like Walsh—came a distant second to the issue of Montana's health. In the span of roughly two seasons, Montana had endured a concussion that landed him in the hospital, surgery to his elbow, bruised ribs that labored his breathing, and a serious back injury that rendered his lower leg numb at times.

"I think if my career was over today, she wouldn't care," Montana said on November 1, 1988. "She just worries that something is going to happen, and I'm going to regret it."

Jennifer even acknowledged deep concern for her husband's health.

"It's not like I beg him to retire," she said. "But I'm a Joe Montana fan be-fore I'm a 49er fan. It kills me to see him get hurt. Games are three, long, mis-erable hours for me."

When the story became big news in the Bay Area, all of the principals—except Young—backtracked. Montana's agent, Bob Woolf, denied that his client had any interest in leaving San Francisco. Walsh also issued a denial, then chastised an "irresponsible" media. He did, however, admit the mistake of not conferring with Montana prior to the announcement that Young would likely start in Week 10.

Montana literally shrugged off a question about being misquoted, then implied that his statements had been taken out of context.

"Some of them, of course. It's normal. It's like being traded. Someone acted like I wanted to be traded. Of course, you only answer a question and it gets written (a different) way."

Although the ongoing conflict that engulfed Walsh, Montana, and even Young—who stayed relatively silent on the issue, simply restating his desire to play and not much else—served as a distraction to the rest of the team, the 49ers were fortunate to have the NFC doormat, the Phoenix Cardinals next on their schedule. Everyone outside of the team's Santa Clara headquarters expected an easy victory. And through two-and-a-half quarters, San Francisco showed no signs of a team in distress.

In uniform, Joe Montana watched from the sidelines as Young recorded 223 yards of offense and set up three field goals and a touchdown that gave the 49ers a seventeen-point halftime advantage.

"I remember leaving the field at halftime thinking, 'This is as good as we've ever looked. This was beautiful,'" Walsh told NFL Films years later. "I was so proud."

Walsh's pride peaked midway through the third period. Near the Cardinals goal line, Young hung in the pocket, then hit Brent Jones in the back of the end zone for a touchdown that seemed to guarantee a blowout victory, the ideal birthday present for owner Eddie DeBartolo Jr., who turned forty-two that day.

But behind Neil Lomax—who guided the Cardinals to a twenty-five-point fourth-quarter comeback the previous November—Phoenix cut the lead to 23–17 with a pair of touchdown passes. A collapse in San Francisco's pass coverage, multiple penalties, and poor starting position for the offense limited the 49ers' options in the final period and consecutive drives ended with three-and-outs.

"We had a big lead," Young said. "When you have a big lead and you're backed up inside the 20, you need to play it close to the vest."

Ahead by six points with less than two minutes remaining and the Cardinals out of timeouts, the 49ers saw a chance to put the game away. On third-and-4 at their own 21, Young scrambled to the left sideline, leaving him with a difficult ultimatum: dive toward the first-down marker and risk landing out of bounds, thus stopping the clock and aiding the Cardinals; or stay in bounds and most likely end up short of the first down.

Young characteristically didn't play it safe. He lunged for the marker.

"I was thinking first down on the play all the way: I get a first down, we win the game. If I was just thinking about the clock, I would have just gone down with the ball. I would have kneeled down at the line of scrimmage."

Officials spotted the ball inches shy of the first-down marker.

"Check the tape, I made it," Young insisted twenty-three years later.

The referees—even after stopping the game to view the Instant Replay—didn't agree. The 49ers punted, Lomax completed four passes, and with three seconds remaining threw a nine-yard touchdown pass to Roy Green. The 49ers squandered their 23–0 third-quarter lead; Young squandered both his chance to be a hero for the second straight week and his golden opportunity to claim the starter's job.

"I didn't get the first down in Phoenix," Young lamented. "That was the place, supposedly, that was the place where I lost it for a couple more years."

According to the *San Francisco Chronicle*'s Glenn Dickey, a columnist very close to the 49ers head coach who co-authored a 1992 book with Walsh, the impact of that loss *was* long-lasting.

"Bill told me later, that if Young had won that game, he would have kept him as the starter."

The franchise's worst collapse since the harrowing 1957 Western Conference playoff loss to Detroit in Kezar Stadium deflated everyone in the 49ers organization. But none more so than Walsh, who during the fourth quarter cracked two ribs in a sideline collision.

"I remember walking in the locker room," the *San Jose Mercury News*'s Mark Purdy said years later. "Walsh was in his little office, and I looked in and he had his head in his hands. He looked up—and Bill's a pretty pale, white guy anyway—but if it's possible to have less than zero color in his face, he did."

"I've never seen Walsh more upset at any time ever," 49ers radio broadcaster Joe Starkey remembered. "We got on the charter going back, and we had a reporter on the plane who worked for our radio station who wanted to ask Bill about the game. And Bill was in no mood to talk to anybody. And he actually told the reporter who kept bugging him up in the first class section. . . . 'One more statement out of you, I guarantee I'm going to the pilot and telling him to land this plane at the nearest airport and you're getting the fuck off the plane.' He was really, really upset."

In his angst, Walsh turned back to Montana for the next Sunday's game against the Raiders, despite the quarterback's achy back, despite the damaged elbow and bruised ribs, despite minimal opportunities in practice, and now, despite the quarterback's recent ongoing struggles with "a form of dysentery" that caused him to lose eleven pounds and become "very weak," according to his head coach.

"He really shouldn't have been out there," Walsh said. "But after losing to [Phoenix], he was willed by the fans and the community and the media and by me to get out there and give it a shot."

Montana returned to the field on a chilly day at Candlestick Park, but the visiting Raiders spoiled his hero's welcome. Montana completed just eleven of his twenty-one first-half pass attempts, Craig found no room to run, and halfway through the final period, the Raiders increased their lead to 9–3. Still, Montana teased the fans with another classic comeback.

At the 3:22 mark of the fourth quarter, the 49ers took possession at their own 33-yard line. Short runs, a twenty-eight-yard pass from Montana to Rice, and two quick completions put the 49ers directly at the base of the Los Angeles red zone. There, on a fourth-and-2, Walsh sent in an ill-conceived, slow-developing, fake-handoff end-around to Rice, who was tackled for a seven-yard loss that sealed the 49ers loss.

The team was humiliated: five consecutive quarters without a touchdown, the first losing streak since 1985, the lowest offensive output at home in team history, slipping to third place in the NFC West, and their playoff shot all but dashed. Much of the blame fell on Montana.

"How long are we going to pretend that Joe Montana is still a great quarterback? Bill Walsh has two quarterbacks. Only one of them is going to improve. If the 49ers are going to have any chance to salvage this season, he has to bite the bullet and go with Steve Young, and forget about Montana's ego or the nostalgia of 49er fans," the *Chronicle*'s Glenn Dickey wrote after the Raiders loss. "Young has the cockiness top quarterbacks need. Montana had it once, in abundance. Now, he's lost his nerve."

But Montana hadn't lost his nerve. He was the same Ringgold Ram who stared down the mighty Monessen Greyhounds, the same numb Notre Dame signal caller who overcame a twenty-two-point fourth-quarter deficit in the Cotton Bowl, the same first-year starter who was unmoved by a twenty-eight-point home deficit to the pitiful New Orleans Saints. As long as Montana was under center, he was still Joe Cool.

"We have to be optimistic. . . . We will probably be the only ones who will be," Montana said. "I know what this offense can do."

To his skeptics, Montana's confidence had to seem far less delusional the following Monday night against Washington. During a 37–21 win over the defending Super Bowl champion Redskins, Montana hit Rice and Brent Jones for touchdowns. And it was his fourth-quarter roll-out touchdown run—after which he violently spiked the football in the end zone—that put the game out of reach.

"I guess vindication is not too strong a word for what he feels," Randy Cross said. "I think he made a point tonight. Joe played the kind of game he is capable of playing. Statistically, he may not have been fantastic. But he took charge."

Even a sprained knee, the result of tripping over tackle Steve Wallace early in the second period, couldn't keep him sidelined for more than two series, one of which ended with a Young interception. Montana returned and drove the team down the field for a third touchdown just before halftime.

X-rays were needed, and the next day Montana—while his one-month-old daughter, Elizabeth, played with his ears—told the media that the knee was "sore and stiff." But the following Sunday he started against the Chargers.

A ninety-six-yard bomb to Rice early in the first quarter as well as a nifty scramble-then-flip-to-Craig for a touchdown pass ignited a forty-eight-point offensive effort that pulled San Francisco within a game of the division lead. And by way of Montana's efficient passing in a 13–3 road win over Atlanta, the 49ers were in line to clinch a wild card berth the next Sunday against New Orleans.

"Joe's performance in the last month made the biggest difference in our offense—no doubt about it," Cross said. "They gave him the ball and said, 'It's yours to do with as you will.'"

Even though the 49ers were within striking distance of an improbable late-season resurrection, the issue of the quarterback controversy lingered. And not just for the press.

"I respect you guys," Walsh not so subtly told a crop of reporters that week. "I like each of you, but you didn't understand Joe Montana's physical state, so you made a quarterback controversy."

"I try not to worry about what happened with Steve," Montana admitted days before the critical divisional showdown. "It takes away from where we've got our sights set. Still, it's hard not to think about it on occasion. Right now, it's in the past, but if I got hurt, the same old thing would crop up. I know that. I try to make do the best I can."

Against the Saints, Montana overcame an early interception inside 49ers territory, and guided the offense to a pair of touchdowns, including a head-first dive into the end zone for his third rushing score of the season. Late in the second quarter, John Taylor found a soft spot in the zone coverage and nabbed a laser from Montana for a sixty-eight-yard touchdown. Connecting on all eight of his second-quarter passes, Montana took his team into halftime ahead 21–10. On the strength of Craig's rushing and stellar defense, the 49ers salted away victory in the second half.

"Any season has its ups and downs," Montana told the press following the game. "As long as you make the playoffs everything's irrelevant."

The win over New Orleans, coupled with the Saints victory over Atlanta the following Sunday, clinched the NFC West title for the 49ers, even before they took the field for the regular season finale in Los Angeles against the Rams. (The Rams and 49ers kicked off at five p.m. Pacific Standard Time, several hours after the end of the Saints–Falcons game, which began at 1 p.m. Eastern Standard Time.)

At several critical points throughout the 1988 season Walsh had opted to sit Montana for multiple series and even complete games, insisting that the veteran needed time to rest and regain his health. Still, in their now-meaningless Week 16 matchup, Walsh—who admitted to knowing about the guaranteed division title prior to the game—kept Montana and most of his starters on the field.

Only after three quarters and eight quarterback sacks did he replace Montana with Young, who was also sacked once in the 38–16 defeat, the fourth at Candlestick that season.

"I've been in the playoffs enough to know whether you're hot or not doesn't make a damn bit of difference," Montana told the media. "It's how you play that next week."

*　*　*

San Francisco's third consecutive NFC West title set up a playoff rematch with the Vikings. Although the Sunday afternoon contest was billed as the 49ers' opportunity to redeem themselves for that previous January's defeat, Joe Montana's personal shot at redemption was the game's most compelling subplot. Not only had he been benched during the gruesome home playoff loss, but injuries had also forced him to miss the regular season rematch, a game in which Steve Young's breathtaking run lifted the club to a spectacular victory.

In his three previous playoff starts (consecutive losses to the Giants in 1985 and 1986 followed by the upset versus Minnesota) Montana, the game's greatest clutch quarterback, completed just 52 percent of his passes for zero touchdowns and four interceptions. Worst of all, under his direction, the 49ers offense scored a total of just nine points in those three games. But with his performance in the first half of the New Year's Day 1989 playoff with Minnesota, Montana made the fans at Candlestick and anyone watching on television forget those previous postseason failures.

Late in the first quarter, three straight completions and a nimble nine-yard Montana scramble put the 49ers near the Vikings goal line. There, Montana faked a handoff to Craig, avoided a blitzing safety, and found Rice in the end zone, the first of a record-setting twenty-two-career postseason touchdowns for the future Hall of Fame receiver.

Ronnie Lott's interception of a Wade Wilson throw gave the ball right back to Montana. On first down, a reverse-handoff to Rice netted twenty-one yards. The trick play not only caught Minnesota off guard, it had the same effect on the ball carrier.

"When I came around on the reverse, Joe was the lead blocker, and it shocked me," Rice said. "The defensive back really got a good blow on him, and I told Joe never do that again."

The supposedly worn-down thirty-two-year-old quarterback later rolled out of the pocket and while still on the run fired a dart to Rice at the near goal line pylon for the second score in two minutes.

As the first half drew to a close, Montana pieced together a seventy-yard touchdown drive, which he and Rice again finished off by way of an eleven-yard play-action pass toward the left corner of the end zone. Montana completed the first half eleven-of-fourteen for 111 yards and three touchdowns.

"Montana played about as sharp as I've ever seen him," Vikings head coach Jerry Burns said.

Partway through the final period, with the 49ers ahead 34–9, Walsh substituted Young for Montana. Only this time, there would be no questions about an impending quarterback controversy at the post-game press conference.

"'I wasn't out to prove anything," Montana said. "I just wanted for us to play well. . . . There's been a lot of pressure on us for not winning the last three years. It relieved a little pressure to win."

Asked about his previous postseason effort, on the same field, against the same team, Montana displayed selective amnesia.

"Too long ago. Bad memories, you forget."

Not quite.

In the locker room, after the 49ers first playoff win since Super Bowl XIX, Montana did something for the first time in his ten-year NFL career. Holding a football—the game ball, that he and Randy Cross decided would be given to head coach Bill Walsh—Montana addressed the entire 49ers team.

"The teams that have beaten another team by a big margin have come back the next week and played terrible. And that is not gonna happen to this ball club," declared an intense Montana. "I ain't bullshitting. We've opened the door, we're going to go through it next week, and we're going to kick ass and take no prisoners the week after."

"We thought we were winning the Super Bowl in '87," Brent Jones remembered years later. "[The Vikings playoff] was one of the most gut-wrenching losses because we felt like we had the Super Bowl type team. And then you went through the whole offseason, and think of what Joe had to listen to: quarterback controversy and all this stuff. And I think it built up in the emotion of him giving a speech [after] that first Vikings game.

"Of all the voices that you're going to hear [after] a game, you're going to hear your head coach, you're going to hear Ronnie [Lott], you might hear an offensive lineman, you might hear Roger Craig say something. And all of a sudden, I hear this voice, and I'm like, 'Who the heck is that?' It's Joe. And he's pretty dang serious. He basically talked about bringing it like we had all season and remember what these suckers did to us last year, and remember the pain that you felt. And we can never let that happen again. It was significant from the standpoint of you knew it meant something to him. You knew the Vikings thing was one thing, and I think also the pent-up frustration from having to deal with all the stuff he had had to deal with for the prior year."

The following week, in the NFC Championship, the 49ers faced the Chicago Bears in another opportunity to exorcize recent demons.

Winners of the "Fog Bowl" a week earlier, Mike Ditka's Bears sounded confident, even cocky the week of their NFC Championship Game showdown. After all, they had beaten San Francisco ten weeks earlier at Soldier Field and believed home field advantage gave them the upper hand: Chicago's lake-effect January weather would surely paralyze the California-based squad. The perceived advantage in climate even allowed the Bears to downplay significant injuries to both of their quarterbacks, Jim McMahon and Mike Tomczak. Asked about the "Bear weather," as Ditka called it, Walsh responded by saying, "The cold won't bother us, but I'm concerned about the wind."

A handful of 49ers players were not: many felt a sense of comfort, knowing that their field general had at least one epic victory in similarly brutal conditions.

"You know something," right tackle Harris Barton said, "that's what I was thinking about when we came out on the field and first felt that cold: Montana's chicken-soup game. I'd seen film clips of it."

On a frigid day featuring minus-twenty-six-degree wind chill and 29 mile per hour winds, Montana and the San Francisco passing game was near flawless. Rice hauled in a pair of long scores in the first half, the defense suffocated the Bears' rushing attack, and when Montana tossed his third touchdown of the day to tight end John Frank, there was no way Chicago and recently inserted backup quarterback Mike Tomczak would recover. San Francisco pounded the Monsters of the Midway 28–3, the largest NFC Championship Game margin of victory in ten years. Against the NFL's top-scoring defense, Montana completed seventeen of twenty-seven attempts for 288 yards and three touchdowns.

"This could have been his greatest game, under the pressure and in these conditions," Walsh boasted.

"People had given up on us six, seven, eight games into the season," Montana said. "But we fought back through all the adversity. It's gratifying to come back from that and perform this way."

San Francisco's third Super Bowl berth in eight years set up yet another rematch of a famous, 49ers postseason battle. The Cincinnati Bengals would again be their Super Bowl opponent. And from the outset, the press cast Super Bowl XXIII as a series of battles between teachers and students: Bengals owner Paul Brown versus Bill Walsh; Walsh versus his former quarterback, offensive coordinator, and friend Sam Wyche; and Wyche versus his former quarterback Joe Montana.

"If it were Sam against anyone else but us," Montana said that week, "we'd all be rooting for Sam."

But the game was against the 49ers and, again, Montana's heightened emotions seeped through in preparation for the enormous game.

"I remember sitting in the back of the [meeting room], the first week of Super Bowl prep week in Santa Clara," said John Paye. "[Joe made] the point of, 'You only get one shot, let's not fuck around when we get to Miami. We need to win. Be focused.' And I remember Randy Cross saying something like, 'It's not about the money: we'll all piss away the money that we're going to earn by going to the Super Bowl. It's about the ring.' And that was basically Joe's point, too: 'Let's get the ring because they can't take that away from us.'"

The extra week off in between the Conference championships and the Super Bowl allowed both coaching staffs—already familiar with one another's schemes—to further prepare for two of the NFL's top offenses. And fittingly, the game turned out to be an extremely physical defensive melee. Through three quarters, neither team scored an offensive touchdown; the 49ers trailed 13–6.

"We didn't play very well," Cross remembered. "We put the ball on the ground, our defense didn't get off the field when it was supposed to, we didn't convert on some third downs. We missed some blocks, I screwed up a snap. We just weren't executing.

"We were really on a roll. We should have gone into that game and strummed them. But it was close, I took it, and always have taken it, and always will take it as our fault it was that close. . . . But that was a very resilient, mentally tough team."

And the player that best epitomized that mental toughness was the 49ers quarterback. On the second play of the final period—after completing back-to-back passes that netted seventy yards—Montana spied John Taylor in the middle of the end zone, but the ball went in and out of the hands of Cincinnati defensive back Lewis Billups.

Unconcerned by the nearly fatal interception, on the very next snap, Montana floated a pass to Rice, who beat Billups to the goal line for the 49ers first touchdown.

After a Bengals punt preceded an unsuccessful forty-nine-yard field goal try by Mike Cofer, Cincinnati's Jim Breech nailed a field goal, the end of a ten-play, time-consuming drive that ate up more than five minutes of the game clock. With only 3:20 remaining, the 49ers were now behind 16–13.

On the home team sidelines at Joe Robbie Stadium, as they both awaited the Bengals kickoff, Steve Young turned to Joe Montana.

"Well, it's set up perfectly for us," Young said.

Young's encouragement came before an illegal block penalty on the ensu-ing kickoff pushed San Francisco's starting position back to their own 8-yard line. Still, Joe Cool once again lived up to his nickname.

"He came into the huddle," Harris Barton recalled. "And I was yelling and screaming, 'Come on, let's go, let's get it going, this is the biggest drive of my life, if we want the ring, we've got to go out and get it.' And he looked at me, and it was during one of those long TV timeouts they have in the Super Bowl. And he looked at me and he goes, 'Hey, [Harris] . . . check it out . . . look over there in that end zone . . . hey there's John Candy.' I go, 'John Candy!?'

"Sure enough, John Candy's sitting there eating some popcorn. I look at him and I look at the clock, there's three minutes to go in the game, the biggest game of the year, and he's so relaxed. Then all of a sudden, the TV timeout ended, and the next thing I know we're marching down the field for the winning drive."

"Did I say anything inspirational?" Montana said. "Oh, no, I was con-cerned with other things. We were calling two plays at a time, and I had to think about what the second one would be. I did say to myself, though, 'Here we go, just like Dallas in '82.'"

The most memorable, heart-pounding drive in Super Bowl history began with three short completions to Craig, tight end John Frank, and Rice. Mini-mal gains on the ground by Craig allowed the 49ers to escape the depths of their own territory but also drained the game clock. Past the two-minute warning, Craig's second rush, a four-yard gain off right tackle, forced San Francisco to spend their first timeout.

During the stoppage of play—extended by a Bengals injury on the field—Montana discussed strategy on the sidelines with Walsh, John Paye, and Young, who spent the majority of the game flashing plays via hand signals to Montana.

"You think Joe Montana isn't going to notice what Cincinnati was doing?" Young asked hypothetically after the game. "The Bengals went away from their game plan. They were playing prevent. We lost a game this year in Phoenix playing prevent, you'll remember."

Fully aware of the change in defensive scheme, Montana began to carve up the Bengals secondary. On first-and-10 at the 35, he found Rice near the sideline for a seventeen-yard gain past midfield. Throwing off his back foot, Montana quickly hit Craig for another thirteen yards. Even an incompletion and an ineligible man downfield penalty that cost San Francisco ten yards couldn't slow down the 49ers.

"Joe Montana during that drive, he displayed all the confidence in the world," left tackle Bubba Paris said, "and he never says anything. He's able to do it through his persona, his confidence, the level, the way that he calls the plays, the way that he explains it in the huddle, the way that he's able to make it all work."

To his ten teammates in the huddle, the crowd of 75,179 at Joe Robbie Stadium, and the estimated television audience of more than 81 million viewers, Montana radiated tranquility. But Montana's impenetrable façade masked his true emotions.

"I hyperventilated to the point of almost blacking out," Montana admitted. "You know how a TV screen gets fuzzy? Well, that's what my vision was like. I was yelling so loudly in the huddle that I couldn't breathe. Things got blurrier and blurrier. One time, I put my hands under center, and I felt like it was taking days to call the play. Everything was in slow motion. When I took my first step back, the fuzz appeared again. By the fifth step, things got so fuzzy I had to throw the ball over Jerry Rice, out of bounds, to clear my head."

Pushed back to second-and-20 at their own 45, Montana and Rice together beat triple coverage from the Bengals on a pass over the middle that easily put the 49ers in position for a game-tying field goal at the 18-yard line. A short throw over the middle to Craig nudged the 49ers eight yards closer, setting up the freeze-frame moment of Super Bowl XXIII, the 1988 season, and perhaps Joe Montana's entire career.

With thirty-nine seconds remaining and the ball at the Bengals 10-yard line, Montana—split backs behind him, Rice coming across the formation in motion—receded into the pocket, briefly surveyed the field, and threaded a pass to the end zone in between two Cincinnati defenders and into the fingertips of John Taylor. Touchdown.

"Joe Montana is not human," Bengals wide receiver Cris Collinsworth said that evening. "I don't want to call him a god, but he's definitely somewhere in between."

6

The Orchestrator

Of all the crazy things I've seen the last few years, this
may be one of the last tests. Maybe it'll be that much
sweeter when it all works out.

—Steve Young, the week of Super Bowl XXIII
in Joe Robbie Stadium

Aboard the team charter to Miami—seven days before Joe Montana's touchdown pass to John Taylor clinched the 49ers 20–16 triumph over Cincinnati in Super Bowl XXIII—offensive lineman Randy Cross joined Bill Walsh in the first-class cabin. There, the thirty-four-year-old, six-time All-Pro—a key piece of three Super Bowl championships—told his head coach that Sunday's game would be his last.

"I think that's a good decision," Walsh told his starting center. "You could play for a few more years, but if you want to go out the right way, that's a good call. You know, in fact, we win this game, there's no telling how much longer I'm gonna coach."

The hint Walsh dropped to Cross wasn't exactly a bombshell. After ten years on the job—the last of which had been tremendously difficult, frustrating, and emotionally draining—speculation that the white-haired genius would retire after the Super Bowl permeated Miami all week. And in the winning locker room following the game, the scene of a choked-up, speechless

Walsh embracing his son, Craig, when asked by CBS's Brent Musberger about his future all but guaranteed that he would step down.

Within days, Walsh announced his retirement at a press conference in Monterey, California. But he wasn't entirely walking away from the organization: Walsh would stay on as vice president of Football Operations.

"It's uplifting to step away on such a high note," Walsh said. "A lot of coaches would like to step aside this way. As long as I keep busy, I don't think there will be any withdrawal."

In June, a banquet at the Sir Francis Drake Hotel on Powell Street was held in Walsh's honor: he requested no press, no television cameras, and a maximum of 350 tickets be sold. Proceeds went to Athletes in Communities, an inner-city youth sports organization created by retired Stanford and 49ers quarterback Guy Benjamin, who also arranged the benefit. Among his friends and local dignitaries, seven of Walsh's past quarterbacks—Benjamin, Steve Dils, Greg Cook, Virgil Carter, Dan Fouts, Steve DeBerg, and Joe Montana—attended.

"I wouldn't be wearing these three rings if it weren't for Bill," Montana said that evening. "He instilled confidence in me right from the start. The other guys have talked about how much he helped them, but I'm the only one lucky enough to have had his coaching for ten years. . . . He knows how to motivate people. I guess that's why he brought in Steve (Young)."

The search for Walsh's successor didn't take long. At the same Monterey press conference, the 49ers named defensive coordinator George Seifert their new head coach. Walsh's former protégé Sam Wyche, as well as University of Miami and soon-to-be Dallas Cowboys head coach Jimmy Johnson were rumored replacements, but ultimately the 49ers decided to promote from within. And Seifert's first order of business was to nip the still brewing quarterback controversy in the bud.

"Joe's our starter," the 49-year-old said at his introductory press conference in early February.

There would be a few additional changes to the 49ers coaching staff. Aside from switching running backs coach Sherm Lewis to wide receivers and adding tight ends to special teams coach Lynn Styles responsibilities, Seifert filled his vacant defensive coordinator role with linebackers coach Bill McPherson. Determining the power structure on the other side of the ball required a more complicated solution.

As the father of the West Coast offense and the 49ers autocrat for a decade, Walsh could not be replaced by a single person. Quarterbacks coach Mike Holmgren assumed the offensive coordinator role: he called the plays, designed the game plans, and oversaw the offense. But Montana's knowledge and experience in the system far exceeded anyone in the entire 49ers organization.

"I think we will depend a great deal on Joe's experience," Seifert said. "There's no question he has a feel for attacking a defense. . . . [But] there are no plans to change this offense. We have an offense that has led us to three Super Bowls. We don't expect any major changes."

The 49ers' journey toward a fourth Super Bowl title began in an increasingly familiar and unsettling fashion: that spring, Montana underwent yet another surgery, this time on the same left knee he had sprained the previous season in the win over Washington.

"Over the years it was just breaking down—just constantly twisting from the throwing motion," he said. "Pieces of the cartilage kept tearing off."

The arthroscopic procedure, which Montana called "as minor as it can get," sidelined him for the team's first minicamp in early May. By the start of training camp two months later, he had completely recovered.

"I feel good. I don't have a wheelchair," Montana quipped. "You always dread going to camp. Then the camaraderie comes right back and the fun on the field and the anticipation of the games coming up. It's all worth it. It's hard to get it out of your blood."

Steve Young's blood was also replete with excitement and anticipation, but not patience.

"I told the coach (Seifert) I'm too prepared, too ready, too everything to sit around," Young said. "But here I am again. I fail at any psychological adjustments at being second-string. That's something I refuse to be very good at—ever."

Although Seifert empathized—"I liken Steve's situation to mine as I worked behind Bill as the defensive coordinator, and yet looked forward to being the head coach . . . it's something you have to live through"—he left no ambiguity and confirmed Montana's entrenched place as the starter.

"I entice [Joe] with money, jewels, all kinds of things to retire, but he doesn't take it," joked Young, who reiterated an amicable relationship with Montana.

A controversy-less preseason in which the 49ers manhandled both the Los Angeles Raiders and Denver Broncos gave way to a difficult start to the 1989 regular season. Each of the team's first three games were cross-country road trips. They won the opener in Indianapolis, then, in a scene reminiscent of January's Florida-hosted Super Bowl, the offense drove seventy yards in the final 3:25 to cap off a 20–16 victory over Tampa Bay. Montana scored the game-winning touchdown, rolling out of the pocket on a play-fake near the goal line, then beating a Buccaneers defender to the end zone. Not only did the touchdown in the final minute increase the 49ers record to 2–0, it hinted at Montana's newfound input in the post-Walsh era.

"Joe wanted to run that play," Holmgren said. "I was concerned that we might be going to that play once too often, because we had used it so much.

But in that part of the field, the defense is really limited because it can't afford to overcommit. The only real way to stop that play is by having one man just commit to following Joe."

Next up, to complete their East Coast odyssey, the 49ers traveled to Philadelphia.

Featuring three of the NFL's best defensive linemen—Clyde Simmons, Jerome Brown, and the incomparable Reggie White—as well as the explosive Randall Cunningham at quarterback, the Eagles were considered a legitimate Super Bowl contender. Head coach Buddy Ryan's track record against San Francisco also suggested the Eagles matched up favorably, in both Week 3 and the race for the NFC championship.

As defensive coordinator, Ryan's Chicago Bears twice suffocated the 49ers, recording twelve sacks of Montana and allowing just six offensive points during regular season contests in 1983 and 1985. Ryan relayed those facts on a local radio show that week. (He conveniently forgot to mention the 1984 NFC Championship Game, when San Francisco defeated the Bears 23–0, collecting 387 yards of total offense in the process.) His strategy for containing Montana was both simple and obvious: "It's hard to throw running on your butt, you know. . . . They're the world champs, but we're not afraid of them."

Several 49ers players posted a photo of Ryan accompanied by those quotes in their lockers that week.

Despite their talent, the Eagles defense wasn't infallible. The trade-off for repeatedly blitzing the quarterback often left cornerbacks in single coverage with wide receivers. The previous week, Philadelphia had allowed thirty-seven points and several big plays to the Redskins passing attack. While the high-risk, high-reward strategy that Ryan employed made for exciting football, it was wildly inconsistent.

"When the pass rush doesn't materialize in Buddy's system," a *Philadelphia Daily News* columnist wrote, "those mismatches stick out like a lady power-lifter at a fashion model's convention."

Montana and Rice needed only six plays to exploit Philadelphia's glaring vulnerability. Less than three minutes into the game, the Eagles sent eight players at Montana, leaving Rice in one-on-one coverage with Izel Jenkins, whom he burned across the middle of the field for a sixty-eight-yard touchdown.

The quick score did not discourage Ryan; it only inspired more pressure from the Eagles defense. Within minutes, Philadelphia started to pound the 49ers and especially their quarterback. By halftime, Montana had been sacked six times and was knocked to the ground at the end of several other pass plays. Late in the third quarter, Montana was hammered by an Eagles lineman just before releasing a pass that was intended for Brent Jones and intercepted by linebacker Al Harris. The turnover set up Philadelphia's fourth field goal of the game, increasing their lead to 21–10. His team headed for their first loss of the season, Montana—indifferent to the score or the beating he'd taken—assumed his Joe Cool persona.

"There's one game that stood out and was by far the greatest game I saw him play, and that was the Philly game," remembered Steve Bono, the 49ers third-string quarterback. "Joe's getting his ass kicked. Reggie White, Jerome Brown, Clyde Simmons, Seth Joyner. . . . Buddy Ryan's 46 Defense is getting after us like nobody's business. And we come out [in the fourth quarter], and he just goes ballistic. We fixed the protection problems, and he's now nailing them."

Early in the final period Montana stood in the pocket long enough to sling a pass to John Taylor but was viciously crunched by Reggie White and safety Eric Everett. As Montana lay on his back, seemingly in tremendous pain—he spent the next few minutes conferring with team doctors—Taylor juked an Eagles defender then streaked down the sidelines for a seventy-yard touchdown. Philadelphia posted a touchdown to regain their eleven-point lead with 8:24 remaining in the game, but Montana was just getting warmed up.

"You look at Joe, and he's about the size of my youngest son," offensive tackle Bubba Paris said in a post-game interview. "When these hungry, husky, man-child pass rushers beat him up and he gets up like nothing has happened, you feel bad. There is a nonverbal communication. He's telling you, 'I depend on you.' Eventually, you feel sorry for him, and you do everything in your heart to not let it happen again."

Montana opened the following series by avoiding more pressure and scrambling nineteen yards for a first down. He then completed six consecutive passes, the last to Brent Jones for an eight-yard touchdown. Minutes later, Montana—who had been sacked for the eighth time on the previous play—danced around several Eagles defenders to complete a thirty-six-yard pass to Taylor. On the next snap, he floated a touchdown pass over Philadelphia linebacker Seth Joyner into the hands of Jones for the twenty-five-yard go-ahead touchdown. And just to put the game out of reach, three plays after a Ronnie Lott interception, Montana perfectly placed a thirty-three-yard touchdown pass over two defenders and into Rice's fingertips.

"It was a satisfying game for a quarterback," said Montana, who in the final period alone completed eleven of thirteen attempts for 227 yards and four touchdowns. "There was a lot of pressure, but that's what it is all about. I am pleased."

Pressed for more detail on his magnificient fourth-quarter performance, Montana delivered a characteristically understated response: "They won the first half, I won the second half."

* * *

Montana and the 49ers didn't win either half the following week during a frustrating 13–12 home loss to the undefeated Rams. In the final minutes, quarterback Jim Everett guided the Los Angeles Rams seventy-three yards for the winning field goal, a drive his head coach, John Robinson, called "Joe Montana-ish."

But the following week in the Superdome it was Montana's turn to be Montana-ish.

Midway through the third quarter, all the 49ers offense could produce was a forty-one-yard field goal by Mike Cofer. Behind 17–3 and in danger of losing a second consecutive divisional game, Montana again caught fire. He hit Rice on a bizarre sixty-yard bomb—it was ruled a touchdown despite an untouched Rice dropping the ball at the goal line as he raised his hand to celebrate—and connected with John Taylor on a twenty-one-yarder that tied the game at 17. New Orleans retook the lead with a field goal, but Montana then tossed his third touchdown of the day—another controversial catch because Taylor never appeared to have control of the ball but was granted the game-winning catch anyway.

"This is bad for the heart," Montana said, referring to his third fourth-quarter comeback in four weeks.

The game was also bad for his already damaged elbow. As was the case a year earlier in the Superdome, a scrambling Montana fell hard on the Astro-Turf, and it became too swollen for him to play: with the 24–20 lead preserved, Steve Young went in to run out the clock.

"Just a little fluid in there," Montana said after his twenty-one-for-twenty-nine, 293-yard, three-touchdown performance. "It should be all right."

But it wasn't: the elbow was swollen, discolored, and very painful to the touch. The following Sunday, Young started in Dallas.

"I get tired of sitting and watching," said Young, who turned twenty-eight years old that week. "I got a lot of practice time this week, and it felt good. I'd like to play."

Against the winless Cowboys—three days removed from trading star running back Herschel Walker—Young's offense managed just one score and entered the fourth quarter locked in a 14–14 tie.

"They were really doubling down on [Rice] and [Taylor]," Young said. "They forced me to be patient."

Rookie head coach George Seifert also exhibited great patience that Sunday. Although Montana did not start, he was in uniform and practiced all week.

"Montana could have played. He told me he was ready if he was needed," Seifert said in a post-game press conference. "It flashed through my mind in the third quarter that I might call on Joe. I would say it was a thought. It didn't get much beyond that."

Early in the fourth quarter, Young faded a short pass to Rice in the left corner of the end zone to spark seventeen unanswered points that gave the 49ers a convincing 31–14 victory. Young completed thirteen of his eighteen attempts for 174 yards and two touchdowns. He also picked up seventy-nine yards on the ground on just eleven carries.

"Not playing is one of the most difficult things. I think I was halfway into the funny farm. I think that's one reason coach let me play, because I was really going nuts," Young said. "I'd love to have another few weeks to show that I've really improved a lot."

Young's wish was not granted, at least not right away.

On Monday, Montana underwent a simple procedure to drain fluid from the elbow. According to Seifert, "Unless something unforeseen happens," Montana would start the 49ers upcoming home game against New England.

That week, however, no one in the Bay Area was very interested in either Montana's achy elbow or Young's eagerness to play. An earthquake measuring 6.9 on the Richter Scale killed sixty-three people and injured several thousand more. Countless more across the San Andreas Fault were terrified, including more than fifty thousand people at Candlestick Park awaiting the start of Game 3 of the World Series. But not newborn Nathaniel Joseph Montana.

Joe Montana, wife Jennifer, and two-week old Nate—daughters Elizabeth and Alexandra stayed at home with a babysitter—were standing with Dwight Clark on a walkway at Candlestick at the time of the natural disaster.

"It sounded like people were stamping their feet and getting excited," Montana said. "Then, all of sudden, things starting shaking. I looked up and could see the upper structure moving. The first thing I thought about was finding some kind of safety for the baby."

Montana's revelation that, during the earthquake, the baby "was mostly sleeping" prompted the *Sacramento Bee* to point out comparisons between Nate and his father, "Joe Cool."

Everyone at Candlestick evacuated the stadium, but not without fans clamoring for Montana's autograph.

"If I'd started that, there would be a lot of people gathering around, and that probably would have been the worst thing," he said.

Structural damage to Candlestick Park not only postponed the World Series game between the San Francisco Giants and Oakland Athletics for ten days, it also forced the 49ers to move their Week 7 matchup with New England to Palo Alto.

As planned, Montana started the game, throwing a second-quarter touchdown to Rice, but a helmet to the knee from Patriots linebacker Kenneth Sims just before halftime sent Montana to the ground. The transplanted crowd watched in horror as the quarterback had to be carted off the field.

"I won't say I saw my season go up in smoke," Eddie DeBartolo Jr. said, "but there was kindling. And there were definitely signs of fire."

Meanwhile, Young wasn't nearly as fraught with concern. Earlier in the week, his growing frustration had seeped out to the media.

"I've seen a lot of things in my career. I started forty-four straight games in the USFL and with Tampa Bay before being traded to the 49ers for a second- and fourth-round draft pick. The last two years, I've started seven games. Sometimes it seems like my career is going backwards. I hate watching. I hate it so much. Before I finally got a start last week because of an elbow injury to Montana, I felt like I was halfway to the funny farm. This can't keep going on."

Still, he rebuffed the reporters who had asked about the prospects of a trade.

"I played on a lousy team before, so I know how difficult it is to get things done. I want to be here. This is a great offense for me, a great organization and a great team. I don't want to shoot myself in the foot. I work at supporting Joe. This is a team game, and I like that aspect of it. If I get mad over this, I should go play golf. . . . Sometimes my ego says I should complain more to show I'm angry about this, but I think you show it more by making something happen every time you're on the field. Maybe it's self-defeating to press Joe so hard because he responds by playing better, but that's good for the team, so it's good for me. Sitting is tough to swallow, but there happens to be a Hall of Famer here. That's reality."

While the 49ers owner sweated over the injury to the team's superstar, Young took the field in a tricky spot. The play that injured Montana resulted in a pass interference penalty which gave San Francisco the ball on the Patriots 1-yard line with time remaining for just one play. Young rolled right, set up far out of the pocket, then nailed rookie tight end Wesley Walls for a touchdown.

"I was supposed to throw to Roger Craig right away, but I ended up rolling the dice a little bit," Young said. "It ended up all right. I didn't feel threatened by the rush so I waited a little longer. Coach Seifert would have choked me if it hadn't worked out."

Young remained on his coach's good side throughout the second half, completing ten of eleven throws for 177 yards and long touchdown passes to Rice and Taylor. Still, the loudest cheer from the fans at Stanford Stadium came in the fourth quarter, when Montana left the locker room and jogged back to the sideline.

"They should applaud," Young said. "I would, too. He'd gone out on a stretcher. It was remarkable to see him back on the sidelines. He's been spectacular."

Two fourth-quarter touchdowns propelled the 49ers to a 37–20 victory, improving their record to 6–1. But again, talk of the quarterback rivalry spread, especially with the puppetmaster behind that controversy in attendance that day, and not without an opinion.

Bill Walsh's tenure as 49ers vice president lasted for just five months. In July, he resigned from the organization and joined NBC as a color commentator. Along with Dick Enberg, Walsh covered the Patriots–49ers game, fittingly at Stanford Stadium, home of the same Cardinal program that he had once coached and would return to three years later.

During the broadcast, Enberg brought up Montana's comments from a September interview with CBS's John Madden in which he compared Walsh's retirement to "driving down the freeway, and you open the window and get a breath of fresh air."

"We were holed up together for ten years straight," Walsh answered, "so I can completely understand."

Later in the day, Walsh beamed with pride while discussing the play of his other former quarterback, Steve Young.

"He's a markedly different quarterback from the one who came here two years ago," he said. "Nothing he did today surprised me, because he's improved each year. You see that in quarterbacks; each training camp makes a big difference in learning what they have to do. He's become a completely different quarterback. He's now looking for that outlet pass, the way Joe Montana does so well."

Young's Montana-like play continued the next Sunday in the Meadowlands. With Montana still sidelined due to the knee injury, Young capped off a ninety-six-yard scoring drive by throwing a short touchdown pass to Brent Jones. Young's joy was shortlived, however: early in the second period, he fumbled a snap, recovered the ball, then twisted his knee upon being wrestled to the ground by linebackers Troy Benson and Kyle Clifton. He limped off the field.

On that Friday, Seifert had declared Montana and his sprained knee available only "in a pinch," so Young was replaced by Steve Bono.

The twenty-seven-year-old UCLA alum—who was planning to retire before the 49ers called him that summer—completed four straight passes, including a forty-five-yard touchdown to Rice that broke a 7–7 tie.

"I have the best job in America," said Bono, whose excitement throughout the game never waned, even though a bat landed on his leg in the fourth quarter. "I get paid good, I work hard [in practice], and I just wait around for a chance to play. I don't think it matters who [the opposing team] is. . . . If I get a chance to play, I'm happy."

An anxious Young begged the head coach to return, and eventually he did, until late in the game when his limping concerned Seifert enough to again replace him with Bono. A series later, somehow Young again convinced Seifert to put him back in. Despite the quarterback carousel, San Francisco defeated the New York Jets 23–10.

"It seems no matter who gets hurt, we have somebody who can come in and get the job done," Rice said. "Joe goes down and Steve Young comes on, or Steve Bono comes on. It's just the way we do things."

Rice's confidence wasn't entirely justified. Although the 49ers had won the previous three games by double digits, the offense still had not dominated an opponent from start to finish. That was about to change, and Montana's return to the playing field was the catalyst.

The swelling in his elbow gone, and his sprained knee at "90 percent or a little more," according to Seifert, Montana started the 49ers' Week 9 Monday night home battle with the New Orleans Saints.

Prior to the game, Montana told his wife that his lone concern was rust, but after four years of marriage, her husband's nonchalant yet self-assured attitude had rubbed off on Jennifer Montana.

"I told her that was the only thing that scared me," Montana said, "because while you can practice well, practice is so much different than anything you experience in a game. But she just told me, 'Don't worry, it's no big deal.'"

Jennifer was right: Montana completed his first eleven throws, tossing three touchdowns in the first half alone.

"When it's made to look easy, you know someone is out there doing a real professional job, whether he's a pianist or a quarterback or whatever," Young said. "I didn't think the knee would bother him. I always tease him that he just goes to the parts shop and gets a new part."

Refurbished, Montana iced a 31–13 victory with a short touchdown run midway through the final period.

"You know, nothing he does surprises me," Brent Jones said. "Except on that touchdown. The old dude ran it in from was it? The 5-yard line? I haven't seen Joe run a 9.5 hundred-yard dash in a while, but he made it in. Of course, you got a big ol' guy like that chasing you, it helps."

"It's not the first time he's played hurt," Roger Craig added. "He's like a Green Beret out there. He'll do whatever it takes to win."

The next week, rather than closing out an NFC West victory with a short touchdown run, Montana opened the 49ers game against Atlanta with one. The "old dude's" arm also made a few plays. Against a secondary featuring rookie superstar Deion Sanders—whom Rice had beat twice to the end zone for scores—Montana misfired on only three passes all day, adding three more touchdowns to his season total. The 45–3 victory improved San Francisco's record to 9–1. Green Bay snapped the six-game winning streak—ten penalties, three fumbles, and Montana's first interception in his previous 149 attempts hamstrung the 49ers all afternoon—but San Francisco soon earned a shot at reclaiming their place as the NFL's premier team. The 9–2 New York Giants were visiting Candlestick Park the next Monday night.

Escalating the hype for the nationally televised showdown, the Giants' Lawrence Taylor publicly disputed Craig's Green Beret/Joe Montana parallel.

"You have to take a quick route to him," the future Hall of Fame linebacker told the *New York Daily News*. "If you get close to Montana, he'll go down. He doesn't like to take a vicious hit."

Questioning Montana's toughness backfired. In the first half he completed seventeen of eighteen passes for 195 yards and three touchdowns. The Giants, behind 24–7, mounted a comeback, scoring twice to pull within seven. More importantly, they finally began to pressure the quarterback: in the third quarter, linebacker Gary Reasons pounded Montana, driving him to the ground, where Montana rolled around in pain. Reasons was penalized for spearing.

Despite damage to his ribs—and a sack-strip by Carl Banks two plays later—Montana refused to exit the game. And on the next drive, during a reverse to Rice, Montana headed up field to block. Ignoring the warning Rice issued to him the previous January during the playoff win over Minnesota, Montana charged into Banks with an aggressive, diving block that sprung Rice for an extra twenty yards.

The play didn't count, however, as a holding call against Jones nullified Rice's long gain. Worse yet, Montana's outstanding, albeit voided block—which the *Sacramento Bee*'s Joe Hamelin described as "arms flapping like a pelican struggling out of the surf"—re-aggravated his ribs and forced him to the sideline for the rest of the series.

"[Team doctors] thought it was a slight concussion," Montana said. "They thought it got started when I was hit under the chin by [Reasons's] helmet. When I got up, I had a faraway look and was kind of pale. And I wasn't fighting to get back in. So they thought something was wrong."

The Giants tied the score in the middle of the fourth period, but by then Montana had returned to a thunderous Candlestick applause.

"Just thinking about Joe getting all banged up and playing was incredible," Jones said. "One time, I didn't know if he was going to get back up, but like he always does, he said, 'I'm OK, I'm OK.'"

With his critic, Lawrence Taylor, now watching from the Giants bench—the All-Pro was sidelined with a sprained knee and ankle—Montana drove the 49ers for the go-ahead field goal then added an insurance touchdown in the closing minutes. An on-the-run, third-down completion with Banks hanging on him kept the game-sealing touchdown drive alive.

"Nobody else in the league could have gotten it off," teammate Matt Millen said. "But on the sidelines, nobody says, 'Boy that was unbelievable.' You say, 'That's Joe. The man is having a career year in a career that's unbelievable."

More specifically, Montana was having a career month. In four November games, he had posted absurd numbers: 76 percent (95-for-125) completion, 1,189 yards, eleven touchdowns, and only one interception.

"I think Joe Montana is the offensive player of the decade," Giants head coach Bill Parcells noted.

* * *

The bruised ribs prevented Montana from practicing early the following week. Contrary to his predecessor, Seifert cringed at the idea of splitting the quarterback duties.

"We've always liked to focus on one guy," he said. "We have the utmost confidence in Steve, so that's not a problem. We just want to have Joe in there if we can. But if he can't practice all week, we won't play him."

Montana was so eager to prove he was healthy that he barged into Holmgren's office Friday morning and did calisthenics for the offensive coordinator to showcase a painless flexibility. That afternoon, Montana returned to the practice field and was named the starter for Sunday's rematch with the Falcons in Atlanta.

"If we felt Joe was going to be hindered at all or play in any pain, he would not have played," Holmgren said. "It's probably unusual (to not have a starting quarterback take snaps until Friday of game week), but Joe is an unusual player. He's hurting a little bit. It's probably one of those things that will last the rest of the season."

Both a weary Montana and the 49ers offense struggled in the first half against Atlanta, scoring just two field goals. Partially redeeming himself for his poor effort in Week 10, Deion Sanders picked off one of Montana's second-quarter passes and returned it inside 49ers territory, putting the Falcons in position for their go-ahead touchdown. On the following drive, while attempting to pick up points before halftime, Montana was struck in the chest by the helmet of Falcons defensive tackle Tony Castillas. Unlike the previous week against the Giants, there would be no dramatic return: Montana spent rest of the game in the locker room.

"Every time I took a breath, I felt a sharp pain above my rib cage," he told a reporter in the parking lot.

Again, Young was thrilled to be given an opportunity.

"In the first three years of my pro career, I started every week, but I didn't have a lineup like this around me," he said. "That's why I get so excited when I play. It's why Joe fights to start every week, I'm sure. He fights to get out here because it's such a great offense to play in."

Behind 10–6 and on the road, Young flourished. He completed his first ten passes, beat Sanders with a thirty-eight-yard touchdown pass to Taylor, and capped off an eighty-yard drive early in the fourth quarter with his first rushing touchdown of the season. The 49ers won their ninth consecutive road game, 23–10.

Montana ducked out of the locker room so the press could not interrogate him, but he personally assured Young that he'd be ready for the next week.

"It's not an easy situation," Young told reporters. "It's very frustrating, but I love this team. It may be one of the greatest ever. . . . Every chance I've ever had to play at least a half, I've played well. I think if I ever get a chance to play a couple of games in a row, I really think I can make things happen."

That chance eluded Young once again: the following Sunday, he returned to his familiar backup role and waited for his turn.

Armed with both a flak jacket and a shot of cortisone, Montana took the field in a critical Week 14 matchup in Anaheim: a win over the Rams would give the 49ers another NFC West title as well as the top seed in the NFC playoffs.

Penalties and two interceptions by Montana—he threw just two in his previous eight starts—put the 49ers in a seventeen-point hole at the end of the first quarter. And even though Montana and Taylor connected on a ninety-two-yard touchdown minutes before halftime, San Francisco still trailed 27–10 heading into the final period.

"We tend to focus more on what we do in the fourth quarter," Montana said.

On cue, Montana completed five passes for sixty-four yards and a touchdown pass to Mike Wilson. A Rams turnover gave the 49ers the ball back on their own 4-yard line. On the very next snap, Taylor ran a post pattern, caught a Montana pass in perfect stride, and, aided by great blocking from Rice, raced ninety-six yards for his second exceedingly long touchdown in three quarters.

Yet another Los Angeles miscue—Ron Brown fumbling the ensuing kickoff—gave San Francisco the ball right back. Trailing 27–23 with less than seven minutes remaining, Montana drained time off the clock with the running game, then found Taylor for fifteen more yards. Three plays later Craig crossed the goal line for the game-winning touchdown.

"This one's pretty satisfying," said Montana, who set a career-high with 458 yards passing. "It gives us the home-field advantage in the playoffs, and that means a lot, to me especially. I don't want any blizzards."

In addition to guaranteeing a snow-less postseason, the win meant Montana could rest and let his myriad of injuries heal. In consultation with the team's doctors, Seifert elected not to play Montana: instead, he watched the next Sunday's game against Buffalo from the sidelines wearing tennis shoes, chinos, and a 49ers jacket.

"I was hoping they wouldn't make that decision," Montana said. "I get paid to play, not to take a week off. It's no fun sitting on the sideline."

Young—who had so often spoken that line—was jubilant.

"Every week has been seemingly the same. I've worked very, very hard to stay sharp despite not playing, and getting the chance to play will be great."

Given the opportunity to play (and even start) a regular season game against any team was a blessing for the impatient quarterback. Nevertheless, a rematch against Jim Kelly—the former USFL MVP turned superstar of the resurgence Bills—added extra motivation for the Week 15 showdown. Four years after the Houston Gamblers overcame a twenty-point deficit to defeat the Los Angeles Express in front of a sparse crowd at the Los Angeles Coliseum, Young would have a shot at paying Kelly back.

But the defacto rematch of a game in which Kelly and Young combined for 829 yards and six touchdown passes didn't resemble that offensive masterpiece. Through three quarters, the two teams had combined for five turnovers and just ten points. Late in the first half, on a fourth-and-goal from the one, Young dove into the end zone, but was not awarded the score. Much like his unsuccessful yet pivotal scramble at the end of the loss to Phoenix the previous year, Young adamantly believed he had crossed the goal line.

"I was up to my waist in the end zone," said Young. "They said I crawled there. I don't know how much [the defense is] going to let you crawl underneath a pile."

Keeping the ball mostly on the ground—forty-two runs against just nineteen passes on the day—the 49ers capitalized on two more Buffalo turnovers, adding two fourth-quarter touchdowns to pull out a 21–10 victory.

"I don't think I'm going to help this team running around too much," said Young, who threw a touchdown to Rice and rushed for another during a two-minute stretch in the fourth quarter, but was also picked off twice. "There were times I could have run today, but I didn't. Look at what Joe does. He's an orchestrator. He's the best at it. He's the best ever at putting the ball in the hands of players and making yards, almost like a great orchestra conductor who can call up the horns if he needs them, the violins. Joe doesn't use his legs a lot. He doesn't need to, but when he has to, he does. I'm a believer in the way it's been done here, and I want to fit in."

For a second straight year, the 49ers regular season finale would have no impact, win or lose, on their playoff positioning. Still, rather than let rust pervade his team, Seifert elected to start all of his superstars, including Montana, against Chicago.

The reeling Bears had started the season 4–0, only to drop nine of their next eleven. On the day before Christmas, they entered Candlestick seeking to snap a five-game losing streak as well as avenge their 28–3 NFC Championship Game loss the previous January. They achieved neither.

Carrying out a rather mundane, unnuanced game plan, Montana produced four drives that ended in field goals and tossed a touchdown to Rice before Young relieved him in the fourth quarter. The 49ers defense—the NFC's second-ranked in points and yards allowed—forced five turnovers and so frustrated head coach Mike Ditka that he not only benched quarterback Jim Harbaugh in the second quarter, he assumed command of the play calling from offensive coordinator Greg Landry.

The uneventful 26–0 San Francisco victory wasn't completely insignificant, however.

Montana, playing without a pregame cortisone shot to his ribs, completed only ten of his twenty-one attempts and was intercepted once. The lackluster statistics weren't entirely Montana's fault. His receivers (including Rice) dropped three passes, and the interception was the result of another drop: when a defender hit Brent Jones, the ball popped up, then into the hands of Chicago's Shaun Gayle.

"Joe is the man, and I felt he played well today," said Rice. "He got the ball downfield; he also ran well today, so he's all tuned up and ready."

"I think we were a little out of sync," Montana explained. "You think it's not hard to get up for a game, but there are a lot of things going on with Christmas and all, and it's pretty easy to let down."

Despite the so-called let-down, Montana made history that day. He finished the 1989 season completing 70.2 percent of his passes, for 3,521 yards, and twenty-six touchdowns against only eight interceptions. According to the NFL's complex, convoluted formula, Montana's 112.4 rating was the best in league history, surpassing Milt Plum's twenty-nine-year-old record.

"I guess records are made to be broken," Plum told Ric Bucher of the *Mercury News*, "and he did it in fine fashion."

Montana, never one to care about his personal statistics, was predictably uninterested.

"You've got to have things going your way for a season like this," Montana said. "Guys have to be making the catches, the line has to block. This record and all the Super Bowls, it's really something you look back on later."

The new passing mark was one of several individual honors Montana deflected attention away from that week. On Wednesday, he was named the NFC's starting quarterback for the Pro Bowl and the *Sporting News* Man of the Year. That same day Montana was also given the Len Eshmont Award, named in memory of an original 49er who passed away from hepatitis in 1957. San Francisco players voted for the annual winner, who "best exemplifies inspirational and courageous play."

After suggesting Chet Brooks and Kevin Fagan were more worthy—"A lot of other guys played with a lot more pain than me"—Montana admitted that the Eshmont carried special meaning because his teammates selected him for the second time in four years. (The miraculous recovery from spinal surgery earned Montana the award in 1986.)

"He inspires people by the way he plays the game," the team's most vocal leader, Ronnie Lott, said. "If everyone had a heart like Joe, we'd have a lot of great leaders in this world and a lot of great people."

*   *   *

One year and five days after their decisive, vengeful win over the Vikings, the 49ers hosted Minnesota for a second-round playoff rematch at Candlestick. And once again, Montana torched the NFL's top-ranked pass defense, collecting 210 yards and four touchdown passes in the first half alone.

Montana's near perfect passing (thirteen-for-sixteen, 210 yards) combined with five Minnesota turnovers built the 49ers an insurmountable lead. They cruised to a dominating 41–13 win.

"[Montana] was doing just like he always does," guard Guy McIntyre said. "Next week, he'll probably do better."

A year earlier, Montana's impassioned speech so inspired (and stunned) his teammates that upon entering the locker room, they all looked to their quarterback for another fiery address.

"I made a fool of myself once," he told them. "I'm not going to do it again."

Still, Montana did reward two of his teammates, blindside tackles Bubba Paris and Steve Wallace, with pleasant, postgame surprises.

During the regular season, the Vikings collected seventy-one sacks, just one shy of the NFL record. Each of their starting defensive linemen, Al Noga (11.5), Henry Thomas (9), and NFL Defensive Player of the Year Keith Millard (18), wrapped up opposing quarterbacks at a considerable pace. But the most feared pass rusher was three-time Pro Bowl defensive end Chris Dole-man, who paced the NFL with twenty-one sacks in 1989.

"Joe told us that if we kept Doleman off him, he'd give us a little some-thing," said Paris, who found two $100 bills in his locker. "I was as ready for him as I have ever been for anybody. I knew I couldn't let him get to Joe."

Doleman didn't. In fact, no Vikings defender did. For the first time in seven weeks, Montana wasn't sacked once. Coincidence or not, San Francisco's twenty-eight-point playoff win was the largest in team history.

"I'd rather win this way," Montana said. "This is a more enjoyable way to win. It's fun when you can take it easy in the second half. You can't make a liv-ing by always having to come back in the fourth quarter."

The easy victory sent San Francisco to a second straight NFC Champi-onship Game. And although they didn't have to brave the "Bear Weather" that allegedly tormented the 49ers a year earlier in Chicago, the climate by the Bay wasn't much better for their matchup against the division rival Los Angeles Rams.

On a cold, wet, muddy day in Candlestick, the 49ers fell behind 3–0 until late in the second period. Starting at his own 13-yard line, Montana com-pleted seven passes, covering sixty-nine yards. Nine seconds remained when Montana, standing calmly in the pocket, surveyed the field, targeted an open-ing, and hit John Taylor midair across the goal line for an eighteen-yard touchdown.

"That was a big boost, scoring right before the half like that," said Mon-tana, who completed twenty-six of his thirty pass attempts. "I think it took a lot out of them."

He was absolutely right. The 49ers shut out the Rams in the second half to earn a date with John Elway's Denver Broncos. Montana's postgame predic-tion for Super Bowl XXIV, however, couldn't have been more wrong.

"We're just happy to be back there, no matter who we play," Montana told the press. "They've been having a pretty good year themselves. It should be a pretty good game. Just seeing the way they've been winning football games and their record, it should be a good ballgame."

"I'll never forget sitting in my box with Bill Walsh before [that Super Bowl] started," owner Eddie DeBartolo Jr. recalled two decades later. "I said, 'Boy, Bill, this is going to be a tough game.' He said, 'I don't think so.'

"The game was about five or seven minutes old. And we had stopped El-way and took the ball, went down the field, and scored, and [Bill] turned to me, and he said, 'You can go home . . . Eddie, they can't cover anybody. We have so many people that are open . . . this game is going to be a blowout. George Seifert can name the score of this game.'"

The score turned out to be 55–10, the most lopsided defeat in Super Bowl history. Montana completed twenty-two of his twenty-nine attempts for 297 yards and five touchdown passes, another Super Bowl record. Following the game, Seifert declared Montana "probably the greatest quarterback to play this game."

Asked about his head coach's cautious declaration, Steve Young agreed.

"Well, he's not looking up at anyone, that's for sure."

The Next One

The 49ers postgame Super Bowl locker room inside the New Orleans Superdome bore no resemblance to the 49ers postgame Super Bowl locker room inside Joe Robbie Stadium twelve months earlier. There were no tears, no sighs of relief, and no emotional exhaustion over the most heart-pounding finish in Super Bowl history: As Eddie DeBartolo Jr. discovered hours earlier, suspense had vacated the Crescent City hours before the final gun sounded.

Instead of supplying details of a nail-biting ninety-two-yard drive or his game-winning touchdown pass in the final seconds, Joe Montana regaled reporters with a cute story that offered far better copy than the actual game played that day.

Equipment manager Bronco Hinek—who three years earlier had granted Steve Young permission to borrow a certain teammate's pair of cleats—had placed two familiar, yet unexpected items inside and next to Montana's locker the morning before San Francisco faced Denver.

Upon arriving in the Superdome dressing room, Montana saw a No. 87 jersey hanging in the empty locker beside his. No 49ers player had worn that number since Montana's close friend and trusty receiver Dwight Clark retired after the 1987 season.

"I smiled when I saw it," Montana said. "It was like a ghost from the past. It brought back some pleasant memories."

Hinek's sentimental showcase continued when Montana looked inside his locker.

Several months earlier, Jennifer Montana had snapped a photograph of her three children. In the picture, daughters Elizabeth and Alexandra each had one of their father's enormous, diamond-encrusted Super Bowl rings on their thumbs, and infant Nathaniel wore a No. 16 T-shirt with the third ring pinned to it. Beneath the picture an engraving read, "OK, Daddy. The Next Ring Is Yours." The framed photo—"My inspiration," Montana called it—stayed in his locker for the remainder of the 1989 season and the 49ers' two home playoff games.

Prior to the team's departure from Santa Clara, Hinek surreptitiously placed the keepsake in Montana's equipment bag.

"I wanted Joe to show up for the game and find it," Hinek said. "You know, a touch of home."

Once he was done telling the story, a reporter asked Montana if he was pleased to know that the championship prize he earned that evening, his fourth, would finally be for him.

"No, I'll give this ring to Jennifer," said Montana. "The next one will be mine."

*   *   *

Although he modestly deflected the claim that he was now the greatest quarterback of all time—"those types of things are reserved for guys no longer playing the game"—Joe Montana enjoyed the aftermath of winning a fourth Super Bowl and third Super Bowl Most Valuable Player award.

Five days later, alongside Eddie DeBartolo Jr. in Monterey, he played nine holes at the Cypress Point Club during the AT&T Pebble Beach National Pro-Am and partied that evening with a few dozen teammates at the owner's nearby house. The next week, he signed a multimillion dollar endorsement deal with a burgeoning athletic shoe company called L.A. Gear. And after a visit to the White House, a trip with his wife to Australia (where Jennifer was filming her regular segment for KPIX-TV's "Evening Magazine" program), and a team vacation to Hawaii, Montana's representatives at IMG began negotiating a new, more lucrative contract.

"In four years, I'll be thirty-eight," he told the *San Jose Mercury News*'s Ann Killion during negotiations that carried on into August. "We'll see how I'm doing physically and mentally. Mentally, I might say to hell with it."

During training camp, Montana and DeBartolo agreed upon the final details over lunch—"bad tuna fish salad," according to the team owner—in the cafeteria at Sierra College. The four-year, $16 million deal made Montana the highest-paid player in NFL history.

"I hope I make it four more to make another one . . . I'd like to. Up until that point, if anything happens before that, it would be (the last). I'm hoping that we have to do it again at the end of four years."

"So am I," DeBartolo replied.

"But I might have a gray beard," Montana joked.

49ers fans may have been comforted by news of Montana's extension, but Steve Young was not.

"However long Joe plays impacts me," he said. "Willing [to wait] is the wrong word. I'm under contract."

In each of the 49ers' two playoff blowouts, Young played the bulk of the final period, and early in the fourth period against Denver, he made his Super Bowl debut. But with the 49ers ahead by forty-five points, few people noticed his two completions or the zigzagging, back-and-forth, eleven-yard scramble he made on a third down that allowed the 49ers to assume the "victory formation" and run the clock down to zero.

Within days of the Super Bowl triumph—and Montana's historic performance—rumors surfaced that Young wanted to be dealt out of San Francisco.

"Steve likes everything about the 49ers except one thing: he likes the players, he likes the coaching, he likes the classy way the organization does things. But it drives him crazy because he isn't playing," Young's agent Leigh Steinberg told the *Chronicle* two days after the 49ers Super Bowl win over Denver. "At some point, Steve will ask Joe what his expectations are. If Joe plans to play only another year or two, it will be worth it for Steve to stick around. But if Joe wants to play another three to four years, well, then it's another matter."

During the spring, Young mostly remained silent on the issue. Published rumors of a trade to Kansas City, Detroit, or New England coupled with reports that the 49ers and Cowboys had discussed a trade for Dallas quarterback Steve Walsh said enough.

By spring and the start of a fourth consecutive minicamp as the team's backup Young finally vented.

"My deep, darkest feeling is that I'd like to be a San Francisco 49er (starter) before I'm forty years old," he said. "The way it's going to go this year is, I'll play a lot, and I'll play very good, and I'll be that much better than I was last year. Because of that, I'll put myself in the position where I'll be just too qualified to be in that (backup) spot."

Caught in a difficult situation—trying to prepare for the future when the present was so glorious—the 49ers front office was equally frustrated. Even with Bill Walsh gone and the team paying Young $1.1 million in 1990 to serve as a backup there was very little interest in giving up the seemingly limitless quarterback.

"One of the things you learn if you stick around the NFL long enough," Young said in May, "is that your life is not your own in a lot of ways. The 49ers have made it clear to me that I'm not going anywhere. All I can do is wait."

Although Young's contract expired after that season—he opted not to sign an extension the previous year—with the NFL's unrestricted free agency still three years away, any club interested in signing him would have to pay San Francisco an enormous compensatory fee of two first-round draft choices.

"We did everything humanly possible to keep Steve happy," Carmen Policy recalled. "Money is one thing, but it can only go so far. Steve was a good soldier, a very, very good soldier. I think Steve was committed to playing for the 49ers and wanted a championship so bad, and I think he sensed this was the way to go about doing that."

For the rest of the 49ers, their fans, and the national media, Young's angst as well as any remnants of his challenge to Montana's job were quickly forgotten by the start of training camp. Instead, focus centered on the 49ers chance to become the first team in history to win three consecutive Super Bowls. Late into the summer the opportunity for a "three-peat" dwarfed any other pro football story, both in the Bay Area and across the nation.

"I haven't heard much said about the three-peat lately," Montana told the press. "It's a part of everybody's mind because we have that opportunity. But we can't look to the end of the season. We have to look at the beginning of the season because we have a lot of tough games."

Having successfully avoided a surgeon's knife for the first offseason in three years, Montana was understandably eager to start the regular season. And his praise for their upcoming opponents was not simply lip service: the 49ers 1990 schedule was brutal, especially down the stretch.

After close wins against New Orleans, Washington, and Atlanta, Montana brought the 49ers back from a seven-point fourth-quarter deficit to topple the Oilers in the Houston Astrodome. The 24–21 comeback set a new NFL record for consecutive road victories, a mark they extended to thirteen the next Sunday, as Montana set a career-high of 476 yards passing and six touchdowns—five of which Jerry Rice caught to tie another NFL record—to blow past Atlanta, 45–35.

"I thought it was going to be a tough day," said Montana. "Initially, I missed two guys wide open and under threw [John Taylor]. I thought, 'Oh no, it's just one of those days.' But it turned out better for us. . . . At times I wouldn't hit people, then there were times when no matter how I threw the ball it was getting there."

Victories over Pittsburgh, Cleveland, Green Bay, and Dallas gave the 9–0 49ers the greatest start in franchise history. Apart from the three-peat, and an

NFL record for consecutive victories (wins in Weeks 10 and 11 snapped the previous mark of seventeen), there was serious talk of joining the 1972 Miami Dolphins as the only team in modern history to finish with an undefeated record.

"Guys don't care about that. We're dragging those records behind us," Montana told a reporter in early November. "The only way we're aware of them is when someone else brings them up. Otherwise, we wouldn't have any idea."

Neither did he have any idea of the individual record on the horizon: Montana was on pace to surpass Dan Marino's single-season record of 5,084 passing yards. If nothing else, he would set new personal bests in every single significant passing statistic. Through nine games, a second-consecutive Most Valuable Player award was Montana's to lose.

Through those same nine games, Young did not attempt a single pass, and his only meaningful appearance bordered on the disastrous.

With less than seven minutes remaining in the fourth quarter of their Week 5 win in Houston, the 49ers trailed 21–17. In search of the go-ahead score, Montana released a pass, only to be crushed by Oilers defensive end Ezra Johnson. Although the hit simply knocked the wind out of him, Montana left the field and Young hastily took his place for the critical third-and-4 at the Oilers 46-yard line. He fumbled the snap, and Oilers defensive end Ray Childress recovered the loose ball.

"We were trying to get the play off anyway, because they were all mixed up," Young said. "The snap problem occurred because [center Jesse Sapolu] thought it was a timeout, and I was trying to get the play off."

Only an ill-advised pre-snap timeout taken by Oilers safety Bubba Mc-Dowell (which went unnoticed by most players, coaches, and fans) kept the turnover from counting. The down was replayed with Montana reentering the game, and on the next snap he threw the game-winning touchdown pass to John Taylor.

"I was so frustrated 'cause certainly I didn't want to be backing up, but that's what it was, and I learned a ton," Young remembered years later. "I saw the best football Joe ever played, and that's some of the best football ever played. . . . So that was good, it was invaluable to have to sit there, to be forced to sit there. But, man, I was frustrated. I knew if I could get on that field, with that team, with that offense that it would be worth it, if I could figure out a way to do it."

To the press and oftentimes his teammates, Young outwardly expressed his frustrations, but he also internalized them. Not playing wasn't just dissatisfying, it also left him riddled with guilt.

Although Young's contracts with the Los Angeles Express and Tampa Bay Buccaneers had banked him millions of dollars, the twenty-seven-year-old didn't flaunt (and barely even spent) his money. For a few years, during the NFL season he lived in room that he rented from teammate Harris Barton.

One day—long after Montana's resurgence in late 1988—Barton sneaked into Young's room to borrow a pair of socks. Inside his roommate's drawer, Barton found thirteen uncashed checks from the 49ers organization, each one for roughly $90,000.

"I didn't feel like I was earning my keep," Young explained years later. "The club got mad at me. They said I was screwing up their bookkeeping."

But stuffing the checks in his sock drawer didn't make Young feel better. Watching—rather than playing—the game he loved left the customarily positive, even perky, quarterback sullen.

"There were many days a few years ago when I'd get to work and want to turn around and go home," Young later said. "It was a difficult time."

If he wasn't playing in games, Young felt that his best chance to improve was to at least be given more repetitions in practices.

"Here was a young, talented guy that wanted his shot," George Seifert recalled two decades later. "Steve was pretty out front about wanting to get an opportunity and knew that if he sat back it may never come. And so he was, I don't think overly aggressive, but he wasn't going to sit there and just let things happen. He wanted to be part of the deal: interacting with coaches on the field or after practices.

"I remember when I was the head coach and Joe was the starting quarterback, one of the vivid things in the back of my mind was that at the end of each practice, Steve Young would always be walking off the practice field and talking: you could tell he was just like a buzzsaw going off to Mike Holmgren. We kid about it now, but at the time I'm sure it was deadly serious to Steve and certainly with Mike. Steve was just a great competitor, himself, and wanted his chance and didn't want to lose his opportunity. And he knew he was facing one of the best quarterbacks or the best quarterback of all time."

Although Young knew Holmgren was both a friend and a great advocate, contrary to conventional wisdom, he didn't always view the presence of his former position coach at Brigham Young as an aid to his goal of more playing time.

"It was comforting; it was a positive," Young said. "But I think it was also a negative because I was trying to compete for every snap, every practice, every chance. I complained to Mike a lot, saying I need more opportunities. And Mike was like, 'Steve, it's *Joe Montana*.' But I think because everyone knew he coached me before that he almost had to go overboard, the other way, so that it didn't look like he was playing favorites. So I think it kind of hurt me that I had known him before."

Young's antsy, anxious demeanor was evident to his teammates. In his 1997 autobiography, *All the Rage*, Charles Haley expressed an irritation, even anger at Young's impatience. And on at least one occasion, Montana became outwardly annoyed with Young over the same issue.

"Joe felt like Steve brought focus onto him as the second string quarterback," John Paye remembered. "I think Joe felt like, 'Hell, I'm the starter; you need to be the backup over here, being quiet and being supportive and not say things in the press or after games.' I think it frustrated Joe, he felt like the focus should have been on the team.

"And as an example, the 49ers played the Rams in a [1989] Monday night game, when John Taylor had two touchdown passes on slant patterns; one was ninety-six yards, the other one was [ninety-two] yards. At that time the Rams were the big rival for the 49ers in-conference. So it was a big, big win for the 49ers to get that win. . . . Steve had done wind sprints after the game on the field, and he was asked about it after the game [by a reporter]. . . . Steve responded, 'I can't put on my uniform and not sweat. I'm a player, I want to play.'

"Things such as that frustrated Joe. I think he was okay with the competition during practices and games. I just think Joe was kind of a quiet guy in terms of the media, and I don't think he appreciated some of those types of comments that Steve made public that he thought should have been more in-house.

"Steve irritated Joe," Paye added. "Steve's very hyper, and Joe is 'Joe Cool.' Steve's hyperness, whether it was on the field where he needed to play and sweat or . . . when we played on AstroTurf, he didn't like the feeling of Astro-Turf because it wasn't real football. So he would take a cup of dirt and he would get his hands in the dirt so he could grip the ball better to throw, so all those little things. Steve had this superhuman athletic body, and he was anxious to run or throw, and Joe was more methodical, Joe Cool."

The blistering pace that Joe Cool had been on at the halfway point of the 1990 season cooled off after Thanksgiving. Hosting the Rams, the undefeated 49ers trailed 21–7 at the half, and on a rainy and wind-swept day at Candlestick their NFL record eighteen-game winning streak eventually came to an end. An unexpected change in defensive strategy helped the Rams win yet another road game against the 49ers. Instead of their normal 3–4 defense, the Rams shifted frequently into a "Bear-style 46," as described by Montana, who fumbled once and threw three interceptions.

During the post-game debriefing, reporters asked Montana if he thought the team—with the undefeated New York Giants visiting Candlestick the following Sunday—overlooked the 4–7 Rams.

"There was no reason for us to look ahead and look past this game. We just didn't take advantage of the opportunities."

Although now neither team was undefeated (the previously 10–0 Giants lost in Week 12 at Philadelphia) the December matchup between the cross-country rivals was tailor-made for ABC's nationally televised Monday Night Football. It would be New York's dominating defense against the 49ers peerless offense. In the end, the Giants defense would win that battle, but San Francisco still found a way to win the game.

New York stifled Montana throughout the game—he completed just twelve of twenty-nine passes for 152 yards and converted only eleven first downs—but his twenty-three-yard touchdown pass to Taylor just before halftime was enough to edge out the Giants, 7–3.

"The key was to get rid of the ball quick after making basic reads," Montana said. "We thought maybe they'd come with more pressure. I guess I might have thrown the ball quicker than I would have ordinarily."

San Francisco's offensive line didn't allow New York a single sack that evening, but the Giants held Rice to just one catch, suffocated the 49ers running game, and repeatedly pressured, hurried, and hit Montana. Despite the outcome, Giants head coach Bill Parcells was encouraged. The four-point loss on the road against the two-time defending Super Bowl champion instilled even more confidence in his club.

"Something tells me we'll meet again in January," Lawrence Taylor told the press.

Even before the victory over the Giants, the 49ers had reason to celebrate. San Francisco's eleven wins coupled with losing records by every other team in their division clinched the 49ers fifth straight NFC West title. And despite pedestrian outputs from both Montana and the offense as a whole the following two weeks, San Francisco won back-to-back road contests against Cincinnati and the Rams to clinch home-field advantage throughout the postseason.

"Our offense didn't play as well as we can," said Montana, who completed just half his pass attempts during the 26–10 Monday night win at Anaheim. "Sometimes we played well, and sometimes we didn't. When we get to the playoffs, we'll have to play with more consistency."

The final two games of the season could neither hurt nor help the 49ers in terms of playoff-seeding, prompting speculation that Montana would sit to avoid any unnecessary risk to the team's superstar.

"Guys get hurt all the time. [Last week Harry Sydney] got knocked out. Brent Jones got knocked out," Montana said. "So are you going to rest [tight end Jamie Williams] so he doesn't get knocked out?"

The other element to the debate—the elephant in the room—was another prime opportunity to accommodate the increasingly frustrated Steve Young. Although meaningless to the team's postseason status, no regular season game was ever meaningless to the backup quarterback who had thrown just one pass all season.

"This is a year in which Steve hasn't gotten a lot of work," Seifert later said during his weekly press conference. "We'll see Steve in the next two games."

Those types of comments—which revealed a compelling desire, even a need to play Young—most annoyed Montana.

"I don't see the Giants or Miami saying, 'We have to get our backup playing time,'" he said that week. "Part of the role, unfortunately, is not getting much playing time. This is the only place I've ever heard of where they want to give backups playing time. Sure it's great for Steve, but it's not part of the role description."

A backup's role, in Montana's mind, was to play in the preseason, during a blowout, or if the starter was too injured to participate or play effectively.

"[People] always say, 'Well, what do you do to help the guys behind you?' I go, 'I don't,'" Montana said years later. "That's not my job, that's the coaches' job, get them ready. My job is to make sure that they're behind me, that they stay there because that means I'm playing well."

"I can tell you that Joe, he did not want to mentor me," Young told ESPN's *Outside the Lines* in 2012. "And I don't blame him."

On the Tuesday before the 49ers last home game of the regular season against New Orleans, Montana assured the press that his health was not an issue: "I feel pretty good. Actually, this is the best I've felt at this time of the year for a while."

That turned out not to be entirely true.

Against the Bengals Montana had sustained a groin injury that he reaggravated eight days later during the win over the Rams. He practiced throughout the week, but on Saturday night noticed bruising and felt significant discomfort. The next morning in the training room at Candlestick Park, both the medical and coaching staffs, concerned about internal bleeding, decided to keep him out of that afternoon's game versus the Saints. A team spokesman told the media that Montana had a lower abdominal injury.

Informed an hour before kickoff that he would make his first start of the season, Young initially operated the 49ers offense to perfection. Experimenting with a no-huddle approach for the first series, Young's crisp passing drove the team to the 1-yard line, where Tom Rathman capped off the game-opening touchdown drive.

New Orleans then pieced together a long touchdown drive of their own, but from that moment on, both offenses shut down. Four sacks and few windows in the Saints secondary slowed down San Francisco's passing game, and Young was forced to bail out of the pocket and scramble several times.

"How he was running, he could have gotten hurt at any time," Saints free safety Gene Atkins said. "I'd say he's got some really good guts to run the ball like he did. One time, when I hit him on the sidelines, I didn't think he was going to get up. He got up real slow. I thought he had a concussion. Quarterbacks don't need to take that kind of beating, because your mind has to be real clear to run the offense."

"Young's a fortunate young man," New Orleans linebacker Vaughan Johnson added. "A couple of times, he almost got decapitated."

A career-high 102 yards rushing—"I didn't have happy feet and run around like a crazy man," Young insisted—was not enough to overcome several penalties and three turnovers. San Francisco scored only three points in the game's final fifty-two minutes.

Behind 13–10 late in the fourth quarter, the 49ers forced a Saints punt and, aided by a fine return from Eric Davis, took possession at midfield with 2:11 remaining. Two productive Young rushes and two more completions pushed the offense to the Saints' 20-yard line. Although the 49ers were well within Mike Cofer's range for a game-tying field goal, Young hoped for more.

"I knew we were going to win the game," he said. "I just knew it."

But while attempting a draw handoff to rookie running back Dexter Carter, the two understudies botched the play—an unclean, awkward exchange forced the football to squirt out. The Saints' Rickey Jackson recovered the fumble, allowing New Orleans to capture a 13–10 victory.

"[Young] gave us a chance to win," tight end Jamie Williams said. "A guy can only do so much."

The starting quarterback took the last-minute miscue and subsequent loss much harder.

"You don't lose around here . . . [losing] is the one thing I can't take. If I'm gonna play, I can't lose. Can't lose. . . . Can't. . . . I can't believe that we lost," Young said.

"On that last drive," he added, "all year long, I play with Joe. I see him drop back, and I yell to him. I felt very comfortable in that situation. I'd be very disappointed if I didn't move the ball downfield into scoring position. . . . It's too bad. We turned the ball over four times. That's exactly what I didn't want to happen."

Still, Young remained supremely confident in both his skills and his future as a franchise quarterback.

"I'll be starting soon," he assured the press. "I feel I'm preparing to start and win in this league. . . . It's just what I believe."

Young had good reason to expect another opportunity to start in place of Montana, whom he talked with for several minutes in the locker room following the loss. Montana's groin injury was, by admission of the 49ers' medical

staff, "sort of a mystery." Seifert even told the press on Monday "I have absolutely no idea if [Joe Montana] will play or what his status is."

To no one's surprise, Montana expressed a desire to play in the regular season finale at Minnesota: "You like not to miss a beat and stay tuned up. We're
playing a good opponent, and it will be a good test for us."

Seifert ultimately opted for the same quarterback schedule that he had intended to use the week before against New Orleans: Montana would play the
first half, Young the second.

Noticeably off-target and unable to overcome spotty pass protection,
dropped passes, and poor field position, Montana recorded just eighty-eight
passing yards and no points during his half under center. He lobbied Seifert to
remain in the game, but the head coach stuck to his plan: Young was the quarterback tasked with overcoming the 10–0 halftime deficit.

Although the game had absolutely no impact on the postseason—the
Vikings had long since been eliminated from playoff contention, and the 49ers
had already secured home-field advantage—the visiting locker room of the
Metrodome was filled with anger and finger-pointing. Consecutive losses were
not the way San Francisco hoped to start their bid for the coveted three-peat.

"There was a lot of frustration at halftime," tackle Steve Wallace said.

A short field goal to open the second half cut into the Vikings advantage,
but Young saved his best for the final period. Two critical runs, including an
eight-yard gain on third-and-7, gave way to a field goal, narrowing the deficit to
just four points. On the next series, two more long scrambles gained thirty-
three yards, setting up Young's go-ahead touchdown pass to Rice. And after
Minnesota quickly regained the lead, Young—for the second time in three seasons—broke the back of the Vikings defense in spectacular, last-minute fashion.

A sack and a holding penalty did not slow down Young's determination.
His passing and a key fourth-down quarterback sneak surged the 49ers into
Minnesota's red zone, and with half a minute remaining in the game Young
slung a pass to John Taylor who raced the last fifteen yards untouched into the
end zone. On the game-winning drive, Young completed six-of-seven attempts for eighty-eight yards.

"To be a good quarterback, you have to do that," Young said. "Joe's obviously been spectacular at it for years, and it's something I just hope has
rubbed off."

* * *

Any questions about Montana's gimpy groin or possible rust from his
shortened participation in the final weeks of the regular season were answered
immediately once the 49ers hit the Santa Clara practice field in preparation
for their divisional round game with Washington.

"Joe Montana on Thursday looked as sharp as I've ever seen him," linebacker Matt Millen said. "In fact, after one play in practice I kind of harked back to last year. That's what it looked like to me. There were times last year when there would be not incompletions in practice. It was scary. It was one of those times when you think, 'Geez, save it for the weekend.'"

Montana—who days earlier had been named the NFL's Most Valuable Player for the second consecutive season—could spare it.

Scoring on their first possession of the game, Washington grabbed a 7–0 lead that Montana's near-flawless passing quickly made vanish. Montana responded with back-to-back lengthy touchdown drives, the second of which was capped off by a touchdown pass to Rice, just beyond the fingertips of All-Pro cornerback Darrell Green. The next series, although pinned deep in his own territory, Montana again baffled the Washington defense. Twice while on the run he hit Roger Craig and Brent Jones for long gains. Next, Montana fired a dart across the middle to Mike Sherrard, his third touchdown pass of the half.

"I knew we should have kidnapped the sucker," Redskins defensive coordinator Richie Petitbon said. "That was my first plan, and no one wanted to go along with it."

Petitbon did, albeit briefly, see his wish of Montana disappearing come true. Just before halftime, with San Francisco targeting their fourth touchdown in four offensive possessions, Redskins defensive lineman Jumpy Geathers pounded Montana underneath the jaw at the end of a pass play. For several seconds—far too long in the minds of the enormous Bay Area crowd—Montana remained doubled over on the ground before hobbling over to the sidelines. Young spelled him for the final play of the first half, which encouraged the Redskins as they headed into the locker room.

"When I saw Steve Young come in, I thought we had a chance," said Geathers. "But Montana came back like Superman."

Montana returned to the field for the entire second half, an uneventful thirty minutes of football, aside from the 49ers 295-pound defensive tackle Michael Carter intercepting a pass and lumbering sixty-one yards for a touchdown late in the fourth quarter.

"We all thank Michael for running time off the clock," Montana joked.

The 28–10 playoff victory returned San Francisco to their seemingly annual spot in the NFC Championship Game, remarkably their sixth appearance in ten seasons. Just as familiar as that gateway to the Super Bowl was the 49ers' opponent, the New York Giants. The teams' four playoff contests during the 1980s had forged a Giants–49ers rivalry that only intensified with the two Monday night classics at Candlestick Park, the most recent being San Francisco's 7–3 victory seven weeks earlier.

"I think we realized there would be a good chance that we would [play them again], yes," Seifert said. "They're going to come out here with a vendetta, and at the same time I think we're going to be a determined club, too."

Matching levels of determination notwithstanding, experts and oddsmakers saw the game as overwhelmingly in San Francisco's favor. Not only were the two-time defending Super Bowl champions at home—where they were 3–0 in NFC title games—but the Giants' already limited offense was far more handicapped than it had been in the December loss, when they scored just three points. Injuries sidelined former Super Bowl MVP quarterback Phil Simms and running back Rodney Hampton.

Even Montana's battle with the flu—in addition to missing the team's final full practice, he was sent home by team doctors prior to a Saturday morning walk-through—was not considered nearly enough to keep the Giants in contention.

"Let's get something straight. This San Francisco team, like four others before it, is phenomenal," the *Washington Post's* Michael Wilbon wrote. "Assuming Montana isn't flat on his back with the flu Sunday, the New York Giants won't come within twenty. This is no slap at the Giants, a fine team that is capable of beating almost anybody as long as LT and Pepper and Carl Banks line up. But in these Niners, we are watching the Yankees of the 1920s–'30s, and Joe Montana is Babe Ruth."

Even the normally modest and cautiously optimistic Montana reveled in the thought of a victory.

"We are very close to a goal and dream that we set last year after the Super Bowl; that is very exciting," he said. "To win three straight Super Bowls would be a tremendous achievement. But really, whoever wins this game goes to this year's Super Bowl. And to me, that is exciting enough."

As was the case in their regular season showdown, the two defenses dominated the first half of the NFC Championship Game. And although Montana completed seventeen of his first twenty-one pass attempts, the Giants pass rush repeatedly forced him to unload the ball early. At one point just before halftime, Leonard Marshall sacked Montana, who uncharacteristically slammed the football to the ground and screamed out in anger.

"We put a lot of pounding on him, and you could tell he was getting frustrated," Taylor said.

"After the second series, when he left from under center, he was already passive, you could see it," added Giants safety Dave Duerson. "He was expecting to get hit. Even when he handed off, he was flinching."

Through the first half, each offense managed just a pair of field goals, but on the 49ers' first offensive snap after halftime, Montana seemingly blew the game wide open with a sixty-one-yard touchdown pass to John Taylor. The Giants clamped down on the 49ers passing game, however, chipped away at the lead via a field goal, and with less than ten minutes remaining in the game, they trailed just 13–9.

Then, on a third down inside 49ers territory, Montana escaped the pocket, paused near the sideline, and cocked his arm to heave a deep pass for Rice, who had shed his coverage. But at the last moment, with one of NFL history's most indelible hits, Giants defensive end Leonard Marshall plowed into Montana at full speed, just before the pass was released.

"We pushed everyone inside to allow Joe to roll out," Steve Wallace explained. "But Joe was naked out there. He got by the first couple of guys, but a split-second later, he got hit from the back."

"Blind side," Marshall explained. "He never had a chance. He sort of cringed. I knew he was hurt."

So did every one in Candlestick Park, including Young who sprinted onto the field and knelt down next to a doubled-over, groggy Montana.

"I just wanted to make sure he was OK," Young said. "It looked worse than normal."

The petrified home crowd watched as team doctor Michael Dillingham, three trainers, and Ronnie Lott quickly joined the consultation. They all hovered over Montana, who rolled over onto his back and lay on the ground.

Soon, Montana was able to stand, and the Candlestick crowd erupted as he rose. But as he wobbled to the sidelines, he looked dazed.

Meanwhile, Marshall's sack of Montana had knocked the football far downfield, where Wallace had recovered the fumble, maintaining possession. Following the third-down play, San Francisco punted, and, aided by a brilliant fake punt, the Giants moved three points closer with yet another field goal.

But the action along the home team's sideline had attracted just as much attention from the fans and the millions watching on television as the game on the field. While Steve Young hastily warmed his throwing arm, a cadre of doctors, trainers, and paramedics—"thirteen very concerned people," the *San Francisco Chronicle* reported—surrounded a stationary Montana, who remained frozen on a wooden bench.

"The report we get on Montana is that the doctors want him to stay right where he is," Pat Summerall informed CBS's viewing audience. "Because the report from the 49ers bench is that *everything* hurts."

Despite the gruesome hit and the sight of the franchise's cornerstone sitting motionless, the 49ers were less than six minutes away from surviving a Giants comeback and advancing to Super Bowl XXV. Ahead 13–12 and in possession of the football, Young's task was simple: "All I had to do was get a couple of first downs: I just had to play quarterback. Just a couple of first downs."

49ers fans may have been terrified at Montana's absence, but seeing Young take his place was actually a greater concern for the Giants defense.

"We were so used to Montana, having watched so much film of him and having played so much against him, that when Young came in late in the game, he was a real problem," Giants safety Greg Jackson said. "He is so mobile back there that you never can let him out of your sight. He worried me."

Aware that the Giants defensive strategy shifted when Young took the field, offensive coordinator Mike Holmgren tried to catch the New York defense off guard. Following a Roger Craig run that nearly resulted in a fumble, Young connected with tight end Brent Jones on a deep pass over the middle that netted twenty-five yards.

"Once we got to midfield, it was down to the clock," Young said. "I thought we were in really good position."

All the 49ers had to do was hold onto the ball. They couldn't.

With 2:41 remaining, Young handed off to Craig, who had carried the ball on each of the previous two plays. The thirty-year-old, hampered by injuries all season, charged into the middle of the line, where nose tackle Erik Howard's helmet knocked the football out of his hands and into the arms of Lawrence Taylor.

While Montana rose to his feet and delicately roamed the 49ers sidelines, a gutsy effort by quarterback Jeff Hostetler—another perpetual backup who had been thrust into the starter's job five weeks earlier—drove the Giants thirty-two yards into position for the winning field goal attempt. On the game's final play, kicker Matt Bahr nailed a forty-two-yarder that simultaneously completed an astonishing win and ended San Francisco's chance at a third consecutive Super Bowl berth.

"I've never heard this locker room quieter than it was after the game," linebacker Mike Walter said. "The only noise in here was the CBS crew whispering as they set up their cameras. We were that close. . . . When you're that close, you go back and look at every play where they got one more yard than they should have."

Outside of the 49ers locker room, however, there was plenty of noise from reporters asking Ronnie Lott, Matt Millen, Jerry Rice, Roger Craig, George Seifert, and countless others about missing out on the three-peat.

"This type of loss really hurts now," said Seifert, "but, in the next few days, I think we'll be very proud of this team . . . when the shock wears off."

Next, the press's attention turned to Montana's injury.

Given the specifics of Marshall's sack—a torpedoing hit into the quarterback's surgically repaired spine—49ers team doctor Michael Dillingham was the first person they cornered.

"Nothing, nothing, nothing," said Dillingham, anticipating such questions.

Montana's chest and hand, however, did suffer damage. He had broken the fifth metacarpal (just below the pinkie finger) on his throwing hand and bruised his sternum, diaphragm, and stomach.

"New X-rays will be taken (Monday) morning," Dillingham said in a press release. "The final plan for treatment (an operation is possible) will be determined later Monday or Tuesday. . . . If we had won today, Joe would not have been able to play in next week's Super Bowl."

Montana himself did not speak in front of the enormous postgame press gaggle. Instead, he issued a written statement through the 49ers public relations department.

"I still don't know what happened. I don't want to sound like a coach, but I have to look at the video. I don't think it was the initial hit. I think it was the ground. . . . I'm still having a tough time breathing deeply."

Eventually, the locker room cleared out, and Montana, his father, and a security guard unsuccessfully tried to sneak past the press into the team parking lot. In the adjacent tunnel, a few reporters spotted him, quickly rushed over, and badgered Montana about the hit and his injuries. Far more coherent than he had appeared on the sidelines hours earlier, Montana continued along his path, cryptically answering their questions.

"By then, Montana was at the end of the tunnel that leads away from the 49ers' locker room, a few steps away from the bullpen of the San Francisco Giants," the *San Francisco Chronicle*'s Ron Thomas wrote. "When he reached the top of the steps, his wife, Jennifer, kissed his cheek and hugged him. Montana smiled at her. Then he walked around to the passenger side of a white Range Rover, a security guard opened the door, and Montana sat down in the passenger's seat. Jennifer drove him away."

Never again would Joe Montana exit Candlestick Park as the starting quarterback of the San Francisco 49ers.

8

A Year Early

Things wouldn't be normal if they weren't bizarre.

—Steve Young, December 1991

Two days removed from the brutal hit delivered by the Giants Leonard Marshall, Joe Montana underwent surgery on his broken right hand. The hour-long procedure, performed by Dr. Michael Dillingham, was to insert two screws into Montana's fractured metacarpal. The screws were to be taken out in March, and after a month of rest and recovery, he would be allowed to resume throwing a football.

Also informed that the injury to his chest and sternum was "nothing major," Montana left Sequoia Hospital in Redwood City in good spirits.

"I actually feel a little better, now that I'm out of the hospital," he said. "The doctors told me the operation was successful. . . . I told them if they made any mistakes, to curl it in so I can still grip a golf club."

But wrapping his hands around a driver or seven-iron wasn't in Montana's immediate future: due to the surgery, he withdrew from playing in early February's AT&T Pebble Beach Pro-Am. Steve Young took his spot that week on the Monterey Peninsula. Even in the offseason, away from the game of football, Young was Montana's stand-in.

Playing alongside fellow Mormon and Brigham Young University Cougar Johnny Miller, Young laced a perfect tee shot down Spyglass Hill's seventh fairway. The 255-yard drive put him in great position to birdie the par-five, slight dogleg right.

Next, Miller approached the tee box and announced to Young and the small gallery, "Now I'll show you how Joe Montana would do it."

The forty-three-year-old former U.S. and British Open champion, who had already won the annual Pebble Beach tournament twice, blasted his tee shot twenty-five yards past Young.

"I guess I got him where it hurts," Miller joked.

Although Miller's ribbing was certainly good-natured, Young couldn't have laughed too hard. He had just finished a season in which he posted new career lows for starts, attempts, completions, and touchdown passes.

And the events in the fourth quarter of the NFC Championship Game loss to the Giants devastated Young: due to Montana's injuries, if the 49ers had not frittered away their last-minute lead, Young would have started Super Bowl XXV against Buffalo the following week in Tampa.

In the parking lot of Candlestick Park, hours after Matt Bahr's field goal ended the 49ers bid for a three-peat, Young asked his agent Leigh Steinberg, "Won't the world cut me some slack?"

"I think that was the worst thing I ever saw Steve go through," Young's teammate and close friend Harris Barton said the next summer.

For Young, the more disheartening news was that Montana was expected to make a full recovery from his relatively minor injuries: a broken bone in the hand carried far less concern than his injured spine or achy elbow.

During that spring of 1991, Young and Steinberg mulled over their options.

A restricted free agent, Young was allowed to sign with any team he wanted, but the 49ers had the right to match any offer and retain him outright. If the 49ers opted not to match the offer, Young's new team would have to send San Francisco two first-round draft choices.

"We really don't have to let him go," Carmen Policy said. "But I'm sure Eddie [DeBartolo Jr.] won't be unreasonable. If it became a negative situation, I'm sure we'd see what we could do to accommodate him."

In late February the press jumped on a rumor that the 49ers were discussing a trade with the Patriots. Young's potential return to his New England roots gave the story credibility until 49ers vice president John McVay, Eddie DeBartolo, and George Seifert vehemently denied the report.

Steinberg quickly pointed out that a trade was impossible. As a restricted free agent, Young technically wasn't the 49ers property.

A month later reports surfaced that Young had visited both the Los Angeles Raiders and San Diego Chargers, but no formal negotiations ever took place.

"Leigh has asked if we're interested, and I've told him we don't have enough to give up to get him," Chargers general manager Bobby Beathard said. "We would have to tear our team apart if we ever did, and I don't seriously believe the 49ers are going to trade him. . . . It will never happen. . . . The 49ers need Steve Young, so I don't think there is anything going on there. There's nothing to get started if they aren't going to trade him."

With every other NFL team similarly scared off by the heavy compensation they would have to pay the 49ers, Young received no offers, and in early May he agreed to a two-year, $4.5 million deal with San Francisco.

"The bottom line is they expect me to play, and I expect to play," Young said at a press conference. "I didn't sign to sit down. We'll work out the ins and outs. This probably is a little bit of a risk, but I rolled the dice on this. We'll just work it out as it goes."

Despite encouragement from his head coach—"George's mind-set was that he needed both [of us]"—Seifert still had to issue one caveat.

"Don't read into this that the job is open," he said. "Joe Montana is our starting quarterback."

Seifert could afford to be confident in that statement: by training camp, Montana, the league's reigning two-time Most Valuable Player was fully recovered from his injuries, telling reporters after the 49ers first preseason game, "I'm good as new."

In that brief exhibition appearance against the Raiders, Montana completed five of six passes, but the greater challenge was taking the game seriously: "I might laugh when I look across the line," he told the press.

The previous winter, every NFL franchise had been required to submit a list of twenty under-contract players whom they would not protect from becoming unrestricted free agents: through the end of March, any other franchise could sign these free agents and not be forced to pay the player's previous team any compensation.

Two names put on the San Francisco's so-called "Plan B" free agent list were key pieces of the 49ers dynasty: Ronnie Lott, who turned thirty-two that spring and had missed significant portions of the previous two seasons with ankle and knee injuries; and twenty-nine-year-old Roger Craig, the feature back who nursed a sore knee throughout 1990, statistically the worst year of his career. Both signed with the Raiders, a club that also lured longtime 49er linebacker Riki Ellison to Los Angeles the previous offseason.

"Bill [Walsh] always had the adage, 'Get rid of a player a year early rather than a year late,'" Carmen Policy later said.

Although he was no longer with the 49ers, Walsh's managerial style had trickled down to the rest of the front office.

"Players, unfortunately, are going to come and go," Montana said in May. "Some will be closer to you than others, like Ronnie and Roger were. You'll miss them; they were definitely a major part of the team. But that's all part of the game. Hopefully, it all works out best for everybody."

The day after defeating Craig and Lott's Raiders in Los Angeles, the 49ers began on a much more exhaustive road trip. As they had two of the previous three seasons (the 1988 visit to London and the 1989 trip to Tokyo), San Francisco would once again participate in the NFL's prolonged, seemingly futile experiment: American football catching on outside of America.

A sixteen-hour flight across fifty-six hundred miles and nine time zones dropped the 49ers in Berlin, Germany, where five days later they played the Chicago Bears in Olympic Stadium, the site of Jesse Owens's famed performance in 1936.

"Last year we didn't play overseas, and we didn't win the Super Bowl," Tom Rathman said. "The two times we played overseas, we won Super Bowls. Maybe it's a good omen."

East German figure skating gold medalist Katarina Witt conducted the pregame coin toss, and from there the 66,876 fans in attendance—some of whom curiously sampled "original Amerikanische chicken wings mit barbecue sauce" in the concession stands—witnessed a one-sided contest as the 49ers stomped Chicago. Both Montana and Young threw touchdown passes in the 21–7 victory.

But soon it became clear that, contrary to Tom Rathman's logic, the trip was not "a good omen."

Home from Germany, Montana and the 49ers returned to the Rocklin County practice field to continue the preseason and prepare for their next exhibition against Denver.

"I started to throw again, and I came and threw one post down the field, and I felt it," Montana later said.

What Montana felt after releasing the forty-yard pass was a slight pain in his throwing elbow, the same throwing elbow that had been operated on in 1988 and had periodically nagged him ever since.

"It had been sore a little bit, and I don't know why it happened right at that point. But on one throw I felt it go. I didn't believe it, so I threw another one."

The 49ers front office and coaching staff were equally unconcerned by the issue, but as a precaution, Montana sat out the next preseason game. No mention of the elbow ailment was released to the press. Everyone simply assumed that rest, not injury, was the reason the thirty-five-year-old sat: the game in Denver was the 49ers' second in four days and third in twelve.

Young took on his stand-in role, one that had become almost routine for the previous four preseasons.

"Young is the perfect exhibition season player," the *San Francisco Chronicle*'s C. W. Nevius wrote in the next morning's edition. "Opposing teams should hire him to go from city to city to take a few snaps and break up the monotony of penalty flags."

"Hey, I'm Mr. July," Young added.

Young lived up to those relatively low expectations, throwing a first-quarter touchdown pass to Jerry Rice and completing nine of his twelve attempts in an easy 24–6 49ers win.

"There was a time, when I felt like I had to prove something on every play. Now I'm comfortable," he said. "It's weird but despite it all, I still think I can help. If it was anyone else (but Montana), I feel like I could work my way in."

Seifert gave his players a well-deserved break, then resumed practice the next morning. Montana took another day off, then joined his teammates on Saturday, only to be sent right back to the sideline.

"Just watching him work, you could see he had lost a little zing," Seifert said. "As to when he will return, I'm not sure. We'll monitor the situation on a daily basis."

Acknowledging Montana's depleted arm strength and the uncertainty over his return let the cat out of the bag, and the troublesome elbow became a huge scoop for the press. Reporters hounded Montana, Seifert, and everyone else about the quarterback's health.

"It's just sore from throwing so much," Montana said. "There's no swelling or anything. As a matter of fact, I was all set to practice when they told me to sit this one out. I didn't argue."

Two days later, Montana started throwing again, but the elbow "flared up a little bit," and he spent another practice in the locker room.

"The trainers and doctors are of the opinions that it's not going to be an ongoing thing," Seifert said, "It's just a matter of getting it over with now."

But the start of the regular season was now just three weeks away. Little practice for Montana and ongoing questions about his injury—recently diagnosed as tendinitis—led to speculation that Young would be under center for the 49ers cross-country road trip to face the defending Super Bowl champion New York Giants.

"[Seifert] said he is not going to have a controversy at all but would look to keep us both sharp," Young said. "I don't know how he's going to do it, but I'm going to be much more involved throughout the season."

When told of Young's statement, Montana called the comments "wishful thinking."

"That's not what was said to me," he remarked. "Reality sometimes is hard for people to grasp. I can understand [Young] wants to play, but that's the way it is here. He had his choice [to leave]."

For nearly three years, George Seifert had tried desperately to avoid the friction and confusion his predecessor, Bill Walsh, had brought to the organization by committing to two quarterbacks. Nevertheless, the issue inevitably resurfaced, then mushroomed toward the end of August.

The 49ers fourth preseason game was at home against San Diego. Despite having not practiced for more than a week and a half, Montana received a cortisone shot in the elbow, then took the field an hour before kickoff to test his arm in an attempt to play. To the delight of the still-arriving crowd at Candlestick, he easily fired twenty-yard passes to a teammate. Upon increasing the distance, however, Montana's passes floated rather than soared, and he quickly ceased throwing.

"And then he did the most curious thing," the *San Francisco Chronicle*'s Lowell Cohn narrated. "He placed his right arm across his stomach—rested it on his belt—and he kept it in that strange position while the other quarterbacks went on with their business. Standing there, removed from the action, Montana was just another injured athlete, a man protecting a wounded arm."

The coaching staff declared him inactive, but remained confident that he was healthy.

"If it was two weeks from now, the opening game, Joe would have played," offensive coordinator Mike Holmgren said. "We might be a little overconservative, but that's OK."

In Montana's place, Young completed eighteen of his twenty-five attempts for 227 yards and a touchdown pass to John Taylor. He also singlehandedly gave the 49ers a first-quarter lead they would never relinquish. On a third-and-long just past midfield, Young scrambled away from pressure, avoided one tackle, broke another, then carried two San Diego defenders on his back as he crossed the goal line for a spectacular forty-seven-yard touchdown run. Later on, in the third period, Young led the 49ers on an eighteen-play, eighty-four-yard drive that ran nearly thirteen minutes off the clock.

"The coach loves to see that kind of thing," Young said. "I knew I was going to start after Joe warmed up and he couldn't go. I just hope in a good way both Joe and I can help the team win the Super Bowl. I know what my role is."

Montana re-tested his elbow two days after the 49ers win over San Diego, but again felt pain and left the field to undergo an MRI: Coach Seifert was informed that the cortisone shot, not the elbow itself, had caused the pain, and there was no ligament damage. Rest, nothing else, was the prescription.

"We're not trying to hide anything," Seifert said. "The doctor never said to me that it's going to be more than something we've just got to get through."

But during its broadcast of the 49ers final preseason game against Seattle, NBC reported that the injury to Montana's elbow was far more severe than the front office admitted. Ahmad Rashad informed viewers that Montana had told him before kickoff that there was a tear in his ligament.

"They're still evaluating it. The doctors have to do a further read because they were primarily looking for ligament damage," Seifert explained later that evening. "As far as it being a serious type of tendon tear, we don't know yet. Our doctors haven't totally evaluated that."

On the sidelines and not in uniform for the exhibition in Seattle, Montana watched Young torch the Seahawks for 165 yards: only one of his eleven passes was incomplete. San Francisco won the game 28–16, finishing their first undefeated preseason in thirty-seven years.

"You only get better if you play as much as I've been," Young said. "I'm ready. But it's just a matter of time before Joe gets healthy. It could be five days or it could be longer."

It would, in fact, be longer. Much longer.

Neither rest, cortisone shots, or even acupuncture could produce any improvement in Montana's elbow. The injury—confirmed by orthopedist Dr. Michael Dillingham as medial epicondylitis, or "golfer's elbow"—finally forced the 49ers to place Montana on the injured reserve list. Per NFL regulations, regardless of any miraculous, seemingly overnight recovery—similar to the one he experienced in 1986—that may occur, Montana would not be allowed to play the first four games of the season.

"We didn't want to force ourselves into a situation where, after a couple of weeks or three weeks, we might press the issue and possibly reinjure Joe's arm," Seifert told the press. "We had to weigh what would happen in two or three weeks if all of a sudden he says he feels super. But even then the doctors have said, 'Even when you feel good, the wise thing is to take another week.' . . . In the opinion of the doctors, this is the length of time we will need for this to become rested and not become an ongoing problem."

Montana, the coaching staff, and fans hoped for his return on September 29, coincidently the day that the 49ers were scheduled to visit Lott, Craig, and the Los Angeles Raiders.

"I don't think I'm being overly optimistic, we have to wait and see, but that's what we're led to believe at this time," Seifert said. "We're not going to force the issue but that's the return date."

Although frustrated at missing his first season-opening start in more than a decade, Montana also remained optimistic when approached by reporters. The pain was "subsiding," in his words, and—based on his extraordinarily fast recovery from back surgery five years earlier—he fully expected to return to the starter's job within a month.

"I don't see why not. I've been through that once before."

Seifert, however, chose not to think that far ahead.

"I just don't want to get into that aspect of it," Seifert said. "Let's just let Steve play quarterback, that's my emotion on the thing. Let him play, let him do his thing, and when we get to that point, hopefully everybody will be saying they're both so great, 'What the hell are you going to do, George?'"

* * *

The 49ers 1991 season began with great promise. In an NFC Championship Game rematch with the New York Giants, Young and Rice connected on a seventy-three-yard touchdown pass to give the 49ers an early advantage in the Meadowlands. But the Giants adjusted. With their roles reversed and Montana signaling in the plays—his elbow was healthy enough at least for that duty—Young completed just twelve passes, missed several wide-open receivers, and was intercepted at a critical moment in the third quarter.

"They really dogged the outside receivers with double coverage," Young said.

In the fourth quarter, San Francisco trailed by only six points and, mixing up runs and passes, Young drove the offense forty-two yards for a go-ahead score. His five-yard touchdown run put the team ahead 14–13. But during a painfully familiar episode, the Giants controlled the clock, chipped away at the defense, and in the final seconds won the game on a Matt Bahr field goal.

"That's twice in a row they've beaten us like this. It's very frustrating," Young admitted. "There's such a premium on winning, and we didn't win. . . . I take the experience with me, but not much else."

Whatever else Young took home with him from East Rutherford boosted his play. In the home opener against San Diego, Young was virtually flawless, setting new career highs for completions (twenty-six), attempts (thirty-six), and yards (348). Three touchdown passes in the span of less than six minutes overcame a small deficit, and San Francisco bested the Chargers 34–14.

But one outstanding performance didn't satisfy the eager-to-please, determined quarterback. After four seasons in San Francisco, Young knew the standard for quarterback play had been set much higher.

"I'd like him to enjoy it a little more," Mike Holmgren remarked. "He's waited a long time for this."

"Everybody wants me to laugh," Young said. "I'm thinking, 'Hey, I gotta work.'"

San Francisco split the next two games, losing by a field goal in Minnesota, then thumping the rival Rams back at Candlestick. During those two weeks, Young continued to shine, completing over two-thirds of his attempts for four touchdowns against just one interception.

"He really has played well," Holmgren said after the win over the Rams. "His production has been good, and he's made good decisions. He's running at good times, not like his first year, when he would take off and run right away."

Everyone was pleased with Young's noticeable progress; everyone except Joe Montana.

"Steve is on a big push for himself," Montana told the *Washington Post* in early September. "And anytime you have a competition, there is always that certain amount of animosity towards each other. I can say we have only a working relationship. That's all it is. After that, he's on my team, but as far as I'm concerned, he's part of the opposition. He wants what I have, and I have to approach it that way. There is no other way to deal with it."

Still, Young was merely the symbol of Montana's angst, not necessarily the cause. More than anything, Montana simply hated not playing; *who* was playing in his place was secondary.

"I don't really care who's behind me," Montana said twenty years later. "If you're not playing well, somebody's going to take your position. So it doesn't matter whether it was Steve Young, Steve Bono, Steve DeBerg, it didn't matter. The biggest competitor I had is with myself. So I didn't really care whether it was Steve Young or not."

But his injured elbow rendered Montana unable to even practice, let alone play in a game. The doctors' recommendation that he rest the elbow prevented him from competing with the person he always considered his chief rival: himself.

"I think Sundays are the toughest for me," he said. "Everybody can miss practice—and they don't mind doing it—but when it comes to Sunday and the game is being played, that's the toughest part. It would almost be better if I had an injury where I couldn't move around. That would be better, but that's not the case."

The greatest quarterback of his, or perhaps any, era now had to prove his worth to the coaches, the media, and the fans. Just the thought of having to audition for *his* job—which he had not willingly abdicated—infuriated the normally placid Montana.

"Inside when things are going tough, I get mad, and it makes me work harder and get tougher," he said. "All I know is that I'm not ready to leave the game or lose the starting job. I'm mad right now, you know? I'm mad because for all that I think I've done, I have to prove that I still belong out there on the field. The best thing for me to do now is to get mad at everything. It gets me going. It fires me up. It's unfortunate that it has to happen that way, but maybe it's better for me at this point in my career."

As Montana stewed on the sidelines and inside the training room, the 49ers carried on without their senior-most member. Next on the schedule was another game against Ronnie Lott and Roger Craig's Los Angeles Raiders, and as awkward as their preseason game may have been, the rematch was far more unsettling.

Early in the first period, San Francisco reached the Raiders 1-yard line, but a false start penalty killed the drive, and they settled for a field goal. From that point the offense went silent. Clamped down by a secondary equipped with Lott's intimate knowledge of their system, 49ers wide receivers were limited to just seven receptions. Young also tossed a pair of costly interceptions, the second of which was a failed attempt to throw the ball away. The careless pass landed in the arms of Raider Howie Long, whom Young tackled by driving his shoulder into the 275-pound defensive end's thigh.

"He's got a big heart. I think he's going to be dead in three years, but I really like the kid," Long said. "He is one of the most fearless SOBs I've ever seen. He throws his (stuff) around out there like there's no tomorrow. The problem is, he ain't gonna be around long. I admire the hell out of him. But maybe he needs to sit in the pocket a little more. . . . He doesn't go out of bounds. He doesn't slide. I talked to him about it about three years ago. I said, 'You gotta stop that.'"

Late in the game, trailing 12–6, the 49ers forced a punt, giving their offense one last shot at victory. Young completed consecutive passes to Rice, Taylor, and Rathman, reaching the Raiders 22-yard line. But his next three passes fell incomplete. As quickly as he stirred up memories of Montana Magic, they vanished.

"You can't buy it," Lott told the press afterward. "Anyone who could buy it would make a lot of money. It's unfair to put those two in the same situation. No one will be like number 16."

Lott's strange day playing against his former teammates—"those are guys I respect, and I always will; I'm really glad it's over with"—became even stranger after the game.

In the 49ers locker room, All-Pro defensive end Charles Haley went "berserk," after the game: both Lott and Craig had been mentors to Haley as a young player, and he took the loss especially hard.

Haley—dehydrated from an extremely humid day in Los Angeles—pulled an IV needle out of his arm, punched a wall, tried to punch Seifert, and then directed his rage at Young, shouting, "I could have fucking won that game in my sleep. . . . You're a motherfucking pussy faggot quarterback! A motherfucking pussy faggot with no balls."

"As the blood gushed from his arm," sports author Jeff Pearlman wrote in his 2008 book *Boys Will Be Boys*, "Haley charged toward Young, arms flailing, legs kicking."

Haley's tirade came to an end only when retired 49ers linebacker-turned-member-of-the-front-office Keena Turner convinced Lott to leave the Raiders locker room (wearing just a towel) to console his former teammate.

"We weren't in the locker room when all this happened," *San Jose Mercury News* reporter Ann Killion recalled years later. "I remember walking into the locker room and—it was a really hot day—Steve was standing in front of this giant, old-fashioned industrial-sized fan that was in the locker room, and he was just standing there letting it blow on him. And whenever I think about that Charles Haley thing. . . . I always think of [Young] standing in front of that fan like trying to cool down and gain his composure. It was kind of a sad little scene."

Just as the proud franchise's tailspin spiraled even further out of control, hope slowly began returning to the Bay Area. Less than twenty-four hours after the loss, Montana threw for the first time in six weeks. Under Dr. Dillingham's supervision, Montana—who said he was too excited to sleep the previous night—tossed a football to conditioning coach Jerry Attaway.

"I threw about forty passes today," Montana informed reporters, all of whom were barred from the workout. "It was only about ten minutes. I'll probably step it up to fifty or sixty tomorrow. I thought I threw with pretty good velocity, but it wasn't anywhere near as hard as I can throw. I'll also try to step up the distance. I was throwing about twenty-five yards today."

"I think if everything goes OK this week, it would be realistic for me to expect to suit up for the next game," he added. "I don't know how comfortable George would feel playing me. How I look in practice probably will determine that."

Pleased by his progress, Montana cautioned the press about his potential return to the struggling team.

"I don't think I'm the savior by any means."

Fans and even some teammates and coaches disagreed.

"What's wrong with us? I could say," one assistant admitted, "but I'm not going to; it would get me into too much trouble."

Thousands, if not millions, craved Montana's return and repeatedly offered him unsolicited assistance.

"[A fan] wrote and said he'd had the same (elbow) problem I did," Montana said. "Then he went out and somehow got bitten by these bees. Then he got a shot for the bee stings, I think. And the pain went away."

Montana may have been desperate to recover—"You just wish it would get worse or get better. The hell is being in the middle, where you don't know"—but he wasn't that desperate. He also chose not to apply the mudpacks a fan mailed to the team's headquarters or the "healing hands" cloths that evangelists sent to him. And he politely ignored one well-meaning woman's advice.

"She said ice was bad, that the worst thing I could do was put ice on my elbow," Montana said while chuckling. "I put ice on it two or three times a day."

Soothed by ice following his Monday workout, Montana threw approximately fifty more passes the next day, rested on Wednesday, then returned to the practice field the following day, gradually increasing the distance. But on Saturday, attempting thirty-five-yard throws, he felt tremendous pain in the elbow—later compared to "a key twisting into flesh"—and an unidentified 49ers official told reporters that "surgery is now a very strong possibility."

"We got lulled into a sense of euphoria," Carmen Policy told the press. "Maybe he did feel as good as he said he did, (but) Joe's situation was not as positive as we'd have liked it to be after Saturday."

Seeking a second then a third medical opinion, Joe and Jennifer met with elbow specialists Dr. James Bennett in Houston, Texas, and Dr. Ben Kibler in Lexington, Kentucky. Both advised surgery to repair a torn pronator teres tendon. The next day, at the Stanford University Medical Center, Dr. Dillingham drilled holes into Montana's elbow and sutured the common flexor tendon back to the bone: until the surgery, Montana's doctors did not know that the tendon had been completely torn off the bone. A similar surgery had been performed eight years earlier on Pittsburgh Steelers quarterback Terry Bradshaw, who at the time was also thirty-five years old and the only other quarterback to start and win four Super Bowls.

"I think he's an extremely professional man," Dillingham said. "His feeling is that he's done the thing to allow him to play next year. He knew he couldn't play this year, so he's taken a surgical risk. He feels he's doing the right thing."

Not everyone was as encouraged.

"Personally, I didn't think he'd ever play again," Seifert admitted twenty years later. "But it was not like, 'My God!' The team was always prepared for that, whether it be Bill Walsh leaving or any one coach or any one player. From Day One, part of our foundation was whoever steps up now, the expectations are to fulfill what had been established prior to that person."

* * *

Fortunately for the 49ers front office, all the drama surrounding Montana—the return to the practice field, aggravating the elbow, seeking multiple medical opinions, and ultimately the surgery—occurred during the team's bye week.

But when Montana's state of elbow limbo finally came to an end and season-ending surgery was announced, the attention shifted back to the 49ers active roster and, specifically, Young.

Five games into the 1991 season, Young—a week shy of his thirtieth birthday—had already made more starts than at any other point in his San Francisco career. Still, the stored up hunger and impatience after four years on the sidelines continued to prevent Young from enjoying himself. Even Montana's place on the inactive roster—the result of his lingering elbow injury—couldn't bring Young peace of mind.

"Anyone who's been around the 49ers this season has witnessed a remarkable change in Young," Lowell Cohn wrote. "In all other seasons, he seemed carefree, would hang around the locker room talking with teammates and media. This season, he has the furrowed brow, the worried look. He says it's because he has to study harder now that he's the starter, although in the past when he was the second banana, he said he prepared just the same as if he were starting. Many believe Young changed because the pressure of starting and being measured against Montana was making him edgy. One 49er veteran said, 'He's made his bed, and now he has to sleep in it.'"

The day after Montana re-injured the elbow, however, Cohn and others noticed an instant turnaround in Young's demeanor.

"He came into the 49ers' locker room after practice yesterday afternoon, and he acted like a man who'd had a weight lifted off his shoulders," Cohn wrote in early October. "He was smiling so broadly, the lights in the room appeared to gleam off his teeth."

Young's smile wouldn't last for long.

That Sunday against the Falcons the host 49ers fell behind 14–0 within five minutes of the opening kickoff. But behind Young, who ran for one score and threw long touchdown passes to Rice and Taylor, they charged back into contention, tying the game at 20 just after halftime.

Not even a hundred-yard kickoff return by Atlanta's Deion Sanders—perhaps fired up by a pregame audience with rap superstar M. C. Hammer, who gave the Falcons locker room a sneak preview of his new single "2 Legit 2 Quit"—could slow the 49ers momentum. Early in the final period, Young vacated the pocket, scrambled six yards to the tip of the goal line, then soared over two defenders, landing face-first for a touchdown run that gave the 49ers a 34–33 edge. The crowd at Candlestick started chanting his name.

"I thought it was going to be the play of the game," tackle Steve Wallace said.

A field goal by Norm Johnson snatched the lead right back for Atlanta, but more than a quarter remained. Young then marched the 49ers to the Atlanta 20-yard line, and from there he could sense victory.

"I thought we had the game won," he said. "Then we lost nine yards on the next play, and we had to throw."

Following Harry Sydney's negative run, Young could not find an open receiver, and with the pass rush bearing down on him, he simply flicked a pass near tight end Jamie Williams. The referees deemed the throw intentional grounding, resulting in a ten-yard penalty and a loss of down.

"So I threw it to the middle of the field toward Jamie and a few other people, not to the side where there was nobody. But we haven't gotten a call all year."

Now faced with a third-and-29 and out of Mike Cofer's field goal range, Young "had to take the chance and gamble."

That gamble resulted in an underthrown pass to Taylor, which was intercepted by Tim McKyer, the former 49er whom Rice had burned for a fifty-seven-yard touchdown earlier in the game. The 49ers defense kept Atlanta out of the end zone, and after another field goal increased the Falcons lead to five points, San Francisco still had one last opportunity. But in the final minute, the 49ers could not cross midfield, and on fourth down Young threw another interception, his third of the day.

"I don't think that the 49ers are what they were," Falcons linebacker Scott Case said in the winning team's locker room. "I'm just glad Joe Montana didn't come on the field at the end."

"We've got to let the Joe Montana thing get away from us. Let it lie," 49ers guard Roy Foster told reporters afterward. "We've got to understand that we've got a quarterback who's capable."

Despite the loss, Young posted tremendous statistics, completing twenty-two passes for 348 yards and two touchdowns. But even more so than the three interceptions or the costly intentional grounding penalty, what concerned the 49ers coaching staff most was Young's penchant for running with a style that Seifert jokingly compared to Bronco Nagurski's.

"There's a concern about it—at the same time that's the way Steve Young moves the football team. And Steve has got to be allowed to play his game," Seifert said. "We told him before the game to play your game and take what they give you. . . . But when he looks at the film there are a couple of plays where he'll see he could have hung in there a little longer and thrown the football."

Another loss dropped the team's record to 2–4: not since 1982 had the 49ers been two games under .500, or in last place in the NFC West. The fans and media—already discouraged by Montana's absence and the departure of revered players Lott and Craig—were unaccustomed to such mediocrity.

"There was so much drama going on in that season," *San Jose Mercury News* reporter Ann Killion later said. "Steve kinda became the scapegoat for all

NOVEMBER 10, 1985: Joe Montana—a fun-loving, practical joker—targets photographer Michael Zagaris with a snowball at the Denver airport one day before the 49ers Monday Night game against the Broncos. Ironically, the next evening at Mile High Stadium, a fan hit 49ers holder Matt Cavanaugh with a snowball just before a field goal try, botching the attempt. San Francisco lost 17–16.

OCTOBER 29, 1983: Trailing 34–31 with eleven seconds remaining, Brigham Young University quarterback Steve Young scrambles for the game-winning touchdown against Utah State. During the final two minutes, Young—who was knocked out of the game in the first quarter due to a concussion—completed three passes and rushed for nineteen yards to set up the winning score.

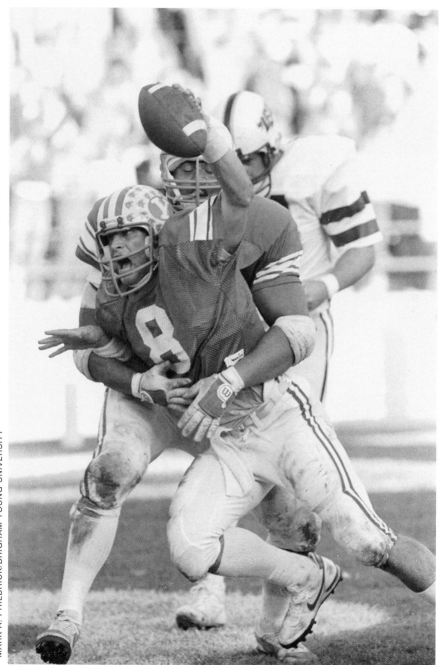

JANUARY 4, 1987: At halftime of San Francisco's 49–3 playoff loss to the New York Giants, Dwight Clark checks on Montana, his teammate and close friend, in a training room at Giants Stadium. "He was pretty groggy," Clark said. A vicious hit from defensive lineman Jim Burt gave Montana a concussion that knocked him out of the game. Montana was held overnight at the Hospital for Special Surgery–Cornell Medical Center.

AUGUST 3, 1987: Montana and Young pose during the 49ers training camp in Rocklin, California. That spring, San Francisco sent two draft picks and $1 million to the Tampa Bay Buccaneers in exchange for Young.

NOVEMBER 22, 1987: Montana throws a pass to fullback Tom Rathman during the 49ers 24–10 victory over the Buccaneers in Tampa Bay. At halftime, Steve Young was honored as the Buccaneers Most Valuable Player for the previous season.

JANUARY 9, 1988: 49ers offensive coordinator Mike Holmgren speaks with Montana and Young, following the 36–24 playoff loss to the Minnesota Vikings at Candlestick Park. In the third quarter of the enormous upset, head coach Bill Walsh replaced Montana with Young, sparking a quarterback controversy that carried on throughout the offseason and into the next summer's training camp.

OCTOBER 30, 1988: With the 49ers trailing Minnesota 21–17 and 2:11 remaining in the fourth quarter, Young scrambles forty-nine yards for the game-winning touchdown. NFL Films president Steve Sabol later called it "the greatest run . . . the greatest individual athletic effort in the eighty-year history of the National Football League."

JANUARY 22, 1989: In the locker room of Joe Robbie Stadium, Jerry Rice, Montana, and Young await the start of Super Bowl XXIII against the Cincinnati Bengals. That evening, with the 49ers trailing 16–13, Montana drove the offense ninety-two yards in the final minutes, tossing the game-winning touchdown pass to John Taylor.

JANUARY 22, 1989: Montana embraces Bill Walsh in the locker room of Joe Robbie Stadium, following the 49ers 20–16 victory over Cincinnati in Super Bowl XXIII. Walsh, Montana's head coach for the previous nine seasons, retired from the NFL later that week.

OCTOBER 22, 1989: Young stands over an injured Montana during the second quarter of the 49ers game against the New England Patriots. After Montana—who sprained his left knee—was carted off the field, Young completed eleven of twelve passes for 188 yards and three touchdowns in the 49ers 37–20 victory at Stanford Stadium.

CIRCA 1990: Young and offensive coordinator Mike Holmgren speak in the locker room during an exhibition game at Candlestick Park. Prior to joining the 49ers, Holmgren spent five years at Brigham Young University where he was Young's quarterback coach for two seasons.

SEPTEMBER 1, 1989: Inside Seattle's Kingdome, Montana and Young share a laugh before the 49ers final exhibition game of the 1989 preseason, a 28–17 loss to the Seahawks.

NOVEMBER 25, 1990: Young and Montana discuss strategy during the 49ers 28–17 home loss to the Los Angeles Rams.

DECEMBER 3, 1990: At halftime of the 49ers Monday Night game versus the New York Giants, Montana and Young study Polaroids of the opposing defense. Montana's twenty-three-yard touchdown pass to John Taylor was San Francisco's only score during a 7–3 victory.

OCTOBER 13, 1991: Early in the fourth quarter, Young soars over two Falcons defenders for a seven-yard touchdown that gave San Francisco a one-point lead. Although Young accounted for four touchdowns and set a career-high with 348 yards passing, the 49ers lost at home to Atlanta, 39–34.

DECEMBER 19, 1992: At Candlestick Park, Young and Montana await the start of a regular season game versus the Tampa Bay Buccaneers. The Week 16 contest marked a milestone for both quarterbacks: Young made his first-ever start against his former team, while Montana suited up for the 49ers after a twenty-three-month hiatus.

DECEMBER 28, 1992: Montana throws a pass during a cold and rainy Monday Night game against the Detroit Lions. Prior to the 24–6 victory, an elbow injury sidelined Montana for nearly two years, during which time Young became the 49ers starting quarterback. Montana completed fifteen of twenty-one attempts for 126 yards and two touchdowns in his final appearance as a 49er.

MICHAEL ZAGARIS

DECEMBER 19, 1992: Against his former team, the Tampa Bay Buccaneers, Young throws the game-winning, fourth-quarter touchdown pass, a 30-yarder to Jerry Rice. The 49ers 21–14 victory clinched homefield advantage in the playoffs and all but locked up Young's first league MVP award.

MICHAEL MALONEY/SAN FRANCISCO CHRONICLE

JANUARY 17, 1993: Young and Montana exit the field at Candlestick Park after San Francisco's 30–20 loss to Dallas in the NFC Championship Game. Three months later, the 49ers traded Montana to the Kansas City Chiefs.

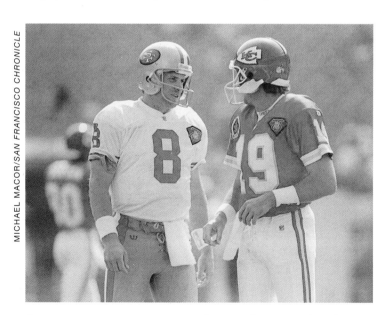

GARY CAMERON/REUTERS

JANUARY 16, 1994: Montana and Marcus Allen (no. 32) celebrate the touchdown that clinched a road-victory over the Houston Oilers in the second round of the 1993 playoffs. Late in the fourth quarter, with the Chiefs ahead 21–20, Montana drove the offense seventy-nine yards on six plays to seal Kansas City's remarkable fourth-quarter comeback.

MICHAEL MACOR/SAN FRANCISCO CHRONICLE

SEPTEMBER 11, 1994: Prior to their regular season showdown in Arrowhead Stadium, Young and Montana exchange pleasantries. Montana completed nineteen passes for 203 yards and two touchdowns in a 24–17 victory over his former team. Young, perpetually harassed by the Chiefs pass rush, was sacked four times and threw two interceptions.

APRIL 18, 1995: With five-year-old son Nathaniel on his lap, wife, Jennifer, holding their two-year-old son Nicholas, and his mother, Theresa, behind him, Montana sits during his retirement ceremony. More than twenty thousand fans attended the star-studded event at San Francisco's Justin Herman Plaza.

JANUARY 29, 1995: Young drops back to pass in Super Bowl XXIX. Against the San Diego Chargers, Young completed twenty-four of thirty-six attempts for 325 yards. His six touchdown passes eclipsed the Super Bowl record set by Momtana five years earlier.

JANUARY 29, 1995: Young clutches the Vince Lombardi Trophy, following the 49ers 49–26 victory over San Diego in Super Bowl XXIX. Young's record-setting performance earned him the game's Most Valuable Player award.

of that. Not just the Joe stuff, for Ronnie [Lott] stuff too, even though that was purely an organizational decision and it didn't have anything to do with Steve. But the way it played out, I think there was a lot of anxiety and unhappiness about this general transition from the greatness to an unknown future. And Steve was a part of that so he probably bore the brunt."

A day after the loss to the Falcons, Young received a phone call from Bill Walsh. The retired head coach and *NBC Sports* analyst invited Young to his Menlo Park home for a chat.

"He took such a beating in that game, and then after what I read in some of the papers, I thought he might want to talk," Walsh said. "We visited briefly, talked about his state of mind, things like that. We visit like that from time to time, as I do with a number of the players. He knows I'm here if he needs me. . . . He's a favorite of mine. So I reminded him that he was a gifted athlete, and that he played a great game. I told him not to apologize for anything."

Walsh's encouragement yielded significant dividends over the following two weeks. In consecutive victories over the 5–1 Lions and 4–3 Eagles, Young was razor-sharp, completing twenty-eight of his thirty-five pass attempts for 333 yards, three touchdowns, and zero interceptions. And with their defense equally dominant, allowing just ten combined points and forcing seven turnovers, the 49ers returned to an even 4–4 record.

"We answered some of our own questions today," Young said following the win over Detroit. "This team needs to develop an attitude of its own—separate from 49er teams of the past. I think we're starting to do that."

The turnaround—for both the 49ers and Young—hit full-stride seven minutes into the team's next game, a rematch with the Falcons in chilly Atlanta. From his own end zone, Young heaved a deep pass for Taylor, who hauled it in near midfield. In pursuit of the ball, Falcons defenders Tim McKyer and Scott Case collided and fell to the ground, giving a free path to Taylor, who outran Deion Sanders to the goal line for a ninety-seven-yard touchdown, the longest in team history.

But near the end of the first half, Young scrambled up the middle for six yards and was yanked to the ground by linebacker Darion Conner. Visibly in pain with a badly sprained left knee, Young spent the second half in the locker room while Steve Bono took command of the offense. After falling behind 10–7 late in the fourth period, Bono completed four passes to push the 49ers into Falcons territory, and with under a minute remaining, tossed a thirty-yard touchdown pass to Taylor that seemingly clinched a victory.

"They had everybody stacked up on the other side," Bono explained. "I let the ball go, and all I could see was John going in. A great, great feeling."

A great feeling that was short-lived. On the final snap, Atlanta's Billy Joe Tolliver—the game's other backup quarterback called upon after Falcons starter Chris Miller suffered a rib injury in the second quarter—launched a Hail Mary into the 49ers end zone. Wide receiver, No. 81 Michael Haynes, with his back to Tolliver, caught the ball on the rebound among a crowd of eight players. Atlanta won, 17–14, sweeping the season series with San Francisco. The play was a bitter moment of déjà vu: eight years earlier, during a November visit to Fulton County Stadium, San Francisco had also lost on a last-second, desperation throw to an Atlanta wide receiver wearing No. 81— Billy "White Shoes" Johnson.

The news was even worse upon the 49ers return to California. An MRI revealed damage to Young's medial collateral ligament, and arthroscopic knee surgery was required. The last operation Young underwent had been a tonsillectomy at age five. For the first time in his life, injury would sideline him from practice, games, and potentially the remainder of the season.

"I expect this will have an impact on his season and not on his future at all," said team physician Dr. Dillingham, who by now had become fairly used to addressing the press.

Dillingham (nicknamed "Dilly") was certainly earning his salary. In addition to performing surgical procedures on the 49ers' two star quarterbacks in the span of one month, Dillingham also directed Montana's recovery and rehabilitation program.

Following the October surgery, Dillingham placed Montana's elbow into a custom-made cast equipped with a locked dial that restricted his range of motion. Seifert described the black device as "very futuristic." Team vice president John McVay called it "Darth Vader–like."

"But I can just take it off," Montana laughed.

By early November, Montana was delicately exercising the elbow.

"Right now, we're just working on flexion and extension," Montana said. "We're starting to strengthen a little bit, the triceps and biceps."

Including the second loss to Atlanta, Montana had now missed nine consecutive 49ers games, the longest absence of his career: even the spinal injury in 1986 had cost him only eight. Since the elbow surgery, he had not even traveled to away games with the team. But due to Young's injury, Montana was recalled to the sideline: they needed him to signal in the plays.[1]

---

[1]The 49ers used hand signals to send in offensive plays from the sideline to the huddle. Provided with the play name from offensive coordinator Mike Holmgren (and before him, Bill Walsh), the backup quarterback flashed intricate hand gestures to the starting quarterback, who in turn called the play to the rest of the huddle.

On the same day as his teammates, Montana flew to New Orleans for the annual trip to play the Saints. It was the first time in-season that Montana visited the Big Easy, knowing he would not be playing on Sunday. The night before the game, Montana, retired teammate Keena Turner, and a few team officials, decided to go out for dinner. Knowing Montana's preference for privacy and his uneasiness with the spotlight, friend and team photographer Michael Zagaris recommended a quiet, secluded place, far removed from the madness of Bourbon Street. Surprisingly, Montana instead suggested a visit to Pat O'Brien's, one of the most popular bars and tourist spots in the French Quarter.

"I didn't want to go to Pat O'Brien's because I knew it would be fucking crazy," recalled Zagaris, the 49ers team photographer for decades. "I remember, we walked in, and these three guys in their late twenties, early thirties, came up to us, and one guy went right up to Joe and stood in front of him like a seven-year-old outside Yankee Stadium. He goes, 'Oh My God! It's You! It's Joe Montana! Fucking Joe Montana! I can't believe I'm here with you!' And the guy was serious. Joe was really cool, but I looked at [Keena Turner] and said, 'We gotta get out of here.'

"Then, someone from Pat O'Brien's said, 'Come with us; we'll take care of you.' So they put us over near a back bar, and they kinda put up a velvet rope or something there. It was a huge mass of people, people trying to press in and reach out and touch him. And Joe was really cool, just having a beer. I think he was taking it in, kinda digging it. And at one point, I said, 'This is like a 1964 Beatles tour; let's get out of here.' Because you really couldn't enjoy yourself, it was more like a spectacle."

Later, Zagaris relayed the story to Mark Purdy, the sports editor of the *San Jose Mercury News*.

"At that point in his time with the 49ers," Purdy said in 2011, "I think maybe Joe needed to do something like that. It's not that Joe needed to sit there in Pat O'Brien's and be worshipped or fawned over or backslapped—I think he just needed the affirmation that after not playing for a while he was still relevant to fans and relevant in the whole NFL universe. It sounds silly, I know. But Joe always had that streak of insecurity inside him, as if he were still that fifth-string quarterback at Notre Dame just trying to get on the travel squad. I think he really thought many fans had dismissed him and moved on to the next thing."

Montana's night on the town didn't end at Pat O's. Unrestrained by a curfew, he and his posse explored the city into the early hours of the next morning.

"It's one of my greatest memories of Joe ever," recalled Jeff Bayer, a 49ers photographer who also traveled with the team on the trip to New Orleans but didn't accompany Montana, Zagaris, and the others to Pat O'Brien's. "I went to five or six places, I forgot who I was with, and everywhere I went, Joe was there. He was in the door already!

"Finally I go back to the hotel, it's six o'clock in the morning. And [49ers chief financial officer Keith Simon] is there with his tie all the way up. And he goes, 'We're just going to open up some new red wine, would you like some!?' Six o'clock in the morning. I said, 'Whatever!' So we're all sitting there at the table, and Joe walks in. And he doesn't have his [Darth Vader elbow brace] on. And Keith's eyes come out of his head. He goes, 'Joe! Joe! Where's your thing?' . . . The gizmo that was supposed to give him flexion. Joe goes, 'Dilly wants flexion? [Violently shaking his arm] I got flexion! I got flexion!'"

Eventually, Montana returned to his room, reattached the brace, and went to sleep. Not long after, he awoke and joined his teammates at the Superdome for a critical showdown with the 8–1 Saints.

For the first time in more than five years, the 49ers started a quarterback other than Joe Montana or Steve Young, who had insisted on joining the team despite surgery three days earlier. While Montana flashed signals in to Bono, Young watched from the coaches' box.

"I said if they're going, I'm going," he explained. "Yeah, they tried to (talk me out of it), but they've been arguing with Joe for ten years and it's never worked."

Both multimillion dollar quarterbacks were helpless to contribute in a dismal 10–3 loss. San Francisco's only points came after safety Dave Waymer returned an interception to the New Orleans 17-yard line, setting up a short field goal. Although Bono played well in the loss (fifteen-for-thirty-one, 131 yards, no interceptions), the offense was unable to overcome three fumbles, a handful of penalties, and the typically loud crowd noise inside the Superdome.

"It was tough for Bono to come into an environment like this," Seifert said. "He did a good job. You could say that without a fumble or two, it's a different ball game. He played with poise."

Under Bono, San Francisco's offense improved just enough the next week to secure a 14–3 victory over Phoenix, then erupted with four first-half touchdowns to tear through the Rams in Anaheim, 33–10. A week later, in a rematch with the division-leading Saints, Bono tossed a pair of fourth-quarter touchdown passes to overcome a seven-point deficit. And seven days later, Bono delivered another comeback triumph in Seattle's Kingdome. Trailing the Seahawks 22–17 late in the final period, Bono and Taylor connected on two passes, the second of which was a fifteen-yard, game-winning touchdown.

"I've been in close games before," Bono said after the win, "but in a situation where you absolutely can't lose the game? No. I haven't. This hasn't all sunk in yet. I just know I can get on the plane and relax."

Many attributed the team's resurgence to Bono, who had won four straight starts and thrown a trio of touchdown passes in consecutive games. Bono attributed the success to a model set by his close friend, Joe Montana.

"It's not that he's told me anything earthshaking or secret," said Bono. "But for two years I've been able to watch him in practice, watch film with him, ask him what he saw, why he did something."

Bono's rise to stardom sparked a once-unimaginable thought within many fans: Could Steve Bono, not Steve Young, actually be a more suitable replacement for and heir apparent to Joe Montana?

Not only was Bono right-handed like Montana, and making roughly one-tenth the salary ($275,000 per season) Young made, but he fit the offense's ideal pocket-passer mold.

"He's got a great arm, good touch, and he can also drill the ball in," Rice added. "He's the type to hang in the pocket, wait on his receivers to really get open. He's similar to Joe."

Bono also shared another Montana trademark.

"He's a lot like Joe. He doesn't say much, but he gets the job done," 49ers tackle Steve Wallace said.

Even Bono's wife, Tina, saw the parallels.

"Sometimes, she'll say, 'I'll see you down there doing all those things, and I still don't think it's you,'" Bono said. "She's so used to Joe, she probably thinks it's him."

While Bono started to grab headlines and attention around the NFL—"Now when Mrs. Bono tries to cash a check at the supermarket, nobody is going to say, 'Are you related to Sonny?'" Dan Fouts joked during CBS's broadcast of the Saints game—Young itched to return to the field.

Rehabilitation of his knee was on schedule. During the surgery, Dr. Dillingham noticed no damage to the cartilage and that the ligament was healing itself. Soon, the cast was removed, and by Thanksgiving Young resumed throwing. He suited up for the victories over New Orleans and Seattle—he did not play—but with the knee still healing, he would be used only in case of an emergency.

"We just have to wait and see how Steve Young is," Seifert said prior to victory over the Seahawks. "I guess the normal thing is the starting player (Young) gets his job back, but we'll just have to wait and see what he can do as a football player."

The health of Young's knee was not the only factor in Seifert's decision. To many, swapping out Bono for Young was problematic: such a change risked sacrificing the team's momentum or any so-called "chemistry" that Bono had developed as the team's quarterback.

"I feel you continue with the guy who's been playing," guard Guy McIntyre said after the win in Seattle. "It's kind of late in the game to try to change anything."

At 8–6, the 49ers were still in contention for a once improbable playoff berth. Wins in their final two games coupled with losses by several other playoff contenders could earn the 49ers a trip to the postseason. So with his club still in the hunt for a playoff spot, Seifert stuck with Bono for the 49ers' Week 16 hosting of the 9–5 Chiefs. And although Bono completed twenty-four of his thirty-three attempts and tossed three more touchdown passes in a decisive win, two days later San Francisco learned they would not participate in the postseason. New Orleans's victory over the Raiders had eliminated San Francisco from the playoff race.

For the 49ers, all that remained in the 1991 season was a home game against the Bears. But for Bono, the season was already over.

In the middle of the third quarter, during the win over Kansas City, a Chiefs defender hit Bono hard. He stayed in the game, and even threw his third touchdown pass of the day on the very next snap, but Seifert replaced him for the following series and the remainder of the day. Young, wearing a bulky knee brace, ended his six-week absence to preserve the 49ers 28–14 victory. And when doctors noticed ligament damage in Bono's knee after they removed his cast, Young was named the starter against Chicago.

"I need to be back on the field," he said. "Not making the playoffs makes it frustrating. Everything else is just part of the season. You're going to take the dents and shots and be in and out, but it's a team game."

Although the game meant far more to the Bears—a win would clinch the NFC Central, the second-seed in the playoffs, and a first-round bye—San Francisco routed Chicago. Young threw three touchdown passes in the game's first twenty minutes and his eight carries for sixty-three yards showed his knee was healthy enough to play.

"People are saying that this offense isn't made for me, but I think it's a beautiful offense for me, and it was tonight," Young said. "People are saying, 'He runs too much for that offense,' but that focuses too much on the running. We've thrown the ball for more yards this year than ever before in 49er history."

In addition to rushing for a two-yard touchdown at the start of the fourth quarter, Young completed twenty-one of thirty-two attempts for 338 yards and three scores. The excellent performance—his sixth multitouchdown passing day and third game with three hundred or more yards through the air—surged Young past Washington's Mark Rypien in the competition for the league's passing title.

"That's not bad," Young said. "It takes the sting out of not being in the playoffs a little bit."

The 52–14 final score enraged Mike Ditka, but not enough to flick off or throw gum toward the fans at Candlestick Park for a second time in four years. Still, despite the victory—which extended the team's winning streak to six and pushed their overall record to double-digit wins for a ninth consecutive season—the 49ers' season was over.

"I thought at the end of the year, we were the best team in football," Brent Jones said years later. "And we weren't going to the playoffs. That was a tough pill to swallow. But I just remember that year there being a lot of tumult. It was tough to have consistency because we had three different quarterbacks. Obviously, Joe, that was a tough season for him. And it was tough for Steve, too, to be handed over the reins and then not be able to be healthy the whole time. But he ended up coming back and being fine."

Young's performance only created more uncertainty for the 49ers heading into the offseason. No one questioned Young's talent, his work ethic, or desire to excel. But neither could anyone overlook the fact that his only season as the 49ers starting quarterback was also the first time in nine years that the team did not make the playoffs.

"A quarterback lives and dies with the success of his team," he acknowledged. "Fair or unfair, that's the way it is."

The NFL's penultimate winner, Joe Montana, had shed his Darth Vader brace in early December and was expected to make a full recovery by mini-camp the next spring. Looking ahead, Seifert tacitly endorsed Montana as the team's 1992 starter.

"He's the incumbent quarterback," said Seifert prior to the Bears game. "Basically, the rule is that a guy doesn't lose his starting spot to injury, if he's capable of doing what he was prior to the injury. That's my answer. That's what my answer has to be."

Bono's presence complicated the situation even further. He had assumed command of a team with a losing record, won five of six starts, and proved to be a solid—and also comparatively inexpensive—backup. With Bono and a healthy Montana, many believed Young would be expendable.

"I feel I had ten starts this year, and I feel very good about the way I played," Young said after the win over Chicago. "I've done everything that I can, and now it's up to the coaches to figure the rest of that stuff out."

9

Pandora's Box

On January 11, 1992, Mike Holmgren took the podium at a press conference in Wisconsin. The forty-three-year-old had just been introduced as the new head coach of the Green Bay Packers.

"[Today is] probably the most exciting day in my life," he said.

A native of San Francisco, Holmgren shared with the press childhood memories of attending 49ers–Packers games at Kezar Stadium during the early 1960s, the start of the Packer dynasty built by Vince Lombardi. Now it was Holmgren's mission to revive the once-proud franchise that had not been to the playoffs in nearly a decade.

"Wherever I've been, I've been a part of successful, winning programs," he said. "I have tremendous confidence in my ability to get the job done. We're going to do things my way. I want [players] to come along with me."

The players Holmgren wanted to metaphorically "come along with" him were those already on the Packers roster. But it was a curious choice of words.

Within weeks, Holmgren hired 49ers assistant coaches Sherm Lewis and Ray Rhodes as his offensive and defensive coordinators, respectively. That same winter, Holmgren and general manager Ron Wolf tried to lure another member of the 49ers organization to Green Bay.

Don Majkowski, the Packers former Pro Bowler, missed half of the 1990 and 1991 seasons due to shoulder and leg injuries, prompting the front office to search for a potential replacement to operate Holmgren's West Coast offense. The 49ers, overloaded with quarterbacks Joe Montana, Steve Young, and Steve Bono, were the obvious place to look.

"If they want to trade any of them, I'll take them in a minute," said Holmgren.

Given the history between Holmgren and Young, speculation shifted toward another reunion of the Brigham Young University coach and quarterback.

"Steve Young is a fine player and a good team guy, but he should be starting somewhere," said Holmgren in late January.

The Packers and 49ers discussed a trade, but again the price for Young—both his salary and the 49ers compensation—was too steep. Instead, Green Bay dealt the Atlanta Falcons a first-round pick for a seldom-used, second-year quarterback named Brett Favre.

"I wasn't terribly concerned about the quarterback, but this gave us a chance to solidify the position," Holmgren told the *Milwaukee Journal*. "Now I've got a young guy I can teach the offense to."

Then, in a line that sounded very familiar, he added, "Don Majkowski is the starting quarterback. I don't think a guy loses his job because of an injury."

Green Bay was not the only team to discuss a trade for Young. That spring, Carmen Policy, John McVay, and George Seifert also listened to offers from Kansas City and the Los Angeles Raiders. But they were not intent on making a deal.

"The image is that the 49ers are shopping Young to anybody who's interested," *San Francisco Chronicle* columnist Glenn Dickey explained in April. "In fact, a better comparison would be with a man who owns a house he doesn't want to sell but puts a price on it that's perhaps double what he thinks it's worth. If somebody comes along who's willing to pay that price, the deal will be made, but in effect, the owner has taken his house off the market."

Leading the NFL in passer efficiency during the 1991 season convinced Young that he could excel as the 49ers starting quarterback. And during the team's second minicamp in early May, he aimed to convince the coaching staff, specifically Holmgren's successor, Mike Shanahan. Off the field, Young also stated his case to the fans and media.

"It's insane. I'm not going to accept number two status," he said. "That would be like running in the Kentucky Derby and then going back to run with the trotters at Yonkers. It's illogical in my mind. There would be no fulfillment in that. No way."

Young knew that his comments wouldn't be well received, and that he had admittedly just opened up a "Pandora's Box." But he didn't care.

"It's just a strange situation to be in. It really is. I made a transition last year, and I really believe I'm ready to take this team all the way, every year for a lot of years."

Inevitably asked for a response, Montana simply tuned out reporters' questions. He couldn't, however, ignore a much more pressing concern: the damage to his elbow.

In March his rehabilitation took a slight detour—arthroscopic surgery on his left knee to clear out loose bits of cartilage—but Montana recovered quickly. By the team's first minicamp in April, his arrival thrilled both fans and his head coach.

"I just saw Joe Montana," Seifert said. "I think we all like that. I really didn't see any particular glitches."

The elbow was even strong enough to endure Montana's newest hobby. That winter, he had learned to play tennis and occasionally battled his former coach Bill Walsh on the court.

"He's been killing me," Montana said. "I don't like to lose to begin with, and he's a lot better than I am. But I'm competing with myself just to get the ball back to Bill so he can hit another one harder at me."

Far more than his backhand or serve, the public was interested in Montana's ability to throw a football. There was stiffness but no pain in his surgically repaired elbow.

"I've been throwing a lot," Montana said. "The farthest I've thrown has probably been out forty-eight to fifty yards at the most. I'm doing things, warming up, throwing the ball, and then going back and letting some go, because I really haven't done it.

"I'm afraid to really snap it off as hard as I can," he added. "That's why I say it's probably pretty close to 100 (percent). . . . I've thrown pretty hard, and I feel it's pretty close, but then it gets to that point where I've got to get through that mental part where I know I can let it go because it doesn't really bother me."

During the team's second minicamp, he showed no such hesitation. One observer noted that he was "humming the ball in practice," and there was little debate as to who would be under center at the beginning of the 1992 season.

"Joe Montana is our starting quarterback," Seifert said, "and as long as he stays healthy and does the things that he's done in the past, which he's shown every indication of doing, I would expect that Joe will be our starting quarterback."

Within a week, however, Montana's elbow needed another surgery, this time to remove adhesions and scar tissue. Once again, the minor procedure was not considered a setback.

"Right from the time I got out [of the hospital] it felt better," Montana later said.

Exhaustive daily exercises—one requiring him to submerge the elbow in a bucket filled with thirty pounds of dry rice—greatly strengthen the ligaments, and he resumed throwing by June. Seifert praised his workouts as "very, very crisp."

As training camp neared, Seifert met with Montana, Dr. Dillingham, and trainer Lindsy McLean—"the Holy trinity," as Seifert called them—and devised a plan for limiting his preseason work. Montana would throw only during the first (morning) practice of the team's two daily sessions: forty passes one practice, sixty the next, forty the next, and so on. Gradually, his velocity and accuracy returned near full strength.

"It's the magic of Joe Montana," Seifert said. "My sense from watching him out there, from his throwing and his reaction and his movement, is that he looks like he's always looked."

As *Sports Illustrated*'s Peter King noted in late July, "Even his opponents expect no less. 'He's like Lazarus,' said Atlanta Falcon cornerback Tim McKyer, who was a 49er teammate of Montana's from 1986 to '89. 'You roll back the stone, Joe limps out, throws off the bandages—and then he throws for 300 yards.'"

Through two weeks of throwing camp, Montana felt fatigue in the elbow and took several days off, but he was expected to play in the team's first exhibition game. He did not: a brief test of the arm discouraged "the Holy Trinity" enough for Montana to sit out against Denver. Afterward, the veteran met with Dr. Frank Jobe, the orthopedic specialist who pioneered the "Tommy John Surgery" that prolonged many baseball careers. Instead of another surgery, a minimum of two weeks rest was prescribed, and Montana sat out the 49ers' next two preseason games.

"Steve Young will start the rest of the exhibition games, and go until Joe is ready," Seifert said in mid-August. "That's the way it is."

Even with Montana sidelined indefinitely, Young couldn't lock down the starter's job. In the preseason win over Denver, linebacker Karl Mecklenburg sacked Young, twisting his back. As a precaution, Young was held out of the team's next game against the Raiders, then returned to the field for the team's third exhibition game against Washington, yet another preseason trip abroad.

"I did my best to talk them into [playing against the Raiders]," Young said. "I'll just go to London in good shape and be well rested. I guess I'm in a different situation now."

In London, where Walsh had officially given birth to the quarterback controversy four years earlier, Young completed twelve of seventeen passes for ninety-five yards. But he was sacked in the end zone for a safety, and the offense was held scoreless during the first half. Steve Bono—whose 5–1 record as a starter the previous season still intrigued fans and reporters—started the second half, threw two touchdowns, and in the final three minutes drove the 49ers into position for a game-winning field goal.

"Some people who watch the 49ers have the nagging feeling that Bono, not Young, is the right man for the 49ers," the *Chronicle's* Lowell Cohn wrote. "This is the line of reasoning: Bono is aware of his limitations and stays strictly within the game plan. This is not the case with Young. When he can't find his primary receiver, he takes off running, and even if he stays put and tries to follow the progression of second and third receivers, he'd really rather be running—he's waging an endless battle against his own nature."

Five days after returning from England, the 49ers visited the Chargers in San Diego. Behind Young, the offense produced just three points and one third-down conversion. Again Bono relieved Young at halftime, and completed fifteen of his twenty-one attempts for 155 yards and a touchdown as the 49ers rallied from a fourth-quarter deficit to win. The whispers for the coaching staff to give Bono, not Young, the starting job grew louder.

"It's always going to be that way around San Francisco just because of the competition, not only at quarterback but in the media itself," Young said. "I think as long as we're efficient, we know that you've got to earn your stripes around here. I've made a living in the preseason in the second half for a lot of years. Steve's played very well. It's great for us. We need both of us."

Despite all of his efforts to avoid the controversy Bill Walsh stirred up, George Seifert now faced an impossible situation. The 49ers had one exhibition game left before the season opener against the Giants and—with Montana's elbow improving enough to resume throwing—there were three viable contenders for the quarterback job.

As if that wasn't troublesome enough, two more personnel issues plagued the club that August. Perennial All-Pro wide receiver Jerry Rice could not agree to a contract and held out, missing the first four weeks of the preseason. And less than one year removed from his frightening meltdown after the loss to the Raiders, Charles Haley caused even more headaches for the organization. In addition to his erratic, occasionally offensive behavior, he feuded with teammates, including linebacker Tim Harris, and openly ignored or disrespected members of the coaching staff.

Rather than risk an encore to the chaotic 1991 season, Seifert and the 49ers front office swiftly imposed order. Rice's contract demands were met, Haley was traded to Dallas, and an unambiguous statement about the team's starting quarterback was made.

"We all know what Joe Montana means to this organization," Seifert told the press, eleven days before the regular season began. "[But] Steve Young is our starting quarterback, and all of my energies and all of the team's energies have got to go in that direction. . . . We hopefully learned a valuable lesson last year, the players and coaches. I feel good about the fact that we have Steve Bono as well. Should something happen, he's a proven, winning quarterback. But Steve Young is our starter, and away we go."

Avoiding any further speculation, the 49ers sent Montana to the injured reserve list for the second straight year. Again, he was ineligible to play in the team's first four games, and was not allowed to practice with the club.

"Talk about a letdown," Montana said. "One minute I think I have a chance to play by the third week, the next I'm out until the fifth game. All these decisions were made without anybody even watching me throw."

But the next decision made by the front office angered Montana even further. Seifert informed the press that for the team's final preseason game, at home versus Seattle, Montana would appear "most likely in the first half of the game for a few plays."

Regardless of whether the decision had been borne out of well-intentioned loyalty or was simply an attempt to cater to the fans paying regular season ticket price for an exhibition game, the token gesture greatly irritated Montana.

"He's not happy about this," Montana's teammate Steve Bono told reporters. "But he has to accept it. We all do. And it's time to rally around Steve [Young]. We will, because we have to."

Despite the announcement that Montana would play sparingly, he did not even suit up for the preseason game.

"Maybe I'm kidding myself, but when it comes down to it, I still feel I'm capable of playing. It's going to be over soon enough," Montana said, referring to his career, "and I can't come back to it."

* * *

Along with game-winning touchdown passes and playoff excellence, absorbing savage hits from New York Giants defenders had become a part of San Francisco 49ers quarterback lore. In the 1986 playoffs, Jim Burt delivered one to Montana. Three years later, in a Monday night showdown at Candlestick, linebacker Gary Reasons's spearing of Montanta injured the quarterback's rib cage. And late in the fourth quarter of the 1990 NFC Championship Game, Leonard Marshall leveled Montana with another infamous pounding.

In Week 1 of the 1992 NFL season, Steve Young received his initiation via not one, but two, brutal rites of passage.

On the fifth play of the season opener in the Meadowlands, just as Young released a pass, defensive end Eric Dorsey drove his helmet into Young's chin, planting the quarterback head-first into the Giants Stadium AstroTurf.

"[It was] the hardest hit I've taken in a long, long time," Young said.

He staggered to the sidelines where he was looked over by Dr. James Klint, the same team physician who attended to Montana after Jim Burt's playoff hit in January 1987. Steve Bono entered the game and threw a touchdown pass that was negated by an offensive penalty.

"I was tryin' like hell to keep them from figuring out what was wrong," Young said. "We're all pretty good actors. I'm not gonna say, 'I'm too hurt,' or 'I don't think I'm good enough to come back in.' You fake it."

Young faked it well enough to convince Klint. After a few plays, Young replaced Bono, then threw a touchdown pass of his own, a three-yarder to Tom Rathman.

"Touchdown pass?" Young asked a few hours later. "I've been reminded of that play, but I don't remember."

In his postgame interviews, Young could not recall the play, perhaps because on the very next series, Lawrence Taylor—who had a habit of ending quarterbacks' careers—sacked Young, delivering what Seifert called, "the knockout punch."

"But that second hit didn't have anything to do with it," Young said. "It was all from the first one. Man, that was a hit. And I was in the pocket!

"I came off the field, and I couldn't remember the third-down play I had just called," he added. "That kind of gave me away. Dr. Klint and I went into the locker room, and he gave me an exam, and that was it."

The previous season, Young had made it through nine games before a knee injury halted his quest to replace Montana. This year his effort stalled less than one quarter into the first game. And as was the case late in 1991, Bono delivered another solid performance in Young's place, completing fifteen of twenty-two passes for 187 yards and two touchdown passes in a 31–14 win.

"We all thought, 'All right, the starting quarterback is out, so we've got this game won,'" the Giants Eric Dorsey said. "I remember that playoff game here in this stadium where Jim Burt knocked Joe Montana out of the game, and we rallied behind that. But this time, their offense rallied behind Bono."

Praise for Bono surged after the game, but Seifert avoided talk of another quarterback controversy. During Monday's press conference he stated that Young, who was "bouncy and with it," would remain the starter but ended his endorsement there.

"At the same time we're fortunate enough to have a fine backup or two and a hell of a quarterback in the wings (Joe Montana) who's on IR," said Seifert. "So it's a good situation, and the club has to be strong enough character-wise and from within. People can't be thin-skinned about all the talk in the media about the controversy. That's all part of this game. We've all got to say, 'That's an issue,' and keep playing."

The 49ers ability to do that would be thoroughly tested the following week: the AFC's best team, the Buffalo Bills, were coming to Candlestick Park. Back-to-back conference champions, Buffalo had won thirty-one of their previous thirty-nine games and featured a roster loaded with All-Pros and future Hall of Famers on both sides of the ball. But the leader was Jim Kelly, Young's counterpart in the "The Greatest Game No One Saw." And in another rematch of their February 1985 showdown between the Houston Gamblers and Los Angeles Express, Kelly and Young entertained once again, this time in front of a much larger crowd at Candlestick Park. Two first-half touchdown passes from Young, who repeatedly avoided an outstanding Bills rush that included five-time All-Pro defensive end Bruce Smith, lifted the 49ers to a 24–13 halftime advantage.

"He's sixty minutes of hell," said Buffalo's Darryl Talley, describing the maddening task of defending Young. "You have to cover the whole field, and then he still scrambles away from you."

Evoking more memories of the now-defunct league's greatest shootout, Kelly and his no-huddle, "K-Gun" offense stormed back. On consecutive series in the third quarter, he tossed touchdown passes to tight end Pete Metzelaars to put the Bills ahead.

"It brought me back to the USFL days when the Gamblers were playing the Express, and we had to come back and win," Kelly said afterward.

Trailing 27–24 late in the third quarter, Young laced a throw over the middle to Taylor, who broke a listless tackle attempt and sprinted to the end zone for a fifty-four-yard touchdown. Then, on San Francisco's next possession, cornerback Nate Odomes baited Young into throwing an interception, and the Bills covered seventy-two yards for the go-ahead score.

With 3:04 remaining in the game, Young still had a chance to tie or even win the game. He drove the 49ers deep into Bills territory, but a holding penalty and Buffalo's defense forced the 49ers to settle for a forty-seven-yard field goal attempt, which struggling kicker Mike Cofer missed.

"It's funny," Young said. "We made some mistakes on offense last week, but when you win a game decisively, those things are forgotten. If we win this today, if we tie it up at the end, then win it in overtime, this is one of the classics. I think I played pretty good football today. I guess we have to play a perfect game next time."

Despite the loss, the 49ers helped make history that day. For the first time in an NFL game, neither team punted once, and the 1,086 yards of combined total offense was the second most since the 1970 AFL–NFL merger. And for just the second time ever, both quarterbacks topped the four-hundred-yard mark. But Young's stat line was far more impressive than Kelly's.

In addition to throwing for more yards and completing more passes, Young did so mostly without two of his top receivers: Rice and Brent Jones were both injured in the opening quarter and did not return. Young also rushed for fifty yards on seven carries.

"Today the defense should have apologized to Steve Young," 49ers linebacker Mike Walter said.

For Young, the loss was frustrating, but so were more questions about the quarterback controversy. During the *NBC Sports* pregame show, O. J. Simpson reported that Rice said he "preferred to catch balls from a pocket passer like Bono."

"I can't fight that," Young said after the loss. "I don't know what to tell you. I think Jerry Rice is the kind of football player who likes to get the ball, and I try to throw it to him. I play for the team. You guys control the (controversy). . . . Around here, the standards are pretty high, and that's OK."

Through two weeks of the NFL season, the man who set those standards, Joe Montana, remained in purgatory. Since being placed on injured reserve, a decision he publicly opposed, Montana had been criticized for statements that suggested a desire to be traded or released.

"If I am 100 percent, I am not the kind of guy who would sit on the bench and happily collect his money," Montana told the *San Francisco Examiner*. "I would rather go to another team and be able to play. I think it's just a natural reaction for a competitor. Show me somebody who likes to be on the bench, and I'll show you somebody who is always on the bench."

The next day Montana met with team president Carmen Policy and eventually backtracked from the statement. The frustration of being placed on the injured reserve despite significant progress in his rehabilitation—throwing pain-free, every other day—had gotten the better of him.

"I didn't think. I was upset about being put on IR and all that. It was kind of a milestone for me to reach. The next thing you know, the bubble burst," he said a few days later. "I worked pretty hard to get to that point. I thought if I just backed up and, you know, took a breath . . . but all of a sudden everything went crazy."

Having eased the minds of 49ers fans, Montana reassured the team's owner in a hallway at Giants Stadium.

"There's no way Joe Montana doesn't want to finish his career in San Francisco, with the 49ers," Eddie DeBartolo Jr. said.

Although the elbow still ached, and he did not dress before the 49ers opener, Montana casually tossed a football with NFL commissioner Paul Tagliabue. And prior to CBS's broadcast, in a pregame interview Montana reiterated his eagerness to play once he was eligible to come off the injured reserve list.

"I've been throwing well," he said. "It's been pain-free throwing the ball. The last couple times I've been trying to throw to spots, like hooks and outs and things. I've got pretty good velocity on it. I feel pretty good. As long as there's no setbacks, everything should go according to schedule.

"I get a little tightness, but no soreness," he added. "No matter what I do, you can't re-create that snap at the end of the thing. We've been working it, trying to work every muscle in that direction, but we can't do it, other than throwing."

Then Montana suffered a major setback. The day before San Francisco hosted the Bills, Dr. Dillingham performed another surgery on the elbow, the third in less than a year. Initially, the "elective procedure to release pressure that was causing some pain and discomfort on the ulnar nerve" was considered minor.

"I had come back from the elbow injury, and I was ready to play, and I could throw, and everything was solid there except one little tiny thing . . . a staple that was holding my tendon," Montana said in 2011. "Every time I threw, it dinged my nerve in my hand. So they went in and removed that, and unfortunately they hit that nerve.

"It wasn't the injury to my elbow that kept me out, it was that when they went in to take that staple out they hit the nerve and the ring finger on my throwing hand went numb, and I couldn't hold on to the ball. So that was more frustrating than anything. . . . That made that year hard because I knew I was ready to play again right then without ever having to miss a beat."

Although he soon resumed throwing, Montana's projected return date, September 29, had to be pushed back. First, Policy labeled the Week 8 visit to Phoenix on November 1 as the target. But as the numbness persisted, Montana stopped throwing, doctors ordered two more weeks rest, and the front office gave up on making predictions. By late October, Montana had already considered the possibility of missing a second consecutive full season.

"I still have a while. I may be back sometime. If not, I'll shoot for training camp."

But he refused to consider retirement.

"I'd love to go out on this field more than anything," Montana told the *San Francisco Examiner* in Candlestick Park. "But if things don't work out, it's business. . . . I could accept a backup role if I wasn't 100 percent. But if I was 100 percent (and the 49ers wanted him to be the backup), then I'd go someplace else if the circumstances were right. Everybody keeps saying, 'You don't want to do that,' but there's nothing like playing. There's no sensation like it. Everybody's trying to talk me out of it, but the competitor in me says sitting on the bench is not the way for me to go out."

* * *

Exactly two weeks after leaving Giants Stadium with a 31–14 victory over the New York Giants, the 49ers walked out of Giants Stadium with another 31–14 victory, this time over the New York Jets. Young threw two touchdowns and ran for a third in the first half, as San Francisco improved to 2–1.

The following week, Young's twenty-six-yard, third-down scramble set up the 49ers lone touchdown in a 16–10 road victory over the Saints. With the game tied heading into the final period, Young's passing converted a string of first downs that kept consecutive drives alive, putting the 49ers in position for two fourth-quarter field goals.

"I think Steve's getting much more of a feel for the system and the players and is more at ease with himself," Seifert said following the win over New Orleans. "He went through a tough time last season, and I think he learned and grew from that."

In another vital divisional game, this time against the Los Angeles Rams, Young completed twenty of his twenty-nine attempts for 247 yards. But his legs propelled San Francisco to victory.

Early in the fourth quarter, cornerback Robert Bailey picked off one of Young's passes and returned the interception for a touchdown that gave the Rams a 17–10 lead. On the next possession, the 49ers were forced to punt and many of the 63,071 in attendance at Candlestick Park began booing.

"When I heard those boos, I was thinking, 'Gee, we better start moving the football,'" Young said. "We've been in this situation before. I'd tried to force a pass to Jerry (Rice) on that interception, but I was sure we could get it back. Heck, with this offense, we can score three touchdowns in ten minutes. I looked at our linemen, and I know they were thinking the same thing. We weren't fazed at all."

Young atoned for the interception by driving the offense to the Los Angeles 8-yard line, then scrambling for the game-tying touchdown. A Rams fumble gave the 49ers the ball back at their own 48 with less than six minutes showing on the clock. Young couldn't find anyone open downfield so he pump-faked, ran to his left, cut inside a string of tacklers, then froze a safety, and headed for the goal line.

"He faked us out," said Anthony Newman, one of the defensive backs Young sidestepped. "He's too big and too strong to arm tackle. You have to take his head off. That was the toughest part out there today. You're busy covering their receivers, you look up, and the quarterback's running straight at you."

The scramble did not entirely mirror his astounding game-winning touchdown run against Minnesota four years earlier. Instead of stumbling over his own feet near the goal line, the lone roadblock to pay dirt was Robert Bailey, the Rams defender whose interception-turned-touchdown a few minutes earlier had brought about boos from the home crowd. At the 7-yard line, Young met Bailey, stiff-armed the 175-pound cornerback, and pulled him into the end zone.

"I don't want to end the play with the football," Young told reporters asking about the thirty-nine-yard touchdown run. "If I do, it's because I have nothing else to do. I hope, I think, that I don't look to run so quickly anymore. I think I've matured a lot in that regard. I'm growing into this job. I feel more solid, more steady. I don't come into a game thinking about rushing for fifty yards. But hopefully the fear will be there for the defense."

A Rams touchdown pass from Jim Everett to Flipper Anderson tied the game at 24, but in the final two minutes, Young's precision passing racked up seventy-seven yards, setting up Mike Cofer's last-second field goal attempt. With time expiring, the ball sailed through the uprights, and San Francisco won, 27–24.

"I've seen San Francisco come back to win games at the end a lot of times with Joe Montana. They've done it plenty," Bailey said. "So we knew what to expect from them. But we still got bitten by the snake."

That snake also bit the New England Patriots the following Sunday—three scrambles and a touchdown pass by Young overcame a slim fourth-quarter deficit—then devoured Atlanta in Week 7. Young's 399 yards and three touchdowns highlighted a thirty-nine-point, revenge-driven blowout of the Falcons, who had swept the season series a year earlier.

"This was fun," Young told reporters.

The crushing win over division foe Atlanta was a fine way to enter the 49ers' bye week. Players rested, spent time with their families, and enjoyed a few days off. Young and teammate Harris Barton attended a Bruce Springsteen concert at the Shoreline Amphitheater in Mountain View, California. And that weekend, if he had wanted to, Young could even watch NBC's broadcast of the first-ever "Theology Bowl": Brigham Young University versus Notre Dame. In South Bend, Montana's alma mater pounded Young's, 42–16.

The 49ers season resumed the next week against the Cardinals, but the night before the game Young became sick with a stomach bug.

"He was pretty barfy," road-trip roommate Brent Jones said.

Noticeably "hoarse, pale, red-eyed, feverish, and dizzy," Young survived pregame warmups, and even the team's opening possession, completing six of eight pass attempts to help the offense cover seventy-nine yards. But near the Cardinals goal line he was sacked and fumbled the ball away.

Young persisted through two more fruitless possessions before pulling himself out of a scoreless tie late in the second quarter.

"I tried to get out there a little bit, but I couldn't keep anything down," an exhausted Young said after the game. "It just hit me on the wrong day. . . . After the first series, I knew I was going to struggle."

Bono took over and threw an interception to safety Dexter Davis, which allowed the Cardinals to add a field goal in the closing seconds of the second period. Behind 10–0, the 49ers offense struggled the rest of the day. Only wide receiver Mike Sherrard's wacky thirty-nine-yard touchdown return—he stripped the ball away from a Cardinals defender who had recovered a fumble by Jones—kept the game close. But another turnover coupled with Phoenix quarterback Chris Chandler's third touchdown pass put an end to San Francisco's five-game winning streak.

The 24–14 defeat made for a deflated 49ers locker room, and the image of an ill Steve Young doubled over in the locker room—"I feel like crap," he told a reporter—was an apt metaphor.

While Young remained weakened by the flu, Montana felt great. Team doctors had just given him permission to resume throwing for the first time in more than a month (they didn't know that he had secretly started throwing indoors the week earlier). Days later, at an "undisclosed location" near his Atherton home (not the team's training facility in Santa Clara), Montana drastically increased his regimen, tossing roughly seventy-five passes to tight end Wesley Walls. Several throws soared forty yards or further.

"I feel real positive about it," Montana said after his fourth day of extensive throwing. "It's hard to say when I've felt this good. I'm very confident about it, but until I get out there and practice or play, that will be the biggest test more than anything. Yesterday was the best day I've thrown. Not just by a little. It's progressed a lot, especially in the last three days."

The news may have delighted loyal 49ers fans, wistful members of the media, and plenty of teammates, including Rice, who was still frustrated with the changes to San Francisco's offense, but not head coach George Seifert.

"If Joe's doing good, great," he told reporters upon learning of Montana's covert workouts. "I've said all along that I think there will be a time when Joe comes back. It's conceivable to me that he'll get into a football game this year, yes, but we all know who the starting quarterback is."

Even Montana conceded that point.

"It's hard to interrupt with what's going on now," he said. "Steve's playing well, and the team's winning. You can't argue with that. I just have to be ready when I have an opportunity to play."

That same week, invigorated by rest, fluids, and vitamins—as well as public endorsements from both his head coach and rival—Young breezed past the Falcons in the brand new Georgia Dome. Three of his eighteen pass attempts went for touchdowns, and the 49ers drubbed Atlanta, 41–3, setting up a momentous showdown with the Saints the following Sunday. Heading into the contest both clubs owned 7–2 records. The winner would have the inside track on the NFC West title.

Through three quarters San Francisco struggled against a rabid New Orleans defense that would finish the season ranked first in sacks and points allowed. Young scored the team's only offensive points on a dazzling ten-yard touchdown scramble that he capped by diving for the pylon.

At the start of the final quarter, the 49ers trailed 20–7, but Young—calling his own plays in the two-minute drill—stormed San Francisco back into contention, completing five of six passes for sixty yards and a touchdown, narrowing the deficit to six points. With four minutes remaining, the offense took possession at their own 26-yard line: to his ten teammates in the huddle, Young projected a command and confidence reminiscent of his predecessor Joe Montana.

"Nobody said anything besides Steve," said Guy McIntyre. "Except Tom Rathman. He just said, 'We're going to do it. We're going to do it.' And we were going to do it."

"We've got a good quarterback," Rathman added. "When the pressure was on, and there was a lot pressure, he had what it takes. He never panicked."

Young carried the offense down the field, this time for sixty-six yards—converting a trio of third downs along the way—then tossed the game-winning score to Jones.

"We will call it four-minute magic, what happened Sunday at Candlestick Park," Art Spander of the *San Francisco Examiner* wrote. "We will call it a remembrance of things past and a glimpse of things possible. We will call it the afternoon Steve Young made us forget Joe Montana and at the same time made us remember Joe Montana."

The following Sunday, Young again reminded 49ers fans of his paragon. For years, one of Montana's greatest legacies had been consistently beating the Los Angeles Rams, especially on the road. Now, in his first trip to Anaheim Stadium as a starter, Young assured a victory over the 49ers' rival, by completing a forty-two-yard fourth-quarter touchdown pass to Rice.

After toppling the Rams, San Francisco embarked on their toughest stretch of the season: three consecutive games against playoff contenders with top-notch defenses: the Eagles, the Dolphins, and the Vikings. Five more touchdown passes from Young helped the 49ers handily win all three and earn the NFL's best record at 12–2.

In Week 16, Young even secured a small piece of revenge against his former team, the Buccaneers. His third touchdown pass of the day gave the 49ers a fourth-quarter lead that quarterback Vinny Testaverde—the draft pick who had triggered Young's departure from Tampa Bay—could not overcome. The 21–14 victory clinched the NFC West title, a first-round playoff bye, and home-field advantage for the 49ers throughout the postseason.

"This year was awesome," Young said after the win. "As far as our regular season goal—we accomplished it. Now the playoffs will be like scaling a mountain, and we're going to try to reach the summit."

It had been an incredible season for Young. In addition to leading the NFL in completion percentage, touchdown passes, and quarterback rating, his 537 yards rushing were second on the club. And later that week, not only did Young earn his first-ever Pro Bowl spot, but he was also voted the winner of the Len Eshmont Award by his teammates.

"There's been a lot said about [Steve] and he's hung in there when things didn't necessarily look real good," linebacker Michael Walter said following the announcement of the team's award for inspiration and courage. "There's been the speculation on how he gets along with Joe, and can he stay in the pocket, and is he really as good as everyone says he is. And for him to come out and have this kind of year it's super. And we've all been witness to what he's done."

But any focus on Young's deeds was short-lived. During the final week of the 1992 regular season, all anyone wanted to talk about was the club's "other" quarterback: Joe Montana was returning to the 49ers' active roster.

Ever since he resumed throwing, Montana's doctors and trainers had continued with a cautious approach to his rehabilitation—the Holy Trinity was terrified of another setback. By November, despite persistent numbness in his finger, his hand had regained its full strength. Montana told reporters he was 98 to 99 percent healthy, "and the rest is just a lack of playing time."

Still, his spot on the injured reserve rendered him unable to even practice with the team. To the coaching staff, he felt practically invisible.

"They ask me, 'How's it going?'" Montana said after a workout in mid-November. "I parked my car by the no parking sign today so they probably know I'm here. . . . I'm ready but things are going well here, so I'm going about keeping myself prepared, and whenever they think it's necessary for me to come back. . . . Steve has been doing well. The team has been playing well. George [Seifert] is not going to do anything to upset the team, and that's understandable."

Near the end of November Montana was placed on the 49ers' practice squad. In the preparation for the game against Philadelphia, he tried his best to simulate the Eagles dynamic quarterback Randall Cunningham. Three weeks later, prior to the game against Tampa Bay, the 49ers waived former San

Jose State running back Sheldon Canley, freeing a spot on the forty-seven-man roster for Montana. In uniform, he served as the 49ers third (emergency) quarterback[1] against the twenty-point-underdog Buccaneers. Fans across the country prayed that Montana would have an opportunity to play.

"I think Joe's return is great," Young said. "I was inspired, and I think the team was also."

The "inspired" 49ers could not easily dispatch the 4–10 Buccaneers, however, squeaking out a seven-point win, deferring the dreams of Montana's return. But not for long. In addition to clinching the division title, a playoff bye, and home-field advantage, the win over Tampa Bay also meant nothing rested on the outcome of the team's regular season finale against Detroit. The 49ers could afford to play Montana.

"I'm anxious to see him play, certainly," Seifert said. "I think it's a situation where Joe has worked hard to get himself in position to where he can get some work and see where he is in his redevelopment.

"Is he best to be the backup?" Seifert asked rhetorically. "Or is [Steve] Bono? You would think, being Joe Montana and what we all remember of Joe Montana, that would be an easy answer. But it's not right now."

Each year from 1988 to 1990, the 49ers' last game of the regular season had been meaningless; with playoff positioning secured, the coaching staff was free to rest Montana and feed a hungry Steve Young several snaps or even a start. Now, the two quarterbacks' roles were reversed. Although Young would start, Montana would relieve him and finally return to the field after twenty-three months. To the fans and media across the nation, the 49ers' 1992 regular season finale was far from meaningless.

"We're looking at this as a positive. We're not looking at it as a threat to Steve Young," Rice said. "Steve, he's been named the quarterback, so I don't think there's any pressure on him. But knowing that Joe can step in if something should happen to Steve, it's a big lift to the team."

For Montana, the prospect of simply playing—taking the field, commanding the huddle, throwing passes in a live game—far exceeded any claim to the role of backup quarterback.

"It'll be interesting," he said that week. "It'll be fun. I think it will definitely be emotional. One thing that has been part of the drive of coming back has been the support I've received from the fans throughout the time I've been

---

[1] The third or "emergency" quarterback was eligible to play without taking a spot on the active roster, but if they entered the game before the fourth quarter neither the first- or second-string quarterbacks were allowed to return to the field.

out. It's been overwhelming. I'm just happy I've got an opportunity to hopefully come back and do something."

Despite the mythology of Joe Cool—steely nerves and ice water in his veins—Montana was tense in the days leading up to the game.

"It was my audition to go somewhere else," Montana said years later. "And that's really what the nervousness was about, not really about playing, just whether I'm gonna be afforded an opportunity to be able to throw the ball and do things that other teams could see that I could still do."

On a typically cold, windy, and rainy Monday night in San Francisco, the 49ers defense allowed Detroit two early field goals before Young took the offense in for a go-ahead touchdown. Ahead 7–6, the 49ers exited the muddy field for halftime. When they returned for the start of the third period, the Candlestick crowd erupted.

"That's when it really hit me what was happening," Brent Jones said, "at the start of the second half when we came out of the locker room and people were going nuts."

With the howling fans on their feet during the entire series, Montana trotted onto the field. He completed his first two passes—short dump-offs to running backs, neither of which yielded a first down.

"I had a lot of expectations for myself," he said. "And I was a little jittery in the beginning, just trying to get a rhythm going, and I couldn't seem to get it going."

As the 49ers punt team replaced the offense, Montana said to Rice, "Man, I'm glad to get that over with."

"Now you can go out and have some fun," Rice replied.

San Francisco's defense stonewalled the Lions throughout the night, giving Montana several opportunities to have fun. But he didn't feel at ease until Detroit defensive linemen Tracy Scroggins and Marc Spindler sandwiched him for a sack midway through the third quarter.

"Once I got knocked around. I felt OK," Montana said. "I took a couple of good hits, which probably more than anything settled me down. I came up throwing and didn't really feel the hit as much as I expected. . . . I felt once I got into the fourth quarter things would turn around. I was over getting the completions and over getting hit a few times and starting to feel a little bit more of the rhythm, a little bit more of how much time I had in the pocket, moving around, feeling the pressure and moving up. So I felt a lot more comfortable as we got further on."

Despite increasingly difficult conditions—in addition to rain, wind, and mud, the absence of offensive starters Harris Barton, Tom Rathman, and John Taylor hampered the 49ers passing game—Montana led the offense to a field goal.

Then, in the fourth quarter, on his rusty, thirty-six-year-old legs, Montana eluded two defensive linemen, scrambled out of the pocket, sidestepped another defender, and picked up sixteen yards.

"I tripped over my own feet and fell right on my face, and all I could do was laugh," he said.

Two plays later, Montana capped off a seventy-four-yard scoring drive with a touchdown pass to Jones. In the end zone, aware that it might be the final touchdown pass the quarterback ever threw as a San Francisco 49er, Jones handed the ball to Montana.

"I gave him the ball and I remember him going, 'Why are you giving me this?'" Jones recalled years later.

A confused Montana—"I didn't know why Brent was giving it to me, I was looking for an official to hand it to"—jogged to the sidelines and high-fived several coaches and teammates, including Young.

"It was a great tribute to Joe, and I was excited to be a part of that," Young said that evening.

On the next series, Montana drove the offense seventy-six yards for another score, an eight-yard touchdown pass to running back Amp Lee.

An awestruck crowd absolutely loved it. So did Montana.

"It took us a little while to get going," center Jesse Sapolu said, "but on his timing patterns, once he got going, it was unbelievable the way he was throwing. You could tell on the first series he was like a kid in a candy store. The last couple of drives, it was vintage Joe Montana. It was such a beautiful picture. All you can do is have a smile on your face."

Montana finished with fifteen completions on twenty-one attempts, 126 yards passing, and two touchdowns. In the 49ers locker room later that evening, it was the 1980s all over again. The press swarmed Montana, who narrated his touchdown passes, talked at length about his mindset, and showered praise on his teammates after another 49er victory.

"I'm just glad it's over," he said.

Back at the Montana family home in Atherton, all four young children—Elizabeth, Alexandra, Nathaniel, and seven-month old Nicholas—were asleep, even though they stayed up as late as possible to watch their father on the ABC broadcast. The next morning, the children woke up their father to ask if he had fun and to talk about the game, the first they had seen in nearly two years.

"You can tell he's my son," the proud father said. "[Nathaniel] was saying, 'Wow, daddy's strong.' Jennifer had a great laugh over that one."

But at his Tuesday press conference, Seifert made sure everyone—his players, the fans, and the media—knew that the stroll down memory lane was a one-night-only viewing. The head coach stated that once the postseason began, only an injury to Young would put Montana back on the field.

That pre-emptive strike delivered, Seifert and the coaching staff went back to work, watching game film of the possible playoff opponents who would be coming to Candlestick Park. By the end of Wild Card weekend (San Francisco's bye week), the defending Super Bowl champion Washington Redskins earned that honor the following Sunday.

"We've been in a playoff atmosphere for a number of weeks now," Young said proudly. "They were all must-win games in our hearts. . . . The high expectations are also good. I enjoy that, and I seem to do pretty well with it. So I don't think there's any problem. . . . You play all the regular season to get here. So now you've got here, and now you have to do it. It's no big deal."

Clearly Young didn't need any more confidence prior to his first-ever playoff start, but nevertheless, he received an additional boost that week. By a huge margin, the *Associated Press* voted him the league's MVP. When asked how it felt to follow Joe Montana, winner of that award twice in the previous three seasons, Young responded with his trademark optimism.

"I guess I decided last year that rather than feeling uneasy with that, that it was great," he said, referring to walking in Montana's footsteps. "You're going to find out how good you can play. And I decided to make it something I really wanted rather than a microscope I was trying to get away from. 'Make it something that I like, and it will make me a better person, a better player.' And obviously winning the MVP, it speaks for itself. . . . I've enjoyed football probably as much as I've ever done in my whole life this year."

Still, in the minds of many across the nation—especially fans at Northern California bars like Ricky's in San Leandro, where a fistfight broke out over the Young–Montana controversy—Young, the league's Most Valuable Player, wasn't even his team's most valuable quarterback.

"I can't help it. I want to see Joe Montana play against the Redskins," Michael Wilbon of the *Washington Post* wrote. "I don't want to see him play as badly as the tacky woman who called San Francisco radio station KNBR and told the talk show host she hoped Steve Young would break his leg between now and Saturday.

"Can't go in with her on that, but what would be the harm in Young coming down with a three-hour virus, right around 4 p.m. Eastern on Saturday, something that would leave him temporarily congested and stuffy just long enough to see The Man in one more playoff game? . . . It's absurd, we know that. But this is what happens when you follow a living, playing legend, the greatest quarterback who ever lived. This is what Steve Young is living with at the moment. I know Joe Montana, young man, and you, sir, are no Joe Montana."

Wilbon almost got his wish. Young disappointed Montana loyalists by playing just well enough to defeat Washington in the NFC Divisional playoff. Still, the narrow victory only came at the end of a truly sloppy day by the Bay, especially for Young.

A week's worth of rain turned the Candlestick Park surface into a quagmire that both head coaches called the worst they had ever seen. Although sod was laid down atop the dirt infield (the stadium also housed Major League Baseball's San Francisco Giants), heavy California rains almost always resulted in a mud-covered playing surface.

Young threw two touchdowns in the first half to give the 49ers a 17–3 lead, but an interception and a fumble (both deep in Redskins territory) allowed Washington to remain in contention. Late in the third period, the 49ers charged inside the Washington red zone, but the drive ended when Young, scrambling through the muddy terrain, fell down and stood back up only to bump into by a teammate. Young dropped the ball, which a Redskin fell on.

"Joe Montana wouldn't be running in the first place," Redskins radio analyst and Sam Huff told the WTEM-AM 570 audience.

The Redskins quickly scored, narrowing the gap to 17–6. And on the very next possession, at the San Francisco 15-yard line, Young pump-faked a wet football, which squirted out of his hands and onto the ground. The Redskins recovered and scored a touchdown three plays later.

A fourth turnover cut the 49ers lead to just four points, but Seifert remained true to his word and kept Young in the lineup.

"I didn't say anything to Steve about the turnovers," he said. "The key to Steve Young, or anybody, for that matter, is you have to forget about the last play and go on to the next. I wasn't worried about Steve. He always bounces back."

But Young almost didn't bounce back. Trying to recover a third fumble, Young dove into the pile and bruised his throwing hand. Suddenly, all eyes turned toward the 49ers sideline.

"Steve was hit then as hard as he was hit the whole game," Seifert said. "He was getting up slow. It just flashed into my mind: 'Joe hasn't been throwing the ball here as of late. What if Steve takes another hit like that?' So I turned to (Montana) and I said, 'Go warm up.'

"I turned back to watch Steve, and Steve was fine. Joe eventually came back, put his jacket on, and quit warming up. There was no thought beyond that to make a change at quarterback. There was no thought at that time."

Claiming he was unaware of a loosening-up Montana, Young promptly conducted a seven-minute, fourteen-play scoring drive that pushed the San Francisco lead to 20–13 just before the two-minute warning. The 49ers hung on for the win, but Young's ugly playoff debut did little to rally the masses heading into the NFC Championship Game.

Fans called in to radio shows and wrote local newspaper editors, insisting that Seifert start Montana the following Sunday. Many sports columnists shared their sentiment. While their collective impatience came as no surprise, Jerry Rice's did.

To more than just the die-hard 49ers fans, the transition from Montana to Young was a work in progress, especially to each of the pass catchers on the 49ers roster. Adjustments took both time and practice.

And although Montana and Young came from dissimilar backgrounds, projected opposite personalities, and epitomized starkly different styles of play—Montana the classic pocket-passer, Young the scrambling, improviser—the most basic element of their quarterback play presented the most tangible obstacle: Montana was right-handed, Young left-handed.

"After developing that chemistry with Joe, I had to put that on the back-burner and just let it go," Rice said in 2011. "You have a different spin on the ball. The ball pretty much spins opposite when it comes out of a lefty's hand. And to really watch Steve, as a receiver, you look back there and see this guy is opposite, everything is backward. It took some getting used to."

A few days after the 49ers playoff win over Washington, *Newsday*'s Bob Glauber questioned Rice about his take on the quarterback situation.

"Joe and I had a chemistry going, and it's going to take some time before I really start to feel comfortable with Steve," Rice said. "I have to say to myself, 'Well, Joe's not going to be back there to make my job a little easier.'"

Montana was (predictably) less candid and much colder when reporters asked whether he had offered Young any counsel or encouragement after his shaky playoff performance against Washington.

"Why should I? Did he say anything to me when he came? If he did, I would have remembered. It's part of the game, pressure."

As he had for years, Young avoided the conflict and chose instead to focus on the positive.

"I've never looked over my shoulder and not seen Joe," he said. "But I just look at it as me keeping the train going and not thinking of Joe as anything negative, like a shadow. I relish the situation. You find out how good you are in situations like these."

If Young did indeed relish the challenge issued by Montana's shadow, he must have been ecstatic when he learned who the 49ers were playing for the right to go to Super Bowl XXVII. Eleven years after "The Catch"— Montana's dynasty-forging touchdown pass to Dwight Clark—the Dallas Cowboys were once again coming to Candlestick Park for the NFC Championship Game.

Flashbacks to that game as well as interviews with Clark, head coaches Tom Landry and Bill Walsh, Everson Walls—the defender over whom Clark caught the ball—and many more appeared in newspapers from coast to coast. But Montana garnered the most attention: he was the only remaining player on either roster from that seminal 1981 NFC championship contest.

"Yeah, I'm, the only one who is here for both games," Montana said. "And it doesn't mean a damn thing."

That wasn't entirely true. To finally escape Joe Montana's shadow, Steve Young would have to repeat one of the beloved quarterback's greatest feats with a healthy Montana in uniform—as well as thousands of nostalgic fans in the stands—glaring at him from the sidelines.

Through one quarter of football, Young appeared capable of doing just that. In front of his childhood hero Roger Staubach—whom the Cowboys brought, dressed in a No. 12 jersey, and positioned as a good luck charm near the Dallas bench—Young tossed a beautiful sixty-three-yard touchdown pass to Rice. But a deflating penalty against the offense canceled out the score, and the 49ers soon punted. The offense regained those points a few series later when Young drove to the 1-yard line, then sneaked the ball across the goal line for the game's first touchdown.

During the next two quarters, however, Dallas took command of the game. The Cowboys young offense—featuring superstars-in-the-making quarterback Troy Aikman, running back Emmitt Smith, and wide receiver Michael Irvin—scored touchdowns in the second and third quarters. Only able to post field goals, the 49ers fell behind 24–13 in the final period.

Young—who had orchestrated fourth-quarter comebacks that year against New England, New Orleans, and the Rams—didn't panic.

"We've done it a couple of times before," Young said. "I felt like we were going to do it again."

On their next possession, Young completed a pass to Jones and scrambled for a few yards to cross into Dallas territory, but with just over ten minutes remaining in the game, Cowboys linebacker Ken Norton Jr. intercepted Young's pass over the middle intended for Jones.

"I thought Norton's body weight was taking him in the other direction," Young said. "But once I threw it and looked out there, I realized he wasn't going where I thought."

In less than two complete playoff starts, Young now had five turnovers. During his previous nine playoff appearances, Montana had turned the ball over just twice. With the season on the line, the league's Most Valuable Player was not playing like one.

The interception only cost the 49ers time, not points. On the ensuing Dallas drive, Cowboys head coach Jimmy Johnson elected not to try a field goal on fourth-and-1 near the 49ers goal line, and a handoff to Emmitt Smith was unable to gain the first down, giving San Francisco the ball back.

Within three minutes, short passes and runs picked up ninety-two yards, and at the Dallas 6, Young dropped back, rolled left—away from former teammate Charles Haley—and slung a touchdown pass to Rice, who was inexplicably covered by a linebacker.

"I was feeling good there," Young said. "Confident, relaxed. We could get the ball back and put the hammer to them."

But the Cowboys immediately silenced an energized Candlestick crowd when Aikman's post-pattern throw to Alvin Harper picked up seventy yards. A 49ers blitz and the slippery field were the perfect storm. Three plays later, the Cowboys scored their fourth touchdown.

"After the long drive, I really thought we were going to pull it out," Young said. "But Dallas came up with the big plays at the end the way we have so many times over the years."

Although 3:43 remained, and the 49ers trailed by only ten (Dallas's extra point was blocked), hopes of a Montana-like miracle quickly dissipated. Young, targeting Rice deep inside Cowboys territory, threw into double coverage and was intercepted again. With less than two minutes left and possession of the ball, the Cowboys ran out the clock, sealing a Super Bowl berth.

Given the narrow loss, the two fourth-quarter turnovers, and the magic Montana had delivered eleven years earlier on the same field against the same opponent, the question was asked: Would Joe Montana have done better?

"Anywhere else, Steve Young is a hero," Jesse Sapolu said. "But he plays here in the footsteps of No. 16, and so anything less than a Super Bowl win is not going to be enough for anybody. It's not fair. But I guess that's life."

Leigh Steinberg—who after seven years had become very close to the Young family—wasn't nearly as accepting. One day after the 49ers NFC Championship Game loss to the Cowboys, he sprang to his client's defense.

"Going 14–2 and advancing to the conference championships, in most other football cities, they'd have a parade," Steinberg said. "In Dallas, they had seventy thousand screaming fans at a pep rally. In San Francisco, we've become so blasé to winning that we just need some time to get some perspective. . . . We well understand the tremendous heritage of success that Joe Montana has had, and Steve has always taken great pains over the past six years to pay suitable homage to Joe's greatness. But it's 1993, and Steve is a free agent, and I simply think it would make sense to pause and watch what transpires."

Young wasn't thinking that far ahead: he was still processing the unbearable loss to Dallas. At the postgame debriefing, he spoke about the crippling holding penalty that cost them the opening touchdown to Rice, the interceptions, and his mood.

"When you realize how hard it is to get here to this point and almost reach the Super Bowl," Young said, "you know, you leave your heart and soul out there. I feel like I'm a walking shell right now. I feel like the inside of me is still out there on the field, trying to win the game."

Then came the inevitable questions about his backup and his backup's legacy.

"If people want it to be me compared with Montana again next year," Young said, "I guess that's the way it's going to be."

No one had a chance to ask Montana any questions. After removing his spot-white, unused uniform in the training room and donning his civilian clothes, Joe Montana—quarterback for the San Francisco 49ers—ducked out of a back entrance, never to return.

10

Dream On

For most NFL players, the offseason meant a time to relax, train for next fall, and decompress after another physically, mentally, and emotionally exhaustive year. But not for Steve Young: "Mr. Hyperactivity" spent springs and summers in Provo, Utah, preparing for the career he thought was his true calling ever since the college freshman matriculated in the fall of 1980.

"When I started at BYU, I never really had the image of myself playing professional football; it never crossed my mind," Young once said. "From the start, from when I started thinking about what my major would be or what I would eventually do, I was going to go to law school, be a lawyer; that was the plan all along."

Instead, Young settled for a life in professional football that made him a multimillionaire before his twenty-fifth birthday. That never stopped him from pursuing his passion for the law. In the summer of 1988, Young enrolled at BYU's J. Reuben Clark Law School, and by September 1992—as a part-time student—he was fourteen credits shy of graduation.

"It wasn't easy getting the other students' respect, and I'm not sure that I've succeeded at it," he said. "But over five semesters I've been able to prove my longevity, that it's not just for fun, that it's a second career for me."

Young's first career had peaked in 1992—he won the league MVP, was named a first-team All-Pro, and brought the 49ers to the doorstep of the Super Bowl. But for the fans in the Bay area, so accustomed to championships, the doorstep was not enough.

Not long after that excruciating NFC Championship Game loss to Dallas, Young resumed his law school curriculum. In April, as his semester neared conclusion, the ever-diligent student retreated from the world in preparation for his final examinations, causing him to miss one of the most bizarre, jarring episodes in NFL trade history.

"Finals, you're kind of underground for a couple weeks," Young said years later. "We were studying, then sleeping, then studying, sleeping, studying. Finally, I got done with my last final, I came out, and one of my friends called me:

'Did you hear? Joe was traded.'

'Really? I had no idea.'

'Yeah, it was a couple days ago!'"

* * *

While Young was busy immersing himself in constitutional law, 49ers team president Carmen Policy was also buried in an avalanche of expert opinion.

"In '93 we got a report from the doctors: 'You may get ten games out of Joe. Maybe twelve. He's not going to finish a season. But maybe, if you play him right and sparingly and rest him, you might have him ready for the playoffs," Policy recalled years later. "I sat with the coach, I sat with all our personnel people, sat with the doctors: 'What is the right thing to do? Give me the information.' And everyone of them said, 'Steve has to be the guy. You've got to go with Steve from this point forward. If you want to keep Joe, keep Joe. He'll be divisive.' Because, how do you take the lead stallion and tell him he's in the back of the truck that's being pulled by the Clydesdales. It probably won't work. But Steve has to be the starter. And they were right."

Policy had other distractions competing for his attention that spring. A new collective bargaining agreement reached in January brought about radical changes to the NFL landscape—specifically a salary cap and the start of unrestricted free agency. The 49ers—the least frugal franchise in professional football—now had to limit the amount of money they spent on player salaries. At the same time, however, they were also allowed to sign (without compensating the player's former team) some of the game's brightest stars. In March and early April, the front office's attention was focused less on their surplus of quarterback talent and more on re-signing their own players, reducing salary, and trying to acquire future Hall of Fame defensive end Reggie White, the game's most highly coveted free agent.

Although San Francisco lost out on White—who instead joined Mike Holmgren in Green Bay—and saw their two premier pass rushers, Tim Harris and All-Pro defensive end Pierce Holt defect, the 49ers did re-sign defensive end Kevin Fagan and added All-Pro safety Tim McDonald.

The move the team made on April 7, 1993, however, had far more impact on the quarterback controversy that had been underway for more than five years. Re-signing unrestricted free agent Steve Bono to a three-year, $5.15 million deal all but guaranteed Joe Montana's departure from San Francisco. Given the new salary cap restrictions, the 49ers could not afford to pay three quarterbacks more than $1 million each per season.

"This permits us to more fully explore the alternatives with Joe," Policy said after the announcement of Bono's deal. "In all likelihood, we're talking about a trade if he leaves."

The 49ers gave Montana and his team of agents at IMG permission to seek a trade, and that spring the Tampa Bay Buccaneers, Kansas City Chiefs, Phoenix Cardinals, Minnesota Vikings, Detroit Lions, New Orleans Saints, and Los Angeles Raiders all expressed serious interest. Soon Phoenix and Kansas City emerged as front runners, and both teams brought Montana to town for a prolonged courtship.

A moribund franchise desperate for star power to increase low season-ticket sales and excite a lukewarm fan base, the Cardinals pitched Montana a robust offer. In addition to a brand new training facility and Gary Clark—the top free agent wide receiver had signed two weeks earlier—they offered Montana a raise to roughly $4.5 million per season.

The city of Phoenix and its residents showered Montana with adoration. He was greeted by screaming fans upon his arrival at the airport, and from there team officials chauffeured him along Highway 10, where a large billboard read, "Arizona. A great place to live and play. The Cardinals welcome Joe Montana." The *New York Times* even reported that a Cardinals fan named Susana Chavez—in anticipation of Montana's acquisition—named her newborn daughter Sara Joe Montana Chavez.

"He's going to go where he feels he has the best opportunity to win," Peter Johnson, one of Montana's agents, said. "It's not the sun. It's not the grass. It's not the turf. It's not the community. This guy would play in Alaska if he thought he could get to the Super Bowl. That's all he cares about."

Prior to his visit to Phoenix, Montana was in Kansas City, meeting with the Chiefs. There he underwent a physical and threw passes for head coach Marty Schottenheimer, general manager Carl Peterson, and the team's new offensive coordinator, Paul Hackett, Montana's former quarterbacks coach in San Francisco from 1983 to 1985.

"I would love to play for the Chiefs," Montana told the press. "I think everything's in place, if everything can be worked out."

The X-factor was the requirement that the 49ers approve any trade, no matter how appealing it was to Montana. Even though he preferred Kansas

City, Phoenix offered San Francisco the highest value—the third overall selection in that April's draft.

"I dealt with [Cardinals owner] Bill Bidwell himself," Policy said. "They were willing to give us the first pick, and they were willing to make sure Joe's happy. Because I'm not only negotiating for us, I'm negotiating for Joe, because I want a package that is going to be as palatable to him as possible. Then Carl Peterson thinks he's going to steal Joe, and he thinks he's going to go to Joe's heart, and they're going to give him a contract, and we're going to give him away, and he's trying to get Joe for nothing. There was an appeal to Eddie, 'If you're going to let him go, let him go on his own terms. He's earned it.' And I was incensed by that, because we're the 49ers; if we're going to let Joe go and take the heat, we have to have compensation. So these are rough times. Strong words, strong conversations going back and forth. So then the compromise was, we'll let him go for less, but it's still got to be a credible deal."

Apart from Montana's desire to find the ideal situation, the 49ers goal of receiving the best compensation, and owner Eddie DeBartolo Jr.'s reluctance to part with his favorite player, there was another roadblock in the negotiations: the role of Dwight Clark.

Since his retirement, the former 49ers wide receiver had risen in the front office, becoming coordinator of football operations during the summer of 1992. Now, he was caught between management and his close friend and longtime teammate.

"Dwight was in personnel," Policy said. "He never wanted to let Joe Montana go, but he would say, 'I don't know where my heart is, where my head is at this point. I just can't let him go. We gotta do everything to keep him. He is the heart and soul of this team.' Dwight almost threw himself on the table to keep him. But he couldn't fight any of the substantive conversation. It was like, how do you cut the heart out of an organization and give it away. That's what we were doing when we let Joe Montana go. [Clark] was that vocal. I said, 'You're too emotional and you feel what we feel and you're letting it get control of you.'"

During the discussions held at the 49ers headquarters in Santa Clara, emotions eventually overwhelmed both parties.

"It was the most surreal feeling I've ever had in that building," one member of the press recalled years later. "Upstairs Jennifer [Montana] was furious with Dwight, because he tried to really shove this [deal] down their throats. He said, 'We're in charge, essentially this is our property, and that's the way it's going to be. It's not going to be anything else but what we want,' and it was pretty unnerving to them."

While Montana made follow-up trips to both Kansas City and Phoenix, negotiations between the 49ers and Chiefs, the 49ers and Cardinals, as well as the 49ers and Montana's representatives continued.

"I cherished draft choices, in particular high draft choices," Carl Peterson said. "Carmen and I laugh about this today: we went back and forth on this. What they wanted, of course, was a first [round draft pick], a second, and a third. And I said, 'Carmen, let's be honest. Joe's thirty-six years old, he's coming off injury. It's just awful for me to give up a first-round draft choice. In fact, you're going to have to give me something back. . . . Carmen would call me and say, 'Carl, I'm a very stubborn Sicilian, and I'm not budging on this.' And I'd say, 'Carmen, I'm a very stubborn Swede, and I'm not budging on this.'"

Ultimately Policy and the 49ers budged. They agreed on a slightly less lucrative deal with Peterson and the Chiefs. San Francisco would send Montana, safety David Whitmore, and a third-round draft choice to Kansas City in exchange for the Chiefs first-round choice (eighteenth overall) that spring. Montana agreed as well.

The next day, Montana flew to Youngstown, Ohio, to personally tell 49ers owner Eddie DeBartolo Jr. about the impending trade.

"This is such a compliment to Joe Montana and Eddie DeBartolo, this story, and it's something you don't find in any sports today," Policy said in 2011.

"I'm flying back," Montana said, according to Policy. "I'm going to tell Mr. D . . . how much I love him; I'm gonna thank him for everything and explain to him how this is the best thing for me, for the 49ers. I'm going, but I'm going happy; not happy that I'm going. And I'll be back. However many years I play, ultimately I'm coming back here. . . .

"Call me and let me know how it goes," Policy told Montana.

Policy then fielded a call from DeBartolo, who was awaiting Montana's arrival.

"I'm going to take one more stab at trying to get him to stay," DeBartolo said.

"Well, OK," Policy said. "But you have to understand it's so tough, Eddie. Him saying no is not a rejection of you."

"I know, but I'm going to take another stab."

"But if he has to go, Eddie, let's make it gracious."

"OK," DeBartolo said.

"So will you call me, let me know how it goes?" Policy asked.

"Yeah."

The next day Policy's phone rang again. It was DeBartolo.

"He's staying!"

"What?" Policy said.

"Joe's staying. We had a long talk last night, we had a few drinks together, he's agreed to stay! Tell George Seifert to get ready, I'm flying him out there;

we're flying back tomorrow, and we'll do a press conference. Set up the press conference."

"OK, but before we set up the press conference," Policy said. "Let's make sure we're all on the same page. This is serious stuff here, we gotta get the team ready, we gotta get the team ready."

Early the next morning, Policy met DeBartolo and Montana's plane at the airport.

"Hey Mr. D! Hi Joe," a member of the airport crew shouted.

"He's staying!" DeBartolo shouted back, pointing to the quarterback.

Along the tarmac, with DeBartolo a few steps away, Policy made eye contact with Montana.

"What happened!?" Policy whispered to Montana.

"I'll tell you later," Montana whispered back.

From the airport, they all went to DeBartolo's home, where Policy pulled Montana aside.

"What happened?"

"[Eddie] was so emotional and he was so sincere and he was so intent, I couldn't say no."

"What!? What do we do now!? Are you staying?"

"Hell no, I'm not staying," Montana said. "But you've got to tell him I'm leaving. I can't tell him I'm leaving."

Neither one told DeBartolo, who instructed George Seifert to appoint Montana the team's "designated starter."

"For what he's done over the years for the 49ers and for the fans," Seifert told the *New York Times* after speaking to his bosses, "he deserves this opportunity. The more you evaluate the situation, this is the logical thing to do."

The national media pounced on the story. Just two months earlier, Seifert had unequivocally declared Young the starter. Now, the vague, newly coined term "designated starter" appeared in headlines of newspapers across the country.

"That's when, again, Steve Young was a great, great team player," Policy said. "Because I called him before that and called Leigh Steinberg before that. I said, 'We gotta do this. We need your cooperation, we need it desperately. And somehow, someway, we'll make it up to you.' And Steve did it. When that announcement came out, he said, 'That's the coach's decision, and I'm ready for training camp.' He handled it like a very big boy."

Young may have been too wrapped up in centuries-old legal rulings to be overly concerned.

"Whatever they need to do, let them do it," Young told Steinberg. "I've got to study."

But deep down, Young burned for some closure after years of pent-up frustration.

"When I got to San Francisco," he said in 2011, "I had started with the USFL and Buccaneers probably forty games and had never sat since I replaced Jim McMahon, and it wasn't like I think I'm cool. If I wasn't playing there's a lot of [other] things I wanted to do. And so after playing and playing well I wasn't going to go back to that again. So it was really up to the 49ers which way they wanted to go, but certainly one of us was going to have to go at that point."

Then, all of a sudden, Young got his wish. The day after Montana returned to San Francisco, Policy approached DeBartolo.

"It was agreed, I'd talk to Eddie that night," Policy recalled. "So we're at Eddie's place, and I said, 'You broke Joe's heart. He couldn't tell you what he wanted to tell you. He came back to tell you [about the trade]. He could not in your presence say no to you, which is a sublime compliment, but which is undeniably a complicated element in everything we're dealing with. The deal is done.' So we all go to Joe's house the next day: Seifert, Dwight Clark, myself, Eddie, Jennifer, Joe. Dwight's crying, Joe's crying, Eddie's crying. I felt like a criminal."

Montana issued a press release—which thanked DeBartolo and the organization, praised Young's performance over the previous two seasons, and shared his eagerness for his future in Kansas City—then met with reporters in Santa Clara the next day. Flanked by Jennifer and both his parents, Montana answered questions with customary humor, joking that all he knew about Kansas City was their legendary barbecues and the encouraging news that "they only have one newspaper there."

The other half of the dais appeared far less cheerful. The ongoing negotiations had rendered Policy and Seifert physically wiped. DeBartolo was also emotionally drained.

"I don't have the relationship with anyone on this team I have with Joe Montana," DeBartolo said. "It transcends football. I feel a deep sadness. This is a personal loss for me."

DeBartolo wasn't alone. When the fifty-minute press conference ended, two hundred fans waiting in the parking lot cheered, "We want Joe! We want Joe!" as a van drove Montana to the airport and a plane bound for Kansas City.

"Babe Ruth got traded, Willie Mays got traded, Joe Montana got traded, Jesus was crucified," Michael Zagaris, the 49ers team photographer, said later. "So who is safe? . . . Nothing is forever."

The entire Bay Area was crushed. Kansas City was overjoyed.

"I remember the rock station here," Chiefs center Tim Grunhard said, "101 The Fox, which covered the games, was playing that old [Warren Zevon] song, 'Lawyers, Guns and Money,' to get Joe Montana to Kansas City."

Although his status as an icon had certainly hastened the deal, to the Chiefs organization Montana's arrival was more than simply a move to sell tickets.

Once a powerhouse of the American Football League and a Super Bowl champion at the end of the 1969 season, the Chiefs had fallen on hard times in the 1970s and '80s. The team missed the postseason every year between 1972 and 1985, and after Hall of Famer Len Dawson retired in 1975, Kansas City offenses were routinely among the worst in the AFC.

Hoping to cure their scoring woes, the Chiefs drafted Clemson quarterback Steve Fuller in the first round of the 1979 draft, fifty-nine selections before the 49ers chose Montana. During his first three seasons, Fuller was sacked more than any quarterback in the NFL's modern era and lost the starting role to backup Bill Kenney. In 1983—the same year that they drafted Penn State's Todd Blackledge with the seventh overall selection—Kenney posted the first four-thousand-yard passing season in team history and earned a Pro Bowl selection. But neither Kenney not Blackledge could produce a playoff victory, and toward the end of the decade the front office brought in a string of established passers nearing the twilight of their careers: Ron Jaworski in 1989, Steve DeBerg in 1990, and Dave Krieg in 1992.

"Even in Kenney's spectacular 1983 season there was never a real feeling that the Chiefs had found their quarterback," said Kent Pulliam, the beat reporter for the *Kansas City Star*. "None of the veterans they brought in were ever deemed a long-term fix."

Under head coach Marty Schottenheimer, the franchise rebounded in the early 1990s. Great defense—anchored by two of the game's premier pass rushers, Derrick Thomas and Neil Smith—propelled the franchise to three consecutive postseason appearances. But they won just one playoff game and still had not claimed a division title since 1971. And with each of the Chiefs' main rivals for AFC supremacy—Jim Kelly's Buffalo Bills, John Elway's Denver Broncos, Dan Marino's Miami Dolphins, and Warren Moon's Houston Oilers—sporting a future Hall of Famer at quarterback, Montana's presence was needed in order to take the Chiefs to the top.

"Even when Joe arrived, he wasn't viewed as a long-term fix," Pulliam added. "But there was an excitement of getting a Super Bowl–winning quarterback— even at the end of his career—and the 1993 season was the most anticipated in Kansas City since the team lost to Miami in their double overtime Christmas Day 1971 playoff game. Finally, even though everyone knew it was short-term fix, the Chiefs had a quarterback who could lead them to the Super Bowl."

As much as his Super Bowl MVPs and playoff excellence, Montana's personality instantaneously attracted fans and teammates to their new quarterback.

"When he came here, we had our first minicamp meeting, and I got to meet Joe, and we decided we'd go out," recalled Tim Grunhard, a fellow Notre Dame alum who had graduated eleven years after Montana left South Bend. "So we went down to Westport, which is an area here in Kansas City where all the bars are at and the nightlife. This was probably a Wednesday night or Thursday night, kinda quiet in Kansas City, and we went up to a place called Kelly's. Went in and had a couple beers, just kinda sitting, getting to know each other.

"And this is before cell phones were real popular. But we noticed that all of a sudden, the bar went from maybe five or six or seven people to twenty, thirty, forty, fifty people. Then we thought we'd pay our bill, go somewhere else, go maybe find a quieter place, and the next thing you know that bar would be filled up too. By the time it was all said and done, hundreds of people were lining the streets of Westport, trying to get a glimpse of Joe Montana. This is the charisma he brought to Kansas City and brought to the Chiefs. He kind of re-invented the Chiefs at that point.

"The one thing I noticed about him right away was that he was a down-to-earth guy, just like talking to a buddy from college. And he really opened himself up to the people that he was with that night," said Grunhard.

Even the man whose job he took, incumbent Chiefs starting quarterback David Krieg, enjoyed spending time with Montana.

"He took me to some nice golf course," Krieg said, "and tried to smooth the water and said, 'Look, I know you played every down last year, that's not easy to do.' And I said, 'Yeah, I know, but if your name wasn't Joe Montana, and you didn't have four Super Bowls, there certainly would be a competition.' But we became really good friends after that.

"I told him, if I played in [the 49er] offense, I would have gone to a Super Bowl or two, easy. It's such a quarterback friendly offense. It's getting the ball out of your hands and putting it in the receivers' hands, let them run with it. I said anybody could throw to John Taylor and Jerry Rice on an eight-yard slant, let them run eighty yards. . . . We gave each other crap all the time. . . . I think he liked the fact that I didn't treat him like Joe Montana. I think he got a kick out of that."

Less than two weeks after acquiring Montana from San Francisco, the Chiefs opened minicamp practices. And although the coaching staff kept a cautious approach to their new quarterback and his fragile elbow by limiting his throwing regimen, that didn't prevent Montana from assimilating into the Chiefs locker room.

Pranks and wisecracks—a Montana trademark from his years in San Francisco—were the quickest means of building team camaradrie. He dropped stink bombs in team meetings, sneaked into teammates' lockers and cut the shoelaces in their cleats, and, along with Derrick Thomas, even "kidnapped" Neil Smith's cherished baseball bat: the Pro Bowl defensive end celebrated each sack with an elaborate homerun swing. And when Smith refused to pay their $50,000 ransom, he found countless boxes of toothpicks in his locker. Only after Smith informed head coach Schottenheimer that he had not recorded a sack since the bat was kidnapped was it returned.

"He was a fun guy to be with," Smith recalled years later. "I always said to people, 'That is the coolest white guy that God ever made.'"

And because Montana lacked a emormous ego or frosty façade that isolated him from the rest of the team, he, too, was a target of taunts and playful mocking. At the team's very first minicamp, safety Bennie Thompson stole Montana's clothes and hid them while he was in the shower. Teammates ribbed Montana upon learning that Grunhard's wife, also a Notre Dame alum, had the quarterback's picture in her high school locker. And they repeatedly teased Montana about his notoriously frail frame.

"They used to look at me and go, 'Wow,'" Montana said in 2011. "Derrick Thomas, he owned part of a soul food restaurant. And a lady used to bring breakfast every morning. I never ordered breakfast. He walked over to me, and he had this huge breakfast on him: two pork chops, grits, potatoes, eggs, bacon. It was a monster meal. He goes, 'The lady who runs the restaurant said you're way too skinny to be playing football, so she thought you'd better eat breakfast everyday.'"

But not every moment of his honeymoon in Kansas City was fun and games. Despite his comfort with offensive coordinator Paul Hackett—a Walsh disciple and former 49er assistant—Montana needed to adjust to a new collection of pass catchers. And they all needed to adjust to him.

"It really took me a couple practices to get used to this," wide receiver J. J. Birden recalled. "I'm in the huddle with Joe, and I'm just like, 'That's *Joe Montana*,' so I went through that for a while. I can recall the very first play we called in practice was 'X-hook,' and I ran a hook and remember Joe hit me in the back of the head [with the ball], and I came back to the huddle and he says, 'OK, now I did that for a reason. You gotta understand: I don't wait until you get open. I expect you to be in an area, and I throw it anticipating that, so you want to get used to getting your head around faster.' And that was the first lesson I got from Joe."

While Birden, Willie Davis, tight end Keith Cash, and the rest of receiving corps learned from and adapted to Montana's style, so too did head coach Marty Schottenheimer.

"I could definitely see there was a tight relationship between Hackett and Joe because of their familiarity," Birden added, "Marty was kind of old school a little bit. He was used to being the guy, making all the decisions.

But I could see that Marty gave Joe a lot more leeway and a lot more trust, knowing that Joe knows this offense. He really accepted Joe's input, and he had a lot more freedom. And I witnessed the opposite the other years because when we got in the huddle, Joe had the ability to change the plays more. . . . He knew the plays so well, and he knew the defenses so well that he was always a step ahead of the defense. I would sit there and watch Joe in the meetings. He would be sitting there studying these plays. And I'd ask him, 'Joe, haven't you been in this offense forever? Don't you know it?' And he goes, 'Oh, yeah, but I always want to make sure that I'm prepared for everything.'"

As if adding one former Super Bowl MVP to the offense wasn't enough, the Chiefs also signed running back Marcus Allen six weeks after acquiring Montana. By the start of training camp, the buzz in Kansas City was unprecedented.

One day in early August at 8 a.m., single-game Chiefs tickets went on sale at Arrowhead Stadium and Ticketmaster outlets. By 8:01 a.m. five hundred were sold; all twelve thousand were gone within two hours.

"No matter what happens this year, it's going to be the most exciting year the Chiefs have seen in a long time," Bob Gretz, the sports director for KCFX-FM, told local business leaders at an August meeting of the South Kansas City Chamber of Commerce. "They are either going to go all the way, and everyone is going to be thrilled, or they won't, and everyone will be mad."

The Chiefs won three of their four exhibition games, with Montana completing twenty-five of thirty-seven passes for 288 yards and two touchdowns in three appearances. By the end of the preseason, Kansas City fans were already dreaming of a Super Bowl berth.

"He's played very, very well," general manager Carl Peterson said at the conclusion of the exhibition season. "He certainly played as well as I would have hoped he could, and better. He's been very impressive through the entire training camp. He's been tremendously productive. He knows this offense, and he still can execute it. His arm is stronger now than when we worked him out in March before I made the trade. We monitored the throws in training camp so that he would never go over one hundred. That was just prudent of us. We started back in the off-season with fifty a day. It was purely precautionary. He's had no problem whatsoever."

Montana's tenure with Kansas City officially began in a familiar place and among two familiar faces. The Chiefs 1993 regular season opened with a visit to Tampa to play the Buccaneers, coached by Sam Wyche, Montana's former quarterbacks coach in San Francisco. Steve DeBerg, once Montana's roommate and fellow 49ers prankster, was the veteran quarterback operating Wyche's version of the West Coast offense.

"We get to the [Tampa Stadium] visiting-team locker room," Chiefs general manager Carl Peterson recalled. "Joe's always got this sneaky smile, smirk. He came into the locker room, and he had done something to play a prank on Steve DeBerg. So he's giggling about it, telling his teammates as he's getting dressed. He puts his foot into his shoe, and it's filled with shaving cream. And there's a little note that Steve DeBerg said, 'You think you got me; I got you.'"

The Week 1 visit to Florida provided another, albeit much more painful, flashback for Montana. During a previous season-opening game in that same stadium, against that same opponent, Montana had twisted his lower spine in 1986, nearly ending his career.

"The back was going to go sooner or later," Montana informed the press that week. "It was degenerative to begin with. I didn't really get hurt in that game. I was running toward the sideline and turned back to throw. It was just the straw that broke my back, so to speak."

In his Chiefs debut, Montana again shredded both the Buccaneers and his former quarterbacks coach, completing fourteen of twenty-one passes for 246 yards and three touchdowns.

"To me, he looks like the same old Joe," Marcus Allen said afterward. "He hasn't changed a bit."

But as was the case seven years earlier when the 49ers dominated the Buccaneers in a 31–7 victory, Montana left Tampa Stadium injured. Midway through the third period, with the Chiefs ahead 17–3, Montana fired an incomplete pass to the end zone that was intended for wide receiver Willie Davis. On the follow-through, Montana smacked his throwing wrist into Bucs linebacker Broderick Thomas's helmet, then tumbled to the ground. His wrist broke his fall. Montana remained in the game, however, and on the next snap, threw a twelve-yard touchdown pass to Marcus Allen, clinching the Chiefs win.

"I knew it wasn't that bad because I threw the next pass," he said. "I could've kept throwing, and I probably could have gone back in. I just told them it was a little sore, and it was starting to swell up a little bit, and they wanted to grab some X-rays."

Krieg relieved Montana, and the Chiefs left Tampa with a 27–3 victory. But the next day, the wrist was noticeably swollen, sore, and sporting a welt. Montana was unable to practice until Friday, encouraging the press to ask him and Schottenheimer about the possibility of Montana and Krieg splitting the quarterback duties for the next game in Houston.

"I would hope they wouldn't do that to David or me," Montana said. "That's a tough way to go."

Sunday came, and erring on the side of caution, the Chiefs sat Montana against the Oilers. Aided by five turnovers and four sacks, Houston annihilated Kansas City, 30–0. Just two games into his career with Kansas City, Montana had exhibited both the agony and ecstasy attached to the great, yet often fragile quarterback's legacy. When healthy, Montana was still an elite passer; sidelined by injury, he was useless.

"You always want to play, especially when you think you can," Montana said. "Marty explained to us that it's a long season."

* * *

"Despite what you may have heard, I learned from Joe and will miss him," Steve Young told the press after emerging from his law school finals cocoon. "We were competitive, but we were part of the same family."

Young solidified his place as the 49ers *pater familias* that summer. After insisting that he harbored no resentment toward DeBartolo, Seifert, or the 49ers for declaring Montana the "designated starter," Young signed a five-year, $26.75 million contract that made him the highest-paid player in NFL history. (A technicality in the NFL free agency system made Young a free agent that summer, but the trade of Montana solidified his place on the roster—Leigh Steinberg explained that "this form of free agency means Steve is about as free as the People's Republic of China.")

The three-year transition from Montana to Young had been neither smooth nor swift, but now, at last, it was complete. And for all their many differences—in personality, background, playing style, and even in the way they threw a football—Young and Montana shared at least one characteristic that earned their teammates' trust, respect, and affection.

"Both guys were so similar, because they were great leaders," Rice said in 2011. "They exemplified confidence in the huddle, and I feel like that's a quality as a quarterback you should have. Joe, he was a prankster; he would put Tiger Balm in jocks, kid around, but when it came down to winning football games, he was very serious, and he always wanted to go out there and win. With Steve, he might have been a little more serious at first, but then the latter part, he was funny, he was dancing a little bit, having a great time on the football field, just enjoying himself. . . .

"The thing that really put them on the map is that they were that competitive, and they wanted to win, and they brought that 'it' factor out of players. They had that little extra where you wanted to win football games for those guys, and you knew that if they had the ball in their hands that they were capable of winning that football game."

In late July, the 49ers opened training camp without Joe Montana for the first time in fifteen years. As Montana's successor, Young scoffed at the notion that—as the unquestioned, unchallenged starting quarterback—he felt less pressure.

"Not at all," Young responded. "I've got a load on my back—to go to the Super Bowl."

Aside from a broken left thumb that sidelined Young for most of the pre-season (and required center Jesse Sapolu to snap the ball to his right hand), the 49ers' Super Bowl mission appeared to be on schedule. Opening their 1993 season with a visit to Pittsburgh to play the defending AFC Central champion Steelers, Young and his broken thumb threw three touchdowns in a 24–13 victory.

"I'm sure he's still sore and it's bothering him, but Steve won't admit it," said Brent Jones, whose fourth-quarter touchdown catch secured the victory. "Think how he's going to be in a few weeks when he feels better."

Jones's assumption made sense, but it never materialized. As the thumb started to heal, the 49ers offense became remarkably inconsistent. On a Monday night in Cleveland, Young threw three interceptions, lost a fumble late in the game, and could not score any points throughout the entire second half of a Browns victory. The following week, Young was nearly perfect, completing eighteen of his twenty-two attempts with three touchdown passes in a key win over Atlanta. But aside from an efficient performance during a home win against Minnesota, Young's offense continued to struggle over the next three weeks. In consecutive road losses to New Orleans and Dallas, San Francisco scored just one touchdown. Through the first six games of the 1993 season, the 49ers had three losses—one more than they recorded during the entire 1992 season—and Young had nine interceptions, two more than he threw all of the previous year.

"We've been getting field goals instead of touchdowns," Young said. "The focus of our offense has to be to put more points on the board. I think we should throw it more into the end zone. To me, the key of our offense is to attack. When we don't attack, we don't look like ourselves."

The main weapon in the 49ers passing attack was obviously Rice, and during their marginal offensive showing, he did not abuse opposing secondaries with his usual frequency. After a two-touchdown effort in the opening win over Pittsburgh, Rice caught just one over the course of the 49ers' next five games. And for the second consecutive season, he didn't post a single one-hundred-yard receiving effort through the 49ers' first six games. Even though Young and Rice were both first-team All-Pros the previous year, now that they were struggling, some members of the press rekindled the 1991 speculation that Young was not the ideal pocket-passing, right-handed quarterback that Rice preferred.

"Everything comes together through repetition," Rice said in 2011. "How you prepare during the week, the extra time you're going to spend off the football field, just getting to know this guy in the classroom. Once you get on the same page with each other, you're able to do incredible things out on the football field. Everything was through hard work and repetition. We got on the same page, [Young] knew my body language, he could look at me, read my eyes. . . . If you practice over and over again and practice at very high level, game situations, you're going to develop chemistry."

Beginning with a Week 8 visit from the Phoenix Cardinals, that chemistry finally developed. The duo connected on a pair of touchdown passes in a 28–14 victory, then, when the calendar turned to November, Rice collected eight more scores in successive blowouts of Tampa Bay, New Orleans, and the Rams.

Rice's touchdown binge propelled the 49ers to six straight victories and first place in the division. And despite a frustrating finish to the regular season—losing three of their final four games each by a field goal—the 49ers earned the second-seed in the NFC playoffs.

"You guys focus on the wrong things," Young told the press after the regular season finale, a 37–34 overtime loss to Philadelphia. "We exploded in Detroit, and we got the home-field advantage. Then we started playing around. It doesn't mean anything. We got beat by the Rams 38–16 the last game in 1988 and won the Super Bowl. We were mowing people down the last three games in 1987 and got knocked out in the first round. . . . We got behind the 8-ball [tonight], but the way we put points on the board gives me confidence."

Adding to Young's confidence were two records he set by season's end. Not only did he become the first player in NFL history to win three consecutive passing titles, and pace the NFL in touchdowns for a second straight year, his 4,023 yards passing bested Joe Montana's franchise record.

"As far as things I feel very good about, those records, they are important," Young said. "Four thousand yards passing. And look how many times I came out this season in the third quarter. It's not an easy thing to do."

A playoff bye allowed San Francisco to rest and prepare for their second-round opponent, the New York Giants, making their first visit to Candlestick since the 1990 NFC Championship Game. But the rematch of that thrilling, last-second New York victory was no contest. Right away, the 49ers overwhelmed an aging Giants team. The defense collected three interceptions, Ricky Watters rushed for a playoff-record five touchdowns, and Young completed seventeen of twenty-two attempts for 226 yards.

"This is as good as we can be without turning the ball over," Young said after his first turnover-free playoff start.

The 44–3 victory earned a second straight berth in the NFC title game and a chance at redemption. Young and the 49ers' road to the Super Bowl would take them through Dallas for a rematch with the defending Super Bowl champion Cowboys. The opening line listed San Francisco as a four-and-a-half-point underdog.

"I've been jumping through hoops for years," Young added. "They keep putting 'em up there, and I keep jumping through 'em. It's tough, trying to keep track of what you're trying to validate."

There was, however, one validation that Young could never lose track of—the 49ers decision to choose him over Montana.

"It's not a dark, looming image," he said. "To me it's a great thing to have to keep things going at the same pace."

To keep pace with Montana, Young needed to guide the 49ers to the Super Bowl—and win there.

* * *

His sprained wrist mostly healed, Joe Montana returned to the Chiefs lineup for Week 3 of the 1993 regular season. Montana's home debut, coupled with a visit from John Elway and the archrival Denver Broncos, made the prime-time episode of Monday Night Football one of the most anticipated events in Kansas City sports history. The sellout crowd was the largest at Arrowhead Stadium in twenty-one years.

"This place will be rocking, and that's a big plus for our football team," Chiefs coach Marty Schottenheimer said. "I don't think you can ever underestimate that."

Minutes after his old singing cronies from the Bay Area—Huey Lewis and the News—performed the national anthem, Montana led the Chiefs downfield for the first of five crowd-pleasing field goals. Behind his crisp passing (twenty-one-for-thirty-six, 273 yards) Kansas City defeated Denver, 15–7.

"It felt great for my first game in Kansas City," Montana said. "I had a little bit of taste of it in the preseason. It's pretty crazy out there. I'm glad they're on my side."

An equally raucous home crowd returned to Arrowhead two weeks later for the Chiefs next home game versus the Raiders. But against this hated AFC West foe, Montana was unable to survive the first half. On his way to another outstanding performance in a Chiefs win—completing seven of nine attempts along with two touchdown passes—Montana injured his hamstring while running toward the sidelines. He limped off the field and did not return.

"You wouldn't mind if you actually got hit," said Montana. "But to get one running out of bounds and the other you reach out to stop your fall and boom! You sprain your wrist."

The second injury to Montana was especially frustrating to a particular subset of the Chiefs' roster.

"We told the offensive line," Carl Peterson said, "that this quarterback behind them was a porcelain doll and that no one, no one should touch him ever. Our offensive line, they were a pretty good offensive line, they killed themselves to protect Joe Montana."

The players charged with protecting the thirty-seven-year-old quarterback used a very simple litmus test to measure their performance: Montana's golf game.

"We're going to make sure that Joe can play golf on Monday," center Tim Grunhard remembered. "That was one of our goals all the time. We always said, 'Hey, Joe, can you play golf today?' when we came in Monday. And if he said no, we didn't do our job. If he said, 'Yes, I can play golf on the off-day,' then we did our job. Joe Montana wasn't too sore to play golf."

Although no fault of the offensive line, Montana's hamstring kept him off the golf course as well as the playing field at Arrowhead Stadium the following week. Without him, Kansas City squeaked out a 17–15 victory over the winless Bengals. Through five games, injuries had sidelined Montana for exactly half (ten of twenty quarters) of the Chiefs season.

The hamstring improved just enough for Montana to return to practice and a critical Week 7 road game against the defending AFC West champion Chargers, the team that had shut out Kansas City 17–0 in the previous year's postseason. Despite Montana's return, late in the fourth the Chiefs seemed headed for another loss to a division rival.

Then, behind 14–10 with less than four minutes remaining, Chiefs defensive end Neil Smith blocked a San Diego field goal attempt, putting the ball back in Montana's hands at his own 20-yard line.

"I was on the edge of my seat," Chiefs defensive tackle Joe Phillips said. "I turned to [teammate Dan] Saleaumua and said, 'We've got the right guy for the job out there, with Joe.'"

Without any timeouts, Montana—who had aggravated his hamstring injury earlier in the game—completed a twenty-two-yard pass to tight end Keith Cash and earned an additional fifteen yards by way of a roughing-the-passer penalty. Three incompletions followed, setting up a pivotal fourth-and-10. At that moment, Montana's Chiefs teammates learned first-hand the origin of their quarterback's nickname, Joe Cool.

"Here he is, out there limping, but he's a leader," Marcus Allen said. "He doesn't show any signs of concern. Why should you?"

While the hometown crowd at San Diego's Jack Murphy Stadium hoped not to witness his patented fourth-quarter magic, Montana hit Willie Davis on the run to convert the fourth down, then connected with Hassan Jones on a twelve-yarder that moved the Chiefs into San Diego's red zone with just over two minutes remaining. Two runs by Marcus Allen covered the remaining nineteen yards, and Kansas City completed the comeback, earning a 17–14 win.

"It's always important to be able to do that as a team," Montana told reporters. "It gives confidence to our offense—and to our defense—that if they can stop them we will still be able to come back. You can't do this with one person."

That assertion, however, lost credibility during the Chiefs next game, a road trip to Miami to face the Dolphins.

In the middle of the night, less than twelve hours before game time, Montana woke his roommate Dave Krieg.

"We were in the hotel room together, and he told me to call the doctors. I was laying in my bed sleeping. I said, 'Hell, why should I call the doctors? If I call the doctors you might play, but if I don't call the doctors, I'll start," Krieg joked. "It must have been some serious pain because he was grabbing for my feet, he was laying on the ground, he was in serious pain. When the doctors came in they thought that was really a serious thing. He said it was the worst pain he'd ever felt."

Taken to a Fort Lauderdale hospital, Montana underwent an emergency procedure and passed two kidney stones. By 8 a.m., he was at the team breakfast, eating a full meal in preparation for kickoff five hours later.

The kidney stones crisis behind him, Montana started against Miami and completed ten of seventeen attempts, but late in the first half, avoiding pressure, Montana scrambled, slowed down, and "jammed my leg into the ground," re-injuring his hamstring. Already behind by two touchdowns, the Chiefs could not overcome Montana's absence and were pounded by the Dan Marino-less Dolphins, 30–10. (Earlier that season, Miami's star quarterback had torn his Achilles tendon, dashing a much-anticipated quarterback showdown.)

An old joke from his time in San Francisco—"What's the difference between Joe Montana and a dollar bill? You can get four quarters out of a dollar bill"—resurfaced in Kansas City.

Montana left Joe Robbie Stadium—the site of his dramatic Super Bowl XXIII victory five years earlier—on crutches and sat out the Chiefs next three games. In his place, Krieg won consecutive starts. Still, no one suggested any quarterback controversy.

"It's a different situation here," Montana said. "There was always this thing, they were trying to make a change back there. I was trying to fight it as long as I could. And here I have a different relationship with David (Krieg). I enjoyed watching him play . . . if you can ever enjoy watching someone else play. . . . I mean if it is possible. You still want to be out there. But if it is your friend out there, it makes a difference."

With the hamstring no longer sore, "just a little weak," Montana returned to the lineup for the Chiefs' late November game against the three-time defending AFC champion Buffalo Bills. And after a slow start, Kansas City tore through the conference's top-rated defense. Three field goals and a pair of touchdown passes lifted the Chiefs to 23–7 victory.

"[With Montana] perhaps subconsciously, some of us play harder," Marcus Allen said after the win, in which the offensive line didn't allow a single sack. "That's no knock against Dave Krieg, but it's just that Joe knows the offense much better."

The following week, despite Montana being worn down by either the flu, a cold, or a Vodka drinking contest with teammates two nights earlier in Kansas City's Country Club Plaza (depending on conflicting reports), the Chiefs dominated Seattle in the Kingdome for their ninth win. Then, a week after nearly snapping a ten-year draught at Denver's Mile High Stadium—Montana's third-quarter touchdown pass to Willie Davis gave the Chiefs a short-lived edge, but the Broncos won—Kansas City overcame a 17–0 deficit to defeat the Chargers at Arrowhead Stadium. But once again, the Chiefs were unable to get four full quarters out of Montana.

Down by three points in the third period, Montana drove the Chiefs near the San Diego goal line then was clobbered by Chargers All-Pro linebacker Junior Seau. Kansas City used a timeout, during which Montana convinced Schottenheimer he was coherent enough to return. On the next snap, a split second before Montana released a pass for J. J. Birden, he endured another brutal hit, this time from defensive end Chris Mims.

"What happened next looked straight out of a cartoon," the *Kansas City Star*'s Jonathan Rand wrote. "Montana, looking like a bird squashed under an elephant, raised his head to peek at Birden, who had caught the ball for a touchdown. While flat on his back, Montana's arms, as if springing from a jack-in-the-box, struck the famous touchdown pose he prefers to display when standing. Mims then playfully tapped Montana's face mask, as if to say, 'Aw, shaddup.'"

"I don't know what he said, but he was laughing and so was I," Montana said. "My head started to hurt, so they took me inside and took a couple of tests. I kept trying to get back out, and they kept trying to hold me."

Diagnosed with a minor concussion, Montana spent the next few series in the locker room then returned late in the fourth quarter and preserved the 28–24 victory.

"Joe was dizzy, lightheaded," Schottenheimer said. "The ballgame . . . was not won by talent. It was won by people with a determination and something in their heart that says, 'I'm not going to be denied.'"

The Chiefs were denied the following week in Minnesota—Montana threw two interceptions in "probably one of the worst games I've had"—but losses by the Raiders and Broncos resulted in Kansas City clinching their first AFC West title in twenty-two years. In the Chiefs' regular season finale against Seattle, Montana and the offense tuned up for the playoffs with a 34–24 win, then looked ahead to their upcoming wild card opponent, the Pittsburgh Steelers.

Under head coach Bill Cowher, a protégé of Schottenheimer's, the Steelers defense had become renowned for pressuring the quarterback, earning the nickname the "Blitzburgh Steelers," and evoking memories of the Steel Curtain dynasty of the 1970s.

"They like to put pressure on you and see if you can make the correct decision in a pretty quick amount of time," Montana said. "And they like to blitz a lot and play zone behind it. They try to bring guys and try to make you think it's hot when it's not really hot."

"Not really hot" proved to also be an apt description of the early January weather in Kansas City: prior to the kickoff at Arrowhead, the temperature was below twenty-five degrees. Montana had previously excelled in frigid environments, but for the only time in his entire career, he wore a glove on his throwing hand. Missing several open receivers, his first seven pass attempts were incomplete.

"I wish I could blame it on the gloves," Montana said, before adding, "but I won't wear them again."

He ditched the gloves and completed a twenty-five-yarder to Willie Davis, but at the end of the play Steelers defensive end Donald Evans planted Montana into the ground. Bruised ribs sent Montana to the sidelines, and Dave Krieg took his place. The thirty-five-year-old backup soon threw a touchdown to a diving J. J. Birden, who had beaten the NFL's Defensive Player of the Year, Rod Woodson. Montana returned for the next offensive series, yet the Chiefs fell behind. Midway through the third period, Pittsburgh led Kansas City 17–7. Montana wasn't worried, however, and neither were his teammates.

"We have more confidence with Joe here," Davis said. "In the playoffs, we feel like we can beat anybody any time because of his experience. This is Joe's show. And you can't give up. Because with him you never can tell what might happen."

After a field goal and a nine-play, eighty-yard Chiefs touchdown drive tied the score, the Steelers reclaimed the lead. Now with less than three minutes to play, Kansas City trailed 24–17.

"I still felt we'd get another opportunity," Montana said.

Tight end Keith Cash provided that opportunity by way of a blocked punt, which gave the Chiefs possession at the Pittsburgh 9-yard line. But the offense gained just two yards on the next three plays, creating a game-deciding fourth-and-goal at the seven. And although it wasn't by way of a John Candy sighting—*à la* Super Bowl XXIII—Montana still found a way to loosen up his teammates.

"I think there was a minute left on the clock, and we were trying to get into overtime," Birden remembered years later. "And Joe told a joke in the huddle, which I thought was really odd, because I was so dang nervous . . . fourth down, whatever it was, and he told a joke! . . . I said, 'You've got to be kidding me. This guy did not just tell a joke at the most intense moment in this game.' But once again it kind of reminded us that this guy has been there, done that, and that was his way to relax us."

"He never really panicked, when other guys were screaming, 'We have to make a play, we have to get back in it!' he was just cool Joe," Keith Cash remembered. "It was almost like his heartbeat just slowed down while everyone else's was speeding up."

On that fourth down with the game on line, Montana sat in the pocket, looked off the safety, and fired a dart that Tim Barnett hauled in at the back of the end zone for the game-tying score. The Arrowhead crowd of 74,515 exploded in cheers.

"We go into the postgame press conference," Peterson remembered, "the media is saying, 'Joe, what were you thinking when you knew this was fourth down, you've got to make the play, you've got to make the throw, what were you thinking?' He stopped, hesitated, 'Was that really fourth down?' He's just tweaking the press. We laughed. He knew exactly what it was; he just knew and had great confidence in what he could do. And he executed it."

In overtime, Montana completed five passes for forty-six yards to put the Chiefs in position for a game-winning field goal attempt, which veteran Nick Lowery nailed from thirty-two yards out.

To a franchise that had just one playoff victory since winning Super Bowl IV in January 1970, Kansas City's 27–24 victory marked a special day. To Joe Cool, it was just another entry in a lengthy volume of post-season heroics.

"Part of the fun of the game is having to deal with pressure," Montana told reporters afterward.

For both Montana and the Chiefs, the pressure only increased a week later in Houston.

The Oilers, who had shut out Kansas City in Week 2, earned the AFC's second-seed, a bye in the first round, and a home playoff game in the second. Under three-time All-Pro Warren Moon, Houston operated one of the league's most explosive passing attacks, but during successive postseasons, their defense had disappeared.

In 1991, they blew a three-score, late third-quarter lead in Denver. A year later in the wild card round, the Buffalo Bills overcame a 35–3 deficit to topple the Oilers in the most spectacular playoff collapse in NFL history. To remedy the problem, Houston hired Buddy Ryan, the architect of suffocating defenses in both Chicago and Philadelphia.

Ryan's first postseason challenge as the Oilers defensive coordinator was Kansas City. His most recent attempt to stifle Montana's offense had resulted in one of the quarterback's greatest comebacks when Montana's four fourth-quarter touchdown passes lifted the 49ers to victory over Ryan's Eagles in Week 3 of the 1989 regular season.

"He beat us with a couple of three-yard passes," he insisted. "They broke tackles and went about a hundred yards apiece."

As he was prior to that 49ers improbable triumph in Veterans Stadium, Ryan once again explained that persistent pressure would both intimidate and neutralize Montana.

"When an eighteen-wheeler runs over you, you have to feel something, I would think," Ryan said.

Through two quarters, Ryan's boasting was justified.

In addition to collecting a blitz-induced interception, the Oilers defense repeatedly knocked Montana to the turf of the absurdly loud Astrodome, which was aptly nicknamed "The House of Pain."

"He doesn't run like he used to, but neither do I," Ryan said. "We got some pretty good licks on him, and he kept getting up like he always does."

During the game, Montana—who needed multiple pregame pain-killing injections for the ribs he bruised a week earlier—was seen holding his wrist as well as his knee, and his surgically repaired throwing elbow swelled up considerably.

By halftime, the Chiefs trailed 10–0.

"No matter how far behind we are," Willie Davis said that day, "the whole team feels we're going to win the game as long as Joe's out there. At any given time, we know he can make the plays and win the game."

On their opening possession of the second half, Montana drove the Chiefs to the Oilers 7-yard line. While rolling out of the pocket, he floated a pass to tight end Keith Cash, who leapt for the grab, crossed the goal line, then celebrated by hurling the football at a nearby poster of Buddy Ryan hanging behind the end zone.

Aided by their own fierce pass rush—which gathered a playoff-record-tying nine sacks—the Chiefs shut out the Oilers during the third period. And despite Montana's fourth-quarter interception deep inside Chiefs territory, the defense didn't allow a single yard, forcing a long field goal attempt. Still, with less than nine minutes remaining, Houston led 13–7.

"If we were close, we always thought we had a chance to win with [Montana] behind center," fullback Kimble Anders remembered. "Through that run during the playoffs it happened, down in Houston, also in the Pittsburgh game, it prevailed that way. Just the confidence that he brought in the huddle, and the way he—it's strange—how he relaxed you. . . . I think he brought that to the huddle, the sense of calmness that he instilled in everybody in the locker room or offensively, that we knew we had a chance to win the game if we just stayed close."

Another huge catch by Cash, followed by a pass interference penalty against Houston put the Chiefs at the Oilers 11-yard line, where Montana targeted J. J. Birden across the middle for the go-ahead touchdown. Derrick Thomas then stripped Moon on Houston's next possession, and Dan Saleau-mua recovered the fumble, putting the ball back in Montana's hands. On the ensuing third-and-16, Montana's perfect backshoulder throw to Davis at the right corner of the end zone beat impeccable coverage by the Oilers' Cris Dishman. The second touchdown pass in less than a minute gave Kansas City a 21–13 advantage.

"Joe threw the ball up, and Dishman never saw it. I saw the ball the whole time. He was going full speed, and I just stopped, turned around, and caught it," said Davis, who had dropped an easy touchdown pass during the Chiefs scoreless first half. "[Montana] never loses his temper out there. He doesn't say he's not going to throw you the ball anymore. He keeps his confidence in you."

Warren Moon matched the touchdown by connecting with Ernest Givins from seven yards out, and with 3:35 remaining the Chiefs' lead was cut to one. Houston's defense then forced a third-and-1 at the Kansas City 30-yard line. The Oilers were one play from getting the ball back.

In the huddle, Montana called "Y-Banana," a play designed simply to gain a few yards.

"What we were trying to do was just get a first down," Montana said. "We knew they were going to blitz. I got hit; the ball went up. . . . A guy who used to play with me said I have a tight wobble, not a tight spiral. All my balls are like that."

Montana's tight wobble was made even wobblier by defensive end William Fuller, who smacked Montana's arm just as he released the pass. But Cash—closely covered by linebacker Eddie Robinson—pulled the fluttering football out of the air and raced forty-one yards for the game's most critical gain. Three plays later, at the Oilers 18-yard line, a handoff to Marcus Allen sealed the Chiefs' second straight fourth-quarter miracle.

"Before Marcus Allen had taken his second step," Carl Peterson recalled, "Joe Montana has his hands raised for touchdown. He knew right then that it was the right call, the right place, and that Marcus was going to hit the seam. I think he celebrated that play as long as any that I can remember ever seeing."

His swollen right arm raised, Montana high-stepped to the end zone to rejoice with Allen and the rest of his teammates over the game-clinching score.

"It feels as good as ever. Obviously, a lot of people have counted you out, saying you'd never make it this far," Montana said. "It feels good to be still in one piece at this point and still playing, and still winning."

The 28–20 victory advanced Kansas City to the AFC Championship Game for the first time in twenty-four years. The following week, in Orchard Park, New York, the Chiefs would play Buffalo. But their potential Super Bowl opponent—if they were to defeat the Bills—drew much more attention from the national press. In Dallas, on that same Conference Championship Sunday, Montana's former team was also playing for the right to go the Super Bowl. A dream matchup of Montana's Chiefs versus Young's San Francisco 49ers teased millions.

"Fans all over the country, maybe all over the world, want to see Joe against Steve in the Super Bowl," 49ers tight end Brent Jones said. "Supposedly, Joe and Steve would want to see it. Anybody who knows how competitive each of them is would understand that. Kind of an ultimate challenge thing."

Publicly, Montana maintained the ultimate challenge was simply reaching a record fifth Super Bowl.

"If we make it, I don't care who makes it [from the NFC]," Montana said. "That's all I'm concerned about. Who cares who the other team is if we have the opportunity to go?"

He did, however, concede that he still cared about many of his former 49ers teammates.

"I keep up with some of the guys," Montana said that week. "I was there for too many years not to."

Of course, reporters wanted to know if his successor belonged to that group.

"How about Young?" one asked.

"No," Montana said, "I couldn't care less."

*   *   *

For the quarterback who had won a Cotton Bowl while battling hypothermia, and an NFC Championship in sub-zero wind chill conditions by Lake Michigan, frigid weather in Western New York was little concern.

In fact, cold was one of Montana's greatest allies in the days prior to the AFC Championship Game against Buffalo: he needed ice to reduce swelling in several different body parts.

"He'll be on the injury list with ribs, wrist, elbow . . . one of the above," Marty Schottenheimer told reporters. "But the elbow thing looks worse than it actually is. It's just a [bursa] sac that's got some fluid in it. It doesn't inhibit him in any way from doing what he needs to do."

Schottenheimer was right: neither the ribs, nor the wrist, nor the elbow would inhibit Montana against Buffalo. Another concussion, however, would.

Although the Bills took a 20–6 advantage into halftime, Kansas City was confident that a third straight comeback was possible. In addition to Montana's presence, the Chiefs were encouraged by their steady play against a stingy defense. Twice in the first half, the offense advanced inside the Buffalo 10-yard line, settling for field goals. And just before the end of the second period, Montana completed five passes through the sleet and wind to guide the offense seventy-five yards. Only a goal line interception—the result of a bobbled pass in the slick conditions—prevented Kansas City from scoring again.

"We realized we were still only two touchdowns out of it at that point, and we were getting the ball back (to start) the second half," Montana said. "So we felt we could move the ball and do similar things."

But less than a minute into the second half, a trio of Bills defensive linemen crunched Montana at the end of a pass play. As All-Pro Bruce Smith dragged him down, Montana smacked his head on the cold, hard AstroTurf. Lying on the ground, Montana clutched the sides of his helmet and winced in pain.

"He was moaning, 'Ohhh . . . ohhh,'" Smith said. "I asked him if he was OK, and he didn't comprehend what I was saying. I realized it was something more serious than him just laying on the ground."

"As soon as I landed," Montana said, "everything went white, and I had a real severe pain inside my head."

In a scene reminiscent of the NFC Championship Game three years earlier, teammates, coaches, and trainers circled Montana. They delicately stood him up, then slowly walked the quarterback to the team bench where he sat very, very still. The diagnosis was a second concussion in six weeks.

"I couldn't remember for most of the third quarter what had even happened, let alone what was going on," Montana said. "I was trying to pay attention, but I couldn't even remember what the score was or how they had gotten twenty points."

Dave Krieg relieved Montana and produced a third-quarter touchdown that cut the deficit to just seven. But Thurman Thomas's third touchdown on the day combined with constant pressure by the Buffalo defense closed out the Chiefs.

"There's pros and cons to having a quarterback like Joe Montana," Tim Grunhard said years later. "The pros were that you believed that if he was in the huddle you had every opportunity to win. But the con is when you lose a guy like that, I think you lose confidence, and I think you lose the innate idea that 'We can win this game if Joe's here, but if Joe's not here, gosh, can we still win?' And it put a little doubt in our minds.

"We had some opportunities in the second half, and we had some opportunities in the first half before Joe got hurt, but it kind of just took the air out of the balloon. When Joe Montana was knocked out, and we went over and looked at him . . . as the offensive linemen we felt like we had let our team down, we let our quarterback get hit, we let him get a concussion. He looked like he was completely out of it. Just looking at him on the sidelines, it looked like he had aged ten years from the beginning of the game, to the time I saw him on the bench. His face looked different, it looked older, he looked tired, and he looked like he was beat up, and we felt responsible for that. I don't think we ever bounced back from it."

The Bills 30–13 victory crushed the possibility of a Montana versus Young Super Bowl. But even if the Chiefs had managed to escape Orchard Park with a victory, a dream matchup still wouldn't have materialized. The 49ers failed to hold up their end of the bargain, as well.

Ten minutes before the end of the Bills-Chiefs AFC Championship Game, the NFC Championship Game opened at Texas Stadium in Irving.

Excitement over a possible Super Bowl showdown with the franchise's former centerpiece had hovered over the 49ers all week, but the veteran team refused to look ahead.

"Yeah, that would be great, just great," Young said. "People have been talking and wondering about it all along, and that's understandable. But for right now our focus is on the Dallas Cowboys, because that's who we play Sunday."

The Cowboys were not simply the next opponent. They were also the team that had defeated San Francisco twice the previous year: in the NFC Championship Game at Candlestick Park, then again nine months later during a Week 7 visit to Dallas.

"After that game we kind of got upset with ourselves," Young said. "Yeah, they beat us, but we made some turnovers and (mistakes) that really cost us. At that point, we decided we're a better team than this; let's turn it around and start playing really top-notch football. And we did."

The Cowboys scored on their opening possession, and although Young and the 49ers offense answered with a nine-play, eighty-yard touchdown drive to tie the game, the second period belonged to Dallas. Behind 14–7, Young was pressured into overthrowing John Taylor, who deflected the ball into the arms of safety Thomas Everett.

"After that pick, I really felt we took control of the game," Everett said. "They never threatened us again, really."

Dallas added two more touchdowns, and by halftime San Francisco trailed 28–7. Not even knocking Cowboys star quarterback Troy Aikman out of the game with a concussion could revive the 49ers.

"This was just a different kind of game altogether," Young said. "Last year it went down to the wire. This year we were playing catch-up in the second quarter. We've rarely been in that situation.

"Dallas got off to the kind of start that we did last week. And against a team like that, every time they score early you have to match it, especially on the road. Football is a strange game. I never thought we'd come down here and get beat by that score."

For the 49ers, very little went right during the 38–21 loss. They committed several costly penalties, forced no turnovers, allowed Dallas to convert on eight of thirteen third-down attempts, and the San Francisco running game—third best in the NFL—was shut down. As a team, the 49ers appeared rattled even before kickoff. That week Dallas head coach Jimmy Johnson had guaranteed a victory, foreshadowing a pregame scuffle between Rice and opposing cornerback Kevin Smith.

Nevertheless, for many, the blame fell squarely on Young, who for the second consecutive season could not deliver San Francisco to the Super Bowl.

"The Montana faithful would rather see the team lose with Montana at quarterback than win with Steve at quarterback," Young's agent Leigh Steinberg recalled years later. "[Montana] never threw an interception. He never lost a game. He took the team to the Super Bowl every year in legend."

Even those with a far more objective perspective realized that 49ers fans carried lofty, often unfair, expectations.

"Many 49ers fans still don't believe in [Young]," the *San Francisco Chronicle*'s Lowell Cohn explained several months later. "They constantly leave messages on my voice mail blaming him for every problem that befalls the team. If an offensive lineman jumps offsides—nullifying a touchdown pass that miraculously came about because Young scrambled for ten seconds behind the line of scrimmage before spotting an open receiver—it was somehow Young's fault. They say that when he called signals, his cadence was irregular, or he got a frog in his throat, or he accidentally counted in French."

Young's teammates, including Jerry Rice and Brent Jones—both of whom consoled him after leaving the field at Texas Stadium—rushed to his defense.

"He doesn't play defense, does he?" Jones facetiously asked a reporter who mentioned the second playoff loss by Montana's replacement.

"The criticism didn't pierce my heart; it just pricked my skin," Young later admitted. "It was an irritation that wouldn't pierce to the core. I appreciate the skeptics and critics because it made me a tougher human being."

But no matter how tough he became, no matter how much his teammates respected or defended him, Young also knew that without a Super Bowl victory, his claim to Montana's throne would never be recognized.

"There was a part of me that thought, 'If I don't help get this team to the Super Bowl, I might have to get out of town.' It doesn't matter what else you're doing, so it was a big deal. You think about everything I've done in college, replacing Jim McMahon: nothing mattered unless you were All-American and went to the Holiday Bowl and won it every time you went. Following Joe was like nothing mattered unless you went to the Super Bowl.

"So in some ways, that's a hard road, but even failing, you're going to do pretty well. So if you actually succeed at it, that's a really great thing."

11

The Monkey on My Back

Near midfield on a sunny, seventy-three-degree September day at Arrowhead Stadium, Steve Young approached Joe Montana. Less than an hour remained before the San Francisco 49ers and Kansas City Chiefs kicked off the second week of each team's 1994 regular season.

"We worked together for a long time," said Young, who jogged thirty-five yards to initiate the conversation. "I swear from the bottom of my heart, there's no animosity. For me not to go over and say hello to Joe after all the years we were together would have been a little awkward."

The pregame exchange between the two quarterbacks—which included a laugh, Young patting Montana on the butt, and courteous wishes of good luck to one another—didn't last long.

"We both had to warm up," Montana said.

While the former teammates spoke ever so briefly, the rest of the Montana clan was on pins and needles.

"I think it was more emotional for my wife," Montana's father, Joseph Sr., said. "I think she took a Valium before the game."

"Nervous? I'm always nervous at game time," Jennifer Montana told reporters. "But I was so confident last night, and I told him so. . . . Because it's him. It means a lot, emotionally. The thing between him and Steve means a lot because it's what you've all been writing all week."

Even Montana couldn't mask an uneasiness about playing his former team.

"It's tough," he said early in the week. "I wish I could look ahead and tell you exactly what it's going to be like, but I really don't know. "I'm sure it's going to be one of excitement and nervousness, like any other game, maybe just a little bit more. It'll be fun to play against them, but I'll be nervous because everybody at home will be watching."

The day before, the thirty-eight-year-old quarterback tried to remain relaxed. He played six holes of golf, hosted a barbeque at his suburban Leawood, Kansas, home for several dozen out-of-town guests, then rode go-carts in the cul-de-sac with the neighborhood children.

But by kickoff, Montana was noticeably anxious.

"That was a lot of pressure on him, a lot," recalled Steve Bono, who had been traded by San Francisco to Kansas City the previous offseason. "That was a really tough week, really tough. He was grinding over that one."

The game was no less difficult or bizarre for the stars on the visiting team.

"It felt like a bad dream," Jerry Rice remembered. "You look on the opposite side, and you see Montana. . . . It just didn't feel right."

The matchup between teams sporting 1–0 records—each a defending champion of their respective Western divisions and the runner-up in their conference the previous season—kicked off just after noon Central Standard Time. And from the outset, the energy pulsating throughout Arrowhead Stadium was palpable.

"That game was incredible," Chiefs wide receiver Danan Hughes remembered. "If there could ever be a measurement of the impact of momentum and intensity of a game before it started . . . the score was 21–0 before we even stepped on the field. That's how we felt. We knew that there was a lot more on the line than just another game. There's no better way—especially with all the tension that you hear and the rumors between Steve and Joe—to show the type of player and person you are than to go against your former team and stick it to 'em. Joe never stood up in a meeting, never made any kind of super pregame speeches or huddle speeches during the week or even in that game."

Armed with his trademark efficiency as well as simple advice by his Kansas City teammates—"Don't have flashbacks and throw it to the guys in the other uniforms," he was instructed—Montana drove the offense to the 49ers 1-yard line. From there, he floated a corner end-zone pass to offensive lineman Joe Valerio, who turned the tackle-eligible play into a touchdown. Montana celebrated the opening drive score by striking his classic arms-raised pose.

"He said the game was nothing special, but we sensed it was," wide receiver Willie Davis said. "When we saw him do that and jump in the air, we knew it was."

Young and the 49ers offense answered, scoring touchdowns on back-to-back second-quarter drives. Behind 14–7, Kansas City rallied prior to halftime. Punter Louie Aguiar pinned the 49ers deep in their own territory and the Chiefs defense targeted Young, who was without two of his starting offensive linemen that day. (In addition to a foot injury that sidelined guard Ralph Tamm, a torn triceps kept left tackle Harris Barton from playing in the game against his former John Candy–lookout from Super Bowl XXIII.) On third down, Young retreated into his own end zone and was sacked by Derrick Thomas, resulting in a safety that awoke the Kansas City crowd.

"It was different than any other game, obviously," Montana said in 2011. "Playing the team where I still should have been, probably a little more motivation on my side and actually on my teammates' side. Them being happy I was there, they were also unhappy that I had to leave. . . . They all probably had that same feeling that it could happen to them someday. They thought about it probably more than or as much as I did as the week went on."

Sparked by the defensive score and another Thomas sack on the first play of the second half, Montana's Chiefs reclaimed the lead midway through the third quarter. An eight-yard touchdown reception by Keith Cash and a successful two-point conversion pass from Montana to J. J. Birden put Kansas City ahead, 17–14. As the second half wore on, the Chiefs front-seven further harassed Young. He threw two interceptions—one the result of a defensive lineman grasping his feet—fumbled the ball away at the end of a short scramble, and avoided Thomas's fourth sack only by drawing an intentional grounding penalty.

"I don't think Joe ever said anything," Chiefs center Tim Grunhard remembered. "I don't think he put that kind of pressure on us. But I think we put that kind of pressure on ourselves. I know the defense—Joe was really close with Derrick and Neil [Smith] and some of those guys—they put pressure on themselves to get to Steve Young and make Steve Young look like that was the wrong decision.

"So the defense really kind of rose up and said, 'We're going to prove that the 49ers and their organization was wrong for letting Joe Montana go.' I would not have wanted to be an offensive player on the 49ers that week. [The Chiefs defense was] like crazed dogs coming after people. All week long that's all they talked about: getting after Young, knocking him down, getting after him, getting after him, getting after him."

In the fourth quarter, a field goal pulled San Francisco within seven—safety David Whitmore, the other former 49er traded to Kansas City the previous year, tackled Young near the goal line on a critical third-and-goal from the two, forcing the 49ers to bring on the kicking unit. With less than four minutes remaining, Young, in search of the game-tying touchdown, found John Taylor for a first down, but the veteran wide receiver fumbled, ending any chance of a Montana-like comeback. The Chiefs ran out the clock to secure a 24–17 victory.

"This had a special meaning because it was my old team," Montana said. "But there is no feeling of vindication or anything. We beat one of the best teams in the league, and that's the most important thing about today. I've got a lot of friends on that team, so that makes today satisfying. But that's my old team. This is the team I worry about now."

With the game over, Montana shook hands with many of his former teammates, including a battered Steve Young.

"There [were] a lot of people around, and I just got a chance to say good luck," Montana said. "He's having a good year and hang in there, you know, maybe we'll see each other again. It's not an easy thing to have a game of this nature and to be on the short end. Just look at his passing and winning record. He's having a great career with them."

Not long after the postgame quarterback summit, Young met with the press in the visiting locker room. As usual, he was upbeat, self-effacing, and flattering of Montana.

"Right up to the end I thought we could come back and win it. I learned from Joe, from the master. Today the master had a little more to teach the student," Young said.

"He's in many ways one of the greatest as far as winning Super Bowls, four. I gotta get there."

Although smiling and optimistic in front of the press, when Young called his parents at their home in Greenwich, Connecticut, his outlook was far different. LeGrande and Sherry weren't at home, so the two-time All-Pro quarterback left a message on their answering machine.

"Joe's a hero, and I'm a schmuck," he said.

Despite a near perfect, winning performance (thirty-one completions for 355 yards and two touchdowns) the next week against the Rams, and two more touchdown passes in a comeback victory over New Orleans, Young's despair peaked at the end of the 49ers Week 5 visit from the Philadelphia Eagles.

Not nearly as ferocious as they had been in years past—their great defense had been poached by free agency—the Eagles arrived at Candlestick looking to snap a five-game losing streak to the 49ers. By the second quarter they jumped out to a 23–0 lead, and only Young's one-yard touchdown run avoided a shutout. The 49ers were trounced, 40–8, the franchise's most lopsided home loss in twenty-seven years.

"I'm in a certain state of shock," said head coach George Seifert. "We didn't come off blocks. We didn't tackle. I'm sure all of us, players, coaches—everybody is wondering what the hell happened."

Young completed just eleven passes, threw two interceptions, and was sacked for a safety. But none of the 49ers played particularly well that day. The defense allowed 437 yards and five touchdowns. The running game averaged barely three yards per carry. Even Jerry Rice dropped a short pass, resulting in Young's first interception. An inability to protect the passer was most troubling: with Barton still sidelined by surgery, the Eagles defense pounded Young, much like the Chiefs had done four weeks earlier.

"It was almost surreal, in a way," Young said afterward. "It was pretty obvious; it was getting to the point, I don't know the right word, where every time I dropped back I was taking a hit."

For that reason, with the Eagles ahead 33–8 late in the third period, Seifert replaced Young—in the middle of a series—with backup quarterback Elvis Grbac.

"Steve took that shot at the end of the second down, and I said to myself, 'To hell with this,'" Seifert explained. "It became obvious to me to take Steve out. If I didn't handle it to everybody's liking it's because I don't have a lot of experience in this situation, and I hope to hell I don't have any more of them."

Young was furious. A few feet behind the head coach, with several players, coaches, and team doctor James Klint, standing in between as a buffer, Young verbally tore into Seifert.

"I felt like he was saying, 'Yeah, everyone got beat up, but you, *you*, it's your fault,'" Young told NFL Films years later. "And I thought, for me, for all the crap I had been through all those years, and you're going to trot out the quarterback to replace me, then trot out [wide receiver] J. J. Stokes to take Jerry's place. Trot someone else out with him.

"But me, I think I just basically broke. And I went down the sideline, and I was looking for a fistfight. I wasn't gonna just have an argument, I was looking to have a fist fight, and I was going to have it with George Seifert. . . . I started saying things and emoting things. . . . I'm surprised that he didn't turn around and fight me. If I were him, I would have turned around and fought me."

Assistant coach Gary Kubiak lured him further away from Seifert, and Young eventually sat on the bench where he vented to Brent Jones.

"I think that there was a connection between the Kansas City game and the Philadelphia game," *San Jose Mercury News* beat writer Ann Killion recalled years later. "Steve was so uncharacteristically off his game. But I think it was this 'F— You' moment like, 'It is not my fault, don't take me out of this game; it's not my fault I'm not Joe Montana. I'm still a good quarterback.'

"It was like something snapped in there, and I think the ground work for that snap was laid in Kansas City, because that was a very tense and emotional game. And again, Steve had to say all the right things and do all the right things . . . it was intense, and I think that could have unraveled their season right then, because it was such a emotional thing as well as such a big loss."

Hours later, in the locker room, Young remained livid about the negative message that he believed the benching had sent. Beyond anything else, the quarterback, who had already been sacked fourteen times that year and was nursing a sore shoulder, didn't want to be labeled fragile or a quitter.

"The funny thing about the whole event, from my teammates' standpoint," Young later said, "was suddenly, I was this fiery leader. I wanted to go home and throw up and think about, 'Are you kidding me? For all these years I've been out here battling and I had to yell at my coach, and now you're ready to follow me?' But it taught me the vital lesson in football: perception is reality. If you're perceived to be something, you might as well be it, because that's the truth in people's minds."

* * *

For the Chiefs, momentum from the emotional defeat of San Francisco carried over the following Sunday in Atlanta. J. J. Birden caught two touchdowns as Montana set a Georgia Dome record with 361 yards passing in a 30–10 win over the Falcons. The 3–0 record matched the franchise's best start since their 1966 AFL championship season.

But Kansas City's offense was dominated the following week by the Rams. Montana threw three interceptions and completed less than half his passes in a 16–0 home loss. Even after a bye week, there was little improvement. Visiting San Diego to play the undefeated Chargers, the Chiefs again were kept out of the end zone during a 20–6 loss. Montana tied a career-high with thirty-seven completions, but on consecutive second-half drives he turned the ball over and three times could not score a touchdown from goal-to-go situations deep inside San Diego territory.

"We would get on a roll and then not be able to get into the end zone," Montana said. "There's always a concern when you don't get into the end zone. We'll find a way."

The schedule intensified eight days later: the Chiefs headed to Denver's Mile High Stadium, where they had lost the annual road game against the Broncos for eleven consecutive seasons. Kansas City had never defeated John Elway in his home stadium.

"The years I was there [1990 to 1994], I think every single time we were leading against Denver," Birden remembered. "And every single time, Elway drove down, and we lost. I mean three, four times. But it was different this time because we felt, we got a shot, we gotta be the last to have the ball. We got Montana, we can do this."

At that point in the season, Montana was not the same sharp passer that his teammates had rallied behind the previous postseason and during the Chiefs undefeated start. A sore shoulder, badly bruised ribs, and a massive purple welt on his hip—each a result of seven knockdowns and two sacks in the loss to San Diego—raised doubts about his ability to play against Denver. He sat out several practices, and critics wondered if his age and wear-and-tear had begun to sap his strength.

"All across Kansas City," Jim Thomas of the *St. Louis Post-Dispatch* wrote that week, "disappointed football fans want to know: How did the Chiefs get so bad so fast? Blame it on the offense. Why does Joe Montana suddenly look 48 instead of 38?"

Jack Elway, the Broncos advanced scout and father of the franchise's star quarterback, offered an answer:

"They're having a tough time putting points on the board, and I don't think Montana, although he had great stats, [has] got the arm strength he had at one time. Knowing that, defenses are keeping everything in front of them," the former Stanford head coach said. "I think I saw a difference last year in Montana's arm strength, and I think I see a difference again this year."

Montana—accustomed to such injury-inspired doubts since major back surgery in 1986—paid no attention.

"My arm is as strong as ever," he said before leaving for Denver.

Early on, during his nineteenth appearance on ABC's Monday Night Football, Montana hardly appeared at full capacity. For a ninth consecutive quarter, the Chiefs were held without a touchdown, and a Montana interception helped the Broncos take a 7–0 advantage.

Soon, however, the Kansas City offense heated up. Montana engineered touchdowns on their next three possessions, giving the Chiefs a seven-point cushion. Elway responded with two touchdown passes of his own to tie the game at 21. The suspense created by the pair of future Hall of Fame quarterbacks peaked late in the final period.

Montana completed passes to tight ends Tracy Greene and Derrick Walker and running back Greg Hill, racking up sixty-four yards. With barely four minutes remaining, kicker Lin Elliott nailed a nineteen-yard field goal. Kansas City now led 24–21, but they had left Elway—nearly as acclaimed for fourth-quarter comebacks as Montana—plenty of time to tie or win the game. And, as the Chiefs feared, after the two offenses traded fumbles, Elway rushed for the go-ahead score with 1:29 remaining.

"It was just a fun game," Montana remembered years later. "It's hard to play in Mile High in the first place, but Denver had a pretty good team. I think it was just fun for everybody watching the end of the game, going back and forth between John and myself, [it] really came down to who had the ball last."

Beneath a full moon, Kansas City took possession at their own 25-yard line. A trio of Montana completions along with a run by Marcus Allen moved the offense to the Denver 47, before an incompletion stopped the clock with just thirty-six seconds remaining. Applying his uncanny patience and calmness in the pocket, Joe Cool connected on two more short throws then hit rookie tight end Tracy Greene in stride for a nineteen-yard pickup over the middle. Kansas City used their final timeout, halting the clock at thirteen seconds.

Along the Chiefs' sideline, Montana strategized with the coaching staff, settled on a play—"X-corner"—then jogged back toward the field to instruct his teammates.

"Just the composure," Birden recalled. "Even when we were in the huddle, he said, 'OK, we got X-corner. Everybody relax, don't worry. If it's not there, I know where to go. Just do your job. Just do your job, I got this.' You could look in his eyes and this guy knows what he's doing."

Montana dropped back, sat in the center of the pocket, and went through his first, then second read. Neither Greene nor Birden were open. He looked right: Willie Davis had squeezed inside two Broncos defensive backs. Montana laced a throw to the near corner of the end zone where only Davis had a play on the ball. Inches from the goal line, the undrafted free agent and former member of the World Football League's Orlando Thunder snagged the ball and tiptoed inside the pylon for the game-winning touchdown.

"I'm the third option on that play," Davis recalled years later. "He throws the ball and had barely looked over there at me: he's looking one-two-three and throws it out, and it was a perfect pass where it had to be because if it was inside, the defensive back would have knocked it down. Fortunately it was outside where I had to reach for it.

"I think the difference was when Joe was there, everything was calm in the huddle. Nobody was pressing. I played there three years before Joe came there, and it was always, 'Here we go again. We score and they come back the last minute with Elway, and they beat us.' This time, there wasn't any of that. It was just, 'Let's get going, guys.' It's just amazing how someone in that position can be calm, keep the whole team calm, and think on your feet, not press."

Mile High Stadium went silent; the visitors' sideline went crazy. Montana struck his famous statuesque arms-raised pose then delivered a fist pump. Nearby, Jennifer Montana and their daughter, standing along the Chiefs sideline, exploded with joy, embracing one another.

"It's nerve-wracking," Montana told the press late that evening. "But it's a lot of fun. We felt we had a good chance. That's all part of the game. You don't like to be in those two-minute situations very often, but it's all part of it."

Much like the win over San Francisco, momentum from the gripping victory over Denver carried over into the following Sunday, and the Chiefs pummeled Seattle in Week 8. But from that point Kansas City struggled, losing three of their next five games. They were blown out by Buffalo and dropped close divisional rematches to both the Chargers and Seahawks. By the end of November, the 7–5 Chiefs were virtually eliminated from the AFC West competition.

The sprained left foot Montana suffered in the third quarter of their 10–9 loss in Seattle only further dimmed Kansas City's playoff prospects. Steve Bono started the next two games; Kansas City lost both.

As the Chiefs' woes mounted, more frustration emerged for Montana in the form of a newspaper article that stated he had already decided to retire at season's end. The *New York Daily News* report, which cited an unidentified source, was picked up by many newspapers, radio stations, and even CNN. In one of the few instances during his long career, Montana became noticeably furious with the media.

"Why should I have to come out here and answer to this only because somebody feels like I'm going to retire?" he asked. "Right now is not the time even to talk about it. They thought I was going to retire last year. I've got a sprained [foot]. Maybe that's what started it. I got a hangnail a couple of weeks ago, but he didn't write anything then. It's ridiculous. It's irritating. Why should I have go to through this at this time of the year? It's annoying.

"We're right in the middle of a race to make the playoffs and get to the Super Bowl. Why would I want to distract from that even if I had decided—and I haven't. You can say anything and use an unidentified source, and you get away with it. That's the bad part about the profession. They don't have to name a name and go back and find the guy. Until you hear it from me, I wouldn't worry about it."

Eventually, with plenty of ice and rest, Montana returned to practice for the 7–7 Chiefs and started the team's critical Week 16 game against Houston. On the tender foot, Montana threw two touchdown passes in a 31–9 victory that set up a momentous game with the Los Angeles Raiders. The winner would earn the AFC's last wild card berth; the loser would miss the postseason.

Still, instead of framing the game as a pressure-packed, winner-take-all battle between longtime division rivals, many in the press covered it from another perspective.

"It has been a fantastic journey," Steve Springer of the *Los Angeles Times* wrote, "from Ringgold High in Monongahela, Pennsylvania, to Notre Dame, from Candlestick Park to Arrowhead Stadium, with four memorable stops along the way to pick up Super Bowl rings. On Saturday, quarterback Joe Montana makes one more stop at the Los Angeles Coliseum to take one more shot at the Super Bowl. If he fails, if the Raiders deny the Kansas City Chiefs a chance at postseason play in the regular-season finale, is that it? Could this be the last time Montana puts on a football jersey, the last time anyone sees his arms raised in his trademark celebration after throwing yet another touchdown pass?

"If Montana can somehow spin that magic for one more month and get by the Raiders and whoever else the American Football Conference playoffs throw in his path, if he can somehow make it back to the Super Bowl and find his old 49er teammates there, if he can somehow pull out one more Super Bowl triumph and beat the man who replaced him in San Francisco, Steve Young, in a dream matchup, if he can pull all that off, then there would truly be nothing left to accomplish. Then, even he might be ready to say, 'That's enough.'"

Against the Raiders, Montana needed just five plays to arouse another tease for the NFL postseason. His forty-seven-yard touchdown pass to Davis, coupled with superb days by the Chiefs defense and former Raiders running back Marcus Allen yielded a 19–9 win and Montana's eleventh trip to the postseason.

"This victory is pretty sweet," he said. "It is sweet because the alternative isn't very pretty."

Despite the great victory, the Montana-retirement-countdown continued. Many believed that the Chiefs' next loss would be the quarterback's final game.

"A lot of people have been predicting my retirement since 1987," he said. "Someone will eventually be right."

As best as he (and his teammates) could, Montana turned his focus away from the retirement talk and toward the Dolphins, Kansas City's wild card opponent. Montana had been sidelined with his sprained foot when Miami topped the Chiefs 45–28 in Week 12. Bono filled in admirably for Montana that day—setting a career high for completions while fighting to a 14–14 halftime tie—but a pair of interceptions allowed Miami to pull away in the second half. With Montana on the field, the rematch at Joe Robbie Stadium was expected to be a much different game.

"It is a new season in the playoffs, and Montana did not play in that first game, so you can toss that out the window," said Dolphins head coach Don Shula.

For the first time since their overhyped, disappointing Super Bowl XIX showdown in Palo Alto, Dan Marino and Joe Montana squared off. And, albeit ten years late, the two Western Pennsylvania natives thrilled both the postseason crowd and ABC's eager television audience. By halftime neither team had punted or turned the ball over and the score was tied at 17. Montana threw for two scores and 178 yards on twelve-of-fifteen passing for 178 yards while Marino completed fourteen of his sixteen attempts for 162 yards and a touchdown.

"You feel like you have to score every time you have the ball in the second half," Marino said. "I've been in a lot shootouts. You just try to not make mistakes that hurt the team."

The Dolphins broke the tie with a touchdown on the opening possession, and late in the third quarter they added a field goal. Behind only ten with more than fifteen minutes remaining and Montana at the helm, Chiefs players expected another playoff comeback, reminiscent of the previous season's triumphs over Pittsburgh and Houston.

Early in the final period Montana drove the offense from their own 29 to Miami's 5-yard line. There, from virtually the same spot inside Joe Robbie Stadium where, six years earlier, he threw his Super-Bowl-winning touchdown pass to John Taylor, Montana dropped back and spied wide receiver Eric Martin on a quick slant over the middle. This time, the opponent's defender, cornerback J. B. Brown, cut in front of the throw and intercepted the ball.

"I was hoping Martin would get inside him," Montana said. "I thought he was going to outfight him, get inside, maybe get a call. It didn't happen."

On the ensuing defensive series, Kansas City forced Miami to punt, giving Montana another chance to reduce the deficit. But once the Chiefs crossed midfield, a second turnover from a former Super Bowl MVP—Marcus Allen had the ball stripped from him by safety Michael Stewart—doomed their comeback bid.

Still, even as the Dolphins drained the fourth-quarter clock to less than four minutes, Montana never gave up. He held out hope for a defensive stop, a Chiefs touchdown, a successful on-side kick, and a chance to tie or win the game.

"He paced the sideline, up and down, up and down, walking behind teammates from one 40-yard line to the other," the *Miami Herald*'s Dan Le Batard observed. "He did this more than a dozen times, uncomfortable that the game was in another man's grip. He licked his fingers, undid his chinstrap, licked his fingers again, took a deep breath, snapped his chinstrap back on, put his head down, undid his chinstrap again. He was not even watching the game. It is as strange a sight as you'll see in sports, Joe Montana nervous."

The Chiefs earned one last possession in the game's final two minutes and from their own 20-yard line, Montana strung together seven completions to move deep inside Miami territory. On a fourth-and-1 with fifteen seconds remaining, his pass to the end zone, intended for Davis, fell incomplete. Montana walked off the field, toward the Chiefs sideline, where he wondered aloud to third-string quarterback Matt Blundin what went wrong.

"His body wasn't running any more, but his mind still was," Blundin said.

Despite the loss and admitting that he felt "low," Montana—barefoot, dressed in a gray T-shirt and shorts—assured reporters that he had, as usual, enjoyed himself.

"It's always fun, the game's fun, that's what it's all about," he said.

Questions about his future, however, took precedence over the exciting quarterback duel. Had Joe Montana played his final game?

"I haven't thought about it," he said. "I didn't think I'd have to think about it. To ask me that now is like asking a fighter after he's lost a championship bout if he'll fight again."

*   *   *

The 49ers disastrous home loss to the Eagles in Week 5 stunned the Bay Area, so much so that KGO-AM (the 49ers flagship station) radio host Bernie Ward conducted an on-air poll asking listeners if George Seifert should be fired and replaced with former Dallas Cowboys head coach Jimmy Johnson. More than seven hundred people called in; 85 percent were in favor of the move.

"Well, I'd like to thank the 15 percent who voted for me," Seifert told the press the next day.

Seifert's job security notwithstanding, the other hot-button issue that arose from San Francisco's 40–8 defeat was Steve Young's atypical sideline outburst, the result of Seifert pulling him from the game in the third quarter. But as serious and potentially destructive as that episode was, Young managed to turn—albeit indirectly—the negative into a positive.

"I kinda chuckled to myself watching him scream and yell at George on the sideline," Brent Jones recalled years later. "It was like, what is he doing? What is his problem? At the time I didn't get it, but then stepping back a day or two, then I understood. [Young thought] 'I don't want all this heaped on me. Joe's gone, Joe's traded, and all of a sudden we've got this new controversy.' . . . It was a great blowing off steam exercise for Steve. And in a strange way, guys kind of said, 'I got a new respect for Steve. He's going to stand up to our head coach.'"

Respect for the 49ers quarterback swelled the next week in Detroit. After San Francisco fell behind 7–0 in the opening quarter, Lions defenders Broderick Thomas and Robert Porcher crushed Young, driving him into the hard AstroTurf. He crawled along the ground, struggled to stand up, and hobbled to the sidelines. The 49ers punted, then quickly surrendered another touchdown.

Despite the gruesome diagnosis, a pinched nerve behind his left knee, Young returned for the 49ers very next series.

"He just keeps bouncing up," Jones said that day. "He's as tough as any quarterback in the league."

The 49ers scored touchdowns on their next three offensive series, and by the fourth quarter, Young's five-yard touchdown pass to Nate Singleton put the game out of reach. San Francisco won 27–21.

"Boy, did he give us a lift when he came back," center Bart Oates added. "You look at the beating he's taken and say, 'How does he do it?' And he just does it."

The next week in Atlanta, Young was near-perfect, completing fifteen of sixteen passes for four touchdowns in a 42–3 pounding of the Falcons. Young was far less agitated this time when Seifert inserted Elvis Grbac into the game partway through the third quarter; or the next week when Grbac took his place during a 41–16 drubbing of the Tampa Bay Buccaneers. Fresh off their bye, the 49ers went to RFK Stadium and walloped the Washington Redskins, to improve to 7–2.

Many attributed the quick turnaround—from dismal offensive showings against Kansas City and Philadelphia to averaging more than thirty-six points during a four-game stretch—to Young's sideline tirade.

"I think more than anything, our team was looking for an identity at that point," Young said that winter. "I don't know if it was a watershed event for the season or not. People have pointed to it. But certainly for me, more than anything, it was that we were humiliated at home. We needed to either put it together or realize we weren't going to be as good as we thought we were. So I think that game was more of a wakeup call, punctuated by the little scene on the sideline."

Although Seifert wasn't quite so certain of its widespread impact, the head coach also believed Young experienced a catharsis that day in Candlestick Park.

"I think the Philadelphia game and Steve expressing himself was good for Steve Young," Seifert said. "I don't know if it was good for the team, but it was good for him. I think now he vents his frustrations as opposed to allowing them to build up within."

Young's new resolve was put to the test during Week 11. The Cowboys—who had defeated the 49ers three times in the previous twenty-two months—were coming to San Francisco. Although they had a new head coach, Barry Switzer, the 8–1, two-time defending Super Bowl champions still had All-Pros Troy Aikman, Emmitt Smith, and Michael Irvin, as well as the NFL's best offensive line and a stacked defense. And thirty minutes into the game, Dallas once again handcuffed the 49ers offense. At halftime, Young had accumulated precisely one passing yard. Only San Francisco's defense—which intercepted Aikman twice—managed to keep the scoring low at 7–7.

"Dallas was coming, and coming hard. They're a great team, no ifs, ands, or buts," said Young. "For a while it wasn't happening. We kind of puffed and puffed early on, and nothing happened. We kind of hung in there because the defense made some big plays."

In the second half Young's fifty-seven-yard play-action touchdown pass to Rice broke the game open, and his bootleg-option scoring strike to Jones late in the fourth quarter pushed the lead to 21–7, sealing the 49ers win. After the score, Young circled the end zone with his right arm raised then leapt through the air into the arms of Ricky Watters, knocking them both to the ground.

"I didn't think Mormons were allowed to dance," his close friend and blindside tackle Harris Barton said after the November 13 victory. "Today, Steve got the monkey off his back."

"Steve Young has taken so much heat for our last three losses when it was really the fault of the defense," safety Merton Hanks added. "That's why today was so big."

Fair or not, Young had been the scapegoat for consecutive NFC Championship Game losses to Dallas, the same franchise that Joe Montana defeated in January 1982 to ignite both the 49ers dynasty and his legend. For Young, the 21–14 regular season victory proved he could beat the NFL's elite team, but doing so in the postseason would mean far more.

With the Dallas demon exorcised, the 49ers continued to cruise through the 1994 regular season. Scoring at least thirty-one points each week, San Francisco won their next five games to clinch the NFC West and homefield advantage throughout the playoffs. During the team's nine-game winning streak followed by a loss in their regular season finale at Minnesota, Young threw the football with historic proficiency: he completed 72 percent of his passes for 2,672 yards, twenty-six touchdowns, and just three interceptions.

As his predecessor Joe Montana had done for years, Young was operating the 49ers offense to its full potential and original design. No longer was he the raw, instinctual athlete masquarading as a quarterback; now he *was* a quarterback, playing the chess game, one move leading to another, not going after the king immediately, four yards here, five yards there, ten yards here.

"You're always a playmaker," Young later said, explaining how he came to understand the role of a quarterback. "What you need to develop is to be an orchestrator. And that is a process that takes a lot of time. The most important piece of you being a quarterback is, 'I want to have this ball out of my hand and into the hands of my teammates. Then you just start to orchestrate the offense, and that just takes time. And in that middle, between playmaker and orchestrator, I call it the vortex, where just hopefully you play long enough to learn fast enough before you get thrown out of town."

By the end of the regular season, Young had tossed thirty-five touchdown passes—surpassing the franchise record that Joe Montana had set seven years earlier—and posted a quarterback rating (112.8) that narrowly edged out Montana's NFL record established in 1989. In a landslide, Young won his second league MVP in three seasons. Those personal accolades pleased, but did not satisfy, the thirty-three-year-old.

"[In 1992] we really were the mature team and ready to go to the Super Bowl again, and Dallas beat us, and it was a lot my fault," Young said years later. "[In 1993] I didn't play well in the Championship Game. So to me, I was winning MVPs but it didn't matter. It literally didn't matter. The only thing that mattered was getting to the Super Bowl."

Young's third attempt to guide the 49ers through the NFC postseason and on to that goal began on January 7, 1995, with a divisional playoff at home against Chicago. Bears' head coach Dave Wannstedt—the former Cowboys defensive coordinator who frustrated San Francisco's offense in the 1992 NFC Championship Game—and his staff had no remedy for the NFL's top-scoring offense.

Trailing 3–0 in the first quarter, San Francisco scored five touchdowns and a field goal on six straight possessions. Minutes into the third quarter, the 49ers were ahead 37–3, and Seifert sat his starters. The only real drama the entire afternoon came just before halftime.

At the Bears 6-yard line, Young retreated into the pocket, recognized a gaping hole in the Chicago defense, ran up the middle, and juked a defender to score the team's third touchdown of the second period. Although Young was already three yards deep in the end zone, Bears safety Shaun Gayle lowered his shoulder, and decked the quarterback, who fell to the turf, stood up, and violently spiked the football at Gayle's feet. Before the ball had even hit the ground, a handful of 49ers charged toward Gayle.

"The whole team just rushed to Steve's defense," said Rice, one of the first to arrive. "Steve Young is the key to our success. We can't let anything happen to him."

An all-out brawl was averted once the referees stepped in.

"I can get in any fights I want with that kind of backup," Young said.

The 44–15 triumph gave way to a third consecutive Dallas–San Francisco NFC Championship Game. And for the 49ers, the third time finally was the charm. Cornerback Eric Davis's forty-four-yard return of a Troy Aikman interception on the third play from scrimmage set up the game's first touchdown. Minutes later, after a Michael Irvin fumble, Young and Watters connected on a twenty-nine-yard swing pass that added another seven points. And when Cowboys returner Kevin Williams fumbled the ensuing kickoff, leading to another score, the 49ers held a 21–0 advantage halfway through the game's opening period.

Dallas kept the game reasonably close, twice cutting the deficit to just ten, but Young's mid-third-quarter touchdown run—a diving effort through three Cowboys defenders to cross the goal line—assured the victory. San Francisco had finally toppled Dallas in the playoffs, and after seven long years of waiting his turn, Steve Young was headed to the Super Bowl as the 49ers starting quarterback.

"Today did it for Steve, and I hope everybody is happy now," said 49ers cornerback Deion Sanders. "Steve has had to survive the pressure established by Joe Montana, but you can't say that anymore. He has far surpassed everything established by Montana, and now he's going to the Super Bowl. I've seen him as an opposing player, but now that I see him day-in and day-out, I think he's the greatest quarterback to ever play the game."

After his final kneeldown officially ended the game, Young—arms raised, the football in his left hand, an enormous grin on his face—trotted around Candlestick Park, hopped a steel barrier, and high-fived the fans, many of whom chanted "Steve, Steve, Steve."

"The same people," Young told NFL Films years later, "that said, 'Joe is the man, and that's never gonna change,' I think suddenly said, 'It's all right. Steve can do it, and Joe can do it, and we're all good cause we're from San Francisco, and we're 49er fans. It was as if everyone's heart grew enough to circle both of us."

In the postgame press conference, a reporter posed the question to Young: "Is the monkey off your back now?"

"Honestly, I swear to you, I haven't felt any monkey," he answered. "If a monkey was there, well, he's light. If you guys say he's gone, great."

Thirteen years after "The Catch," Young had now emulated Joe Montana's crowning achievement: defeating the Dallas Cowboys in an NFC Championship Game at Candlestick Park. The victory earned Young and the 49ers a berth in Super Bowl XXIX and ironically enough a visit to the stage of perhaps Montana's greatest victory. For the world championship, the 49ers would play the San Diego Chargers in Miami's Joe Robbie Stadium, site of Montana's last-minute, ninety-two-yard, Super Bowl–winning touchdown drive six years earlier. But the game's venue was not the only reason the specter of Montana hovered over Young the two weeks prior to the Super Bowl.

Three days before the game, Bill Walsh penned a column for the *Fort Lauderdale Sun-Sentinel*. The man who had brought Young to San Francisco nearly eight years earlier simply stated what everyone already knew.

"I think this is the last step for Steve to be considered one of the greatest quarterbacks in history because he has done everything else," Walsh wrote. "The people in San Francisco have not welcomed Steve because of their total commitment and adoration for Joe Montana. Steve has had to swallow a lot of mean media coverage. The sports talk shows have become so big, and the talk shows have been ugly with him. There has been ugly coverage and ugly demonstrations at 49ers games. I don't think Steve will ever unseat Joe as the Bay Area's quarterback, but this will establish something for him if he can win. I think Joe will always be the person 49er fans adore."

That had begun to change with the victory over Dallas in the NFC championship game, but Walsh, Young, and every football fan knew that a loss in the Super Bowl—in which the 49ers were eighteen-and-a-half-point favorites over their in-state counterparts—would completely invalidate that triumph. Joe Montana never lost a Super Bowl.

Just as Young found it impossible to avoid the press's questions about and comparisons to his predecessor, Montana also could not avoid media scrutiny in the two weeks prior to Super Bowl XXIX. As the most decorated player in Super Bowl history *and* San Francisco's greatest sports hero, everyone wanted to know Montana's take on the impending championship game. And naturally, anything that came out of his mouth regarding Young's 49ers brought about controversy.

Asked for whom he was rooting, Montana named the Chargers.

"I'm an AFC guy now. That's where I'm playing. Of course, I've still got ties with Eddie (DeBartolo) and a couple guys on the team. I hope Eddie wins it for his dad," said Montana. "I'm an AFC guy now, but I've got a lot of friends on both teams."

Although Montana's new allegiances irritated several former teammates— "If you ask me, that's a little weak. . . . I've done nothing but root for Joe and the Chiefs," Brent Jones said—Young paid no attention.

"For so long, I tried to say the politically correct thing regarding my 49ers life after Joe Montana," he told the Super Bowl media that week. "But now, and maybe it's part of a new Niners openness brought to our team by Deion Sanders and William Floyd, I'm saying, 'Just grant me whatever you think I've earned, no matter how it compares to what Montana did in a San Francisco uniform.' Joe was amazing, but maybe folks will come to think I'm not so bad, either. I'm no longer worrying about the Montana shadow and how it affects me. I mean, can a shadow really stretch all the way from Kansas City to San Francisco?"

Rather than obsess about Montana, his comments, or the historical crossroads that lay ahead, Young immersed himself in game plans and the San Diego Chargers defense.

"Steve Young prepared like nobody I've ever been around," 49er offensive coordinator Mike Shanahan later said. "He left no stone unturned in anything he ever did. He was so bright and so conscientious, so when he got ready for a game, he got ready, but for [Super Bowl XXIX] when he got ready it was at another level.

"Thursday's practice, not one ball hit the ground. That doesn't happen very often. I'm talking about from when you start off with warmups, your pat-and-go, the ball never hit the ground, to seven-on-seven and team-drill. That doesn't happen very often when you're practicing a full practice for a couple hours."

"Mike Shanahan and I," Young later said, "wanted to make a statement about the 49ers: Yeah, we've been to the Super Bowl before, but you've never seen this one before."

By Super Bowl Sunday, Young, Shanahan, and the 49ers offense instantaneously made their statement.

On the third play from scrimmage, Young faked a handoff to William Floyd and lobbed a pass deep downfield in between two Charger defenders. At the 12-yard line, Rice caught the ball, kept stride, and crossed the goal line for the game's first score. Less than four minutes later, Young again split the Chargers secondary, this time connecting with Watters, who hauled in the football at the San Diego 35-yard line, broke two tackles, and raced toward the end zone, giving the 49ers a 14–0 lead.

"We practiced well all week," Young said afterward. "People said it was anticlimactic after the Cowboys win. But we hit the road running. Mike Shanahan came up with a great game plan. We showed them some things that they hadn't seen. And you could see that the first two touchdown passes were things that worked just perfectly."

Young tossed three more touchdowns during the second and third quarter to ensure a 49ers blowout, but the denouement came early in the final period. Ahead 42–18, San Francisco's offense crossed into the Chargers' red zone. On a third down from the San Diego 7-yard line Young took a three-step drop, looked left, and flicked a quick slant throw to Rice, who had cut inside a cornerback. Rice snatched the ball and rolled into the end zone. It was Young's sixth touchdown pass of the evening, surpassing the Super Bowl record that Joe Montana set in the 49ers' 55–10 blowout of the Denver Broncos five years earlier.

After the next offensive series, rookie Elvis Grbac replaced Young, who swapped his helmet for a 49ers ball cap and watched the remaining six-plus minutes from the 49ers sideline. As the clock wound down, Young, Rice, and his teammates were all smiles.

"Someone take the monkey off my back, please!" Young screamed. Linebacker Gary Plummer and offensive tackle Steve Wallace fulfilled his request, yanking the invisible and metaphorical monkey off the back of his jersey. The pantomime—captured by NFL Films cameras—became synonymous with Super Bowl XXIX and, in many ways, Young himself.

"I regret ever saying that," Young said in 2011. "Because I didn't live with that on my back. That's not the way I lived it. That's not the way I played it.

Pretty early on—probably because of my experience with Jim McMahon—I realized that part of the greatness of the opportunity was that they were there. It wasn't a burden, it was a tremendous boost. The challenge was so great that it was energizing.

"And so when I did that, I remember the second it happened, I was like, 'I hope no one caught that on film,' because I never said that, I never thought of it that way. It was just out of excitement, I think. You're just having fun. And that was the memory for everybody, and it certainly wasn't for me. And I regret it, I really do, because in many ways it didn't reflect how I went through it."

For his singular performance, Young was named Most Valuable Player of San Francisco's 49–26 Super Bowl victory over the Chargers. Celebration of the franchise's fifth world championship spilled over into the locker room beneath Joe Robbie Stadium. There, NFL commissioner Paul Tagliabue presented the Vince Lombardi Championship Trophy to 49ers owner Eddie DeBartolo Jr., who handed it to Young. With Rice's arms wrapped around his quarterback, Young raised the gleaming monument in the air.

When his brief screams of delight were finished, Young addressed his teammates.

"Every guy in here made a commitment," he said out of breath. "You know you did. There were times when it was dark. It was really dark, but we turned back and into each other's face and committed to each other. You knew we had to do it this way. This is the greatest feeling in the world, is it not? I share this with every one of you guys. Everyone in this room made a commitment and were there. And no one can ever, *EVER*, take it away from us. *EVER!*"

Young again held up his prize, kissed the silver football at the top, then tightly hugged the trophy with both arms, swaying back and forth. Eventually (well past midnight Eastern Standard Time) Young handed the trophy off to his teammates, addressed hundreds of reporters, showered and dressed, then resumed his postgame press junket.

"I knew it was important at that time to have him do as many of these interviews as he could in this moment of ultimate triumph," Young's agent Leigh Steinberg said in 2011. "He became dehydrated, because it was hot and muggy. . . . He had played a draining game where he was sweating and losing water, and he never rehydrated. He had a few soft drinks in the locker room, but he was talking the whole time. At first he did the session of traditional interviews, but then we walked out on the field, and he probably did forty more interviews, and it went on for hours. I could see his face turning white. I could see him progressively becoming more and more dehydrated, more and more drained."

Along with Steinberg and Steinberg's most promising new client, Penn State quarterback Kerry Collins, Young boarded a limousine headed to the

49ers' hotel, site of the team's victory party. Less than a mile from the Miami Airport Hilton, Young alerted his agent that he felt nauseous.

"He's pale and white, and there's no color in his face, and then he proceeds to throw up all over Kerry Collins's shoes."

In search of fresh air after purging the contents of his insides, Young—whom paramedics hooked up to an IV of saline solution—exited the limousine and walked the final quarter-mile along Blue Lagoon Drive to the hotel.

"Joe Who?" someone shouted once he arrived at the hotel.

"No, don't do that," Young responded. "Don't worry about that. That's the past. Let's talk about the future."

12

Here We Go Again

In the fall of 1992, several months before he was dealt to the Kansas City Chiefs, Joe Montana was unofficially banned from the San Francisco 49ers training facility—"I was told being around was a distraction to the team." Still on the team's injured reserve list and therefore unable to train or compete as he was accustomed to, Montana embarked on a new hobby. Achy elbow and all, he started flying lessons.

"It gave me a chance to do something I had wanted to do for a long time," Montana said.

The trade to Kansas City the following spring did not quell his budding passion. When he wasn't playing or studying the opponents' defense and Paul Hackett's game plans, Montana's endless competitive nature drove him to practice and learn about aviation. Fittingly he brought the same passion and determination that he applied toward football to the skies.

Although barrel rolls and 7.6-G speeds caused him to black out during a ride-along flight with a United States Navy Blue Angel, Montana was hooked. He passed his written test just before reporting to Chiefs training camp in the summer of 1994, then began studying for his instrument rating qualification. And on his regular Tuesday off-day, Montana trained under Steve Grantham, a flight instructor at the Kansas Aircraft Corporation.

"It gives you something to get away and have a relief from the pressure of the NFL," he said. "It is fulfilling. You get a lesson. They tell you what you are going to do. You go up and do these maneuvers and don't feel very good about

233

them. But at the end you start feeling a little better about what you have accomplished that week."

Just a few weeks after guiding the Chiefs to their captivating Monday night victory over John Elway's Broncos, Montana, Grantham, *Kansas City Star* beat writer Kent Pulliam, and the newspaper's photographer Joe Ledford, climbed into a single-engine Beechcraft Bonanza 836.

With a hood shielding his peripheral vision—a training method instructors use to force students to rely on their instruments rather than their eyes—Montana checked off his safety procedures, taxied down the runway, and took off above rural Kansas. Familiar with his instructor's advice—to scan the horizon and think "three steps ahead"—Montana commanded the cockpit, practiced left turns, and ascended to upwards of thirty-five hundred feet.

More than an hour into the lesson, while Pulliam and Ledford nervously watched from behind the cockpit, Montana steered the plane back toward the Johnson County Executive Airport, received permission from the tower, put the landing gear down, and touched down on the runway, earning his teacher's praise.

"I brought an airplane down the other day in twenty mile per hour winds and driving rain, and when we landed, my instructor gave me a high-five," Montana said the following spring. "I looked at him and said, 'You mean I did all of that myself?'"

Within days of the Chiefs abrupt end to the 1994 season, the 27–17 playoff loss in Miami, Montana eagerly returned to the air: his wife had bought him a single-engine Malibu Mirage just a month earlier.

"When he's in the air, that's the only time he has that same glow as when he's playing football, maybe even a bigger glow," said Jennifer, who came to develop enough confidence in her husband's skills to fly with him and even bring their four children along. "His eyes get really big, and they sparkle, and he talks about side winds and things like that. It'll never make up for playing in the game, but it'll help ease the emptiness."

That January of 1995, in between fishing, golf, and more flying lessons in Vero Beach, Florida, Montana again underwent surgery. The week that Steve Young's six touchdown passes lifted the 49ers to their fifth world championship, surgeons cleared out "loose bodies" and cartilage bits in Montana's left knee. On the morning of Super Bowl XXIX, ESPN reported that the surgery took far longer and was much more extensive than his doctors originally thought. There were also rumors that the knee—which Montana damaged during the Chiefs Week 17 win over the Raiders—would need a lengthy rehabilitation program and a second procedure later that month.

"It's not true," Chiefs public relations director Bob Moore said in February. "It was nothing more than a usual, routine thing that a number of our players undergo every year. But like everything with Joe Montana it gets blown out of proportion to what actually occurs."

Questionable health of the soon-to-be thirty-nine-year-old quarterback fueled the speculation that Montana was leaning toward retirement.

As he had after the loss in Miami, Montana remained publicly silent on the issue, but he did seek advice from his former head coach.

"He hasn't made up his mind," Bill Walsh said in late January. "I advised him to just wait. I think he can get a better perspective on things if he does."

But as the NFL offseason began and free agency, the draft, and minicamp neared, several unnamed sources guaranteed Montana's retirement.

"He came in to see me," Chiefs team president Carl Peterson recalled in 2011. "We talked about it. He said, 'I'm thinking about the future, I've had a number of concussions, I've got four children—two boys—I want to be able to throw the football to them, to coach them as they grow up. I'm really debating about what to do.'"

"I said, 'Joe, let me tell you what. I've been in this business awhile. Just hearing you and what you're saying, and how you say it. . . . I think you may have already retired in your mind. I've seen this before with players, I know how difficult it is to give it up, to walk away. You still are pretty darn healthy. I think you need to go home and talk to Jennifer and make a good decision. There's no rush. I would appreciate when you do you'll let me know so we can make plans.'"

In late March, the Montanas sold their Hallbrook Farms home to Chiefs team doctor Cris Barnthouse, whom Montana had outbid for the house two years earlier. A week later, the *Kansas City Star* discovered that Jennifer was organizing a huge party for her husband in San Francisco. And when the Chiefs signed free agent quarterback Rich Gannon to a two-year, $1.4 million contract the next day, Montana's looming retirement became obvious.

Still, many weren't convinced.

"I'm not believing anything until I hear it," said Carl Crawley, Montana's midget league head coach back in the 1960s.

"I can't believe Joe would retire before he thinks it's necessary," Carmen Policy told the *Sacramento Bee*. "As far as I'm concerned, if he can run, he won't quit."

Montana remained—to the end—coy with reporters who asked if the rumors were true.

"I can't say it ain't, or it is," he said after leaving a San Jose restaurant.

But the next day, all major media outlets confirmed the news: the following week, an outdoor event in downtown San Francisco was to commemorate "Joe Montana Day." He would speak to the fans and reporters, attend a luncheon, then fly to Kansas City for an official Chiefs press conference.

"At the end of the year, his friends in Kansas City were telling me that Joe was just tired, really tired," Dave Huffman, Montana's college center and close friend told reporters. "This shouldn't surprise anybody."

There were, however, a few surprises regarding the guest list for the celebration.

Among the principals in attendance would be San Francisco mayor Frank Jordan, John Madden, Carmen Policy, George Seifert, Roger Craig, Ronnie Lott, Eddie DeBartolo Jr., and Bill Walsh, the master of ceremonies. And despite the mutual hostility and bitterness left over from the trade two years earlier, Jennifer extended—on her husband's behalf—an invitation to Dwight Clark.

"There was a period when there was some tension just because it was such a bad scene when he left," said Clark. "It was a difficult time for everyone, and I don't think either one of us knew how to handle it. He was in another city with another team. There was just a natural division there, and it's over. I talked to him at length, and it was time for it to be over."

But it was another invitee who stirred up the most intrigue. Someone pretending to be Montana's agent, Peter Johnson, had called Steve Young and invited the newest Super Bowl MVP to the party. Young accepted, and his agent, Leigh Steinberg, called Johnson's office to ask, "What's Steve's role in the ceremony?"

"He has no role," an assistant responded, "because he is not invited."

Even in retirement, Joe Montana was not far from a prank.

"I didn't call Steve; it was all a hoax," Johnson told reporters who learned of the bogus invite days before the celebration. "Joe invited a few other of his old teammates but not Steve, certainly not Steve."

On Tuesday morning, April 18, 1995, fans funneled into Justin Herman Plaza. Parking was shut off between Washington Street and Mission Street as well as Market Street and Steuart Street. By late morning the crowd had reached over twenty thousand, many of whom were dressed in Montana jerseys or carried signs, including one that read "Joe is God."

"A packed, friendly mob that filled the plaza, hung from trees, looked down from office buildings and the Hyatt Regency's fire escapes, and spilled onto the Embarcadero and Market Street," the *San Francisco Chronicle* reported.

A few adventurous spectators even climbed atop the intricately designed Vaillancourt Fountain to catch a glimpse of the star-studded event.

Before noon the invited NFL royalty, as well as Montana's family and friends, walked on stage in front of an enormous inflatable football. Several addressed the crowd.

"I remember getting booed like hell," Chiefs president Carl Peterson said years later. "Carmen [Policy] got back at me. I think he introduced me as 'the man that stole Joe Montana from San Francisco.' The boos are all right then. I'm thinking, what can I say here? And I said, 'Listen, San Francisco. We from Kansas City just want to say this: Thank you for loaning us the greatest export from the wonderful city of San Francisco that's ever been, here, now, or in the future: Joe Montana. And the whole thing changed. They applauded, and I was able to get through my whole speech."

After Madden, Policy, Peterson, DeBartolo, and Mayor Frank Jordan—who presented Montana with a key to the city—each spoke, Walsh retook the podium and introduced the man of the hour. Montana stood up, shook his former head coach's hand, pulled notecards from the breast pocket of his blue suit, and waited for the boisterous cheers to subside.

"I really and truly thought this day would never come when I'd say that word, retirement," Montana told his fans, which erupted into a chorus of boos. "It's like living a dream for me. It started throwing a football through a tire on a swing and then playing in the Super Bowl. My dream, like most dreams, you end up waking up. It's like a wakeup call for me. It's time to move on."

Montana again thanked the crowd, then handed the scene back over to Walsh and waved to his grateful fans.

"It was a lot of fun, to a certain degree," Montana said in 2011. "Part of it was sort of—I won't say a downer—but only because you knew that things were ending, and we had had so much fun and excitement in San Francisco and just playing the game that it was like a reality that that was not going be a part of my life any longer. And that's what I think was probably the most depressing part of it. But on the whole it was fun seeing everybody. And it was a fun day, as much as it could be."

Earlier in the week, Montana's youngest daughter, eight-year-old Elizabeth, approached her father noticeably upset. She had heard the media reports that he was being forced into retirement, either due to the growing list of injuries, his advanced age, or the rumor that Jennifer "wants him home," a claim Montana adamantly denied.

"Nobody made you retire, Daddy," Elizabeth told him. "You made your own decision."

"She doesn't like to lose at anything, either," Montana said.

*   *   *

To Steve Young, the spring of 1995 also marked a transitional point in his career and life. For the first time in seven years, his April was not consumed by final exams. The previous year, he and 139 other students graduated from BYU's J. Reuben Clark Law School.

"My father says he is very happy that I am finally qualified to get a real job," Young said following commencement in Provo.

Young had, of course, remained at his other job as NFL quarterback and led the 49ers to a Super Bowl title nine months later. But afterward, he continued to pursue a career in law and began studying for the California and Utah Bar exams.

"I want to do something in criminal law," he said. "I loved my legal negotiations classes. . . . I got a sense of adrenalin not unlike the adrenalin I get from football."

By the summer of 1995, Young finally reached, and won, the elusive, Super Bowl that defined his legacy, but his adrenaline rush returned every time he stepped on the football field, even during a preseason game that August.

In an exhibition rematch of that January's Super Bowl, the 49ers played the Chargers, and minutes into the game, Young drove his offense deep into San Diego territory. On a third-and-10, he dropped back to pass, stayed in the pocket, and ducked under blitzing safety Rodney Harrison, who ripped his helmet off trying to make the tackle. Rather than run out of bounds or slide to the ground, Young scrambled to his left, faked a pass, then turned upfield and cut to the inside. Eventually, he dove headfirst to the ground—shielding his head with his arm—gaining nine yards.

"Best play I've seen in four years," said fullback William Floyd. "Here you have the premier quarterback in the NFL, and he's playing like he's still trying to prove something."

Once the regular season started, Young set out to prove that his 49ers could repeat as world champions, a feat Joe Montana's 49ers had achieved just six years earlier. And after five weeks, they were on track for another Super Bowl berth.

Although the Denver Broncos had previously hired away offensive coordinator Mike Shanahan—"The greatest play-caller, motivator, he was unbelievable, I cried when he left," Young later said—San Francisco opened with four wins in five games. Young had picked up right where he left off following his marvelous effort in Super Bowl XXIX. During that stretch, he tossed eleven touchdowns and averaged nearly three hundred yards passing per game.

"To finally [win a Super Bowl], it was like you know how hard it is, how many things have been against you; it's pretty exciting. I'd gotten so that I really kind of enjoyed the journey," Young said in 2011. "I'd worked at it so long and hard that just the moment when I realized that I'd gotten there, I couldn't believe it. It was great. It was a lot of fun. It was relieving, too. . . . It was fun to be in a new place in your game, where you're not just dealing with how you haven't been to the Super Bowl. It was fun to play for a little while without having that on your résumé."

Despite the 49ers hot start, Young's new liberated, upbeat attitude quickly began to crumble. Through five games, he had been physically battered and bruised. In the season opener at New Orleans, Young—who tossed a fifty-yard touchdown pass to Rice less than a minute into the game—was sacked for a fourth time in the first half. Finishing off the play, Saints defensive tackle Joe Johnson tackled Young from behind, severely spraining the quarterback's neck. He missed less than a full quarter and returned for the second half. And his touchdown pass midway through the third quarter put the game out of reach.

Although it bothered him in the coming weeks, the neck sprain didn't sideline Young again. A mangled shoulder, however, did. In Week 2, Falcons linebacker Jessie Tuggle smashed Young near the sideline, bruising his throwing shoulder. His ability to throw hampered, Young nonetheless played through the pain, extending his streak of consecutive starts to a league-best fifty-two games.

"It's been weak and hard to get warmed up," he said entering the team's bye week following a Week 5 win over the Giants. "There's still slight pain, but it's getting better. I was really struggling in the New England game. But that's football. Football's brutal. It's good to get a week off and get it completely healed. I'll rest it and come back stronger."

In the 49ers next game, a road trip to Indianapolis, Colts cornerback Ray Buchanan grabbed Young's throwing arm during a pass attempt. The hit re-injured Young's shoulder sprain, but once again he refused to leave the game in spite of tremendous pain.

"You can't throw the ball real hard," the battle-scarred veteran explained. "But I felt effective. I said to George [Seifert], 'I feel I can go in and do the job,' and I felt like I went in and did the job. When you stay in the game, you risk further injury. That's the name of the game. There's no way you should ever say, 'I'm going to sit on the bench because I could risk further injury.' It's the nature of football."

Late in the fourth quarter, with barely a minute remaining and the 49ers trailing by one point, three-hundred-pound Colts rookie Ellis Johnson rammed Young into the RCA Dome AstroTurf.

"I hit right on it," Young said. "If I'd never had anything wrong with my shoulder, that hit would have done it anyway."

Young missed just one play, somehow convincing the head coach and team doctors that he was ready, and he returned to push the offense closer toward a game-winning field goal attempt. But the forty-five-yard kick sailed wide right and the 49ers lost, 18–17.

"In warm-ups I felt dramatically better than in the last three weeks," said Young, who completed 70 percent of his passes. "I felt I was on the road to recovery. Then I took some bangs. The last one could've done some damage."

Young was right. An MRI revealed—in addition to the already partially torn rotator cuff—a deep bone bruise. Team doctor Michael Dillingham told Seifert, "Don't plan on having Steve Young for a four-week period."

With Young forced to the sidelines, third-year quarterback Elvis Grbac took his place.

"I'll work with him all week," Young said. "He's studied hard. In his mind, the only thing he hasn't done is taken the snaps. But he's ready mentally to play now."

Again, Young was right. In his first career start, Grbac, an eighth-round draft pick, torched the first-place St. Louis Rams, completing eleven of fourteen passes for 119 yards and two touchdowns. A proud Young—"I can't tell you how happy I am for him"—watched from the sidelines wearing jeans, tennis shoes, and a headset connected to the coaching staff.

But Young, who had spent several painful and frustrating years of his prime watching, not playing, did not enjoy his return to the 49ers bench. And he knew that mentoring Grbac to play well in his absence might help keep him there.

"It was funny how it flipped on its head," Young told ESPN in 2012. "Other quarterbacks would come in and all of a sudden I was on the other side of it. And I was like, 'Well, this is not as easy as I thought it was, you know.' I always thought Joe should help me more; I handled it a lot of ways like Joe did."

The 49ers struggled over the next two weeks, scoring just seven points in consecutive divisional losses to New Orleans and Carolina: in the two games, Grbac threw four interceptions, one of which former 49ers cornerback Tim McKyer returned ninety-six yards for a touchdown. Following the embarrassing home loss to the expansion Panthers, Rice told reporters, "It's up to the vets to rally around this guy."

They did, despite being thirteen-and-a-half-point underdogs, on the road, against their annual NFC Championship Game rival, the Dallas Cowboys.

On the 49ers second offensive play, Grbac—with Charles Haley pounding him in the face—hit Rice on an eighty-one-yard touchdown pass. Then, before halftime, the Michigan alum marched the offense ninety-two yards in eleven plays to take the 49ers into halftime with a 31–7 lead.

"Living with white-hot heat has a way of forging strength in a man," Young said, referring to the media's recent criticism of Grbac.

Grbac's one-yard rushing touchdown midway through the fourth quarter clinched the upset and earned the understudy respect from his teammates, nationwide acclaim, and—underneath the headline "Elvis Lives"—a cover spot on the next week's issue of *Sports Illustrated*.

"Harris Barton told me this kind of game could make my career or break my career," said Grbac. "So I just said, 'Screw it.' And I decided to shock the world."

Prior to the game in Dallas, Young hoped he might return—"I intend to play football Sunday"—but his head coach wasn't so certain.

"Who knows?" said Seifert. "And maybe (Young) won't be able to play the next week either against Miami. Or maybe he will be able to play against the Cowboys."

Young resumed throwing in the middle of the week, immediately experienced significant pain, and less than twenty-four hours after San Francisco's 38–20 victory, underwent arthroscopic surgery on his throwing shoulder. Another three to four weeks of rest was prescribed.

Growing concern about the thirty-four-year-old Young's health, coupled with Grbac's great game (twenty-for-thirty, 305 yards, two touchdowns) on the road against the NFL's top scoring defense, spawned a familiar quarterback conundrum.

"We'll evaluate the situation," a smiling Seifert told the press at his weekly Tuesday press conference. "Seems like I've been through this once before, doesn't it? Here we go again?"

Seven days later, on a Monday night in Miami's Joe Robbie Stadium, Grbac completed thirty-one of forty-one attempts for 382 yards and four touchdowns in San Francisco's 44–20 pounding of the Dolphins.

Once again, a reporter asked Seifert the question: Was a quarterback controversy brewing?

"Not yet," Seifert replied.

Epilogue

FOREVER YOUNG

In the end, no quarterback controversy between Steve Young and Elvis Grbac would surface late in the 1995 season. Far from it. Young reclaimed his starter's role in late November and won four games in a row, clinching the NFC West crown. At the end of the regular season, the only anomaly on Young's stat sheet was a 92.3 quarterback ranking: several points shy of winning a fifth straight NFL passing title.

Young resumed his supremacy in that category the next season. He won the passing title again in 1996, repeated in 1997, and the following January once again guided his team to the precipice of the Super Bowl. But Mike Holmgren's Green Bay Packers entered rainy, muddy Candlestick Park and toppled the 49ers 23–10 in the 1997 NFC Championship Game.

"There's a feeling like if we don't win the championship, maybe we shouldn't even have training camp. It feels like that. . . . It's bitter, but I'll be damned if we're not going to make that trek again. That's the reason for playing—to be in games like this," said Young, who after the loss explained to reporters that he wanted to continue playing "until I die."

Twelve months later, Young finally bested Holmgren, his former quarterbacks coach turned offensive coordinator, whose Packers had knocked the 49ers out of the playoffs each of the previous three years. In one of the most riveting postseason games of all time, Young and Brett Favre traded scores in a wild card shootout at Candlestick.

With eight seconds remaining, the 49ers trailed 27–23. Young dropped back to pass from the Green Bay 25-yard line, stumbled after stepping on his center's foot, then squeezed a pass through four defenders into the grasp of leaping wide receiver Terrell Owens. The game-winning touchdown was dubbed "The Catch II."

"We got a monkey off our back," 49ers head coach Steve Mariucci said. "And the way it happened, that we came from behind, and made a play at the very end makes it all very exciting."

The playoff victory proved to be Young's last. San Francisco was beaten the following Saturday in Atlanta and the next year, in Week 3 of the regular season, a seventh (reported) career concussion eventually forced him to quit the game at the age of thirty-eight.

"It's a good time to retire," an emotional Young said during a June 2000 press conference. "It's a celebration for me. I don't want anyone to misinterpret, I'm not forlorn about this. For the record, I know I can still play. The fire still burns, but not enough for the stakes to go back out. The truth is I have plenty of football left in me, but I have done what I set out to do, and I think that over time, that is what settled on me most. I have attained all the goals, even more than I could have ever dreamed of."

Upon retirement Young took a studio analyst position with ESPN. He also worked tirelessly to advance his charity. The Forever Young Foundation, established in 1993, benefits physically, emotionally, and financially-challenged children in the United States and Africa.

By August 2005, in his first year of eligibility, Young was enshrined in the Pro Football Hall of Fame with Dan Marino, Benny Friedman, and Fritz Pollard. Introduced by his father, and standing beside his bronze bust, Young addressed thousands of fans from the stage in Canton, Ohio.

"When I first came to San Francisco," he said. "I soon realized that I was watching the Michelangelo that Sid Gillman had years ago prior spoken about. It was art in action, and I was privileged to be holding the palette. Joe Montana was the greatest QB that I had ever seen. I was in awe. I was tempted many times by the opportunity to play for other teams, but I was drawn to the inevitable challenge to live up to the standard that I was witnessing. I knew that I was a decent player, and for some reason God blessed me with the big picture knowledge that if I was ever going to find out just how good I could get, I needed to stay in San Francisco and learn, even if it was brutally hard to do.

"I had the faith that the opportunity would create itself at the appropriate time. I was tough to live with during some of those years, but as I look back I am thankful for the struggles and trials that I had and for the opportunities that were given to me. When the opportunity for me opened up, being a regular quarterback was no longer an option, I would have gotten booed out of Candlestick so fast that I had to rise to the new standard of performance that Joe set. I many times thought about quitting as I heard boos during my sleepless nights, but I feared calling my dad. I knew what he would say: 'Endure to the end, Steve.'"

Three years later, on October 5, 2008, at halftime of the 49ers home game against the New England Patriots, the franchise permanently retired Young's number. With the wistful crowd of 67,650 cheering, a placard featuring Young's name and number eight was unveiled beneath the upper deck at Candlestick Park. There it hung, twenty-some feet from Joe Montana's number sixteen.

On a stage erected atop Bill Walsh Field—the coaching legend had passed away the previous summer and the playing surface at Candlestick Park was named in his honor—Young spoke to his fans.

"The Faithful are the reason we're all here," Young said, beside his pregnant wife Barbara, their three children, and former teammates such as Jerry Rice, Brent Jones, Steve Wallace, and Harris Barton. "Every time I've raised my hands [signifying a touchdown], I raised them to you."

"It's a lot of emotions about a lot of years," he said after the ceremony. "Great times. Hard times. Significant times to me, growing up. I said to Jerry (Rice), 'It's when you were at your best.' It's not that my life isn't sublime now and great in many ways. It was a significant time in sports history as well. There'll never be a time like that again. I'm just grateful."

"It's the sounds, and smells, the memories. It's Pavlovian," Young added. "Honestly I feel like I want to play."

The mediocre 49ers—who would fail to make the playoffs for a sixth straight year—could have used him.

J. T. O'Sullivan, the 49ers fifth different starting quarterback in thirteen games, threw a pair of crippling second-half interceptions inside San Francisco territory. They fell 30–21 to the dynastic New England Patriots, a team attempting to overcome the loss of quarterback Tom Brady. The two-time Super Bowl MVP tore his knee in Week 1 and missed the rest of the season.

Matt Cassel, a seventh-round draft choice from the University of Southern California who never started a collegiate game, struggled in his first month as Brady's replacement. Although the Patriots defeated San Francisco the day of Young's jersey retirement, Cassel threw two interceptions, then showed little improvement the following week in San Diego. But upon the Patriots return from their West Coast road trip, Cassel and the New England offense flourished.

Named AFC Offensive Player of the Week, he completed 75 percent of his attempts and passed for three touchdowns in a blowout of Denver. Then, after winning two of his next three starts, he made NFL history.

During a narrow loss to the Jets, he tossed three touchdowns and threw for four hundred yards. Ten days later—again earning the AFC Offensive Player of the Week award—Cassel threw three more touchdowns and racked up 415 passing yards, becoming only the fifth quarterback ever to record at least four hundred yards passing in consecutive games.

"Everything I do in the games has to do with [Tom Brady's] guidance," Cassel said that week. "He took me under his wing when I was a punk rookie, and he was a superstar. He's been great to me this year. I emulate him every day when I go out to practice or to play a game."

The 48–28 victory over Miami kept New England on pace for a wild card berth and just one game back in the race for AFC East crown. And with Cassel throwing eight touchdowns and just one interception, New England won back-to-back road games in Seattle and Oakland then annihilated the NFC West champion Arizona Cardinals, 47–7.

At 10–5, head coach Bill Belichick's Patriots remained in contention for a playoff spot. A win in Week 17, and either a Baltimore or Miami loss would earn New England a sixth consecutive trip to the playoffs. But a postseason berth wasn't the only uncertainty on the horizon.

"If they do make the playoffs," Harvey Araton of the *New York Times* wrote, "if Matt Cassel plays into January the way he has more Sundays than Bill Belichick could have hoped for, how long before one of the more intriguing quarterback controversies begins—the great Brady coming off reconstructive knee surgery versus the younger, more mobile Cassel, whose market value is soaring."

Cassel led the Patriots into Buffalo for Week 17, and despite fifty-five-mile-per-hour winds, completed six of eight passes during a 13–0 victory over the Bills. Although ultimately were kept out of the postseason, Cassel's rise—3,693 yards, twenty-one touchdowns, 63.4 completion percentage—prompted many in the media to wonder if the younger, less physically damaged Cassel might challenge Tom Brady for the starter's job.

"This is Tom's team," Cassel said in late January. "The Patriots have been Tom's team. He's built that franchise up with his own two hands. He's the guy, and he was the MVP the year before, I realize that. He's been such a mentor for me that I would say, 'No, there is no quarterback competition.'

"[But, I've] earned the right to play in the National Football League and to be a starter in the National Football League; there's no doubt," Cassel added. "And as a competitor, that's all you can hope for is to go out and continue to play and do what you do."

Five weeks later, before any quarterback controversy threatened to sidetrack the New England dynasty, the Patriots traded Cassel to the Kansas City Chiefs.

Acknowledgments

The acknowledgments section for books of this sort often feature some variation of the "so many people went into this project" statement. It's terribly clichéd. And true.

Several friends and family members were fantastic from the very start of this project, which began in March 2011. But my beautiful and brilliant wife, Dr. Sarah Lazarus, deserves top billing here. She consented to, then endured the return of, "Book Writing Adam," the one who works odd hours, stares at his laptop screen far too long, and talks about 1980s football as if it were Camelot or the Holy Roman Empire. Thank you so much, Sarah, for every minute you championed this project.

I also owe tremendous gratitude to my parents, Joan and Dr. Hillard Lazarus—the latter of whom was promoted from "assistant-ish" on my last book to "editor-ish" for this book—as well as my sister-in-law, Brenna Broadnax, and my nieces, Maya and Jasmine, who hosted me during my research trip to Northern California.

The interviews for this book were absolutely critical and I greatly appreciated everyone's time, effort, and insight. (A full list of these interviews appears on page 293.) But a few deserve special mention: thank you so very much to Joe Montana, Steve Young, Jerry Rice, Eddie DeBartolo Jr., Carmen Policy, Steve Bono, John Paye, Brent Jones, Guy McIntyre, Steve Wallace, Mark Purdy, Don DeVore, Carl Crawley, Chuck Smith, Paul Timko, Rich Goldberger, David Sarskus, Allen Veliky, and Dr. Jeff Webb.

I had tremendous help contacting and arranging discussions with those many interviewees, and the following people were instrumental on that front: Michelle Knox, Sasha Taylor, Glenn Dickey, Carl Peterson, Scott Bogdan, Tony Wyllie, Bob Moore, Jude A. Kelly, Valerie Panou, Amy Swander, Dan Brown, Modesto "Moe" Ruggiero, Shirley Johnson, Brian Santiago, Duff Tittle, Rusty Guy, and especially my godfather, Darrell "Buddy" Lazarus.

I also extend my thanks to the people who helped (literally) make this book happen. My mentor from graduate school, the Pittsburgh *Post-Gazette*'s Tom O'Boyle, introduced me to Jane Dystel at Dystel & Goderich, and she passed along my name to John Rudolph, who became my literary agent and remains a great advocate for me and this project. Thank you to all three, especially John.

Da Capo Press and, specifically, Jonathan Crowe also deserve my endless appreciation for recognizing this book's potential. Jonathan was a superb and passionate editor and sounding board until handing the project over to Bob Pigeon with about six minutes remaining in the fourth quarter. Bob and all the staff at Da Capo are each outstanding professionals and great at what they do. The same goes for Lori Hobkirk, Beth Fraser, and Cynthia Young who headed up production, copyediting, and design, and were so paitent and accommodating to me regarding my many, many requests to tweak the manuscript.

Several people also provided tremendous help in tracking down the wonderful photographs inside the book. Thanks to Rick Romagosa and Bill Van Niekerken at the *San Francisco Chronicle*; Jami C. Smith at the *San Jose Mercury News*; Kent Johnston at the *Atlanta Journal-Constitution*; David Pillinger at Reuters; Dave Zilka at the Monessen Public Library; Sara at the Dekalb County Public Library in Decatur; Mark A. Philbrick at Brigham Young University; Sam, Steve, and J. P. at LightSource Studios; and Jeff Bayer. And a special shout-out to Michael Zagaris for the hours I spent at his home looking through his magnificent collection of negatives and prints as well as all the followup calls and e-mails. Thanks so much, Z-Man, for the time, stories, and laughs.

—*Adam Lazarus*, June 2012

Notes

PROLOGUE

1 Tampa Bay didn't: "Young Hastily Fills Shoes of Montana," *Sacramento Bee*, May 18, 1987.

1 Hi, Joe: Charles Bricker, "Big Step for Young—Out of Joe's Shoes," *Fort Lauderdale Sun-Sentinel*, Sept. 27, 1992.

1 This was definitely not: Ibid.

2 Steve, when you're finished: Will McDonough, "Spirited Performance Finally Exorcises the Ghost of Montana," *Boston Globe*, Jan. 30, 1995.

CHAPTER 1: CRYSTAL JOE

3 It was like this guy: Author interview with Carmen Policy, Oct. 24, 2011.

3 It's funny: Joe Montana and Bob Raissman, *Audibles: My Life in Football* (New York: Avon Books, 1986), 218.

3 secret" surgery: Tom FitzGerald, "Joe Montana Had 'Secret' Surgery," *San Francisco Chronicle*, June 13, 1986.

4 He had persistent pain: Ibid.

4 It felt good: Tom FitzGerald, "Smith Cut by Browns Despite Florida Ruling," *Philadelphia Daily News*, July 22, 1986.

4 It's nothing serious: Tom FitzGerald, "Montana Twists Ankle—3 Other 49ers Injured," *San Francisco Chronicle*, Aug. 14, 1986.

4 I don't want to talk: Tom FitzGerald, "Vandals Attack Joe Montana's Car," *San Francisco Chronicle*, Aug. 16, 1986.

5 I'm not worried about: Tom FitzGerald, "Ex-Redskin Jerry Smith Has AIDS," *Fort Lauderdale Sun Sentinel*, Aug. 26, 1986.

5 [It] is getting better: Tom FitzGerald, "49ers Put Wright on Injured List," *San Francisco Chronicle*, Sept. 5, 1986.

5 We were roommates: Author interview with Steve DeBerg, Mar. 1, 2012.

5 I could almost: Montana and Raissman, *Audibles: My Life in Football*, 47.

5 We Want Steve Young: Larry Guest, "DeBerg's Debacle Wasn't 1-Man Show," *Orlando Sentinel*, Sept. 8, 1986.

6 I was very pleased: "49ers Deflate DeBerg and Defeat the Buccaneers," *Los Angeles Times*, Sept. 8, 1986.

6   There was a little disbelief: Tom FitzGerald, "Montana Feels Well Enough to Want Pizza," *San Francisco Chronicle*, Sept. 17, 1986.

6   Montana's injury doesn't: Lowell Cohn, "Let's Hope the Rams Go Easy," *San Francisco Chronicle*, Sept. 12, 1986.

7   I should be there: Michele Himmelberg, "Surgery Set for Montana," *Orange County Register*, Sept. 15, 1986.

7   in order to create: David Perlman, "Montana Has Surgery on Injured Back," *San Francisco Chronicle*, Sept. 16, 1986.

7   Because of the 49ers': Author interview with Art Spander, April 26, 2012.

7   I can safely say: Author interview with Mark Purdy, April 27, 2012.

8   He's still sleepy: FitzGerald, "Montana Feels Well Enough to Want Pizza."

8   Everything looks great: David Perlman, "Months of Therapy Predicted for Montana," *San Francisco Chronicle*, Sept. 17, 1986.

8   That sounds good for Joe: Charles Brickner, "Montana's Surgery Goes Smoothly," *San Jose Mercury News*, Sept. 16, 1986.

8   We'll have to wait: "Montana Out for Season; His Career Threatened," *New York Times*, Sept. 15, 1986.

8   I thought he: Paul Zimmerman, "The Ultimate Winner," *Sports Illustrated*, Aug. 13, 1990.

9   start and play: "49ers Go After Oilers' Everett as Replacement for Montana," *Toronto Star*, Sept. 18, 1986.

9   I do not believe: FitzGerald, "Montana Feels Well Enough to Want Pizza."

9   The absolute soonest: "Montana May Play This Year," *Newsday*, Sept. 23, 1986.

10   I definitely had fear: Lowell Cohn, "'Nervous' Joe Is Ready," *San Francisco Chronicle*, Nov. 7, 1986.

10   This is like anything: Michael Janofsky, "Montana Returns with Sackful of Questions," *New York Times*, Nov. 9, 1986.

11   We had to make: Michael Janofsky, "Montana Back, Ready to Start," *New York Times*, Nov. 5, 1986.

11   I thought something: Cohn, "'Nervous' Joe Is Ready."

11   It was crushing: Ibid.

11   He was different: Author interview with Eddie DeBartolo Jr., Nov. 8, 2011.

11   When he stepped: Author interview with Steve Bono, Oct. 25, 2011.

12   A lot of times: Jim Jenkins, "Montana's Back . . . In Top Form," *Sacramento Bee*, Nov. 10, 1986.

12   The phrase I used: Author interview with Mark Purdy, Oct. 27, 2011.

12   crazy: George Usher, "Cowboys Keep the Faith in Pelluer," *Newsday*, Nov. 10, 1986.

12   I told Joe from: Ibid.

12   It was just the fact: "Montana Back—In Near Perfect Form," *Aiken Standard*, Nov. 10, 1986.

13   The new Joe Montana: Frank Litsky, "Players; Montana Cautiously Proceeds," *New York Times*, Dec. 2, 1986.

13   his throws as if: Lowell Cohn, "Joe's Human After All," *San Francisco Chronicle*, Dec. 2, 1986.

13   He hasn't had the scintillating: Gerald Eskenazi, "Montana in Passable, Not Super, Form," *New York Times*, Dec. 5, 1986.

13   Most successful: Chris Dufresene, "After a Miraculous Recovery From Back Surgery, Joe's Play Has Been Less Than a Miracle," *Los Angeles Times*, Dec. 17, 1986.

13   I think the return: Phil Hersh, "Montana Leads 49ers to Title," *Chicago Tribune*, Dec. 20, 1986.

14   I've never done: Ibid.

14   I'm probably a little: Scott Ostler, "Miracle-Maker Montana Is Back—So Are 49ers," *Los Angeles Times*, Dec. 20, 1986.

14   The game will be: Lowell Cohn, "Coming Back from Failure," *San Francisco Chronicle*, Jan. 2, 1987.

15   We don't try to: Sam Smith, "With 'The Play' Mediocrity Passed into Greatness," *Chicago Tribune*, Jan. 2, 1987.

15   If I had put that one: Tom FitzGerald, "The Play Rice Won't Forget," *San Francisco Chronicle*, Jan. 5, 1987.

15   When you hit people: Tom FitzGerald, "Sticks 'N' Slams: What Great D's Are Made Of," *San Francisco Chronicle*, Jan. 5, 1987.

15   He saw me coming: John McClain, "Notes," *Houston Chronicle*, Jan. 5, 1987.

16   He was pretty groggy: Michael Janofsky, "Montana Is Hospitalized for Concussion," *New York Times*, Jan. 5, 1987.

16   He has a concussion: Ibid.

16   He feels fine except: "Montana Released from Hospital," *Houston Chronicle*, Jan. 6, 1987.

16   This game reminds us: David Bush, "A 49er Era Comes to a Close," *San Francisco Chronicle*, Jan. 6, 1987.

17   Joe's situation does concern: "Walsh Calls Loss to Giants a 'Sobering' Experience," *Orange County Register*, Jan. 6, 1987.

17   He is going to: David Bush, "Montana Released from Hospital," *San Francisco Chronicle*, Jan. 6, 1987.

17   With Montana, who: "It'll Be Denver, Giants, Patriots' Berry Predicts," *Chicago Tribune*, Jan. 6, 1987.

17   I saw no minuses with Vinny: Will McDonough, "Ditka Gone After 1987," *Boston Globe*, Jan. 18, 1987.

18   Word out of the Niners: Will McDonough, "Are Bears Rearmed for '87?" *Boston Globe*, Mar. 8, 1987.

18   the new Joe [Montana]: Jerry Greene, "Don't Expect Young to Back Up Montana," *Orlando Sentinel*, Mar. 18, 1987.

18   We're assuming he'll: Charles Bricker, "Montana Is Put on the Spot," *San Jose Mercury News*, Mar. 18, 1987.

18   I think Joe can be: Greene, "Don't Expect Young to Back Up Montana."

CHAPTER 2: THE COMEBACK KID

19   I was bitten: Bob Oates, "Today, Survival Is the Game that NFL Quarterbacks Are Playing, and the 49ers' Leader Has Certainly Survived Worst," *Los Angeles Times*, Aug. 9, 1987.

19   Playing ball in: Paul Zimmerman, "Born to Be a Quarterback," *Sports Illustrated*, Aug. 6, 1990.

20   Working is for: Bob Oates, "Joe Montana's Not the Type Who Would Let the Big Sky Fall In," *Los Angeles Times*, Jan. 21, 1982.

20   When Joey wasn't: Ibid.

20   I weighed 130: Brian Herman, "Joe Montana Not a Surprise to His Parents," *Monessen Valley Independent*, Oct. 26, 1977.

20   It was just: Author interview with Joe Montana, Nov. 30, 2011.

20   He was a real: Ibid.

21   I told Joe's dad: Author interview with Carl Crawley, Oct. 3, 2011.

21   I've only missed: Herman, "Joe Montana Not a Surprise to His Parents."

21   Joe Banana: Montana and Raissman, *Audibles: My Life in Football*, 141.

21   For me, competing: Zimmerman, "Born to Be a Quarterback."

21   He was a frail: Author interview with Chuck Smith, Oct. 3, 2011.

22   Abramski wasn't: Author interview with Paul Timko, Oct. 3, 2011.

22   When we went: Author interview with Keith Bassi, Oct. 22, 2011.

23   Montana has the: Brian Herman, "Two Changes Bring New Life to Ringgold," *Monessen Valley Independent*, Oct. 3, 1972.

23   In his senior: Zimmerman, "Born to Be a Quarterback."

23   If you ever wondered: Montana and Raissman, *Audibles: My Life in Football*, 3.

23   I liked Ara: Ibid., 10.

24   Forystek throws a: David Condon, "Devine 'Imbued with ND spirit,'" *Chicago Tribune*, July 2, 1975.

24   plenty nervous: Bill Jauss, "NU Scores on Irish, Then Cave in 31–7," *Chicago Tribune*, Sept. 28, 1975.

24 I was excited: Montana and Raissman, *Audibles: My Life in Football*, 13.

25 I thought both: "AF Finds Way to Lose to ND," *Colorado Springs Gazette Telegraph*, Oct. 20, 1975.

25 Once we got going: Roy Damer, "Irish Squelch Rumor, Air Force 31–30," *Chicago Tribune*, Oct. 19, 1975.

25 That season was: Montana and Raissman, *Audibles: My Life in Football*, 16.

25 [He was] just: Zimmerman, "Born to Be a Quarterback."

26 He's a dedicated: Roy Damer, "Lisch Solidifies Spot as No. 1 Irish QB," *Chicago Tribune*, May 1, 1977.

26 was wishy-washy: Montana and Raissman, *Audibles: My Life in Football*, 10–11.

26 I think there: Author interview with Merv Johnson, Aug. 18, 2011.

26 When we lost: Zimmerman, "Born to Be a Quarterback."

27 We had them: Author interview with Keena Turner, Dec. 12, 2011.

27 Forget it, fellows: David Condon, "Purdue Upset Ends in Montana," *Chicago Tribune*, Sept. 25, 1977.

27 I won the quarterback: Montana and Raissman, *Audibles: My Life in Football*, 20.

28 It was almost: Ibid., 27–28.

28 We saw Joe sitting: Author interview with Kris Haines, Aug. 23, 2011.

28 Rick Slager was: Zimmerman, "Born to Be a Quarterback."

28 When Joe came: Sal Maiorana, "CBS SportsLine Historian."

28 The coaches just: Author interview with Vagas Ferguson, Sept. 22, 2011.

29 It couldn't have: Maiorana, "CBS SportsLine Historian."

29 Reporters were: Montana and Raissman, *Audibles: My Life in Football*, 31–32.

29 I can remember: Gil Brandt, "The 1978 College Football All-America Preview," *Sport*, Sept., 1978.

30 We kept going: Harley Tinkham, "To This Point, Steve Dils Hasn't Come Back to Haunt the 49ers," *Los Angeles Times*, Mar. 7, 1990.

30 Where'd you get: Tom FitzGerald, "Before Joe, You Could Pick Your Seat," *San Francisco Chronicle*, Apr. 19, 1995.

30 Bill came out: Author interview with DeBartolo, Nov. 8, 2011.

31 [DeBerg taught me]: Author interview with Montana, Nov. 30, 2011.

31 Coach Walsh was: Author interview with DeBerg, Mar. 1, 2012.

31 I was lucky: Montana and Raissman, *Audibles: My Life in Football*, 54–55.

32 DeBerg has the: Michael Madden, "Patriots Notebook: Cavanaugh Hurting, So Grogan Will Start," *Boston Globe*, Nov. 27, 1980.

32 He said he: Will McDonough, "They Had No Heart in San Francisco," *Boston Globe*, Dec. 1, 1980.

32   Joe was simply: David Harris, *The Genius: How Bill Walsh Reinvented Football and Created an NFL Dynasty* (New York: Random House, 2008), 122.

32   There was a purpose: Author interview with Montana, Nov. 30, 2011.

33   I wanted to play: *The Top 100: NFL's Greatest Players.* #4: Joe Montana.

33   Our confidence: "49ers Advance to Super Bowl with a Late Rally," *Toronto Globe and Mail*, Jan. 11, 1982.

33   I was thinking: Mark Heisler, "Montana: I was Thinking of Throwing the Ball Away,'" *Los Angeles Times*, Jan. 11, 1982.

34   I talked to: "Montana Wants More Rings," *Toronto Globe and Mail*, Jan. 26, 1982.

34   Dan Marino's a: Dave Anderson, "The 49ers' Astronaut," *New York Times*, Jan. 21, 1985.

34   I think when: Author interview with Carmen Policy, Oct. 24, 2011.

35   Bill never would: Author interview with Guy Benjamin, Nov. 10, 2011.

35   I think Joe: Charles Bricker, *San Jose Mercury News*, Sept. 1, 1985.

36   The pain was: Montana and Raissman, *Audibles: My Life in Football*, 213–14.

36   Joe wouldn't: Michael Madden, "49ers' Year? Well . . . ," *Boston Globe*, Dec. 30, 1985.

36   I looked into: Cooper Rollow, "Dynasty Dreams Vanish," *Chicago Tribune*, Dec. 30, 1985.

36   The only time: John McClain, "Bad Giants Blast 49ers to Sideline," *Houston Chronicle*, Dec. 30, 1985.

36   It unquestionably: Rich Cimini, "49ers Are Making No Excuses," *Newsday*, Dec. 30, 1985.

CHAPTER 3: GREAT EXPECTATIONS

37   But the coach's: Mark Purdy, "Young Continues to Take Right Steps to Grow Into Role," *San Jose Mercury News*, Oct. 5, 1992.

37   twenties-aged woman: Steve Young's enshrinement speech transcript, Pro Football Hall of Fame Enshrinement Ceremony, at the Pro Football Hall of Fame Field at Fawcett Stadium, Aug. 7, 2005.

37   She started: Purdy, "Young Continues to Take Right Steps to Grow Into."

37   the low rent: Jack McCaullum, "The Steve and Gordon Show," *Sports Illustrated*, Nov. 14, 1983.

38   I grew up: Mike Kiley, "No More Backup for Bucs' Young," *Chicago Tribune*, Nov. 8, 1986.

38   We thought we: Joan Ryan, "Long Road to the Top," *San Francisco Chronicle*, Jan. 6, 1995.

38   always played with: Greg Garber, "The No. 1 QB," *Hartford Courant*, Jan. 2, 2000.

38   He had the: Woody Anderson, "Forever Young," *Hartford Courant*, Aug. 7, 2005.

38   Steve was never: Jack Cavanaugh, "From the Sandlots of Greenwich to the Super Bowl," *New York Times*, Jan. 29, 1995.

39   I remember looking: Author interview with LaVell Edwards, Oct. 4, 2011.

39   If you want: Michael Janofsky, "Brigham Young: A Special Style On and Off the Field," *New York Times*, Nov. 6, 1983.

39   After five days: Anderson, "Forever Young."

40   I really liked: Author interview with Ted Tollner, Nov. 4, 2011.

40   I thought [Steve: Ibid.

40   a Catholic with: Gene Wojciechowski, "He Was Like Rocker in Mormon Tabernacle Choir at BYU," *Los Angeles Times*, Jan. 25, 1986.

40   I really didn't: Rick Telander, "Superb!" *Sports Illustrated*, Feb. 6, 1995.

40   Their private lives: Author interview with Tollner, Nov. 4, 2011.

41   I am not Jim: N. Brooks Clark, Jill Lieber, Douglas S. Looney, Craig Neff, John Papanek, and Pat Putnam, "19: Brigham Young," *Sports Illustrated*, Sept. 1, 1982.

41   He had a real: Charles Bricker, "Young Fares Best Letting Coaching Staff Call Plays," *San Jose Mercury News*, Aug. 17, 1987.

41   I played my heart: "BYU Tandem May Be Nation's Best," *Boston Globe*, Sept. 4, 1983.

42   We were getting: Author interview with Edwards, Oct. 4, 2011.

42   Expectations were: Steve Young with Greg Brown, *Steve Young: Forever Young* (Boulder, CO: Taylor Trade, 1996).

42   He just worked: Author interview with Robbie Bosco, Sept. 13, 2011.

43   A year ago: Janofsky, "Brigham Young: A Special Style On and Off the Field."

43   I don't wear a: Will Grimsley, "BYU Was Lucky to Land Steve Young," *Kokomo Tribune*, Dec. 24, 1983.

43   Ever since I've: Ibid.

43   This is the future: Sam Farmer, "When Steve Was Young," *San Jose Mercury News*, June 12, 2000.

44   We obviously: Author interview with Sam Wyche, Aug. 31, 2011.

44   self-made billionaire: "Sports People," *New York Times*, July 22, 1984.

44   First of all: Author interview with Leigh Steinberg, Sept. 16, 2011.

45   They knew he: Ibid.

45   always be humble: Chris DuFresne, "Young Spurns Express' Fat Offer for Now," *Los Angeles Times*, Mar. 4, 1984.

45   I don't want: Jack McCallum, "The Man with the Golden Arm," *Sports Illustrated*, Mar. 12, 1984.

46 The big money: Ryan, "Long Road to the Top."

46 You signed a: Laury Livsey, *The Steve Young Story* (Roseville, CA: Prima Publishing, 1996), 130.

46 He woke up: Ryan, "Long Road to the Top."

46 I felt good about: William R. Barnard, "Playing Well Isn't Good Enough for Young, or Express," *Clearfield Progress*, Apr. 2, 1984.

46 He was inconsistent: Chris DuFresne, "Express Beats the Odds . . . Takes on Gamblers," *Los Angeles Times*, Feb. 24, 1985.

47 We had to whisper: Paul Zimmerman, "Ping-Pong Football," *Sports Illustrated*, Dec. 21, 1992.

47 What can I say: George White, "The Kelly Show: Fun in February," *Houston Chronicle*, Feb. 25, 1985.

47 Get rid of him: "Steve Young Overrated—Trump," *Los Angeles Times*, July 19, 1985.

48 You half expected: Chris DuFresne, "The Result of Express vs. Arizona Game: 8,200 and for Those Keeping Score, Outlaws Defeat L.A., 21–10 at Pierce College," *Los Angeles Times*, June 16, 1985.

48 I wasn't mad: Peter King, "No Longer Young and Restless at QB," *Syracuse Post Standard*, Aug. 15, 1988.

48 In a period of: Michael Janofsky and Robert McG. Thomas, "Young Can Talk," *New York Times*, July 20, 1985.

48 This is a new: Jerry Greene, "Tampa Bay Signs Young for 6 Years, $6 Million," *Orlando Sentinel*, Sept. 11, 1985.

48 I didn't have any: Author interview with Leeman Bennett, Sept. 9, 2011.

49 I made it to the: Livsey, *The Steve Young Story*, 174–175.

49 We never had: Ibid., p. 177.

49 I don't think: John Weyler, "Steve Young: The Express Lane to Tampa Hasn't Been So Smooth," *Los Angeles Times*, Oct. 4, 1986.

49 I'd rather get: Tom Zucco, "Mini-Camp Day One: Perkins Meets the Bucs," *St. Petersburg Times*, Feb. 28, 1987.

50 He was like a: Author interview with DeBerg, Mar. 1, 2012.

50 As time goes: Mike Flanagan, "Scrambling Young Could Find Himself Itching for Trouble," *St. Petersburg Evening Independent*, Nov. 26, 1985.

50 Steve would: Livsey, *The Steve Young Story*, 177.

50 I have no resentment: Jerry Greene, "It's Time for DeBerg to Start Shooting Back," *Orlando Sentinel*, Sept. 3, 1986.

50 Young quarterbacks: Jerry Greene, "Tampa Bay Buccaneers," *Orlando Sentinel*, Sept. 4, 1986.

51 I think Young put too: Ibid.

51   probably the worst: Jerry Greene, "Bucs Throw Away Opener," *Orlando Sentinel*, Sept. 8, 1986.

51   We feel awfully: Bob Fowler, "Young Helps Bucs End Road Ways," *Orlando Sentinel*, Sept. 22, 1986.

51   My findings: Tom FitzGerald, "49ers' Young Will Visit Old Haunts," *San Francisco Chronicle*, Nov. 19, 1987.

52   Coach Perkins and: "People," *Houston Chronicle*, Mar. 1, 1987.

52   A quarterback's image: Jerry Greene, "Bucs' QB Young in Limbo Over Testaverde Situation," *Orlando Sentinel*, Mar. 1, 1987.

52   I went to [owner: Author interview with Steinberg, Sept. 16, 2011.

52   I explained to Steve: Author interview with DeBerg, Mar. 1, 2012.

52   So the thought: Author interview with Steinberg, Sept. 16, 2011.Ï

CHAPTER 4: STIRRING SOMETHING UP

53   I must be a: Author interview with Steve Young, Oct. 26, 2011.

53   Bill's trying to: Author interview with Policy, Oct. 24, 2011.

54   If I had wanted: Lowell Cohn, "Joe's Feeling Real Good—You Hear That, Steve?" *San Francisco Chronicle*, May 15, 1987.

54   I remember the: Author interview with Young, Oct. 26, 2011.

54   Steve was the least: Author interview with John Paye, Oct. 28, 2011.

55   When I was in: Author interview with Young, Oct. 26, 2011.

55   was bouncing around: Charles Bricker, "Snap Is Back," *San Jose Mercury News*, Aug. 2, 1987.

55   I feel confident: Tom FitzGerald, "Young Has Moments in 49ers Win," *San Francisco Chronicle*, Aug. 10, 1987.

56   There were times: Author interview with Paye, Oct. 28, 2011.

56   He still thinks too: Charles Bricker, "Young Fares Best Letting Coaching Staff Call Plays," *San Jose Mercury News*, Aug. 17, 1987.

57   We've got a long: Bill Sullivan, "Final Dress Rehearsal Shows Niners Imperfections," *San Jose Mercury News*, Sept. 5 1987.

57   We were that bad: Tom FitzGerald, "49ers Shut Down in Opener," *San Francisco Chronicle*, Sept. 14, 1987.

57   He wasn't quick or: Charles Bricker, "Niners Look Dismal in 30–17 Loss," *San Jose Mercury News*, Sept. 14, 1987.

57   I wasn't tired: Ibid.

57   Sam is clearly the brightest: Charles Bricker, "49ers Bill Walsh Puts Genius Tag on Cincinnati's Sam Wyche," *The Vindicator*, Sept. 20, 1987.

58   Hey, I want to: Lowell Cohn, "Don't Think, Just Punt," *San Francisco Chronicle*, Sept. 21, 1987.

58 A punt definitely is: Mark Maloney, "Bengals Botch the Clock, 49ers Beat It," *Lexington Herald-Leader*, Sept. 21, 1987.

58 The guard and offensive tackle: Ron Thomas, "Esaison Had a Premonition," *San Francisco Chronicle*, Sept. 21. 1987.

59 I was supposed to go: Maloney, "Bengals Botch the Clock, 49ers Beat It."

59 Guys were throwing: Jim Jenkins, "The Catch II," *Sacramento Bee*, Sept. 21, 1987.

59 Vintage Joe Montana: Author interview with Steve Wallace, Sept. 13, 2011.

59 I think we all agreed: Tom FitzGerald, "NFL Players Begin Their Strike," *San Francisco Chronicle*, Sept. 23, 1987.

59 There is always: Tom FitzGerald, "Striking 49ers Are Restless, Meet Upshaw," *San Francisco Chronicle*, Sept. 28, 1987.

60 The main reason I'm: "Many Striking Players Losing Faith in Upshaw," *Orlando Sentinel*, Oct. 3, 1987.

60 We want to avoid: Ron Thomas, "Walsh Tells Some 49ers to Stay Out," *San Francisco Chronicle*, Oct. 3, 1987.

60 This isn't going to affect: C. W. Nevius, "Ten 49ers May Cross Line Today," *San Francisco Chronicle*, Oct. 7, 1987.

60 I was a friend: Charles Bricker, "Losing Some of His Luster," *San Jose Mercury News*, Oct. 3, 1987.

60 It just so happens: Author interview with Wallace, Sept. 13, 2011.

61 Yeah, there was dirt: Jeff Schultz, "A Trick but Not a Threat," *San Jose Mercury News*, Oct. 26, 1987.

61 [Young] miscalled the formation: Ibid.

62 Everything went right: Jeff Schultz, "TV Cameras Bring Francis to His Knee," *San Jose Mercury News*, Nov. 9, 1987.

62 He is very doubtful: Ron Thomas, "Montana 'Very Doubtful' for Saints Game," *San Francisco Chronicle*, Nov. 13, 1987.

62 slipped Ray Wersching: Tom Zucco, "Young to Have Hand in 49ers' Fortunes Sunday," *St. Petersburg Times*, Nov. 14, 1987.

62 Yep, Ray's a rich: Ibid.

62 Joe is a legend: Ron Thomas, "Young Gets Nod—He's Starting," *San Francisco Chronicle*, Nov. 14, 1987.

62 I know better than: Tom Zucco, "Young Rammed Himself Back to 49ers' Bench," *St. Petersburg Times*, Nov. 17, 1987.

63 You don't look so good: Jeff Schultz, "Young Says He's Only Confused by Getting Quick Hook," *San Jose Mercury News*, Nov. 16, 1987.

63 When Walsh had to: Lowell Cohn, "Battered Sub Back on Bench," *San Francisco Chronicle*, Nov. 16, 1987.

63 It's always: Schultz, "Young Says He's Only Confused by Getting Quick Hook."

64   I can't say the Saints: Charles Bricker, "Niners' Loss Is Gift-Wrapped," *San Jose Mercury News*, Nov. 16, 1987.

64   There was a lot: Jeff Schultz, "Young's Return Is Low-Key," *San Jose Mercury News*, Nov. 22, 1987.

64   This means a lot to: Mike Payne, "Getting Bucs MVP Award Makes Steve Young's Day," *St. Petersburg Times*, Nov. 23, 1987.

64   They played more: "Buccaneers Leave Rice Unattended and Get Burned by the 49ers, 24–10," *Los Angeles Times*, Nov. 23, 1987.

65   I thought I answered: Ed Meyer, "Kosar Is a Notch Below Montana,'" *San Jose Mercury News*, Nov. 30, 1987.

65   [Kosar] is big, he's: Ron Thomas, "Walsh Lays it On—Browns 'Awesome,'" *San Francisco Chronicle*, Nov. 25, 1987.

65   Sometimes: Author interview with John McVay, Aug. 22, 2011.

65   Those aren't the: "Records No Big Deal to Montana," *San Francisco Chronicle*, Dec. 7, 1987.

66   We'll just have to: Jim Jenkins, "The Showdown: How the 49ers and Bears Compare," *Sacramento Bee*, Dec. 13, 1987.

66   I said, 'There goes: Ron Thomas, "49ers' Turner May Be Lost for Season," *San Francisco Chronicle*, Dec. 16, 1987.

66   When Joe went: Jeff Schultz, "Montana Is Hurt, But It's Not Serious," *San Jose Mercury News*, Dec. 15, 1987.

66   I think it: Skip Myslenski, "49ers Show They Have More than Montana and Rice," *Chicago Tribune*, Dec. 15, 1987.

67   Any time anybody: Mike Kiley, "Exhibit A: Bears Trash Ditka's Gum All They Can Make Stick Against 49ers," *Chicago Tribune*, Dec. 16, 1987.

67   I'm not just resting: Lowell Cohn, "Young Didn't Miss a Beat," *San Francisco Chronicle*, Dec. 15, 1987.

67   You can't sit: Myslenski, "49ers Show They Have More than Montana and Rice."

67   It seemed like the: Tom FitzGerald, "49ers Wrap Up the Falcons," *San Francisco Chronicle*, Dec. 21, 1987.

68   I felt like I was: Ibid.

68   We decided before: Chris Dufresne, "Rams Swamped by the 49ers, 48–0," *Los Angeles Times*, Dec. 28, 1987.

68   It would [have] been: Ron Thomas, "The Best QB Combo in the NFL," *San Francisco Chronicle*, Dec. 28, 1987.

69   Yeah, that was part: Jim Jenkins, "San Francisco Best in West? 49ers Leave No Doubt," *Sacramento Bee*, Dec. 28, 1987.

69   I hope so: Scott Ostler, "Quarterback Controversy That Is Nice, for a Change," *Los Angeles Times*, Dec. 28, 1987.

69   as long as Joe: Ibid.

70   We spent a lot of: Jim Jenkins, "49ers Changing Gears to Get Ready for Vikings," *Sacramento Bee*, Jan. 4, 1988.

70   I'm getting tired: Robert Sansevere, "49ers Don't Intimidate Vikings Doleman," *Minnesota Star Tribune*, Jan. 5, 1988.

70   [Joe Montana] ain't no great: Ibid.

70   games are played: Steve Aschburner, Robert Sansevere, "49ers' Paris Has Tame Response to Doleman's Tough Talk," *Minnesota Star Tribune*, Jan. 5, 1988.

70   Steve could come: Jim Jenkins, "Young, Eager and Back on the Bench," *Sacramento Bee*, Jan. 9, 1988.

70   The emphasis with Joe: Ibid.

71   I could sense: Skip Myslenski, "Vikings Surprise 49ers," *Chicago Tribune*, Jan. 10, 1988.

71   I don't think he's: Chris Dufresne, "Carter, Vikings Catch 49ers by Surprise, 36–24," *Los Angeles Times*, Jan. 10, 1988.

71   I just threw it behind: Scott Ostler, "Joe Was Spectator When the Time Was Right for a Montana Miracle," *Los Angeles Times*, Jan. 10, 1988.

71   It was frustrating: Jay Lawrence, "49ers QB Is Benched for First Time as Pro," *Orange County Register*, Jan. 10, 1988.

71   I told him I didn't: Paul Zimmerman, "Upset!" *Sports Illustrated*, Jan. 18, 1988.

71   You're always surprised: Mark Blaudschun, "In a Switch, Montana Takes a Seat in Second Half," *Boston Globe*, Jan. 10, 1988.

71   He was (angry) : Jeff Schultz, "A Compromised Position," *San Jose Mercury News*, Aug. 28, 1988.

72   The 49ers thinking was: Author interview with Wallace, Sept. 13, 2011.

72   Young changed everything: Jerry Greene, "Vikings' Key: Twin Cities, Twin Titles," *Orlando Sentinel*, Jan. 10, 1988.

72   Our offense just: Jeff Schultz, "Young Made Good Pitches, but Future Is Out of His Control," *San Jose Mercury News*, Jan. 10, 1988.

72   quarterback talk: Ostler, "Joe Was Spectator When the Time Was Right for a Montana Miracle."

72   We go through certain: Ibid.

CHAPTER 5: JOE COOL AND MR. HYPERACTIVITY

73   Geri and I are: Jeff Schultz, "Walsh Denies He Lost Power in Job Shuffle," *San Jose Mercury News*, Mar. 26, 1988.

73   There is no third: Ibid.

73   [Eddie DeBartolo] was: Author interview with Policy, Oct. 24, 2011.

74   [Bill] certainly had his: Author interview with David Harris, Oct. 4, 2011.

74 take more control: Will McDonough, "Walsh, DeBartolo at Odds?" *Boston Globe*, Mar. 20, 1988.

74 I won't mislead you: Jim Jenkins, "Montana Trade Rumors Fly, So Do Denials," *Sacramento Bee*, Mar. 17, 1988.

74 have a narrow mind: Gordon Forbes, "49ers in No Rush to Deal Montana," *USA Today*, Mar. 30, 1988.

75 runs my organization: Charles Brickner, "Montana Trade Rumors Irk Walsh," *San Jose Mercury News*, Mar. 17, 1988.

75 After we get through: Author interview with Policy, Oct. 24, 2011.

75 Eddie, if it's going: Gordon Forbes, "49ers in No Rush to Deal Montana," *USA Today*, Mar. 30, 1988.

75 [Joe's] a friend of: Ibid.

75 And I am not: C. W. Nevius, "It's Got to Be Joe," *San Francisco Chronicle*, Aug. 8, 1988.

76 We'd do things: Ibid.

76 I'm in a position: S. L. Price, "Montana's Still Same Old Joe," *Sacramento Bee*, July 16, 1988.

76 I've learned a lot: Bob Hill, "Despite Deeds, Montana Challenged by Young," *Sun Sentinel*, July 30, 1988.

76 Joe last year was: Hill, "Despite Deeds, Montana Challenged by Young."

76 We have a quarterback: Jeff Schultz, "Miami Dumps Niners," *San Jose Mercury News*, Aug. 1, 1988.

76 I guess it's sort: Ibid.

77 I ran a reverse in: Ron Thomas, "49ers Lose to Miami—Young Sharp," *San Francisco Chronicle*, Aug. 1, 1988.

77 I'd rather face: Bob Hill and Steve Hummer, "Archer's Number Unlisted, but Dolphins Make Right Call," *Sun Sentinel*, Aug. 1, 1988.

77 I think it would: Charles Bricker, "Walsh Continues to Walk QB Tightrope," *San Jose Mercury News*, Aug. 3, 1988.

77 You never thought: Author interview with Brent Jones, Oct. 24, 2011.

78 the best technician: "Walsh Faced with Nice QB Dilemma Decision Time Starts Sunday vs. Dolphins," *Orlando Sentinel*, July 29, 1988.

78 I know they were: Author interview with Bob Gagliano, Aug. 18, 2011.

78 I had approached: Ibid.

78 Controversy has disrupted: Joan Ryan, "S. F. Quarterback Controversy Comes to You Courtesy of Coach Bill Walsh," *Deseret News*, Aug. 7, 1988.

79 I think Joe was really: Ralph Wiley, "State of Montana," *Sports Illustrated*, Aug. 15, 1988.

79 It took a lot of: Charles Bricker, "Young Is Gaining Ground," *San Jose Mercury News*, Aug. 14, 1988.

79   It seemed like we: Jeff Schultz, "49ers Struggle, then Win 27–21," *San Jose Mercury News*, Aug. 27, 1988.

79   It's not my job to: Jim Jenkins, "It's a Win and a Loss for 49ers QB Young," *Sacramento Bee*, Aug. 27, 1988.

80   A lot of times quarterback: C. W. Nevius, "Young Must Stand By— Impatiently," *San Francisco Chronicle*, Aug. 27, 1988.

80   nervous: Author interview with Guy McIntyre, Oct. 24, 2011.

80   I think a sense: Author interview with Jones, Oct. 24, 2011.

81   People always think: Ibid.

81   It's not that there: Author interview with Montana, Nov. 30, 2011.

81   I remember in training camp: Author interview with Jones, Oct. 24, 2011.

81   We're friends, Steve: Wiley, "State of Montana."

81   [Joe] was so competitive: Author interview with Steinberg, Sept. 16, 2011.

82   As a journalist: Author interview with Anonymous.

82   Montana will start: Jenkins, "It's a Win and a Loss for 49ers QB Young."

82   There's room for improvement: Ibid.

82   helicopters: Charles Bricker, "Montana Hurts Elbow, May Miss Next Game," *San Jose Mercury News*, Sept. 5, 1988.

82   the size of a tennis: Jim Jenkins, "Saints Take 49ers to Limit, and Lose," *Sacramento Bee*, Sept. 5, 1988.

83   Young was shaky: Ibid.

83   I felt that I could have: Paul Zimmerman, "Better Late than Never," *Sports Illustrated*, Sept. 19, 1988.

83   90 percent: Jeff Schultz, "Young Expected to Start for Injured Montana," *San Jose Mercury News*, Sept. 11, 1988.

83   Be ready to play: Mark Purdy, "Will QB Relays Last All Season?" *San Jose Mercury News*, Sept. 12, 1988.

83   I wasn't sure he: Ibid.

84   76 All Go: Paul Zimmerman, "Better Late Than Never," *Sports Illustrated*, Sept. 19, 1988.

84   the ugliest play in football: Ibid.

84   Just as we planned: "Less-Than-Minute Rice Burns Giants, as 49ers Win, 20–17," *Los Angeles Times*, Sept. 12, 1988.

84   I really wanted to: Jim Jenkins, "Neither QB Is Thrilled with Shuttle," *Sacramento Bee*, Sept. 12, 1988.

84   Joe's really been a man: Glenn Dickey, "Quick Start Has Surprised Even Walsh," *San Francisco Chronicle*, Sept. 16, 1988.

84   I'm not going to: Charles Bricker, "Montana's Feeling Heat—And Walsh Is Last to Know," *San Jose Mercury News*, Sept. 20, 1988.

85   The wind had to be really: Mike Spence, "Wind Has Laugh at 49ers' Expense," *Colorado Springs Gazette*, Oct. 10, 1988.

85   It's no big deal: Charles Bricker, "Montana Departs 2 Times," *San Jose Mercury News*, Oct. 10, 1988.

85   It was the wind: Ibid.

85   We Want Joe: Jack Sheppard, "Young's Big Chance Turns Into Fiasco," *St. Petersburg Times*, Oct. 10, 1988.

85   The receivers (Jerry: Ibid.

86   It was a good pass: Mike Spence, "Denver's Wilson Returns From the Dead," *Colorado Springs Gazette*, Oct. 10, 1988.

86   There's no excuses: Thomas George, "Bronco Interception Helps Top 49ers," *New York Times*, Oct. 10, 1988.

86   Next week, if we score: Dan Vierria, "49ers Pointing Fingers at Inept Offense," *Sacramento Bee*, Oct. 10, 1988.

86   Nobody likes to be: Jeff Schultz, "For Montana, Clutch Passing and a Break Drive Away Pain," *San Jose Mercury News*, Oct. 17, 1988.

87   That was a great pass: Ibid.

87   Look, there's definitely: Michele Himmelberg, "The 49ers Held Their Breath When Montana Took Breather," *Orange County Register*, Oct. 17, 1988.

87   We really need Steve: Glenn Dickey, "Passing a Key to Bears Game," *San Francisco Chronicle*, Oct. 24, 1988.

88   You've got to feel: Mike Conklin, "Shocked 49ers Just Shake Their Heads," *Chicago Tribune*, Oct. 25, 1988.

88   totally fatigued: Mark Purdy, "QB Controversy Has 3 Versions," *San Jose Mercury News*, Oct. 25, 1988.

88   Fatigued? No: Ibid.

88   If I was hurting: Ibid.

88   "(Montana's) readiness: Jeff Schultz, "Young Might Start Sunday," *San Jose Mercury News*, Oct. 26, 1988.

89   be fine: "San Francisco Signs QB Gagliano—Oops, No It Didn't," *Orlando Sentinel*, Oct. 29, 1988.

89   Steve looks good: Jeff Schultz, "Young Will Start for Niners," *San Jose Mercury News*, Oct. 29, 1988.

89   It's tougher for Steve: Ibid.

89   (The Vikings) have: Ron Thomas, "Young Will Start; Montana Hurt," *San Francisco Chronicle*, Oct. 29, 1988.

89   I guess I wasn't much: Charles Bricker, "49-Yard Run Lifts Young out of Montana's Shadow," *San Jose Mercury News*, Oct. 31, 1988.

90   Joe helped me through: Mark Purdy, "It's Time for Walsh to Slam Door on Revolving," *San Jose Mercury News*, Oct. 31, 1988.

90   It was a good throw: Ron Thomas, "Reserve Receivers Rescued the 49ers," *San Francisco Chronicle*, Oct. 31, 1988.

91   [Tim Newton] had: Robert Sansevere, "Young Breaks Vikings' Tackles, Hearts," *Minnesota Star-Tribune*, Oct. 31, 1988.

91   Woody gave me: Bricker, "49-Yard Run Lifts Young out of Montana's Shadow."

91   Anytime I was on: Author interview with Young, Oct. 26, 2011.

91   Steve's running style: Lowell Cohn, "No Stumblebum in the Second Half," *San Francisco Chronicle*, Oct. 31, 1988.

92   I was so embarrassed: Author interview with Young, Oct. 26, 2011.

92   Mr. Hyperactivity: Bricker, "49-Yard Run Lifts Young out of Montana's Shadow."

92   Steve is a frustrating: Ibid.

92   I don't know: Bricker, "49-Yard Run Lifts Young out of Montana's Shadow."

92   Joe is one of the: Purdy, "It's Time for Walsh to Slam Door on Revolving."

92   Montana Feels He May: Front Page Headline, *San Francisco Chronicle*, Nov. 1, 1988.

93   I can't say, but I: C. W. Nevius, "49er Star Says He's Confused," *San Francisco Chronicle*, Nov. 1, 1988.

93   I would hate it: Nevius, "49er Star Says He's Confused."

93   too caught up: Ibid.

93   I think Joe is: Ibid.

93   I've never been a big: Ibid.

93   As long as he's healthy: Ibid.

93   Why don't they tell: Ibid.

93   I think if my career: Ibid.

93   It's not like I beg: Ibid.

93   irresponsible: C. W. Nevius, "Walsh Tries to Patch It Up with Joe," *San Francisco Chronicle*, Nov. 4, 1988.

94   Some of them, of course: Jeff Schultz, "Reporters Blitz Montana," *San Jose Mercury News*, Nov. 3, 1988.

94   I remember leaving the: *America's Game: 1988 49ers*, NFL Films.

94   We had a big lead: Jeff Schultz, "49ers Get Burned in Desert," *San Jose Mercury News*, Nov. 7, 1988.

94   I was thinking first: Jeff Schultz, "Young's Decision Backfires," *San Jose Mercury News*, Nov. 7, 1988.

95   Check the tape: Author interview with Young, Oct. 26, 2011.

95   I didn't get the first: Ibid.

95   Bill told me later: Author interview with Glenn Dickey, Nov. 3, 2011.

95   I remember walking: Author interview with Purdy, Oct. 27, 2011.

95   I've never seen Walsh: Author interview with Joe Starkey, Oct. 27, 2011.

95   a form of dysentery: Steve Springer, "Thrown Off," *Los Angeles Times*, Nov. 12, 1988.

95   very weak: Ibid.

95   He really shouldn't: *America's Game: 1988 49ers*, NFL Films.

96   How long are we going: Glenn Dickey, "The Game By Numbers," *San Francisco Chronicle*, Nov. 14, 1988.

96   We have to be optimistic: Jeff Schultz, "Raiders Clamp Down on 49ers," *San Jose Mercury News*, Nov. 14, 1988.

96   I know what this: Mark Purdy, "The Once-Mighty Are Falling Apart," *San Jose Mercury News*, Nov. 14, 1988.

96   I guess vindication: Jeff Schultz, "Niners Make Right Turn, 37–21," *San Jose Mercury News*, Nov. 22, 1988.

97   sore and stiff: Ron Thomas, "Walsh's Mixed Feelings on Win," *San Francisco Chronicle*, Nov. 23, 1988.

97   Joe's performance in: Lowell Cohn, "Storm Blows Over, Joe's Cool Again," *San Francisco Chronicle*, Dec. 9, 1988.

97   I respect you guys: Lowell Cohn, "Walsh Comes Back to Life," *San Francisco Chronicle*, Dec. 12, 1988.

97   I try not to worry: Cohn, "Storm Blows Over, Joe's Cool Again."

97   Any season has its: Mark Whicker, "The Quarterback Now Rams' Worry," *Orange County Register*, Dec. 12, 1988.

98   I've been in the playoffs: Tom Jackson, "Meaningless, Yet Disquieting," *Sacramento Bee*, Dec. 19, 1988.

98   When I came around: Ron Thomas, "For Rice, Another Stellar Effort," *San Francisco Chronicle*, Jan. 2, 1989.

99   Montana played about: Robert Sansevere, "Ouch! 49ers Sack Vikings, 34–9," *Minnesota Star-Tribune*, Jan. 2, 1989.

99   I wasn't out to prove: Bud Geracie, "Montana Plays Like Star He Is," *San Jose Mercury News*, Jan. 2, 1989.

99   Too long ago: Ibid.

99   The teams that have beaten: *Greatest Ever Series: Players*, NFL Films, 1995.

99   We thought we were: Author interview with Jones, Oct. 24, 2011.

100 Bear weather: Mark Whicker, "True Grit," *Austin American Statesman*, Jan. 10, 1989.

100 The cold won't bother: Paul Zimmerman, "Those Rice Capades," *Sports Illustrated*, Jan. 16, 1989.

100 You know something: Ibid.

100   This could have been: "Montana Earns Walsh's Praise," *San Francisco Chronicle*, Jan. 9, 1989.

100   People had given up: Rob Borges "Montana, SF Leave Bears in Cold, 28–3," *Boston Globe*, Jan. 9, 1989.

100   If it were Sam against: Jeff Lenihan "Montana vs. Wyche: pupil against teacher," *Ocala Star- Banner*, Jan. 21, 1989.

101   I remember sitting: Author interview with Paye, Oct. 28, 2011.

101   We didn't play very: Author interview with Randy Cross, Aug. 26, 2011.

102   Well, it's set up: Mark Purdy, "The Last-Gasp Drive: All Guts, All Glory," *San Jose Mercury News*, Jan. 23, 1989.

102   He came into the huddle: *Greatest Ever Series: Players*, NFL Films, 1995.

102   Did I say anything: Paul Zimmerman, "Joe Cool," *Sports Illustrated*, Jan. 30, 1989.

102   You think Joe Montana: Purdy, "The Last-Gasp Drive: All Guts, All Glory."

102   Joe Montana during that: *Greatest Ever Series: Players*, NFL Films, 1995.

103   I hyperventilated to: Jill Lieber, "The Fab 5," *Sports Illustrated*, Jan. 29, 1990.

103   Joe Montana is not human: Purdy, "The Last-Gasp Drive: All Guts, All Glory."

CHAPTER 6: THE ORCHESTRATOR

105   Of all the crazy: Denise Tom, "Young's Latest Test of Faith," *USA Today*, Jan. 20, 1989.

105   I think that's: Author interview with Cross, Aug. 26, 2011.

106   It's been 10 years: "Walsh Resigns as 49ers' Coach," *Doylestown Intelligencer*, Jan. 27, 1989.

106   I wouldn't be: Glenn Dickey, "Glimpse Into a QB 'Club,'" *San Francisco Chronicle*, June 10, 1989.

106   Joe's our starter: Jim Jenkins, "Seifert Ends QB Turmoil," *Sacramento Bee*, Feb. 10, 1989.

107   I think we will: "'Niner coaching staff goes through shakeup," *Ellensburg Daily Record*, Feb. 10, 1989.

107   Over the years it: Ron Thomas, "Montana Watches 49ers Workout From Sideline," *San Francisco Chronicle*, May 25, 1989.

107   as minor as: Ibid.

107   I feel good: Ron Thomas, "Montana's Ready to Roll" *San Francisco Chronicle*, July 21, 1989.

107   I told the coach: Ron Thomas, "Pining Away," *San Francisco Chronicle*, July 22, 1989.

107   I liken Steve's: Ibid.

107   I entice [Joe] with: Ibid.

107   Joe wanted to: Glenn Dickey, "Right Plays, Right Players," *San Francisco Chronicle*, Sept. 18, 1989.

108   It's hard to throw running: Ron Thomas, "49ers 'DL'—Dissatisfied List—Is Growing," *San Francisco Chronicle*, Sept. 22, 1989.

108   When the pass: Ron Thomas, "How Will the 49ers Defend Cunningham?" *San Francisco Chronicle*, Sept. 23, 1989.

109   There's one game: Author interview with Bono, Oct. 25, 2011.

109   You look at Joe and: Don Pierson, "Montana Superman in 49ers' Comeback," *Chicago Tribune*, Sept. 25, 1989.

109   It was a satisfying: Greg Logan, "Montana Stands Tall at End," *Newsday*, Sept. 25, 1989.

109   They won the first half: Ron Borges, "Montana Ignites the 49ers, 38–28," *Boston Globe*, Sept. 25, 1989.

110   Joe Montana-ish: C. W. Nevius, "Rams' Drive Looked Familiar," *San Francisco Chronicle*, Oct. 2, 1989.

110   This is bad for the: "Montana Brings Back 49ers Again, 24–20," *Los Angeles Times*, Oct. 9, 1989.

110   Just a little fluid: Jim Jenkins, "49ers Get Great Breaks in a Good Win," *Sacramento Bee*, Oct. 9, 1989.

110   I get tired of sitting: Mike Weaver, "Montana's Elbow Shows Improvement," *San Jose Mercury News*, Oct. 13, 1989.

110   They were really doubling down: Ron Bergman, "Cowboys, Too, Force Young to Be Patient," *San Jose Mercury News*, Oct. 16, 1989.

111   Montana could have: Ibid.

111   Not playing is one: Ron Thomas, "49ers Stumble Past Cowboys," *San Francisco Chronicle*, Oct. 16, 1989.

111   Unless something unforeseen: Pat Sullivan, "The Burden of Expectations," *San Francisco Chronicle*, Oct. 17, 1989.

111   It sounded like: Jim Jenkins, "Smallest Montana Kept His Composure," *Sacramento Bee*, Oct. 20, 1989.

111   was mostly sleeping: Ibid.

111   If I'd started that: Ibid.

112   I won't say I saw: Ric Bucher, "49ers' Win Proves Painful," *San Jose Mercury News*, Oct. 23, 1989.

112   I've seen a lot: Ron Borges, "Young Isn't Sitting Pretty," *Boston Globe*, Oct. 21, 1989.

112   I played on a lousy: Ibid.

112   I was supposed to: Ron Borges, "Young Gives Team a Lift," *Boston Globe*, Oct. 23, 1989.

113 They should applaud: Ibid.

113 driving down the freeway: "People in Sports," *Houston Chronicle*, Sept. 7, 1989.

113 We were holed up: Tom Gilmore, "Walsh Overcomes Early Mistakes," *San Francisco Chronicle*, Oct. 23, 1989.

113 He's a markedly different: Glenn Dickey, "Emergence of Young Saving 49ers," *San Francisco Chronicle*, Oct. 23, 1989.

113 in a pinch: Ron Thomas, "Millen Final Draws First Start as 49er," *San Francisco Chronicle*, Oct. 28, 1989.

113 I have the best job: Scott Vigallon, "Neither Jets Nor a Bat Can Spoil Special Day for Bono," *San Jose Mercury News*, Oct. 30, 1989.

114 It seems no matter: "Bono Helps 49ers Defeat Jets, 23–10," *Los Angeles Times*, Oct. 30, 1989.

114 90 percent or a: Ibid.

114 I told her that was: Mark Purdy, "Mr. Spare Parts Makes It Look Easy," *San Jose Mercury News*, Nov. 7, 1989.

114 When it's made to: Ibid.

114 You know, nothing he: Ibid.

114 It's not the first time: Dave Carpenter, "Montana, 49ers Blast Saints 31–13," *Aiken Standard*, Nov. 7, 1989.

115 You have to take: "Taylor out to lasso Montana," *Newsday*, Nov. 23, 1989.

115 arms flapping like: Joe Hamelin, "Montana Just Doesn't Quit," *Sacramento Bee*, Nov. 28, 1989.

115 [Team doctors] thought: Steve Jacobson, "This One Lived Up to Hype," *Newsday*, Nov. 29, 1989.

115 Just thinking about Joe: "Montana's Quick Start Leads to Different End for Niners," *Daily Intelligencer*, Nov. 29, 1989.

116 Nobody else in the: Jacobson, "This One Lived Up to Hype."

116 I think Joe Montana is the: "Montana's Quick Start Leads to Different End for Niners."

116 We've always liked: Glenn Dickey, "Wondering About Montana, Craig," *San Francisco Chronicle*, Dec. 1, 1989.

116 If we felt Joe was: Mark Purdy, "Insurance QB Pays Dividends," *San Jose Mercury News*, Dec. 4, 1989.

117 Every time I took a: Pat Sullivan, "Montana Feeling Some Pain," *San Francisco Chronicle*, Dec. 5, 1989.

117 In the first three years: Purdy, "Insurance QB Pays Dividends."

117 It's not an easy: "Young Triggers Frisco's Comeback Win, 23–10," *Altoona Mirror*, Dec. 4, 1989.

117 We tend to focus: Art Thompson III, "Same old story: Montana leads comeback," *Orange County Register*, Dec. 12, 1989.

118 This one's pretty satisfying: Mike Penner, "This Land Is His Land, From San Francisco to Disneyland," *Los Angeles Times*, Dec. 12, 1989.

118 I was hoping they: Mike Weaver, "Young's Start May Not Aid Bills," *San Jose Mercury News*, Dec. 16, 1989.

118 Every week has been: Ibid.

118 I was up to my waist: "Buffalo defeats Buffalo," *Syracuse Herald-Journal News*, Dec. 18, 1989.

118 I don't think I'm going: Art Spander, "Young Helps 49ers to Victory, Returns Again to Shadows," *San Francisco Examiner*, Dec. 18, 1989.

119 Joe is the man: Ron Thomas, "Mixed Feelings About Game, Win," *San Francisco Chronicle*, Dec. 25, 1989.

119 I think we were: "49ers 26, Bears 0, Montana Sets Record," *San Francisco Chronicle*, Dec. 25, 1989.

119 I guess records: Ric Bucher, "49ers Are Bad News for Bears," *San Jose Mercury News*, Dec. 25, 1989.

120 You've got to have: Bob Sakamoto, "49ers Starting to Feel Like Winners," *Chicago Tribune*, Dec. 25, 1989.

120 best exemplifies inspirational: "Day of Honors for Montana: Teammates award him Eshmont," *Modesto Bee*, Dec. 21, 1989.

120 A lot of other guys: Tim Keown, "Teammates Also Honor Montana," *Sacramento Bee*, Dec. 21, 1989.

120 He inspires people: Ibid.

120 [Montana] was doing: Dave Hyde, "Gone With the Win—Joe Has Another Game," *Sun Sentinel*, Jan. 7, 1990.

120 I made a fool of myself: Ibid.

121 Joe told us that if: Mike Weaver, "Paris, Wallace Keep Doleman at Bay," *San Jose Mercury News*, Jan. 7, 1990.

121 I'd rather win this way: Craig Dolch, "Montana Saves Late Heroics for Another Game," *Palm Beach Post*, Jan. 7, 1990.

121 That was a big boost: Bill Sullivan, "Broncos, 49ers Bourbon Street bound," *Houston Chronicle*, Jan. 15, 1990.

121 We're just happy to: Todd Phipers, "Elway Has Earned 49ers' Respect," *Denver Post*, Jan. 15, 1990.

121 I'll never forget: Author interview with DeBartolo, Nov. 8, 2011.

122 probably the: Mark Heisler, "Comfy Joe Could Have Won this From Easy Chair Quarterback," *Los Angeles Times*, Jan. 29, 1990.

122 Well, he's not looking: Ibid.

CHAPTER 7: THE NEXT ONE

123   I smiled when I: Ray Didinger, "Thanks to Joe, 49ers Run Rings Around Broncs," *Philadelphia Daily News*, Jan. 29, 1990.

124   OK, Daddy. The: Ibid.

124   My inspiration: Ibid.

124   I wanted Joe: Ibid.

124   No, I'll give this: Ibid.

124   those types of things: Steve Woodward, "MVP; Performance adds to Montana lore," *USA Today*, Jan. 29, 1990.

124   In four years, I'll: Ann Killion, "Montana to Get $13 Million Deal, Reports Say," *San Jose Mercury News*, July 26, 1990.

124   bad tuna fish: Ric Bucher, "Montana's New Deal Tops NFL Scale," *San Jose Mercury News*, Aug. 10, 1990.

125   I hope I make: Ibid.

125   However long Joe: Ibid.

125   Steve likes everything: Glenn Dickey, "Young's 49ers Days Could Be Over," *San Francisco Chronicle*, Jan. 31, 1990.

125   My deepest, darkest: Jim Jenkins, "Young to Remain as Montana's Backup," *Los Angeles Times*, May 13, 1990.

126   One of the things: Jim Smith, "Steve Young Lays in Perpetual Wait with 49ers," *Los Angeles Times*, May 27, 1990.

126   We did everything humanly: Author interview with Policy, Oct. 24, 2011.

126   I haven't heard much: Don Pierson, "49ers anything but complacent," *Chicago Tribune*, Sept. 9, 1990.

126   I thought it was: Ann Killion, "49ers' Attack Throws Falcons," *San Jose Mercury News*, Oct. 15, 1990.

127   Guys don't care: Ric Bucher, "49ers Big for a Top-Playing Record," *San Jose Mercury News*, Nov. 13, 1990.

127   We were trying: Ric Bucher, "Oilers Fumbled By Calling for a Timeout," *San Jose Mercury News*, Oct. 9, 1990.

127   I was so frustrated: Author interview with Young, Oct. 26, 2011.

128   I didn't feel like: Thomas Boswell, "At Long Last, Demons Be Gone," *Washington Post*, Jan. 30, 1995.

128   There were many: Dan Le Batard, "'The Best Quarterback, Bar None,'" *Miami Herald*, Jan. 30, 1995.

128   Here was a young: Author interview with George Seifert, Sept. 21, 2011.

128   It was comforting: Author interview with Young, Oct. 26, 2011.

129   Joe felt like Steve: Author interview with Paye, Oct. 28, 2011.

129   Steve irritated Joe: Ibid.

129 Bear-style 46: Ric Bucher, "'Different Fronts' Set Montana Back," *San Jose Mercury News*, Nov. 26, 1990.

129 There was no reason: Michael Martinez, "Bumbling 49ers See Streak End at 18," *New York Times*, Nov. 26, 1990.

130 The key was to get: Mark Whicker, "They played hard, but what was settled?" *Orange County Register*, Dec. 4, 1990.

130 Something tells me: Don Pierson, "Defense gets 49ers past Giants," *Chicago Tribune*, Dec. 4, 1990.

130 Our offense didn't: Tim Tuttle, "49ers even score with Rams by reviving a stale offense," *Orange County Register*, Dec. 18, 1990.

130 Guys get hurt all: Ann Killion, "Montana Says He Sees No Need to Take a Break," *San Jose Mercury News*, Dec. 19, 1990.

131 This is a year in: "Some Relief Planned for Montana's Arm," *Toronto Globe and Mail*, Dec. 19, 1990.

131 I don't see the Giants: Killion, "Montana Says He Sees No Need to Take a Break."

131 [People] always say: Author interview with Montana, Nov. 30, 2011.

131 I can tell you: ESPN *Outside the Lines*, Aired April 2012.

131 I feel pretty good: Killion, "Montana Says He Sees No Need to Take a Break."

132 How he was running: Lowell Cohn, "Nightmarish Wake-up Call for Young," *San Francisco Chronicle*, Dec. 24, 1990.

132 Young's a fortunate: Ann Killion, "Young's Confidence Alone Can't Beat Saints," *San Jose Mercury News*, Dec. 24, 1990.

132 I didn't have: Cohn, "Nightmarish Wake-up Call for Young."

132 I knew we were: Killion, "Young's Confidence Alone Can't Beat Saints."

132 [Young] gave us a: Ibid.

132 You don't lose: Joe Hamelin, "Understudy Takes Loss Hard," *Sacramento Bee*, Dec. 24, 1990.

132 On that last drive: Cohn, "Nightmarish Wake-up Call for Young."

132 I'll be starting: Killion, "Young's Confidence Alone Can't Beat Saints."

133 sort of a mystery: Ric Bucher, "Montana Ailment Not Serious," *San Jose Mercury News*, Dec. 26, 1990.

133 I have absolutely: Ira Miller, "Did the 49ers Try Hard Enough?" *San Francisco Chronicle*, Dec. 25, 1990,

133 You like not to: Ann Killion, "Montana Hopes to Play Sunday," *San Jose Mercury News*, Dec. 27, 1990.

133 There was a lot: Jim Jenkins, "Young Follows 49ers' Old Script," *Sacramento Bee*, Dec. 31, 1990.

133 To be a good: Ric Bucher, "Knack Is Back for Niners," *San Jose Mercury News*, Dec. 31, 1990.

134 Joe Montana on: Don Seeholzer, "49ers Have All the Answers," *Orange County Register*, Jan. 13, 1991.

134 I knew we should: Don Pierson, "Montana Makes More History," *Chicago Tribune*, Jan. 13, 1991.

134 When I saw Steve: Craig Davis, "The State of Montana: It's Hottest in Jan," *Sun Sentinel*, Jan. 13, 1991.

134 We all thank Michael: John McClain, "NFL Playoffs/49ers, Bills Zip into Conference Finals," *Houston Chronicle*, Jan. 13, 1991.

135 I think we realized: "49ers Were Expecting Rematch with Giants," *San Antonio Express-News*, Jan. 14, 1991.

135 Let's get something: Michael Wilbon, "An Upset at Candlestick? Another Quake's as Likely," *Washington Post*, Jan. 20, 1991.

135 We are very close to: Thomas George, "Montana Is Center of Attention for 49ers," *New York Times*, Jan. 18, 1991.

135 We put a lot of pounding: Ann Killion, "Hit on Montana Signals the End for Niners," *San Jose Mercury News*, Jan. 21, 1991.

135 After the second series: Don Pierson, "A Super Sunday for New York," *Chicago Tribune*, Jan. 21, 1991.

136 We pushed everyone: Charles Bricker, "Giants Save Greatest Hit for Craig," *Sun Sentinel*, Jan. 21, 1991.

136 Blind side: Michael Wilbon, "What a Way to Lose—What a Way to Win," *Washington Post*, Jan. 21, 1991.

136 I just wanted to make: Killion, "Hit on Montana Signals the End for Niners."

136 13 very concerned people: Ron Thomas, "Montana Fractured His Hand," *San Francisco Chronicle*, Jan. 21, 1991.

136 The report we get on: *CBS Sports*, Jan. 20, 1991.

137 All I had to do: "49ers End Hard Year Bitterly," *Syracuse Post-Standard*, Jan. 21, 1991.

137 We were so used: "Prayerful Giants couldn't bear to look at winning field goal," *Atlanta Journal-Constitution*, Jan. 21, 1991.

137 Once we got to midfield: "49ers End Hard Year Bitterly."

137 I've never heard: Wilbon, "What a Way to Lose—What a Way to Win."

137 This type of loss: John Weyler, "49ers Watched These Last-Second Heroics," *Los Angeles Times*, Jan. 21, 1991.

138 Nothing, nothing: Ron Thomas, "Montana Fractured His Hand," *San Francisco Chronicle*, Jan. 21, 1991.

138 New X-rays will: Ibid.

138   I still don't know: Mike Freeman, "Super Two: Giants at 0:00, Bills at Every Turn," *Washington Post*, Jan. 21, 1991.

138   By then, Montana: Thomas, "Montana Fractured His Hand."

CHAPTER 8: A YEAR EARLY

139   Things wouldn't be: Peter King, "The NFL: The End Zone," *Sports Illustrated*, Dec. 30, 1991.

139   nothing major: Ann Killion, "Montana to Undergo Surgery," *San Jose Mercury News*, Jan. 22, 1991.

139   I actually feel: Ric Bucher, "Quit? 'No Way,' Montana Insists," *San Jose Mercury News*, Jan. 24, 1991.

140   Now I'll show you: Pedro Gomez and Dan Hruby, "Lemmon Says It's His Year," *San Jose Mercury News*, Feb. 1, 1991.

140   I guess I got him: Ibid.

140   Won't the world cut: Ann Killion, "NFL Life Won't Pass Him By," *San Jose Mercury News*, Aug. 30, 1991.

140   I think that was the worst thing: Ibid.

140   We really don't: Jim Jenkins, "Seifert Looks at his Team," *Sacramento Bee*, Mar. 20, 1991.

141   Leigh has asked if: T. J. Simers, "Chargers Talk to Steve Young," *Los Angeles Times*, Mar. 30, 1991.

141   The bottom line is: "Young Signs for $4.5 Million, Becoming Highest-Paid Backup," *St. Petersburg Times*, May 4, 1991.

141   George's mindset was: Jim Jenkins, "Young Agrees to Contract," *Sacramento Bee*, May 4, 1991.

141   Don't read into: Gomez, "Young Signs for $4.5 Million, Becoming Highest-Paid Backup."

141   I'm good as new: Bob Oates, "Montana Looks as Good as New, but 49ers Don't," *Los Angeles Times*, July 30, 1991.

141   I might laugh: Gary Swan, "49ers' Sydney Sidelined By Possible Broken Toe," *San Francisco Chronicle*, July 27, 1991.

141   Bill always had the: Author interview with Policy, Oct. 24, 2011.

142   Players, unfortunately, are: Denise Tom, "Montana: Change Inevitable," *USA Today*, May 9, 1991.

142   Last year we didn't: Jarrett Bell, "Berlin Breaks the Monotony," *USA Today*, July 29, 1991.

142   original Amerikanische: "49ers Pass Bears Quickly, 21–7," *Washington Post*, Aug. 4, 1991.

142   I started to throw: Gary Swan, "Long Post Pass Hurt Montana," *San Francisco Chronicle*, Aug. 29, 1991.

142   It had been sore: Ibid.

143   Young is the perfect: C. W. Nevius, "Steve Young: 49ers' Prince of Preseason," *San Francisco Chronicle*, Aug. 8, 1991.

143   Hey, I'm Mr.: Ibid.

143   There was a time: Ibid.

143   Just watching him: "Sanders Deal Done, Newspaper Reports," *Newsday*, Aug. 12, 1991.

143   It's just sore from: Ibid.

143   flared up a little: "Pittsburgh Steelers," *Orlando Sentinel*, Aug. 16, 1991.

143   The trainers and: Gary Swan, "Montana Out Again with Sore Elbow," *San Francisco Chronicle*, Aug. 16, 1991.

143   [Seifert] said he is: Greg Logan, "Young to Play More? Joe Says It Ain't So," *Newsday*, Aug. 18, 1991.

143   wishful thinking: Ibid.

144   That's not what: Ibid.

144   And then he did: Lowell Cohn, "Should We Be Worried About Joe?" *San Francisco Chronicle*, Aug. 20, 1991.

144   If it was two: Ibid.

144   The coach loves to: T. J. Simers, "Chargers Can't Stop 49ers or Young, 24–13," *Los Angeles Times*, Aug. 20, 1991.

144   We're not trying: Ann Killion, "Montana Suffers Setback," *San Jose Mercury News*, Aug. 22, 1991.

145   They're still evaluating: Nancy Gay, "Dim Outlook on Montana," *San Jose Mercury News*, Aug. 24, 1991.

145   You only get better: "49ers End Preseason Unbeaten," *Los Angeles Times*, Aug. 24, 1991.

145   golfer's elbow: David Perlman, "How to Treat an Elbow Like Joe Montana's," *San Francisco Chronicle*, Aug. 28, 1991.

145   We didn't want: Gary Swan, "Montana Will Miss First Four Games," *San Francisco Chronicle*, Aug. 28, 1991.

145   I don't think I'm: Ibid.

145   subsiding: "Montana Vows to Keep Job," *New York Times*, Aug. 29, 1991.

146   I don't see why: Larry Weisman, "Montana Expects to Return as Starting QB in Four Weeks," *USA Today*, Aug. 29, 1991.

146   I just don't want: Nancy Gay, "Montana's a Patient Patient," *San Jose Mercury News*, Aug. 29, 1991.

146   They really dogged: Dan McGrath, "The Bottom Line is Simple: Giants Won It," *Sacramento Bee*, Sept. 3, 1991.

146   That's twice in a: Ibid.

146 I'd like him to: Rick Reilly, "The Young 49ers," *Sports Illustrated*, Sept. 30, 1991.

146 Everybody wants me: Ibid.

147 He really has played: Glenn Dickey, "Judge Young by His Results," *San Francisco Chronicle*, Sept. 20, 1991.

147 Steve is on a big push: Mike Freeman, "Age Creeping, Montana Fears He's Being Phased Out for Young," *Washington Post*, Sept. 10, 1991.

147 I don't really care: Author interview with Montana, Nov. 30, 2011.

147 I think Sunday's are: Ibid.

147 Inside when things: Ibid.

148 He's got a big heart: Tom Jackson, "Young Has a Fan in Long," *Sacramento Bee*, Sept. 30, 1991.

148 You can't buy it: Chris DuFresne, "Raiders Win This Young Man's Game," *Los Angeles Times*, Sept. 30, 1991.

148 those are guys I respect: Bruce Jenkins, "With Mixed Emotions, Lott Was a Force," *San Francisco Chronicle*, Sept. 30, 1991.

148 berserk: Richard Weiner, "49ers even called Lott for help," *Peninsula Times-Tribune*, Oct. 13, 1991.

148 I could have fucking: Jeff Pearlman, *Boys Will Be Boys: The Glory Days and Party Nights of the Dallas Cowboys Dynasty* (New York: HarperCollins, 2008), 113.

148 As the blood: Ibid., 113.

149 We weren't in: Author interview with Ann Killion, Dec. 6, 2011.

149 I threw about forty: Terry Blount, "Montana Resumes Throwing / Injured 49ers Leader Hopes for Quick Return," *Houston Chronicle*, Oct. 1, 1991.

149 I think if everything: Ibid.

149 I don't think I'm: Tom Weir, "Montana Passes First Throwing Test, Eager to Practice," *USA Today*, Oct. 1, 1991.

149 What's wrong with: Steve Bisheff, "He's Not Just a Regular Joe," *Orange County Register*, Sept. 30, 1991.

149 [A fan] wrote: Mark Purdy, "Surgery or Not, Montana Will Be Back," *San Jose Mercury News*, Oct. 4, 1991.

149 You just wish: Ibid.

150 She said ice was: Ibid.

150 a key twisting: Gordon Forbes, "Montana hopes to speed recovery," *USA Today*, Nov. 12, 1991.

150 surgery is now: "Montana Faces Surgery; Career Is in Jeopardy," *Seattle Post-Intelligencer*, Oct. 7, 1991.

150 We got lulled into: Ibid.

150 I think he's an extremely: Ann Killion and Nancy Gay, "Operation Montana Goes Well," *San Jose Mercury News*, Oct. 10, 1991.

150 Personally, I didn't: Author interview with Seifert, Sept. 21, 2011.

151 Anyone who's been: Lowell Cohn, "Young Knows It's Definitely His Team Now," *San Francisco Chronicle*, Oct. 8, 1991.

151 He came into the: Ibid.

151 I thought it was: Gary Swan, "Young Sees the Errors of His Way," *San Francisco Chronicle*, Oct. 14, 1991.

152 I thought we: Mark Purdy, "A Bad Trend Haunts Young," *San Jose Mercury News*, Oct. 14, 1991.

152 So I threw it to: Ibid.

152 had to take: Ibid.

152 I don't think: Ibid.

152 We've got to let: Swan, "Young Sees the Errors of His Way."

152 There's a concern: Gary Swan, "New Emotions for Flat 49ers," *San Francisco Chronicle*, Oct. 15, 1991.

152 There was so much: Author interview with Killion, Dec. 6, 2011.

153 He took such a: Nancy Gay, "Walsh Coaches Young: Keep Chin Up," *San Jose Mercury News*, Oct. 17, 1991.

153 We answered some: Ron Reid, "Niners Pound Lions," *Philadelphia Inquirer*, Oct. 21, 1991.

153 They had everybody: Bruce Jenkins, "Bono's Day: From Bench to Temporary Hero to Starter," *San Francisco Chronicle*, Nov. 4, 1991.

154 I expect this will: Gary Swan, "Possible Surgery May End Young's Year," *San Francisco Chronicle*, Nov. 5, 1991.

154 very futuristic: Gary Swan, "Montana May Join 49ers on Sideline," *San Francisco Chronicle*, Nov. 8, 1991.

154 Darth Vader like: Ibid.

154 But I can just: Ann Killion, "49ers' Injured QBs Find No Comfort on Sideline," *San Jose Mercury News*, Nov. 11, 1991.

154 Right now, we're: Gordon Forbes, "Montana hopes to speed recovery," *USA Today*, Nov. 12, 1991.

155 I didn't want to go: Author interview with Michael Zagaris, Nov. 3, 2011.

155 At that period: Author interview with Purdy, Dec. 6, 2011.

155 It's one of my greatest: Author interview with Jeff Bayer, Oct. 29, 2011.

156 I said if they're: Killion, "49ers' Injured QBs Find No Comfort on Sideline."

156 It was tough for: "Saints Had Real Fire in Their Eyes," *Los Angeles Times*, Nov. 11, 1991.

156   I've been in close: Mark Purdy, "Ball Belongs in Bono's Hands," *San Jose Mercury News*, Dec. 9, 1991.

157   It's not that he's: Ann Killion, "Man of the Hour," *San Jose Mercury News*, Dec. 6, 1991.

157   He's got a great: "People in sports," *Houston Chronicle*, Dec. 5, 1991.

157   He's a lot like Joe: Clare Farnsworth, "'Oh No, Bono' Third String QB Becomes a 49er Savior," *Seattle Post-Intelligencer*, Dec. 5, 1991.

157   Sometimes, she'll: Bruce Jenkins, "Revived 49ers Should Keep Bono at QB," *San Francisco Chronicle*, Dec. 2, 1991.

157   Now when Mrs. Bono: "So they say . . . ," *Austin American Statesman*, Dec. 5, 1991.

157   We just have to: Don Pierson, "49ers Aren't Well But They're Looking Swell," *Chicago Tribune*, Dec. 3, 1991.

158   I feel you continue: Purdy, "Ball Belongs in Bono's Hands."

158   I need to be back: Susan Fornoff, "Injury Finishes Bono for Year," *Sacramento Bee*, Dec. 20, 1991.

158   People are saying: Gary Swan, "Young, Offense Click Again in His Return as Starter," *San Francisco Chronicle*, Dec. 24, 1991.

159   That's not bad: Ann Killion, "For QB Young, It's the Same Old Story," *San Jose Mercury News*, Dec. 24, 1991.

159   I thought at the end: Author interview with Jones, Oct. 24, 2011.

159   A quarterback lives and: Don Bosley, "Young Plans to Challenge Montana in '92," *Sacramento Bee*, Dec. 24, 1991.

159   He's the incumbent: Ann Killion, "Could Montana End His Career with Another Team?" *San Jose Mercury News*, Dec. 16, 1991.

159   I feel I had ten: Swan, "Young, Offense Click Again in His Return as Starter."

CHAPTER 9: PANDORA'S BOX

161   [Today is] probably the: Bob McGinn, "Holmgren Confident He Will Succeed Here," *Milwaukee Journal*, Jan. 12, 1992.

161   Wherever I've been: Ibid.

162   If they want to trade: Art Spander, "Holmgren Says if 49ers Decide to Trade a QB, He Wants One," *Deseret News*, Jan. 30, 1992.

162   Steve Young is: Jim Jenkins, "Montana Hopes to Test Arm Soon," *Sacramento Bee*, Jan. 24, 1992.

162   I wasn't terribly: Bob McGinn, "Wolf Pulls the Trigger on His Master Plan: Trades 1st-Rounder for Falcons Backup," *Milwaukee Journal*, Feb. 12, 1992.

162 The image is that: Glenn Dickey, "Good Choices Without Deals," *San Francisco Chronicle*, Apr. 27, 1992.

162 It's insane. I'm: Dennis Georgatos, "Young Boldly Stakes Claim to 49ers Starting QB Spot," *Salt Lake City Tribune*, May 9, 1992.

162 Pandora's Box: Ibid.

162 It's just a strange: Ibid.

163 I just saw Joe: Wayne Washington, "Joe Throws," *San Jose Mercury News*, Apr. 11, 1992.

163 He's been killing me: Art Spander, "Montana Ready to Quiet Skeptics," *Meriden Connecticut Record-Journal*, May 10, 1992.

163 I've been throwing: Nancy Gay, "Montana Is 'Pretty Close to 100 Percent,'" *San Jose Mercury News*, Apr. 4, 1992.

163 humming the ball: Bruce Jenkins, "Time for 49ers to Say So Long to Steve Young," *San Francisco Chronicle*, May 11, 1992.

163 Joe Montana is our: Nancy Gay, "Welcome to Camp Complain," *San Jose Mercury News*, May 9, 1992.

163 Right from the time: Wayne Washington, "Montana Is 'Crisp' in Workout," *San Jose Mercury News*, June 2, 1992.

164 very, very crisp: Ibid.

164 the Holy trinity: Peter King, "Qb or Not Qb?" *Sports Illustrated*, July 27, 1992.

164 It's the magic of: Ibid.

164 Even his opponents: Ibid.

164 Steve Young will: "Redskins, 49ers Loaded with Nagging Questions," *Baltimore Sun*, Aug. 15, 1992.

164 I did my best to: John Schumacher, "Young Will Play Sunday," *Sacramento Bee*, Aug. 10, 1992.

165 Some people who watch: "Just When Young Thought It Was Safe . . . ," *San Francisco Chronicle*, Aug. 20, 1992.

165 It's always going to: John Schumacher, "Bono Lifts 49ers 20–14," *Sacramento Bee*, Aug. 22, 1992.

165 We all know what: "49ers Send Haley to Cowboys, Name Young Starter," *San Francisco Chronicle*, Aug. 27, 1992.

166 Talk about a: Jim Jenkins, "Policy: Montana Won't Request a Trade This Year," *Sacramento Bee*, Sept. 3, 1992.

166 most likely in the: Wayne Washington, "Montana Throws, But Young Is Starter," *San Jose Mercury News*, Aug. 27, 1992.

166 He's not happy: Nancy Gay, "Young Did His Time Waiting in the Wings," *San Jose Mercury News*, Sept. 4, 1992.

166 Maybe I'm kidding: Teri Thompson, "Can Montana Make Another Comeback?" *Alberta Lethbridge Herald*, Aug. 30, 1992.

166 [It was] the hardest: Bruce Jenkins, "49ers' Biggest Problem—No Bad QB's," *San Francisco Chronicle*, Sept. 7, 1992.

167 I was tryin' like: Ibid.

167 Touchdown pass?: Mark Purdy, "Young Woozy," *San Jose Mercury News*, Sept. 7, 1992.

167 the knockout punch: Greg Garber, "He'll Pass for a Substitute," *Hartford Courant*, Sept. 7, 1992.

167 But that second hit: Jenkins, "49ers' Biggest Problem—No Bad QB's."

167 I came off the field: Purdy, "Young Woozy."

167 We all thought: Ibid.

167 bouncy and with it: Gary Swan, "'Bouncy, With-It' Young Will Start Against Bills," *San Francisco Chronicle*, Sept. 8, 1992.

167 At the same time: Ibid.

168 The Greatest Game No: Jim Kelly Welcoming Committee speech transcript, 2005 Pro Football Hall of Fame Enshrinement Ceremony, at the Pro Football Hall of Fame Field at Fawcett Stadium, Aug. 7, 2005.

168 He's sixty minutes: Mark Purdy, "Young Sparkles in Loss to Bills," *San Jose Mercury News*, Sept. 14, 1992.

168 It brought me back: Vic Carucci, "Bills' Offense Outguns 49ers," *Buffalo News*, Sept. 14, 1992.

168 It's funny: Purdy, "Young Sparkles in Loss to Bills."

169 Today the defense: Paul Zimmerman, "Ping-pong Football," *Sports Illustrated*, Sept. 21, 1992.

169 preferred to catch balls from: Purdy, "Young Sparkles in Loss to Bills."

169 I can't fight that: Ibid.

169 If I am 100 percent: Frank Cooney, "Montana Rejects Bench-Sitter Role," *San Francisco Examiner*, Sept. 2, 1992.

169 I didn't think: John Schumacher, "Montana Doesn't Expect to Step Right In," *Sacramento Bee*, Sept. 7, 1992.

169 There's no way: Gordon Forbes, "Montana Won't Go Quietly," *USA Today*, Sept. 9, 1992.

169 I've been throwing: Schumacher, "Montana Doesn't Expect to Step Right In."

170 elective procedure: John Schumacher, "Another Setback: Montana Has Surgery," *Sacramento Bee*, Sept. 13, 1992.

170 I had come back: Author interview with Montana, Nov. 30, 2011.

170 I still have a while: "Montana Not Giving Up Comeback," *Chicago Tribune*, Oct. 25, 1992.

170 I'd love to go out: Joan Ryan, "An Ordinary Joe . . . at Home," *San Francisco Examiner*, Nov. 5, 1992.

171 I think Steve's getting: Ann Killion, "New 49ers Era Dawns with Young at Helm," *San Jose Mercury News*, Sept. 29, 1992.

171 When I heard those: John Weyler, "With Young on the Run, There's No Need for Joe's Show," *Los Angeles Times*, Oct. 5, 1992.

171 We've been in this: Glenn Dickey, "Young Didn't Back Down," *San Francisco Chronicle*, Oct. 5, 1992.

171 He faked us out: John Schumacher, "Young Is 49ers Escape Route," *Sacramento Bee*, Oct. 5, 1992.

172 I don't want to end: Weyler, "With Young on the Run, There's No Need for Joe's Show."

172 I've seen San Francisco: Tim Kawakami, "Montana's Not in There, but They're Still Standing," *Los Angeles Times*, Oct. 5, 1992.

172 This was fun: "49ers, Rice Pay Back Falcons 56–17," *Austin American Statesman*, Oct. 19, 1992.

172 He was pretty barfy: Nancy Gay, "'Lightheaded' Young Felled by Nasty Flu Bug," *San Jose Mercury News*, Nov. 2, 1992.

172 hoarse, pale, red: Ibid.

173 I tried to get: Ibid.

173 I feel like crap: Lowell Cohn, "Young Wasn't the Only One Who Felt Sick," *San Francisco Chronicle*, Nov. 2, 1992.

173 undisclosed location: Gary Swan, "Montana Making Progress," *San Francisco Chronicle*, Nov. 7, 1992.

173 I feel real positive: John Schumacher, "Montana Says He Is Ready for Action," *Sacramento Bee*, Nov. 7, 1992.

173 If Joe's doing: Swan, "Montana Making Progress."

173 It's hard to interrupt: Schumacher, "Montana Says He Is Ready for Action."

174 Nobody said anything: Art Spander, "Young Can Play Savior Game, Also," *San Francisco Examiner*, Nov. 16, 1992.

174 We've got a good: Ibid.

174 We will call it: Ibid.

175 This year was: "49ers Are Best in the NFC," *Los Angeles Times*, Dec. 20, 1992.

175 There's been a lot: Gary Swan, "Young Wins Eshmont Award," *San Francisco Chronicle*, Dec. 21, 1992.

175 and the rest is: Gary Swan, "49ers Notes: Montana: I'm Ready When They Are," *San Francisco Chronicle*, Nov. 19, 1992.

175 They ask me, 'How's: Ibid.

176 I think Joe's return: "49ers Are Best in the NFC."

176 I'm anxious to: Don Pierson, "Montana to Get Shot Against Lions," *Chicago Tribune*, Dec. 22, 1992.

176 We're looking at: "Expect This for Montana's Return: Emotion," *Orlando Sentinel*, Dec. 26, 1992.

176 It'll be interesting: Ibid.

177 It was my audition: Author interview with Montana, Nov. 30, 2011.

177 That's when it: Mark Purdy, "Montana Was Just Himself in Return," *San Jose Mercury News*, Dec. 29, 1992.

177 I had a lot of: Nancy Gay, "Second-Half Show: Montana Quality Relief," *San Jose Mercury News*, Dec. 29, 1992.

177 Man, I'm glad to: Scott Ostler, "QB Quandary? It's Really No Problem," *San Francisco Chronicle*, Dec. 29, 1992.

177 Once I got knocked: "Montana Doesn't Disappoint in Return," *Indiana Gazette*, Dec. 29, 1992.

178 I tripped over my: Ibid.

178 I gave him the: Author interview with Jones, Oct. 24, 2011.

178 I didn't know why: Purdy, "Montana Was Just Himself in Return."

178 It was a great: Gary Swan, "Young Steps Aside" *San Francisco Chronicle*, Dec. 29, 1992.

178 It took us a little: "QB Quandary? It's Really No Problem."

178 I'm just glad it's: Purdy, "Montana Was Just Himself in Return."

178 You can tell he's: Gary Swan, "Seifert: Young Is Still No. 1," *San Francisco Chronicle*, Dec. 30, 1992.

179 We've been in a: Gary Swan, "49ers vs. Redskins: 2 QBs With Something to Prove," *San Francisco Chronicle*, Jan. 6, 1993.

179 I guess I decided: Gary Swan, "Young Named Most Valuable Player by AP," *San Francisco Chronicle*, Jan. 7, 1993.

179 I can't help it: Michael Wilbon, "Make It So for Joe," *Washington Post*, Jan. 6, 1993.

180 Joe Montana wouldn't: *In their Own Words: Steve Young*, NFL Films.

180 I didn't say anything: Dale Robertson, "Young Overcomes Jitters, 'Quirky' Errors," *Houston Chronicle*, Jan. 10, 1993.

180 Steve was hit then: Gary Swan, "A Learning Experience for Young," *San Francisco Chronicle*, Jan. 11, 1993.

181 After developing that: Author interview with Jerry Rice, Dec. 19, 2011.

181 Joe and I had a: Bob Glauber, "Rice No Young Fan," *Newsday*, Jan. 15, 1993.

181 Why should I?: Paola Boivin, "Joe vs. Steve," *Daily News of Los Angeles*, Jan. 8, 1993.

181 I've never looked: Selena Roberts, "Critics Just a Way of Life for Young," *Orlando Sentinel*, Jan. 15, 1993.

182 Yeah, I'm, the: Kevin Mannix, "Fans Shouldn't Whine about Orthwein," *Boston Herald*, Jan. 17, 1993.

182 We've done it a: Vito Stellino, "Young Had a Shot at Montana-Like Comeback," *Baltimore Sun*, Jan. 18, 1993.

182 I thought Norton's: Terry Blount, "Young Comes Up Short of Glory," *Houston Chronicle*, Jan. 18, 1993.

183 I was feeling good: Bob Verdi, "Frustrating End to Young's Year," *Chicago Tribune*, Jan. 18, 1993.

183 After the long drive: Blount, "Young Comes Up Short of Glory."

183 Anywhere else, Steve: Bill Plaschke, "It's Back into the Shadow of No. 16," *Los Angeles Times*, Jan. 18. 1993.

183 Going 14-2 and: "Agent Suggests Young Become Ex-49er," *Salt Lake Tribune*, Jan. 19, 1993.

184 When you realize: Mark Purdy, "Not Young's Fault, But He Will Be Blamed," *San Jose Mercury News*, Jan. 18, 1993.

184 If people want it to: Bob Verdi, "Frustrating End to Young's Year."

CHAPTER 10: DREAM ON

185 When I started at: Scott Ostler, "Steve Young's Next Role—The Defender," *San Francisco Chronicle*, Sept. 9, 1992.

185 It wasn't easy: Ibid.

186 Finals, you're kind: Author interview with Young, Oct. 26, 2011.

186 In '93 we got a: Author interview with Policy, Oct. 24, 2011.

187 This permits us: Gerald Eskenazi, "Bono's Reward Sends Message to Montana," *New York Times*, Apr. 8, 1993.

187 Arizona. A great: Gary Swan, "Cardinals Court Montana," *San Francisco Chronicle*, Apr. 10, 1993.

187 He's going to go: Ibid.

187 I would love to: "Football," *Los Angeles Times*, Apr. 9, 1993.

188 I dealt with [Cardinals: Author interview with Policy, Oct. 24, 2011.

188 Dwight was in: Ibid.

188 It was the most surreal: Author interview with Anonymous.

189 I cherished draft: Author interview with Carl Peterson, Dec. 22, 2011.

189 This is such a: Author interview with Policy, Oct. 24, 2011.

189 I'm flying back: Ibid.

190 For what he's done: Tom Friend, "By Popular Demand: Montana Reconsiders," *New York Times*, Apr. 19, 1993.

190 That's when, again: Author interview with Policy, Oct. 24, 2011.

190 Whatever they need: Lee Benson, "Who's on First? 49ers Seem to Be on Pluto," *Deseret News*, Apr. 20, 1993.

191 When I got to: Author interview with Policy, Oct. 24, 2011.

191 It was agreed: Ibid.

191 they only have: Lowell Cohn, "Montana Bids Good-by to Bay Area," *San Francisco Chronicle*, Apr. 22, 1993.

191 I don't have the: Ibid.

191 We want Joe: Gary Swan, "DeBartolo on Joe: 'A Personal Loss,'" *San Francisco Chronicle*, Apr. 22, 1993.

191 Babe Ruth got: Author interview with Zagaris, Nov. 3, 2011.

191 I remember the: Author interview with Tim Grunhard, Sept. 22, 2011.

192 Even in Kenney's: Author interview with Kent Pulliam, Mar. 19, 2012.

192 Even when Joe: Ibid.

193 When he came: Author interview with Grunhard, Sept. 22, 2011.

193 He took me to: Author interview with Dave Krieg, Sept. 15, 2011.

194 He was a fun: Author interview with Neil Smith, Jan. 24, 2012.

194 They used to look: Author interview with Montana, Nov. 30, 2011.

194 It really took me: Author interview with J. J. Birden, Dec. 22, 2011.

194 I could definitely: Ibid.

195 No matter what: Lewis W. Duiguid, "Outlook Bright for Chiefs, Chamber Told," *Kansas City Star*, Aug. 26, 1993.

195 He's played very: Terry Price, "A closer look, Chiefs bet on Montana," *Hartford Courant*, Aug. 29, 1993.

196 The back was going: Ibid.

196 I knew it wasn't: Adam Teicher, "Hot Hand Survives Impact," *Kansas City Star*, Sept. 5, 1993.

196 I would hope: Kent Pulliam, "Montana Says He's OK," *Kansas City Star*, Sept. 11, 1993.

197 You always want: Adam Teicher, "Montana Stays on Sidelines When Chiefs Take Long View," *Kansas City Star*, Sept. 13, 1993.

197 Despite what you: Jerry Greene, "Despite Controversy, Young 'Will Miss' Montana,'" *Orlando Sentinel*, Apr. 24, 1993.

197 this form of free: "Free agent Young seeks hefty deal with 49ers," *Austin American Statesman*, June 17, 1993.

197 Both guys were: Author interview with Rice, Dec. 19, 2011.

198 Not at all: David Leon Moore, "49ers' Young Has Tough Act to Follow," *USA Today*, June 26, 1993.

198   I'm sure he's still: "Young Wins One for a Thumb," *New York Times*, Sept. 6, 1993.

198   We've been getting: Nancy Gay, "Young Is Critical of Play-Calling," *San Jose Mercury News*, Oct. 21, 1993.

198   Everything comes: Author interview with Rice, Dec. 19, 2011.

199   You guys focus: Art Spander, "Niners in Trouble No Matter What Young Says," *Rocky Mountain News*, Jan. 9, 1994.

199   As far as things: Ibid.

199   This is as good: "Bills Shade Raiders; San Francisco Rips Giants," *Alton Telegraph*, Jan. 16, 1994.

200   I've been jumping: Ken Rosenthal, "Young Gets Victory, Not Validation," *Baltimore Sun*, Jan. 16, 1994.

200   It's not a dark: Nancy Gay, Ann Killion, Bud Geracie, and Victor Chi, "For Once, Hard Hit Doesn't KO Young," *San Jose Mercury News*, Jan. 16, 1994.

200   This place will: Jim Thomas, "Montana, Elway Duel Tonight in KC," *St. Louis Post-Dispatch*, Sept. 20, 1993.

200   It felt great for: Woody Paige, "No Touchdowns: Montana's Chief Concern," *Denver Post*, Sept. 21, 1993.

200   You wouldn't mind: Kent Pulliam, "For Montana, Frustration Is Bigger Pain," *Kansas City Star*, Oct. 6, 1993.

200   We told the offensive: Author interview with Peterson, Dec. 22, 2011.

201   I was on the edge: Bernie Wilson, "Chiefs' Rally Grounds Chargers," *Salina Journal*, Oct. 18, 1993.

201   Here he is: Gib Twyman, "Players Are Enchanted By New Magic," *Kansas City Star*, Oct. 18, 1993.

202   It's always important: Kent Pulliam, "Montana Is Quick to Spread the Credit in Big Victory," *Kansas City Star*, Oct. 18, 1993.

202   We were in the hotel: Author interview with David Krieg, Sept. 15, 2011.

202   jammed my leg: Adam Teicher, "Hamstring caps ugly day," *Kansas City Star*, Nov. 1, 1993.

202   What's the difference: "Injuries hurt Chiefs' Montana," *Hays Daily News*, Nov. 2, 1993.

202   It's a different: Kent Pulliam, "All Chiefs Eyes Look to Comeback," *Kansas City Star*, Nov. 26, 1993.

202   just a little: Ibid.

203   [With Montana] perhaps: Randy Covitz, "Montana Leaves the Final Curtain for Krieg after Finishing off Bills," *Buffalo News*, Nov. 29, 1993.

203   What happened next: Jonathan Rand, "Montana Won't Let KC Quit," *Kansas City Star*, Dec. 20, 1993.

203   I don't know what: Ibid.

203   Joe was dizzy: "KC survives with wobbly Montana," *Salina Journal*, Dec. 20, 1993.

203   probably one of: Curt Brown and Jeff Lenihan, "Hits and Misc," *Minnesota Star Tribune*, Dec. 27, 1993.

204   They like to: S. A. Paolantonio, "Troublesome Steelers to Battle Chiefs Today," *Philadelphia Inquirer*, Jan. 8, 1994.

204   I wish I could: Adam Teicher, "Montana Warms Up with Gloves Off," *Kansas City Star*, Jan. 9, 1994.

204   We have more: Bernie Miklasz, "Montana Turns Back the Clock One More Time," *St. Louis Post-Dispatch*, Jan. 9, 1994.

204   I still felt we'd: "Joe Works Overtime," *Newsday* and *Baltimore Sun* (combined editions), Jan. 9, 1994.

205   I think there: Author interview with Birden, Dec. 22, 2011.

205   He never really panicked: Author interview with Keith Cash, Jan. 5, 2012.

205   We go into the: Author interview with Peterson, Dec. 22, 2011.

205   Part of the fun: Dave Goldberg, "Chiefs Perform Great Escape," *Salina Journal*, Jan. 9, 1994.

206   He beat us: Milt Northrop, "Oilers Resting Title Hopes on Buddy System," *Buffalo News*, Jan. 15, 1994.

206   When an 18-wheeler: Ibid.

206   He doesn't run: Jim Litke, "Montana Still Able to Perform in Crunch Time," *Salina Journal*, Jan. 17, 1994.

206   No matter how far: Michael Martinez, "Montana Blitzes Houston Still Standing," *San Jose Mercury News*, Jan. 17, 1994.

206   If we were close: Author interview with Kimble Anders, Dec. 14, 2011.

207   Joe threw the ball: Martinez, "Montana Blitzes Houston Still Standing."

207   What we were: Jonathan Feigen, "Wobbly pass flattens Oilers," *Houston Chronicle*, Jan. 17, 1994.

207   Before Marcus Allen: Author interview with Peterson, Dec. 22, 2011.

208   It feels as good: Jim Thomas, "KC KOs Oilers 28–20, Montana's TD Passes Rally Chiefs," *St. Louis Post-Dispatch*, Jan. 17, 1994.

208   Fans all over: Don Pierson, "Montana Out to Defy Odds Again," *Chicago Tribune*, Jan. 21, 1994.

208   If we make it: Ken Murray, "Montana takes aim at Bills, but Young Is secondary target," *Baltimore Sun*, Jan. 21, 1994.

208   I keep up with: "Rice Has Heard Enough of Montana-Young Debate," *San Jose Mercury News*, Jan. 20, 1994.

208   He'll be on the: Doug Tucker, "Montana Feels Price of Victory," *Salina Journal*, Jan. 18, 1994.

209 We realized we: "Anders' Bobble Drops Curtain on Chiefs' Comeback Hopes," *Baltimore Sun*, Jan. 24, 1994.

209 He was moaning: Rich Cimini, "Bills Ready to Give Us More Thrills," *Newsday*, Jan. 24, 1994.

209 As soon as I: John McClain, "Bills Make It 4 in Row with a KO of KC Joe," *Houston Chronicle*, Jan. 24, 1994.

209 There's pros and: Author interview with Grunhard, Sept. 22, 2011.

210 Yeah, that would: Curt Sylvester, "Young vs. Montana? 49ers QB Is Low-Key on Matchup," *Montreal Gazette*, Jan. 22, 1994.

210 After that game: Gary Swan, "49ers Set to Avenge Losses to Cowboys," *San Francisco Chronicle*, Jan. 17, 1994.

210 After that pick: Fred Mitchell, "Hand it to Cowboys, They're Unnerving," *Chicago Tribune*, Jan. 24, 1994.

211 This was just: Randy Moss, "Loss hard for Young to accept," *Dallas Morning News*, Jan. 24, 1994.

211 The Montana faithful: Author interview with Steinberg, Setpember 16, 2011.

211 Many 49ers fans: Lowell Cohn, "49ers' Young Must Consider Age Factor," *San Francisco Chronicle*, July 19, 1994.

211 He doesn't play: Ann Killion, "Young Doesn't Deserve to Be Blamed for One-Sided Loss," *San Jose Mercury News*, Jan. 24, 1994.

212 There was a part: Author interview with Young, Oct. 26, 2011.

CHAPTER 11: THE MONKEY ON MY BACK

213 We worked together: Jim Thomas, "Pregame Show: Steve and Joe Shake, Say Hello," *St. Louis Post-Dispatch*, Sept. 12, 1994.

213 We both had: Ibid.

213 I think it was: "Chiefs Report," *Kansas City Star*, Sept. 12, 1994.

213 Nervous? I'm always: Paul Zimmerman, "Shoot-Out in Kansas City," *Sports Illustrated*, Sept. 19, 1994.

214 It's tough: Adam Teicher, "Montana vs. 49ers: It's Difficult to Hide," *Kansas City Star*, Sept. 6, 1994.

214 That was a lot: Author interview with Bono, Oct. 25, 2011.

214 It felt like: Author interview with Rice, Dec. 19, 2011.

214 That game was: Author interview with Danan Hughes, Jan. 5, 2012.

214 Don't have flashbacks: Adam Teicher, "Joe Cool Despite Hoopla," *Kansas City Star*, Sept. 12, 1994.

214 He said the game: Tom Keegan, "Pays Back Former Mates with 2nd-Half Rally, 24–17," *Baltimore Sun*, Sept. 12, 1994.

215 It was different: Author interview with Montana, Nov. 30, 2011.

215   I don't think Joe: Author interview with Grunhard, Sept. 22, 2011.

216   This had a special: Neil Hohlfeld, "Cool Montana, Chiefs Ice 49ers," *Houston Chronicle*, Sept. 12, 1994.

216   There [were] a lot of: Thomas George, "It Took Montana and His Entourage to Pull it Off," *New York Times*, Sept. 12, 1994.

216   Right up to the end: Zimmerman, "Shoot-Out in Kansas City."

216   He's in many ways: *Top 10 Quarterback Controversies in NFL History*, NFL Films.

216   Joe's a hero: Joan Ryan, "'Long Road to the Top,'" *San Francisco Chronicle*, Jan. 6, 1995.

216   I'm in a certain: Art Spander, "Eagles Bring Niners Down to Dreadful Past," *Ottawa Citizen*, Oct. 3, 1994.

217   It was almost: Scott Ostler, "Young's Head Still Spinning," *San Francisco Chronicle*, Oct. 3, 1994.

217   Steve took that: Bob Padecky, "Young Correctly Expresses Anger," *Santa Rosa Press Democrat*, Oct. 3, 1994.

217   I felt like he: *America's Game: 1994 49ers*, NFL Films.

217   I think that there: Author interview with Killion, Dec. 6, 2011.

218   The funny thing: *America's Game: 1994 49ers*, NFL Films.

218   We would get: Jim Thomas, "'Night Train' Derails Chiefs Means," *St. Louis Post-Dispatch*, Oct. 10, 1994.

218   The years I was: Author interview with Birden, Dec. 22, 2011.

219   All across Kansas: Jim Thomas, "KC's Offense Dies with Allen Over (The) Hill," *St. Louis Post-Dispatch*, Oct. 11, 1994.

219   They're having: Tom Kensler, "Disarming News: Joe Lacking Zips," *Denver Post*, Oct. 11, 1994.

219   My arm is as: "Sore Montana Unsure He'll Play in Denver," *Montreal Gazette*, Oct. 15, 1994.

219   It was just a: Author interview with Montana, Nov. 30, 2011.

220   Just the composure: Author interview with Birden, Dec. 22, 2011.

220   I'm the third: Author interview with Willie Davis, Jan. 9, 2012.

220   It's nerve-wracking: Joseph Sanchez, "Montana Hits Davis for Winner," *Denver Post*, Oct. 18, 1994.

221   Why should I: Kent Pulliam, "Joe Says It Ain't So," *Kansas City Star*, Dec. 3, 1994.

221   It has been a: Steve Springer, "Options Open for Montana," *Los Angeles Times*, Dec. 22, 1994.

222   This victory is: Thomas George, "The Chiefs Travel to Los Angeles and Show They Are Still Players," *New York Times*, Dec. 25, 1994.

222   A lot of people: Adam Teicher, "Montana Expects to Play Next Week," *Kansas City Star*, Dec. 25, 1994.

222   It is a new season: Thomas George, "Montana vs. Marino Offers a Wild Ride," *New York Times*, Dec. 27, 1994.

223   You feel like: Kent Pulliam, Bob Dutton, and Adam Teicher, "Chiefs Report," *Kansas City Star*, Jan. 1, 1995.

223   I've been in a: Bob Dutton, "Miami Quarterback Outduels Montana in Playoff Shootout," *Kansas City Star*, Jan. 1, 1995.

223   I was hoping: Larry Doran, "Montana Blinks First in Duel with Marino," *New York Times*, Jan. 1, 1995.

223   He paced the: Dan Le Batard, "Not-So-Cool Joe: I'll Be Back for '95," *Miami Herald*, Jan. 1, 1995.

223   His body wasn't: Ibid.

224   low: Ibid.

224   It's always fun: "Game, 'Always Fun' for Montana," *Logansport Pharos Tribune*, Jan. 1, 1995.

224   I haven't thought: Ibid.

224   Well, I'd like to: Brian Murphy, "More Bad News for Offensive Line," *Santa Rosa Press Democrat*, Oct. 7, 1994.

224   I kinda chuckled: Author interview with Jones, Oct. 24, 2011.

224   He just keeps: Art Spander, "At Last, 49ers' Young Earns Respect, Even in San Francisco," *Pittsburgh Post-Gazette*, Oct. 16, 1994.

225   Boy, did he: Brian Murphy and Michael Silver, "Another Day, Another Beating for Young," *Santa Rosa Press Democrat*, Oct. 10, 1994.

225   I think more than: Selena Roberts, "Young Finally Makes 49ers His Own," *Minnesota Star Tribune*, Dec. 23, 1994.

225   I think the Philadelphia: Author interview with Killion, Dec. 6, 2011.

225   Dallas was coming: "Young Answers Critics Against Dallas," *Salina Journal*, Nov. 14, 1994.

226   I didn't think: Bill Plaschke, "49ers Strut Past Cowboys," *Los Angeles Times*, Nov. 14, 1994.

226   Steve Young has: Ibid.

226   You're always a: *In Their Own Words: Steve Young*, NFL Films.

227   [In 1992] we: Author interview with Young, Oct. 26, 2011.

227   The whole team: Dave Goldberg, "When Bear Late-Hits Young, Niners Get Really Restless," *Deseret News*, Jan. 8, 1995.

227   I can get in: Victor Chi, "Young, Gayle Bury Gavel," *San Jose Mercury News*, Jan. 8, 1995.

228   Today did it: John P. Lopez, "Young Relishes Elusive Win," *Houston Chronicle*, Jan. 16, 1995.

228 Steve, Steve, Steve: C. W. Nevius, "Young Knows Very Well How Big a Win It Was," *San Francisco Chronicle*, Jan. 16, 1995.

228 The same people: *America's Game: 1994 49ers*, NFL Films.

228 Is the monkey off: Mike Penner, "Joe Who?" *Los Angeles Times*, Jan. 16, 1995.

228 Honestly, I swear: Ibid.

228 I think this is: Bill Walsh, "Young Needs a Win to Establish Greatness," *Fort Lauderdale Sun-Sentinel*, Jan. 26, 1995.

229 I'm an AFC: Mark Soltau, "Torn Montana wouldn't mind if Chargers won," *San Francisco Examiner*, Jan. 22, 1995.

229 If you ask me: "Team a Bit Miffed with Joe's Loyalty," *San Francisco Chronicle*, Jan. 26, 1995.

229 For so long: Hubert Mizell, "Now, Just One More Tiny, Little Thing," *St. Petersburg Times*, Jan. 27, 1995.

229 Steve Young prepared: Author interview with Mike Shanahan, Jan. 5, 2012.

230 Mike Shanahan: *America's Game: 1994 49ers*, NFL Films.

230 We practiced well: Fred Mitchell, "49ers Heart and Soul Climbs 'Mountaintop,'" *Chicago Tribune*, Jan. 30, 1995.

230 Someone take: *America's Game: 1994 49ers*, NFL Films.

230 I regret ever saying: Author interview with Young, Oct. 26, 2011.

231 Every guy in here: *America's Game: 1994 49ers*, NFL Films.

231 I knew it was: Author interview with Steinberg, Sept. 16, 2011.

232 He's pale and: Ibid.

232 Joe Who? : Rick Telander, "Superb!" *Sports Illustrated*, Feb. 6, 1995.

CHAPTER 12: HERE WE GO AGAIN

233 I was told being: Kent Pulliam, "Trying to Master Another Air Game," *Kansas City Star*, Nov. 16, 1994.

233 It gave me a: Ibid.

234 three steps ahead: Ibid.

234 I brought an airplane: Bill Plaschke, "Montana Goes Home to Say Goodbye," *Los Angeles Times*, Apr. 19, 1995.

234 When he's in: Michael Silver, "All Hail the King," *Sports Illustrated*, Apr. 24, 1995.

234 loose bodies: Kent Pulliam, "Montana Surgery Went Long," *Kansas City Star*, Feb. 2, 1995.

234 It's not true: Ibid.

235 He hasn't made: Kent Pulliam, "Walsh Tells Montana to Take Time," *Kansas City Star*, Jan. 27, 1995.

235 He came in to: Author interview with Peterson, Dec. 22, 2011.

235 I'm not believing: Bill Plaschke, "Joe Expected to Say It's So Next Week," *Los Angeles Times*, Apr. 11, 1995.

235 I can't believe: Jim Jenkins, "Heisler, Clark Eye an Encore," *Sacramento Bee*, Apr. 5, 1995.

235 I can't say it: "Joe Will Say It's So," *Sacramento Bee*, Apr. 12, 1995.

236 At the end: Ibid.

236 There was a: "Montana and Clark Hook Up Once Again," *Los Angeles Times*, Apr. 15, 1995.

236 What's Steve's role: Tom Friend, "Montana, Cool to the End, Says Goodbye," *New York Times*, Apr. 19, 1995.

236 I didn't call Steve: "Young's Bogus Invitation," *San Francisco Chronicle*, Apr. 18, 1995.

236 A packed, friendly: Edward Epstein, "50,000 See Montana Pass Into Retirement," *San Francisco Chronicle*, Apr. 19, 1995.

236 I remember getting: Author interview with Peterson, Dec. 22, 2011.

237 I really and truly: Leonard Shapiro, "Super Montana Puts Away His Cape," *Washington Post*, Apr. 19, 1995.

237 It was a lot: Author interview with Joe Montana, Nov. 30, 2011.

237 Nobody made you: Shapiro, "Super Montana Puts Away His Cape."

237 She doesn't like: Ibid.

237 My father says: "Law Degree Makes Young Eligible to Land a 'Real Job,'" *Salt Lake Tribune*, Apr. 23, 1994.

238 I want to do: "Lions Sign Krieg as Backup," *Spokesman-Review*, Apr. 23, 1994.

238 Best play I've: Ron Kroichick, "Helmetless Young Finally Gets 49ers' Offense Running," *Sacramento Bee*, Aug. 14, 1995.

238 The greatest play-caller: Author interview with Young, Oct. 26, 2011.

238 To finally [win: Ibid.

239 It's been weak: Brian Murphy, "Young's Play Shows He's Hurting," *Santa Rosa Press-Democrat*, Oct. 2, 1995.

239 You can't throw: Eric Gilmore, "Young Endures Pain as Flu, Colts Defense Pound Quarterback," *Contra Costa Times*, Oct. 16, 1995.

239 I hit right on: Don Bosley, "Young's Arm, S. F. Fortunes Are Dangling," *Sacramento Bee*, Oct. 16, 1995.

239 In warm-ups I: Scott Ostler, "Season Hinges on Young's Shoulder," *San Francisco Chronicle*, Oct. 16, 1995.

239 Don't plan on having: Don Pierson, "Young to Miss 4 Weeks May Not Clash with Cowboys," *Chicago Tribune*, Oct. 17, 1995.

240 I'll work with: Dennis Georgatos, "49ers' Stage Belongs to Elvis," *Fresno Bee*, Oct. 18, 1995.

240 I can't tell you: John Crumpacker, "Reassembled Line Still Comes Through," *San Francisco Examiner*, Oct. 23, 1995.

240 It's funny how: ESPN *Outside the Lines*, aired April 2012.

240 It's up to the: Gwen Knapp, "Stars go dark when they're needed most," *San Francisco Examiner*, Nov. 6, 1995.

240 Living with white: Bob Padecky, "49ers Answer One Question: 'How about Them Cowboys?'" *Santa Rosa Press Democrat*, Nov. 13, 1995.

240 Harris Barton told: Brian Murphy, "Grbac Has His Big Day," *Santa Rosa Press Democrat*, Nov. 13, 1995.

240 I intend to play: John Crumpacker, "Young Says He Intends to Play, but Doctors Will Have Final Say," *San Francisco Examiner*, Nov. 7, 1995.

241 Who knows?: Art Spander, "Young's Status a Sore Spot," *San Francisco Examiner*, Nov. 10, 1995.

241 We'll evaluate: Bruce Adams, "It's Definitely Elvis' Show Now," *San Francisco Examiner*, Nov. 14, 1995.

241 Seems like I've: Bob Burns, "Seifert Basks in the Glow of Sunday's Shocking Win," *Sacramento Bee*, Nov. 14, 1995.

241 Not yet: Jim Thomas, "Young Back Aboard 49ers' Express," *St. Louis Post-Dispatch*, Nov. 23, 1995.

EPILOGUE: FOREVER YOUNG

243 There's a feeling: "No victory dance for Steve Young," *Santa Fe New Mexican*, Jan. 12, 1998.

243 until I die: Paul Sullivan and Don Pierson, "Retiring Not Even a Notion for Oft-Battered Young," *Chicago Tribune*, Jan. 12, 1998.

244 We got a monkey: Brian Murphy, "49ers Get the Catch II," *Santa Rosa Press Democrat*, Jan. 4, 1999.

244 It's a good time: Kevin Lynch, "Young Goes Out in Style" *Santa Rosa Press Democrat*, June 13, 2000.

244 When I first came: Steve Young's enshrinement speech transcript, 2005 Pro Football Hall of Fame Enshrinement Ceremony, at the Pro Football Hall of Fame Field at Fawcett Stadium, Aug. 7, 2005.

245 The Faithful are the: Tom FitzGerald, "Forever Eight; Hall of Fame QB Gets to See Jersey Retired," *San Francisco Chronicle*, Oct. 6, 2008.

245 It's a lot of emotions: Ann Killion, "The Thrill Is Back," *San Jose Mercury News*, Oct. 6, 2008.

245 It's the sounds: FitzGerald, "Forever Eight; Hall of Fame QB Gets to See Jersey Retired."

246 Everything I do in: Peter King, "Monday Morning Quarterback: Weekend of the QB: Big Ben, Favre, Cassel All Shine in Week 12 Wins," SportsIllustrated.com, Nov. 24, 2008.

246 If they do make: Harvey Araton, "As Stakes Grew, Jets' Gambler Came Up Short," *New York Times*, Dec. 23, 2008.

246 This is Tom's: Erin McHugh, "Cassel Insists: This Is Tom's Team," GateHouse News Service, Jan. 23, 2009.

246 [But, I've] earned: McHugh, "Cassel Insists: This Is Tom's Team."

PHOTOS

He was pretty groggy: Michael Janofsky, "Montana Is Hospitalized for Concussion," *New York Times*, Jan. 5, 1987.

The greatest run . . . the greatest: "Top 10 Mobile Quarterbacks in NFL History," *NFL Films*.

Original Interviews Conducted by the Author

Kimble Anders
Keith Bassi
Jeff Bayer
Guy Benjamin
Leeman Bennett
J.J. Birden
Steve Bono
Robbie Bosco
Michael Brantley
Keith Cash
Roger Craig
Carl Crawley
Randy Cross
Willie Davis
Eddie DeBartolo Jr.
Steve DeBerg
Don DeVore
Glenn Dickey
Riki Ellison
LaVell Edwards
Vagas Ferguson
Bob Gagliano
Rich Goldberger
Tim Grunhard
Kris Haines
David Harris
Jonathan Hayes
Danan Hughes
Merv Johnson
Brent Jones
Ann Killion
Dave Krieg
Guy McIntyre

John McVay
Joe Montana
Mike Ornato
Steve Ortmayer
Ara Parseghian
John Paye
Carl Peterson
Jeff Petrucci
Carmen Policy
Kent Pulliam
Mark Purdy
Bob Raissman
Jerry Rice
David Sarskus
Marty Schottenheimer
George Seifert
Mike Shanahan
Ray Sherman
Chuck Smith
Neil Smith
Art Spander
Joe Starkey
Leigh Steinberg
Chris Symington
Paul Timko
Ted Tollner
Keena Turner
Steve Wallace
Louis Wong
Sam Wyche
Steve Young
Allen Veliky
Michael Zagaris

Index

Marshall, Leonard, 135, 136, 166
Martin, Chris, 91
Martin, Doug, 70
Martin, Eric, 223
Mays, Stafford, 70
McConkey, Phil, 83
McDonald, Tim, 186
McDonough, Will, 18
McDowell, Bubba, 127
McIntyre, Guy, 4, 60, 80, 91, 120, 158, 174
McKyer, Tim, 152, 153, 164, 240
McLane, Mark, 24
McLean, Lindsy, 164
McLemore, Dana, 67
McMahon, Jim, 40–41, 88
McPherson, Bill, 106
McVay, John, 65, 154
Mecklenburg, Karl, 164
Metzelaars, Pete, 168
Miami Herald, on Montana, 223
Millard, Keith, 70, 71, 91, 120
Millen, Matt, 116, 134
Miller, Chris, 154
Mills, Sam, 82
Milwaukee Journal, interview with Holmgren, 162
Mims, Chris, 203
Mitchell, Dave, 27
Montana, Alexandra, 111, 124, 178
Montana, Elizabeth, 111, 124, 178, 237
Montana, Jennifer, 11, 12, 93, 111, 114, 124, 138, 178, 188, 213, 220, 234
Montana, Joseph, Sr., 19–21, 213
Montana, Joseph Clifford "Joe," Jr.
 awards and honors, 33, 120, 124, 134, 179
 back surgery, 7–9
 childhood, 19–21
 elbow injury, 143, 150, 170

 as 49ers backup quarterback, 176–177
 high school, 21–23
 as host of *Saturday Night Live,* 17–18
 interest in flying, 233–234
 "Joe Montana Day," San Francisco, 235–237
 with Kansas City Chiefs, 193–197, 200–224
 knee surgery, 107, 234
 NFL Players Association strike, attitude toward, 59–61
 NFL records, 65, 119, 127
 at Notre Dame, 23–29
 playing style and personality, 80–81
 post-back surgery return to 49ers, 11–14, 54–59
 quarterback controversy, 76–78
 relationship with DeBartolo, 75
 relationship with DeBerg, 5
 relationship with Walsh, 34–35
 relationship with Young, 81, 129
 retirement, 237
 on role of backup quarterback, 131
 sharing quarterback role, 31–32, 166, 169–170, 176
 signing with 49ers, 31
 on the town in New Orleans, 155–156
 Walsh's coaching style and, 32–33
 on Young, 51, 147, 216
Montana, Nathaniel Joseph, 111, 124, 178
Montana, Nicholas, 178
Montana, Theresa, 8, 19–20, 21
Moon, Warren, 205, 207
Moore, Bob, 234
Moroski, Mike, 5, 10
Morris, Joe, 15